UNIVERSIDADES, por el artista argentino,
MARINO DI TEANA

MASTERING SPANISH

MASTERING

D. C. HEATH AND COMPANY
Lexington, Massachusetts

SpANish

LAUREL H. TURK
DePauw University

AURELIO M. ESPINOSA, JR.
Stanford University

Drawings by JEANETTE P. SLOAN

Maps by JAMES LEWICKI

PREFACE

Mastering Spanish is a second-year college program. It is designed to further the development of the language through review of the fundamentals of Spanish structure, to emphasize oral and reading comprehension, and to provide opportunity for self-expression in speaking and writing. Students who have completed one year of college Spanish or its equivalent in secondary school will find additional material which is essential for a good command of the language.

To fulfill these aims, the text consists of four preliminary lessons, twelve regular lessons, six *Lecturas*, a short section on Spanish letter writing, five appendices, and end vocabularies. The maps and illustrations provide the basis for a great variety of topics which supplement the material on the cultural background of the Spanish American countries. Throughout the text, emphasis is placed on the acquisition of a practical vocabulary and on the active use of the language. The sixteen dialogues deal with situations from daily life and are within the experience of present-day students.

Mastering Spanish is a continuation of Turk and Espinosa, *Foundation Course in Spanish, Second Edition*, Heath, 1970. However, it is written so that it may be used as a logical extension of most basic, first-year programs. It provides ample material for a one-semester course which meets four times per week. In a course meeting three days per week, some of the exercises and/or *Lecturas* may be omitted without detriment to the over-all effectiveness of the text. If it is used in conjunction with other reading material in addition to the *Lecturas*, it may be necessary to carry over a few lessons into the second semester.

The four preliminary lessons are devoted largely to a review of all the simple and compound indicative tenses and polite and familiar command forms of the verb. This stress on verb forms is recognized as a necessity if the student is to gain complete mastery of the language. Each of the four lessons consists of a brief dialogue, with a list of new words and phrases and a section of oral exercises, a section on pronunciation, and a verb review, followed by varied drill exercises. In addition to the specific focus on developing a firm command of the verb forms, the preliminary lessons contain strategies to facilitate and reinforce comprehension and speaking. The entire verb review contained in the four preliminary lessons may be taken up before *Lección primera*, or certain sections may be assigned in conjunction with the regular lessons.

The twelve regular lessons contain: (1) a practical dialogue, with a list of new words and expressions and a section of oral exercises developed in the same way as those of the preliminary lessons; (2) a section on pronunciation and intonation (through *Lección ocho*); (3) *Notas gramaticales*, with *Ejercicios* placed after the explanation of grammatical points; and (4) a *Resumen*, which contains additional oral drills and short English sentences to be expressed in Spanish, and which summarizes the major points taken up in the lesson.

Throughout the text the headings as well as the directions are given in Spanish. In the *Pronunciación* and *Notas gramaticales* sections, however, the explanations are given in English to insure comprehension. Additional grammatical terms and expressions for use in the classroom and laboratory are listed in Appendix B.

The pronunciation material constitutes a basic and effective survey of Spanish phonology. This section is included through *Lección ocho* to insure that the student will continue to apply the principles involved in good Spanish pronunciation.

The *Notas gramaticales* give a systematic, logical, and pragmatic review of the fundamentals of Spanish structure. They are advanced in scope and include points frequently omitted in other texts. However, they retain their basic nature and emphasize general practice rather than exceptions. An important feature of the *Notas gramaticales* is that each major structure is immediately followed by appropriate and adequate drills. Wherever feasible, these exercises are devised so that they may be done orally by the student. The device of placing the exercises immediately after the grammatical summary enables the student to center his attention on the particular point under discussion and to review a maximum number of points in a relatively short time. This method of presentation also permits an easy division of each lesson into assignments. The sentences in the exercises are purposely kept short to encourage rapid drill work. The vocabulary of the drills is most often limited to words of high frequency, permitting the student to focus on the structure under consideration.

Since reading for pleasure is one of the primary goals in learning a foreign language, and because variety in reading materials is essential in the attainment of this goal, there are six *Lecturas*, which appear at two-lesson intervals, beginning after *Lección dos*. The *Lecturas* deal with the development of Spanish America from the *conquistadores* to the problems that confront Latin America today. A sixteen-page section in full color illustrates the *Lectura* on art in Spanish America. (Spanish art is featured in *Foundation Course in Spanish*.)

Preceding the reading material in each *Lectura* there are three sections: (1) *Estudio de palabras*, which is helpful to the student in the recognition of the meaning of new words and in relating them both to

English and to other Spanish words; (2) a list of idiomatic expressions not previously introduced, which acquaints the student with them before he reads the selection; and (3) *Aspectos gramaticales*, which deals with certain grammatical points found in the reading selection and which, for the most part, are not explained in the regular lessons.

The *Lecturas* are followed by two sections designed to develop further skill in oral expression and writing. These sections contain exercises and text segments which emphasize the innovative use of oral Spanish within a framework of motivating contextual content. The material for written practice spans a broad spectrum of exercises, such as dictations, written reports, compositions, structurally oriented translations, etc. Stress is again placed on developing expression and fostering the student's ability to use Spanish.

A *Repaso general* follows *Lección doce*. This review encompasses additional exercises covering many of the major grammatical elements in the text as well as the *Lecturas*.

For those who may wish to carry on social or commercial correspondence in Spanish, some commonly-used phrases and formulas are given in the special section on letter writing, called *Cartas españolas*.

Appendix A contains a summary of Spanish pronunciation, with an explanation of terms used; Appendix B includes lists of expressions used in the classroom and the laboratory, grammatical terms, punctuation marks, and the abbreviations and terms used in the text; Appendix C gives the cardinal and ordinal numerals, the months of the year, the days of the week, the seasons, dates, and ways to express the time of day; Appendix D contains the regular verb paradigms and complete lists of verbs with various types of irregularity used in the text, as well as a few additional verbs which may be encountered in later study of Spanish; and Appendix E includes lists of the reflexive verbs used in the text, verbs which are followed immediately by an infinitive without a preposition, and those which require certain prepositions before an infinitive.

The Spanish–English vocabulary is intended to be complete with the exception of a few proper and geographical names which are either identical in Spanish and English or whose meaning is clear, a few past participles used as adjectives when the infinitive is given, some of the titles of literary and artistic works mentioned in the *Lecturas*, the Spanish examples translated in the *Cartas españolas* section, and a few diminutives given in *Lección diez*. Idioms are listed under the most important word in the phrase, and, in most cases, cross listings are given. Irregular plural forms of nouns and adjectives are included only for those forms which are used in the plural in the text. The English–Spanish vocabulary contains only the English words used in the English–Spanish exercises.

As an aid to the teacher and student, an innovative tape program accompanies the text, covering the dialogues, most of the oral exercises, and certain sections of the *Lecturas*.

The authors wish to express their deep appreciation for the valuable suggestions and constructive criticism offered by Mr. Val Hempel, Executive Editor, and Miss Josefa Busó, Senior Editor, of the Modern Language Department of D. C. Heath and Company.

L.H.T.
A.M.E., Jr.

CONTENTS

RECORDINGS FOR TURK AND ESPINOSA:

MASTERING SPANISH

    TAPES

        NUMBER OF REELS: 8 7″ double track

        SPEED: $3\frac{3}{4}$ ips

        RUNNING TIME: 8 hours (approximate)

MASTERING SPANISH

PRIMERA LECCIÓN PRELIMINAR

Presente de indicativo de los verbos regulares. Verbos que tienen formas irregulares en el presente de indicativo. Verbos que cambian la vocal radical en el presente de indicativo

EN EL DEPARTAMENTO DE ESPAÑOL

(Carlos habla con la secretaria del Departamento de Español.)

CARLOS.	Buenos días, señorita Flores. ¿Cómo está usted?
SRTA. FLORES.	Muy bien, Carlos. ¿Y usted?
CARLOS.	Muy bien, gracias. ¿Puede decirme si el profesor Valdés está en su oficina?
SRTA. FLORES.	Todavía no. Llega a las ocho y cuarto. ¿Por qué no le espera usted unos minutos?
CARLOS.	Quiero saber si me permite asistir a su clase de español este semestre. ¿Sabe usted si la clase es grande?
SRTA. FLORES.	Le interesa a usted la clase que comienza a las nueve, ¿verdad? Creo que tengo aquí la lista de los alumnos. ¿Quiere verla?
CARLOS.	*(Después de examinar la lista.)* ¡Caramba! Mi novia está en la clase.
SRTA. FLORES.	En ese caso no sé si va a admitirle.
CARLOS.	Allí viene el profesor. ¡A ver si tengo suerte! Voy a hablarle.

    admitir[1] to admit   **el departamento** department
    asistir a (+ *obj.*)[2] to attend **la lista** list, roll (*class*)
    ¡caramba! gosh! confound it! **el semestre** semester
    el caso case

A. Busquen en el diálogo las frases que correspondan a las siguientes:

1. Spanish Department. 2. Good morning. 3. How are you? 4. Not yet.
5. at a quarter after eight. 6. a few minutes. 7. whether he will permit me to
attend his Spanish class. 8. You are interested in the class that . . . 9. After
examining the roll. 10. Let's see . . . ! 11. I am lucky (fortunate). 12. I am going
to speak to him.

**B. Aprendan el diálogo de memoria (*Memorize the dialogue*) para poder
repetirlo con el profesor (la profesora) o con uno de sus compañeros.**

C. Para contestar en español:

Preguntas sobre el diálogo

1. ¿Cómo se llama la secretaria del Departamento de Español? 2. ¿Qué le
pregunta Carlos a la señorita Flores? 3. ¿A qué hora llega el profesor Valdés a
su oficina? 4. ¿Qué quiere saber Carlos? 5. ¿Qué examina Carlos? 6. ¿Qué
contesta la señorita Flores cuando le dice Carlos que su novia está en la clase?

Aplicación del diálogo

1. ¿Cómo está usted? 2. ¿Cómo se llama el profesor (la profesora) de esta clase?
3. ¿A qué hora empieza esta clase? 4. ¿Cuántos alumnos hay en esta clase?
5. ¿Qué estudiamos en esta clase? 6. Si usted llega tarde, ¿le permite entrar el
profesor?

PRONUNCIACIÓN

American–Spanish pronunciation. The differences in pronunciation between
American Spanish and Castilian or Peninsular Spanish are matters of some concern
to teachers and students of Spanish. Since Spanish is spoken in so many different

---

[1] Only the words and expressions not used in the dialogues in *Foundation Course in Spanish, Second Edition,*
Heath, 1970, are listed after the dialogues in this text. [2] See pages 304–305 for the abbreviations used in this
text.

areas, it is only natural that there should be differences from country to country. In general, however, the pronunciation of educated persons differs only in two important respects:

1. In American Spanish (and also in southern Spain) **c** before **e** or **i**, and **z**, are not pronounced as interdental *th* (as in northern and central Spain), but as a dental **s**,[1] not unlike the English *s* in *sent*.

2. In some parts of Spain, and quite generally in Spanish America, **ll** (pronounced somewhat like *lli* in *million* in other parts of Spain) is pronounced as the *y* sound in *yes*, with somewhat stronger friction than in English *y*.

In both cases the two variants are accepted as standard forms of pronunciation. Because of the geographical situation of our country in the Western Hemisphere, it seems natural to use the so-called American–Spanish pronunciation of these sounds in this book.

Certain other traits of American Spanish (and of some parts of Spain) are considered popular or regional and are generally avoided by educated persons. Some of these are: the aspiration of **s** final in the word or the syllable, that is, to pronounce **s** in such circumstances as English *h*: **ehtoh campoh** for **estos campos**; the confusion of **l** and **r** when final in the word or the syllable: **comel** for **comer**; the pronunciation of **y** (and **ll**) as English *z* in *azure*; the retention of aspirate **h**, as in Old Spanish: **jumo** for **humo** (with silent **h**); the pronunciation of Spanish **j** and **g** before **e** or **i** as English *h*. All these forms should be carefully avoided.

Review the sounds of **c** before **e** or **i**, of **s**, and of **y** (pages 294–296) and pronounce after your teacher:

1. difícil	hacer	necesitar	oficina	lección
2. almorzar	empezar	comienza	razón	conduzco
3. caballo	ellos	hallar	llegar	llover
4. ayer	leyendo	yo	y ella	y usted
5. semestre	asistir	vender	humo	jamón

PARA REPASAR (*For Review*)

In order to help you understand and use Spanish more readily, you will need to review some of the verbs and expressions used earlier in your study of the language.

I. REPASO DE LAS FORMAS DEL PRESENTE DE INDICATIVO DE LOS VERBOS REGULARES

In Appendix D, page 310, review the forms of the present indicative tense of regular verbs. Some common verbs are:

---

[1] A few basic phonetic terms will be introduced in this text, to allow for greater accuracy in the description of Spanish speech sounds. For a definition of the terms used, see Appendix A, pages 291–292.

comprar   *to buy*
esperar   *to wait (for), hope*
hablar   *to speak, talk*
llevar   *to take, carry*

mirar   *to look (at)*
necesitar   *to need*
tomar   *to take, drink, eat*
trabajar   *to work*

aprender (a + *inf.*)   *to learn*
   (*to* + *inf.*)
comer   *to eat*

comprender   *to understand*
vender   *to sell*

abrir   *to open*
escribir   *to write*

permitir   *to permit, allow*
vivir   *to live*

a. Repitan la frase; luego, al oír un sujeto nuevo, substitúyanlo en la frase, cambiando la forma del verbo cuando sea necesario:

1. *Los estudiantes* toman café.
   (*Yo, Jorge y yo, Tú, Usted, Ustedes, Ana y María*)

2. *Roberto* no comprende la pregunta.
   (*Yo, Nosotros, Tú, Ricardo y Marta, Ustedes, Bárbara*)

3. *José* aprende a hablar español.
   (*José y yo, Yo, Ustedes, Tú, Ramón y Luis, Ella*)

4. ¿Abres *tú* las ventanas?
   (*ustedes, yo, Carolina, los muchachos, tú y yo, él*)

b. Para contestar afirmativamente en español:

1. ¿Hablas español?
¿Hablan ustedes español?
¿Espera Elena el autobús?
¿Trabajas mucho?
¿Necesitan ellos más tiempo?
¿Compran ustedes muchas cosas?

¿Aprendes el español?
¿Aprenden ustedes a hablar bien?
¿Come Luisa a las seis?
¿Abren ustedes la puerta a veces?
¿Asistes a la clase de español?
¿Escribo yo en la pizarra?

Para contestar negativamente:

2. ¿Compras papel en la biblioteca?
¿Espera José a Marta?
¿Comes temprano todas las noches?

¿Comen ustedes a las cinco?
¿Escriben ustedes el diálogo?
¿Escribo yo una composición?

II. ALGUNOS VERBOS QUE TIENEN FORMAS IRREGULARES EN EL PRESENTE DE INDICATIVO

Some common verbs which have irregular forms in the present indicative are:

decir *to say, tell*	**digo**	**dices**	**dice**	decimos	decís	**dicen**
estar *to be*	**estoy**	**estás**	**está**	estamos	estáis	**están**
haber *to have* (aux.)	**he**	**has**	**ha**	**hemos**	habéis	**han**
ir *to go*	**voy**	**vas**	**va**	**vamos**	vais	**van**
oír *to hear*	**oigo**	**oyes**	**oye**	oímos	oís	**oyen**
poder *to be able, can*	**puedo**	**puedes**	**puede**	podemos	podéis	**pueden**
querer *to wish, want*	**quiero**	**quieres**	**quiere**	queremos	queréis	**quieren**
ser *to be*	**soy**	**eres**	**es**	**somos**	**sois**	**son**
tener *to have, possess*	**tengo**	**tienes**	**tiene**	tenemos	tenéis	**tienen**
venir *to come*	**vengo**	**vienes**	**viene**	venimos	venís	**vienen**

A number of irregular verbs have regular forms in the present indicative tense, except in the first person singular: **dar**, *to give* (**doy**); **hacer**, *to do, make* (**hago**); **poner**, *to put, place* (**pongo**); **saber**, *to know* (a fact) (**sé**); **salir**, *to go out, leave* (**salgo**); **traer**, *to bring* (**traigo**); **ver**, *to see* (**veo**). Also irregular only in the first person singular are **conocer**, *to know* (a person) (**conozco**); **escoger**, *to choose* (**escojo**). See Appendix D, page 321, for accented forms in the present indicative tense of **enviar**, *to send*, and of **continuar**, *to continue*, and page 320 for forms of verbs ending in **-uir**: **huir**, *to flee*.

a. Lean en español, supliendo (*supplying*) la forma correcta del verbo entre paréntesis en el presente de indicativo:

1. (decir) ¿Qué le _____ tú a Juan? Yo no le _____ nada. 2. (estar) ¿Dónde _____ yo ahora? Usted _____ cerca de la mesa. 3. (poder) ¿_____ ustedes esperar unos minutos? Sí, _____ esperar un rato. 4. (dar) ¿_____ tú un paseo con Isabel? No, no _____ un paseo con ella. 5. (traer) ¿Me _____ tú regalos a veces? No, nunca te _____ regalos. 6. (hacer) ¿Qué _____ usted esta tarde? No _____ nada. 7. (ver) ¿_____ ustedes estos mapas? Sí, los _____ bien. 8. (querer) ¿_____ tú ir a hablarle ahora? No, no _____ hablarle esta mañana. 9. (saber) ¿_____ usted si mi novia está en la clase? No, no _____ si ella está en la clase. 10. (oír) ¿_____ ustedes cantar a alguien? No, no _____ cantar a nadie. 11. (conocer) ¿_____ tú a mi tía? Sí, la _____ muy bien. 12. (salir) ¿_____ yo de casa temprano? Sí, usted _____ a las siete y media. 13. (ir) ¿_____ usted a asistir a esta clase? Sí, _____ a asistir a esta clase este semestre. 14. (venir) ¿Quién _____ a ayudar a Pablo? Yo _____ a ayudarle esta noche. 15. (tener) ¿_____ usted suerte hoy? Sí, siempre _____ suerte. 16. (ser) ¿_____ tú estudiante? Sí, _____ estudiante de esta universidad. 17. (enviar) ¿Le _____ usted algo a Marta? Sí, le _____ un regalo a veces. 18. (continuar) ¿_____ ustedes leyendo la novela? Sí, _____ leyendo varias páginas cada día.

b. Para expresar en español:

1. I leave at a quarter after eight.   2. I don't know whether John is coming.   3. I see many cars in the street.   4. I go to the library.   5. I choose several books. 6. I put the books on the table.   7. We hear the music.   8. We bring records to class.   9. We are lucky.   10. Do you (*fam. sing.*) want to attend this class?   11. Do you (*fam. sing.*) say that the secretary is in the office?   12. Do you (*pl.*) say that you can wait a few minutes?   13. Do you (*pl.*) want to talk with the teacher soon? 14. There come the teachers.   15. They cannot talk now.   16. Why don't you (*fam. sing.*) continue reading the short story?

III. VERBOS QUE CAMBIAN LA VOCAL RADICAL (*Stem-changing verbs*)

Some verbs of Class I are:

almorzar (ue) *to take (eat) lunch*	jugar (ue) *to play* (a game)
cerrar (ie) *to close*	pensar (ie) *to think;* + inf. *intend*
comenzar (ie) *to commence, begin*	perder (ie) *to lose, miss*
devolver (ue) *to return, give back*	recordar (ue) *to recall, remember*
empezar (ie) *to begin*	sentarse (ie) *to sit down*
encontrar (ue) *to encounter, find*	volver (ue) *to return, come back*

cerrar: **cierro cierras cierra** cerramos cerráis **cierran**
volver: **vuelvo vuelves vuelve** volvemos volvéis **vuelven**
jugar: **juego juegas juega** jugamos jugáis **juegan**

Some Class II verbs are:

divertirse (ie, i) *to have a good time, amuse oneself*	sentir (ie, i) *to feel, regret, be sorry*
preferir (ie, i) *to prefer*	dormir (ue, u) *to sleep*

sentir: **siento sientes siente** sentimos sentís **sienten**
dormir: **duermo duermes duerme** dormimos dormís **duermen**

Some Class III verbs are:

conseguir[1] (i, i) *to get, obtain*	seguir[1] (i, i) *to follow, continue*

[1] See Appendix D, pages 318–320, for the first person singular present indicative of verbs with changes in spelling including those ending in **-guir**: **conseguir** (**consigo**), **seguir** (**sigo**).

pedir (i, i)   *to ask (for), request*   servir (i, i)   *to serve*
reír (i, i)   *to laugh*   vestirse (i, i)   *to dress oneself, get dressed*
repetir (i, i)   *to repeat*

> pedir: **pido pides pide** pedimos pedís **piden**
> reír: **río ríes ríe** reímos reís **ríen**

a. Repitan la frase; luego, al oír un sujeto nuevo, substitúyanlo en la frase, cambiando la forma del verbo cuando sea necesario:

1. *Jaime* empieza a leer el diálogo.
   (*Yo, Vicente y yo, Ellos, Tú, Usted, Usted y él*)

2. *Los muchachos* piensan ir al cine.
   (*Tú, Enrique, Dorotea y yo, Yo, Ustedes, Ella*)

3. *Nuestros amigos* lo sienten mucho.
   (*Mi hermana, Tú, Yo, Ella y yo, Mis tíos, Usted*)

4. ¿Juegan *ustedes* al fútbol?
   (*usted, tú, Ramón y Luis, nosotros, yo, tu hermano*)

5. ¿Cuánto tiempo duerme *Juanita*?
   (*tú, yo, ustedes, tu hermanito, él y yo, los niños*)

6. *Yo* siempre repito las frases.
   (*Los estudiantes, Margarita, Inés y yo, Ustedes, Usted, Tú*)

7. ¿Le pide *usted* a Clara un favor?
   (*Isabel, tú, yo, ellos, ustedes, nosotros*)

b. Para expresar en español:

1. I close the door.   2. We close the books.   3. Paul begins to talk in Spanish.
4. Do you (*pl.*) intend to see the film?   5. Mary and I return at a quarter after five.
6. The boys have a good time, don't they?   7. I ask for books in the library.   8. John and I prefer to go to the park.   9. Do you (*fam. sing.*) sleep seven hours each night?
10. I always repeat the words.   11. Many students continue studying until midnight.
12. My mother serves coffee or chocolate.

SEGUNDA LECCIÓN PRELIMINAR

El pretérito y el imperfecto de indicativo
de los verbos regulares. Verbos que tienen
formas irregulares en el pretérito de indicativo.
Verbos que cambian la vocal radical, Grupos II
y III, en el pretérito. Verbos que tienen formas
irregulares en el imperfecto de indicativo

UN DÍA DE MALA SUERTE

(Carlos encuentra a un compañero de clase en el vestíbulo de la Residencia de Estudiantes.)

JUAN. ¡Hola, Carlos! No te vi en clase esta mañana. ¿Qué pasó?

CARLOS. ¡Un desastre! Tuve que ir al centro porque no encontré en la librería el libro de texto para la clase de español.

JUAN. ¿Lo hallaste en el centro?

CARLOS. ¡No, Juan! Además, como tengo clases esta tarde, tuve que volver en taxi.

JUAN. ¿Dónde almorzaste?

CARLOS. Almorcé en el Centro de Estudiantes. Por cierto, pagué ochenta centavos por una hamburguesa malísima.

JUAN. Te busqué para invitarte a almorzar conmigo, pero no estabas en tu cuarto.

CARLOS. Anoche supe que necesitaba este libro. A propósito, ¿de qué habló el profesor esta mañana?

JUAN. De los usos de los tiempos. Como ves, no perdiste nada.

CARLOS. ¡Hombre! ¡La parte más difícil de la lección! Bueno, tengo que irme. No quiero llegar tarde a clase. Hasta luego.

el compañero de clase classmate (*m.*)
el desastre disaster, catastrophe
la hamburguesa hamburger
la librería bookstore

el libro de texto text, textbook
por cierto certainly, of course
el tiempo tense
el uso use

A. Busquen en el diálogo las frases que correspondan a las siguientes:

1. in the lobby of the Student Residence Hall.   2. I had to go downtown.   3. the text(book) for the Spanish class.   4. (Did you find it) downtown?   5. by (in a) taxi. 6. I ate lunch at the Student Center.   7. I paid eighty cents for a very poor (bad) hamburger.   8. Last night I learned (found out) that I needed this book.   9. By the way.   10. Well, I have to go (leave).   11. to be late for class (to reach class late). 12. See you later (Until I see you).

B. Aprendan el diálogo de memoria para poder repetirlo con el profesor (la profesora) o con uno de sus compañeros.

C. Repasen y estudien las expresiones siguientes para emplear algunas de ellas en el diálogo citado, o para usarlas en un diálogo nuevo basado sobre el modelo:

ayer por la mañana (la tarde)
   yesterday morning (afternoon)
el batido de leche milk shake
la compañera de clase classmate (*f.*)
el cuarto de estar living room, lounge
el emparedado de jamón (queso)
   ham (cheese) sandwich
ir a casa to go home
ir a casa de (Ana) to go to (Ann's)

ir de compras to go shopping
ir en coche (autobús) to go by car (bus)
nada de particular nothing special
¿qué hay de nuevo? what's new?
¿qué hiciste? what did you do?
los usos del imperfecto (pretérito) de indicativo uses of the imperfect (preterit) indicative

PRONUNCIACIÓN

A. Spanish **b** (and **v**), **d**.   Each of these consonants (**b** and **v** are pronounced exactly alike) has two different sounds, a voiced stop sound, and a voiced continuant sound.

When initial in a breath-group, or when after **m** or **n** (also pronounced **m** in this case), whether within a word or between words, Spanish **b** (or **v**) is a voiced bilabial stop, like English *b* in *boy*, but somewhat weaker.   In all other positions, it is a voiced bilabial continuant; the lips do not close completely as in stop **b**, but allow the breath to pass between them through a very narrow passage.   When between vowels the articulation is especially weak.   Avoid the English *v* sound.

At the beginning of a breath-group or when after **n** or **l**, Spanish **d** is a voiced dental stop, like English *d*, but with the tip of the tongue touching the inner surface of the upper teeth, rather than the ridge above the teeth, as in English.   In all other cases the tongue drops even lower and the **d** is pronounced as a voiced interdental continuant, like a weak English *th* in *this*.   The sound is especially weak in the ending **-ado** and when final in a word before a pause.

Pronounce after your teacher:

1. bueno	caramba	vamos	venir	un vaso
2. saber	muy bien	novia	no volvió	¿quiere verla?
3. dormir	¿dónde?	aprender	el día	el dinero
4. cansado	admitirle	verdad	usted	le dice

B. In Appendix A, pages 292–293, review the division of words into syllables, and word stress; then write the last two exchanges of the dialogue on page 8, dividing them into breath-groups and into syllables, and underlining the syllables that are stressed.

PARA REPASAR

I. REPASO DE LAS FORMAS DEL PRETÉRITO Y DEL IMPERFECTO DE INDICATIVO DE LOS VERBOS REGULARES

Review, in Appendix D, pages 310-311, the forms of the preterit and imperfect indicative tenses of regular verbs.

Repitan la frase; luego, al oír un sujeto nuevo, substitúyanlo en la frase, cambiando la forma del verbo cuando sea necesario:

1. *Yo* no esperé a Tomás.
   (*Tú, Ud.,*[1] *Los estudiantes, Elena, Luisa y yo, Uds.*[1])

2. *Felipe* aprendió bien el diálogo.
   (*José y yo, Yo, Uds., Tú, Ana y Luis, Ella*)

3. *Ellos* miraban el mapa de México.
   (*Ella, Yo, Tú, El profesor, Isabel y yo, Uds.*)

4. *Mis padres* vivían en la Argentina.
   (*El señor Díaz, Yo, Mi hermano y yo, Tú, Uds., Ud.*)

---

[1] In writing, **usted** and **ustedes** may be abbreviated to **Ud.** and **Uds.**, or **Vd.** and **Vds.**

II. ALGUNOS VERBOS QUE TIENEN FORMAS IRREGULARES EN EL PRETÉRITO DE INDICATIVO

Some common verbs are:

decir: **dije dijiste dijo dijimos dijisteis dijeron**
hacer: **hice hiciste hizo hicimos hicisteis hicieron**
querer: **quise quisiste quiso quisimos quisisteis quisieron**
venir: **vine viniste vino vinimos vinisteis vinieron**

andar: **anduve adnuviste anduvo anduvimos anduvisteis anduvieron**
estar: **estuve estuviste estuvo estuvimos estuvisteis estuvieron**
poder: **pude pudiste pudo pudimos pudisteis pudieron**
poner: **puse pusiste puso pusimos pusisteis pusieron**
saber: **supe supiste supo supimos supisteis supieron**
tener: **tuve tuviste tuvo tuvimos tuvisteis tuvieron**

traer: **traje trajiste trajo trajimos trajisteis trajeron**

dar: **di diste dio dimos disteis dieron**
ir, ser: **fui fuiste fue fuimos fuisteis fueron**
ver: **vi** viste **vio** vimos visteis **vieron**

In the forms listed above note that:

(1) Four verbs have **i**-stems and six have **u**-stems. There are no written accents on any of the forms, and in the first eleven verbs the first person singular ends in **-e** and the third person singular ends in **-o**.
(2) The third person singular of **hacer** is **hizo**; the third person plural ending of **decir** and of **traer** is **-eron**.
(3) **Ir** and **ser** have the same forms.

A few verbs have special meanings in the preterit tense. The preterit of **saber** usually means *learned, found out*: **Anoche supe eso**, *Last night I learned that*; that of **tener** often means *got, received*: **Yo tuve una carta**, *I got (received) a letter*; that of **querer** often means *tried*: **Juan quiso hacer eso pero no pudo**, *John tried to do that but he couldn't*; that of **querer** used negatively often means *refused to, would not*: **Ellos no quisieron esperar**, *They refused to (would not) wait.*

a. Para contestar afirmativamente:

1. ¿Tuviste que ir al centro?
2. ¿Tuvo que ir Carlos también?
3. ¿Hiciste una excursión ayer?
4. ¿Hizo Juan un viaje a México?
5. ¿Diste un paseo con Luisa?
6. ¿Dieron Uds. un paseo ayer?
7. ¿Fuiste de compras con Pablo?
8. ¿Fueron Uds. en taxi?

b. Para contestar negativamente:

1. ¿Estuviste en casa anoche?
2. ¿Trajeron Uds. fotos a clase?
3. ¿Pudiste trabajar mucho ayer?

4. ¿Vio Carlos un partido de fútbol?
5. ¿Vinieron Uds. a clase el sábado?
6. ¿Le dijiste la verdad a Carolina?

c. Repitan la frase; luego, repítanla otra vez, cambiando la forma del verbo al pretérito de indicativo:

1. Yo no hago nada por la mañana.
2. José y yo no vemos a nadie.
3. María no quiere ir al cine.
4. Los jóvenes no pueden esperar.
5. ¿Adónde vas en autobús?
6. ¿Qué ves en el cuarto de estar?

7. Oigo cantar a alguien.
8. ¿Quién te trae muchos regalos?
9. Mis padres no dicen eso.
10. Pongo los paquetes sobre la mesa.
11. Mi madre tiene que volver en taxi.
12. Él no sabe nada de particular.

d. Para expresar en español:

1. Mr. Díaz, what did you do yesterday afternoon?   2. Johnny, where did you go this morning?   3. Did you (*pl.*) bring the magazines to class?   4. I couldn't find my textbook last night.   5. Charles came to work at ten o'clock.   6. When did you find out that Paul went to New York?   7. I know that he made the trip by plane. 8. John said that he encountered (**a**) Mary downtown.

III. OTROS TIPOS DE VERBOS QUE TIENEN FORMAS IRREGULARES EN EL PRETÉRITO DE INDICATIVO

1. Certain **-ar** verbs have changes in the first person singular preterit:

buscar:	**busqué** buscaste buscó, *etc.*
llegar:	**llegué** llegaste llegó, *etc.*
empezar (ie):	**empecé** empezaste empezó, *etc.*

Recall that verbs ending in **-car** change **c** to **qu**, those in **-gar** change **g** to **gu**, and those in **-zar** change **z** to **c** before the ending **-e** (**-é**). **Empezar** is also a stem-changing verb, Class I, as are three of the following verbs.

acercarse *to approach*	entregar *to hand (over)*	practicar *to practice*
almorzar (ue) *to eat lunch*	jugar (ue) *to play* (a game)	sacar *to take (out)*
comenzar (ie) *to commence*	pagar *to pay (for)*	tocar *to play* (music)

2. Certain verbs ending in **-er** and **-ir** preceded by a vowel replace unaccented **i** by **y** in the third person singular and plural of the preterit. Accents must be written on the other four forms. **Caer**, *to fall*, and **leer**, *to read*, have the same changes as **creer**, *to believe*, and **oír**, *to hear*.

creer: creí **creíste creyó creímos creísteis creyeron**
oír: oí **oíste oyó oímos oísteis oyeron**

3. Verbs ending in **-ducir** and **-uir** (except **-guir**) have irregular forms in the preterit, and also in the present indicative. Review the forms of the models **conducir**, *to drive, conduct*, page 320, and **huir**, *to flee*, page 320.

a. Escriban cada frase otra vez, cambiando la forma del verbo al pretérito de indicativo; luego, lean la frase nueva en voz alta *(aloud)*:

1. Yo no almuerzo hasta la una. 2. Llego tarde al partido. 3. Me acerco rápidamente a la ventanilla. 4. Pago tres dólares por mi billete. 5. Le entrego el dinero al empleado. 6. Entro y busco un asiento. 7. Empiezo a sacar fotos de los jugadores. 8. Saco ocho o diez fotos.
9. Por la mañana juego al golf. 10. Por la tarde toco unos discos primero. 11. Después, busco mi libro de español. 12. Por fin comienzo a estudiar. 13. Leo bien toda la lección. 14. Practico el diálogo varias veces. 15. A las cinco conduzco mi coche a casa de Ramón.

b. Repitan la frase; luego, repítanla otra vez, cambiando la forma del verbo al pretérito de indicativo.

All verbs in this exercise to be changed are stem-changing verbs, Class I; remember that the stem vowel of these verbs does not change in the preterit:

1. Ellos empiezan a examinar la lista. 2. Yo cierro las puertas. 3. ¿No cierras tu libro? 4. ¿No vuelven Uds. a las cinco? 5. Jorge le devuelve el dinero a su amigo. 6. Ella no recuerda el diálogo. 7. Carlos y yo lo recordamos muy bien. 8. Ellos pierden el autobús. 9. Carlos nunca piensa en Juanita. 10. ¿Se sienta Felipe en la sala de clase?

c. Para contestar afirmativamente:

1. ¿Buscaste el libro de texto?
2. ¿Tocaste la guitarra anoche?
3. ¿Jugaste al fútbol el sábado?
4. ¿Condujiste el coche al centro?
5. ¿Almorzaron Uds. a las doce?
6. ¿Oyeron Uds. la orquesta ayer?
7. ¿Creyeron Uds. lo que dijo ella?
8. ¿Leyeron Uds. la novela?

IV. VERBOS QUE CAMBIAN LA VOCAL RADICAL, GRUPOS II Y III, EN EL PRETÉRITO

Stem-changing verbs, Class II and Class III, change **e** to **i** and **o** to **u** in the third person singular and plural of the preterit.

	3rd Sing.	*3rd Plural*
sentir:	**sintió**	**sintieron**
dormir:	**durmió**	**durmieron**
pedir:	**pidió**	**pidieron**

a. Repitan la frase; luego, repítanla otra vez, cambiando la forma del verbo al pretérito:

1. Los muchachos se divierten. 2. María se divierte también. 3. Ricardo prefiere ir al Centro de Estudiantes. 4. Ellos prefieren no acompañarle. 5. Mi padre duerme la siesta. 6. Juan consigue un puesto. 7. ¿Le pide Ud. a él alguna cosa? 8. Los niños nunca me piden nada. 9. Mi hermano se viste rápidamente. 10. Mis hermanas se visten despacio. 11. ¿Sigue Ud. por este camino? 12. ¿Repiten ellos el diálogo?

b. Para expresar en español:

1. They sleep well; they slept well. 2. Tom has a good time; he had a good time. 3. Jane asks for the book; she asked for the book. 4. My mother serves coffee; she served coffee. 5. The teacher repeats the question; he repeated the question. 6. Henry continues working there; he continued working there. 7. I do not drive my car downtown; I did not drive my car downtown. 8. I take a nap; we took a nap. 9. I obtained a job; my brother obtained a job also. 10. I ate lunch in the Student Center; Charles ate lunch there also.

V. VERBOS QUE TIENEN FORMAS IRREGULARES EN EL IMPERFECTO DE INDICATIVO

All verbs in Spanish have regular forms in the imperfect indicative tense except **ir**, **ser**, and **ver**. Their forms are:

ir:	**iba**	**ibas**	**iba**	**íbamos**	**ibais**	**iban**
ser:	**era**	**eras**	**era**	**éramos**	**erais**	**eran**
ver:	**veía**	**veías**	**veía**	**veíamos**	**veíais**	**veían**

Repitan la frase; luego, repítanla otra vez, cambiando la forma del verbo al imperfecto de indicativo:

1. Yo no sé nada de particular.   2. Carlos siempre tiene suerte.   3. Marta no está en su cuarto.   4. No queremos llegar tarde.   5. Van a la biblioteca todas las noches. 6. Vamos a la iglesia los domingos.   7. Es un día hermoso.   8. Las clases no son grandes.   9. Los vemos todos los días.   10. Yo los veo a menudo.

TERCERA LECCIÓN PRELIMINAR

El futuro y el condicional de los verbos regulares. Verbos que tienen formas irregulares en el futuro y en el condicional. Los tiempos compuestos. Formas del participio presente

LA GRABADORA DE ROBERTO

(*Tomás encuentra a un compañero de clase en el Centro de Estudiantes.*)

TOMÁS. Ricardo, ¿dónde has estado? Te llamé por teléfono esta tarde y nadie contestó.

RICARDO. He estado en el cuarto de Roberto. Su papá le ha regalado una grabadora de cinta portátil.

TOMÁS. ¿De veras? ¡Roberto no me ha dicho nada de eso!

RICARDO. Esta noche pensamos grabar la conferencia del profesor Valdés. ¿Podrás ir con nosotros a la conferencia?

TOMÁS. ¡Encantado! Así no tendremos que tomar notas. ¿A qué hora iremos?

RICARDO. Para llegar a tiempo, habrá que salir a eso de las siete.

TOMÁS. Muy bien. Pasaré por tu cuarto un poco antes de las siete. Hasta la vista.

RICARDO. Hasta la vista, Tomás.

la cinta tape
la conferencia lecture
  ¡encantado, -a! (I'll be) delighted to!
la grabadora (de cinta) tape recorder

grabar to tape, record
portátil portable
regalar to give (*as a gift*)

A. Busquen en el diálogo las frases que correspondan a las siguientes:

1. I telephoned you. 2. a tape recorder. 3. Really? 4. Tonight we intend to tape the lecture. 5. Delighted to! 6. Thus we shall not have to take notes. 7. At what time shall we go? 8. In order to arrive on time. 9. it will be necessary to leave at about seven o'clock. 10. I shall come (pass) by your room a little before seven. 11. I'll see you later (Until I see you).

B. Aprendan el diálogo de memoria para poder repetirlo con el profesor (la profesora) o con uno de sus compañeros.

C. Preparen un diálogo original, de unas seis líneas, para recitar en clase, empleando las frases y preguntas siguientes como elemento inicial:[1]

1. CARLOS.   Tuve que ir al centro esta mañana.
   TOMÁS.   ¿Fuiste en coche?

2. SRTA. FLORES. Este joven quiere saber si le permite Ud. asistir a una de sus clases.
   SR. VALDÉS.   ¿Cuál de mis clases le interesa?

3. JUAN.   María, ¿quieres traerme un vaso de agua, por favor?
   MARÍA.   ¿No prefieres un refresco?

PRONUNCIACIÓN

Intonation.   Review the section on intonation in Appendix A, pages 297–298.   In a series or enumeration, which may consist of three or more members (nouns, adjectives, phrases or clauses), each member of the series constitutes a separate breath-group. The intonation pattern varies depending on the position of the series in the sentence.

a. If the series begins the sentence, all the breath-groups end with a slight fall of the voice except the last group, in which the voice rises to a pitch above the normal tone (level 3).

b. If the series occurs at the end of a sentence, the last two groups follow the pattern of the contrasting rise and fall of a declarative sentence of two members, but the preceding groups all end with a fall of the voice slightly below the normal tone.   If the series is left incomplete (that is, if the last two members are not connected by the conjunction **y**), all the groups will end with a slight fall in the voice.   Practice the following examples:

[1] Review of dialogues on pages 1 and 8 will be helpful to the student in preparing the new dialogues.

Series at the beginning:

Los lunes, los
    martes y los
    jueves ceno
    en casa.

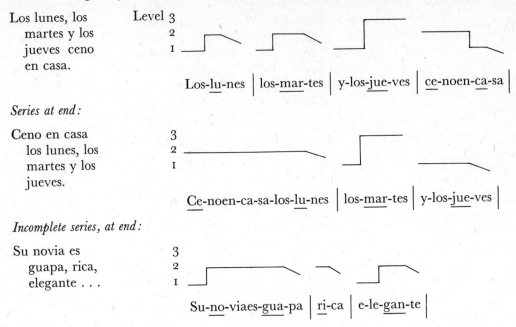

Series at end:

Ceno en casa
    los lunes, los
    martes y los
    jueves.

Incomplete series, at end:

Su novia es
    guapa, rica,
    elegante . . .

PARA REPASAR

I. REPASO DE LAS FORMAS DEL FUTURO Y DEL CONDICIONAL DE LOS VERBOS REGULARES

In Appendix D, page 311, review the forms of the future and conditional indicative
tenses of regular verbs.

Repitan la frase; luego, al oír un sujeto nuevo, substitúyanlo en la frase,
cambiando la forma del verbo cuando sea necesario:

1. *Inés* los llevará a casa.
    (*Yo, Tú, Mis hermanas, Marta y yo, Ustedes, Mi amiga*)

2. *Mis padres* no venderán el coche.
    (*Mi tío, Ella y yo, Tú, Ustedes, Yo, Ana*)

3. *Nosotros* asistiremos a la conferencia.
    (*Mis amigos, Usted, Tú, Yo, Tomás, Él y yo*)

4. *Ella* hablaría con otros estudiantes.
    (*Yo, Ustedes, Nosotros, Tú, José, Ellos*)

5. *Yo* no comería hasta las seis.
    (*Nosotros, Las muchachas, Él, Tú, Ustedes, Mi padre*)

II. VERBOS QUE TIENEN FORMAS IRREGULARES EN EL FUTURO Y EN EL CONDICIONAL

Verbs irregular in the future and conditional indicative tenses are:

Infinitive	*Future*	*Conditional*
1. haber	habré, -ás, -á, etc.	habría, -ías, -ía, etc.
poder	podré, -ás, -á, etc.	podría, -ías, -ía, etc.
querer	querré, -ás, -á, etc.	querría, -ías, -ía, etc.
saber	sabré, -ás, -á, etc.	sabría, -ías, -ía, etc.
2. poner	pondré, -ás, -á, etc.	pondría, -ías, -ía, etc.
salir	saldré, -ás, -á, etc.	saldría, -ías, -ía, etc.
tener	tendré, -ás, -á, etc.	tendría, -ías, -ía, etc.
valer	valdré, -ás, -á, etc.	valdría, -ías, -ía, etc.
venir	vendré, -ás, -á, etc.	vendría, -ías, -ía, etc.
3. decir	diré, -ás, -á, etc.	diría, -ías, -ía, etc.
hacer	haré, -ás, -á, etc.	haría, -ías, -ía, etc.

The future and conditional tenses have the same stem, and the endings are the same as for regular verbs. Note that the irregularity is in the infinitive stem used: in group (1) the final vowel of the infinitive has been dropped; in (2) the final vowel of the infinitive has been dropped and the letter **d** inserted to facilitate the pronunciation; and in (3) contracted stems are used.

a. Formen frases completas empleando las palabras **Carlos dice que** como elemento inicial, y cambiando el infinitivo en cursiva (*in italics*) a la forma correcta del futuro:

1. *tener* que trabajar el lunes.
2. *poder* ir a la conferencia.
3. *salir* de casa a las ocho.
4. *hacer* una excursión el domingo.
5. *poner* las cosas en el coche.
6. *haber* mucha gente en el teatro.
7. *haber* que salir a las siete.
8. no *venir* a vernos mañana.
9. no *querer* acompañarnos al cine.
10. *valer* más esperar hasta otro día.

Repitan el ejercicio, empleando las palabras **Carlos dijo que** como elemento inicial, y cambiando el infinitivo en cursiva a la forma correcta del condicional.

b. Para expresar en español:

1. Will you (*fam. sing.*) be able to go to the lecture? 2. We shall not have to take notes. 3. The boys will leave home at about seven o'clock. 4. It will be necessary

to arrive on time. 5. At what time will you want to return home? 6. Where will you put the packages? 7. Mary said that she would be able to tape the lecture. 8. Martha and Ann said that they would come a little before eight. 9. Tom recalled that there would be another lecture tomorrow night. 10. We said that we would not have time (in order) to hear the two lectures.

III. FORMACIÓN DE LOS TIEMPOS COMPUESTOS

The compound tenses are formed by using the appropriate form of the auxiliary verb **haber** with the past participle. In Appendix D, page 313, review the present perfect, pluperfect, preterit perfect, future perfect, and conditional perfect indicative tenses. The following past participles are irregular:

abrir:	**abierto**	*opened*	hacer:	**hecho**	*done*
decir:	**dicho**	*said*	ir:	**ido**	*gone*
describir:	**descrito**	*described*	morir:	**muerto**	*died*
descubrir:	**descubierto**	*discovered*	poner:	**puesto**	*put, placed*
devolver:	**devuelto**	*given back*	romper:	**roto**	*broken*
envolver:	**envuelto**	*wrapped*	ver:	**visto**	*seen*
escribir:	**escrito**	*written*	volver:	**vuelto**	*returned*

Also note the written accent on the following forms: **caer, caído**; **creer, creído**; **leer, leído**; **oír, oído**; **reír, reído**; **traer, traído**.

a. Para contestar afirmativamente:

1. ¿Has abierto la puerta?
2. ¿Has escrito la composición?
3. ¿Has envuelto el paquete?
4. ¿Has puesto la maleta en el coche?
5. ¿Ha roto Juan el vaso?
6. ¿Han dicho Uds. la verdad?
7. ¿Han visto Uds. la película?
8. ¿Habían ido Uds. al cine?
9. ¿Habían devuelto Uds. los libros?
10. ¿Habían oído Uds. la orquesta?

b. Repitan la frase; luego, repítanla dos veces más, cambiando la forma del verbo al pluscuamperfecto (*pluperfect*) y al futuro perfecto de indicativo (y observando la posición del pronombre usado como objeto del verbo):

1. Yo le he devuelto el dinero. 2. Luisa no les ha dicho eso. 3. ¿Han vuelto ellos a casa? 4. ¿Quiénes los han visto? — Nosotros los hemos visto. 5. ¿Adónde has ido? 6. Carlos nos lo ha traído.

c. Lean la frase en español; luego, repítanla cuatro veces, cambiando la forma del verbo al imperfecto, al pretérito, al futuro y al perfecto presente de indicativo:

1. Yo busco a Tomás.   2. Ellos no traen nada.   3. Yo empiezo a leer el diálogo.
4. Él y yo abrimos las ventanas.   5. Marta se pone el sombrero.   6. ¿Vas tú a la conferencia?

d. Para expresar en español:

1. Where have you (*fam. sing.*) been?   2. I have been at (in) the bookstore.   3. Have you (*pl.*) heard the tape?   4. We have not had time (in order) to go to the laboratory.
5. Have you seen my tape recorder?   6. I had seen it in the classroom.   7. John said that he had returned before seven o'clock.   8. Helen had not told me that.

IV. REPASO DE LAS FORMAS DEL PARTICIPIO PRESENTE

Review the forms of the present participle in Appendix D, page 310.   Some verbs which have irregular present participles are:

caer:	**cayendo**	*falling*		oír:	**oyendo**	*hearing*
creer:	**creyendo**	*believing*		poder:	**pudiendo**	*being able*
decir:	**diciendo**	*saying, telling*		traer:	**trayendo**	*bringing*
ir:	**yendo**	*going*		venir:	**viniendo**	*coming*
leer:	**leyendo**	*reading*				

In stem-changing verbs, Class II and Class III, the stem vowel **e** becomes **i** and **o** becomes **u** in the present participle.   Examples:

sentir:	**sintiendo**	*feeling*	dormir:	**durmiendo**	*sleeping*
pedir:	**pidiendo**	*asking*			

Repitan la frase; luego, repítanla otra vez, substituyendo el verbo con la forma correcta del presente de indicativo del verbo **estar** seguida del (*followed by the*) participio presente:

1. Mi padre lee el periódico.   2. Nosotros miramos el mapa.   3. Roberto aprende la lección.   4. María escribe una carta.   5. Los estudiantes oyen los discos.   6. Mi mamá duerme la siesta.   7. Carlos trae unas flores para Juanita.   8. Juan come con sus amigos.

CUARTA LECCIÓN PRELIMINAR

Formas de mandato correspondientes a «usted, ustedes».

Formas de mandato correspondientes a «tú».

Formas de mandato correspondientes a «vosotros, -as»

EN EL CUARTO DE ROBERTO

(*Ricardo y Tomás entran en el cuarto de Roberto.*)

ROBERTO.   Pasen ustedes.   ¿Qué tal, Tomás?   No sabía que venías.   Me alegro mucho de verte.

TOMÁS.   ¡Hola, Roberto!   Me han dicho que tienes una grabadora nueva.   Me gustaría verla.

ROBERTO.   Me la ha regalado mi padre.   (*Dirigiéndose a su compañero de cuarto.*) Jaime, para la máquina por un momento.   No se oye nada.   Pues, aquí la tienes.

TOMÁS.   ¡Qué bonita es!   ¡Qué suerte has tenido!

RICARDO.   ¿Por qué no grabamos una cinta en español?

ROBERTO.   Es muy fácil.   Acércate al micrófono.

RICARDO.   Con la grabadora podremos preparar mejor las lecciones de español . . .

JAIME.   Hemos estado grabando cintas toda la tarde.   ¿Por qué no salimos a tomar un refresco primero?

TOMÁS.   No olviden que tenemos que ir a la conferencia del profesor Valdés esta noche.

JAIME.   ¡Hombre!   Tienes razón.   Y queremos llevar la grabadora.

RICARDO.   Pues, ¡apúrense!   No tenemos mucho tiempo.

apurarse to hurry (up)
el compañero (**la compañera**) **de
cuarto** roommate (*m.* and *f.*)
dirigirse a to turn to, direct
oneself to, address (*a person*)

la máquina machine
el micrófono microphone
parar *trans.* to stop
¿qué tal? how are you? how
goes it?

A. Busquen en el diálogo las frases que correspondan a las siguientes:

1. (they) enter Robert's room.   2. Come in (*pl.*).   3. I am very glad to see you.
4. I should like to see it (*f.*).   5. Turning to his roommate.   6. stop the machine for
a moment.   7. We can't hear anything (Nothing is heard).   8. Well, here it is.
9. How pretty it is!   10. How lucky (fortunate) you have been!   11. Approach the
microphone.   12. all afternoon.   13. Why don't we go out to take a cold drink?
14. You are right.   15. hurry up (*pl.*)!

B. Aprendan el diálogo de memoria para poder repetirlo con el profesor (la
profesora) o con uno de sus compañeros.

C. Para contestar en español:

Preguntas sobre el diálogo:

1. ¿Dónde se encuentran Tomás y Ricardo?   2. ¿Por qué han ido al cuarto de
Roberto?   3. ¿Quién le ha regalado la grabadora a Roberto?   4. ¿Qué han estado
haciendo toda la tarde Roberto y Jaime?   5. ¿Adónde piensan ir esa noche?
6. ¿Qué piensan llevar a la conferencia?

Aplicación del diálogo

1. ¿Tiene usted una grabadora de cinta portátil?   2. ¿Qué podemos preparar
mejor con la grabadora?   3. ¿Ha grabado usted cintas en español?   4. ¿Por qué
es útil tomar notas durante las conferencias?   5. ¿Tiene usted un compañero (una
compañera) de cuarto?   6. ¿Por qué es difícil estudiar a veces en los cuartos de los
estudiantes?

PRONUNCIACIÓN

Intonation. Review the section on intonation in Appendix A, pages 297–298,
paying special attention to the remarks on interrogative sentences and exclamations.
A few additional observations follow.

a. The intonation pattern used to express special interest in an exclamatory sentence may also be used in questions (especially in those beginning with an interrogative word) and in declarative sentences. The voice rises above the normal tone when the last accented syllable is reached (level 3), and falls below the normal tone in the following syllable (or within the accented syllable, if no unstressed syllable follows). In a declarative sentence this pattern may be used to give special emphasis to any word of the breath-group.   Examples:

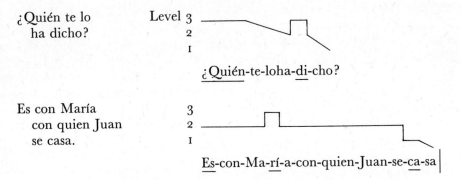

¿Quién te lo ha dicho?

Es con María con quien Juan se casa.

b. The pattern described in the preceding section is typical of commands and requests. The latter differ in that in commands the intervals between accented and unaccented syllables is greater than in requests; furthermore, in requests, the entire breath-group is usually uttered on a higher tone.   Examples:

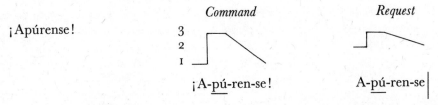

¡Apúrense!

c. If an interrogative sentence consists of two breath-groups, the first group ends below the normal tone.   Example:

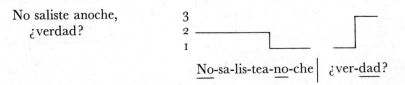

No saliste anoche, ¿verdad?

Write the interrogative and exclamatory sentences of the dialogue of this lesson, dividing them into breath-groups and into syllables, and outline the intonation patterns.

PARA REPASAR

I. FORMAS DE MANDATO CORRESPONDIENTES A «USTED, USTEDES»

Examples of polite commands are:

tome Ud.	} *take*	coma Ud.	} *eat*	abra Ud.	} *open*	**siga** Ud.	} *continue*
tomen Uds.		coman Uds.		abran Uds.		**sigan** Uds.	

In Spanish the stem for the polite command of all verbs, except the five which are given below, is that of the first person singular present indicative. The endings for the command forms of **-ar** verbs are **-e**, **-en**; for **-er** and **-ir** verbs the endings are **-a**, **-an**. **Usted** and **ustedes** are regularly expressed with the verb and are placed after it; in a series of commands, however, it is not necessary to repeat **usted** or **ustedes** with each verb. To express a negative command, place **no** before the verb: **No lo traiga usted**, *Don't bring it.*

In the case of reflexive verbs the pronoun **se** must be attached to affirmative polite commands, and it must precede the verb in negative commands. An accent mark must be written on the stressed syllable when **se** is attached to a command form: **Siéntese usted**, *Sit down*; **No se siente usted**, *Do not sit down.*

In reality, the polite command forms are those of the third person singular and plural of the present subjunctive tense, which will be discussed later. Review once more the first person singular present indicative of irregular and stem-changing verbs in Primera lección preliminar. Also, remember that verbs ending in **-car, -gar, -zar** (see page 12) change **c** to **qu**, **g** to **gu**, and **z** to **c** when the ending is **-e**: **busque(n) usted(es)**, **llegue(n) usted(es)**, **empiece(n) usted(es)**.

The five verbs (the polite command forms of **haber** are not used in Spanish) whose command stem is not that of the first person singular present indicative are:

Inf.	*1st Sing.* *Pres. Ind.*	*Sing.* *Command*	*Plural* *Command*	
dar	**doy**	**dé** Ud.	den Uds.	*give*
estar	**estoy**	**esté** Ud.	**estén** Uds.	*be*
ir	**voy**	**vaya** Ud.	**vayan** Uds.	*go*
saber	**sé**	**sepa** Ud.	**sepan** Uds.	*know*
ser	**soy**	**sea** Ud.	**sean** Uds.	*be*

a. Repitan la frase; luego, repítanla otra vez, cambiando el mandato al plural:

1. Pase usted, por favor. 2. Espere usted unos minutos. 3. Aprenda usted el diálogo. 4. Escriba usted la composición. 5. Siéntese usted ahora. 6. No le permita usted entrar. 7. No siga usted cantando. 8. Tráiganos usted refrescos.

b. Lean la frase en español; luego, cámbienla a la forma de mandato correspondiente a **usted**, según los modelos.

MODELOS: Juan abre la puerta.   Juan, abra Ud. la puerta.
          Juan no cierra el libro.   Juan, no cierre Ud. el libro.

1. Roberto entra en el cuarto. 2. Ricardo trae la grabadora. 3. Jaime busca una cinta. 4. Ana acerca el micrófono. 5. Carlos no para la máquina. 6. Luisa no empieza a leer. 7. José no sigue leyendo en inglés. 8. Miguel va a la conferencia. 9. Elena está en casa a las diez. 10. Tomás no sale a tomar café. 11. Inés no les pide un favor. 12. Jorge pone los libros sobre la mesa.

c. Para expresar en español de dos maneras (*in two ways*): primero, empleando la forma de mandato correspondiente a **Ud.**, y luego la forma correspondiente a **Uds.**:

1. Open the windows. 2. Learn the dialogue. 3. Repeat the sentence. 4. Return before four o'clock. 5. Don't arrive late. 6. Don't take the photos yet. 7. Don't drive the car tonight. 8. Don't go to the movie, please.

II. FORMAS DE MANDATO CORRESPONDIENTES A «TÚ»

Familiar singular commands are:

AFFIRMATIVE	NEGATIVE	AFFIRMATIVE	NEGATIVE
toma (tú)	no tomes (tú)	**vuelve** (tú)	no **vuelvas** (tú)
come (tú)	no comas (tú)	**pide** (tú)	no **pidas** (tú)
abre (tú)	no abras (tú)	busca (tú)	no **busques** (tú)

The affirmative familiar singular command has the same form as the third person singular of the present indicative in all verbs, except the nine listed below. This form is often called the singular imperative. The subject pronoun **tú** is omitted except for emphasis.

The negative familiar singular command is the familiar second person singular of the present subjunctive tense; that is, add **-s** to the third person singular present subjunctive.

The nine verbs which have irregular familiar singular command forms are:

decir:	**di**	no **digas**	ir:	**ve**	no **vayas**
hacer:	**haz**	no **hagas**	poner:	**pon**	no **pongas**

salir:	**sal**	no **salgas**		valer:	**val** (vale)	no **valgas**
ser:	**sé**	no **seas**		venir:	**ven**	no **vengas**
tener:	**ten**	no **tengas**				

In the case of reflexive verbs the pronoun **te** must be attached to affirmative familiar singular commands and it must precede the verb in negative commands. An accent mark must be written on the stressed syllable when **te** is attached to a singular command form of more than one syllable:

levantarse:	**levánta**te (tú)	*get up*	no te **levantes** (tú)	*don't get up*
sentarse:	**siénta**te (tú)	*sit down*	no te **sientes** (tú)	*don't sit down*
vestirse:	**víste**te (tú)	*get dressed*	no te **vistas** (tú)	*don't get dressed*
ponerse:	**pon**te (tú)	*put on*	no te **pongas** (tú)	*don't put on*
irse:	**ve**te (tú)	*go away*	no te **vayas** (tú)	*don't go away*

a. Lean la frase en español; luego, cámbienla a la forma de mandato correspondiente a **tú**; después, expresen el mandato negativamente:

1. Juan abre la puerta. 2. Ana cierra las ventanas. 3. Dorotea graba cintas ahora. 4. Luis sale despacio. 5. Roberto viene conmigo. 6. Marta se sienta en esa silla. 7. Juanito se viste ahora. 8. Tomás se pone los guantes. 9. Elena se va pronto. 10. Enrique se acerca al coche.

b. Para expresar en español empleando la forma correspondiente a **tú**, primero afirmativa y luego negativamente:[1]

1. Write the composition. 2. Come with the other students. 3. Do that before tomorrow. 4. Return the books today. 5. Stop the machine. 6. Get up before eight o'clock. 7. Sit down near the table. 8. Put on your hat.

III. FORMAS DE MANDATO CORRESPONDIENTES A «VOSOTROS, -AS»

Familiar plural commands are:

	AFFIRMATIVE	NEGATIVE		AFFIRMATIVE	NEGATIVE
tomar:	tomad	no toméis	cerrar:	cerrad	no cerréis
comer:	comed	no comáis	volver:	volved	no volváis
abrir:	abrid	no abráis	hacer:	haced	no **hagáis**

[1] Adverbs of manner are often formed by adding **-mente** (compare the English suffix *-ly*) to the feminine singular of adjectives; when two or more such adverbs are used in a series, **-mente** is added only to the last one.

To form the familiar plural command (the plural imperative) of all verbs, drop **-r** of the infinitive and add **-d**.   For the negative familiar plural command, use the second person plural of the present subjunctive.   The subject **vosotros, -as,** is usually omitted.

In addition to the stem change of **e** to **ie** and **o** to **ue** in all three singular forms and in the third person plural in the present subjunctive of Class I and Class II verbs, and of **e** to **i** in the same forms of Class III verbs, the stem vowel **e** also changes to **i** and **o** to **u** in the first and second persons plural of the present subjunctive of Class II and Class III verbs.   (In Appendix D, pages 322–324, see the complete conjugation of stem-changing verbs.   The first person plural form will not be used until the subjunctive mood is discussed later.)

	1st Plural *Pres. Subj.*	*2nd Plural* *Pres. Subj.*	*Affirmative* *Imperative*	*Negative* *Imperative*
sentir:	**sintamos**	**sintáis**	sentid	no **sintáis**
dormir:	**durmamos**	**durmáis**	dormid	no **durmáis**
pedir:	**pidamos**	**pidáis**	pedid	no **pidáis**

In forming the familiar plural commands of reflexive verbs, final **-d** is dropped before the reflexive pronoun **os**, except for **idos** (**irse**).   All **-ir** reflexive verbs except **irse** require an accent on the **i** of the stem of the verb: **vestíos.**

	AFFIRMATIVE	NEGATIVE
levantarse:	levantaos	no os levantéis
sentarse:	sentaos	no os sentéis
ponerse:	poneos	no os **pongáis**
vestirse:	vestíos	no os **vistáis**
irse:	**id**os	no os **vayáis**

Recall that in this text we have followed the practice, which is common in Spanish America, of using **ustedes** with the third person plural present subjunctive in familiar plural commands.   Since the familiar plural forms are used in much of Spain, they are needed for recognition in reading.

a. Cambien el infinitivo a la forma de mandato correspondiente a **vosotros, -as**; luego, expresen el mandato negativamente:

1. Hablar en inglés. 2. Comer antes de las seis. 3. Escribir las cartas hoy.
4. Venir a verme mañana. 5. Quitarse los zapatos. 6. Ponerse los guantes.
7. Vestirse pronto. 8. Acercarse al coche.

b. Para expresar en español, empleando la forma de mandato correspondiente a **vosotros, -as**:

1. Talk more slowly.   2. Look at the map.   3. Say that in Spanish.   4. Sit down
to the right.   5. Don't put on your (**los**) gloves yet.   6. Don't leave the room.
7. Have a good time tonight!   8. Do that tomorrow morning.

LECCIÓN PRIMERA

Usos de «estar» y «ser».   La construcción
reflexiva para expresar el sujeto indefinido y
para expresar la voz pasiva.   La «a» personal.
«Conocer» y «saber»

UN NUEVO[1] ESTUDIANTE EXTRANJERO

(Carlos habla con Pablo en la sala de clase antes de la llegada del profesor.)

CARLOS. ¡Hombre!   ¿Dónde has estado?   ¡Creía que estabas enfermo!

PABLO. He tenido que acompañar a su primera clase a un nuevo estudiante extranjero.

CARLOS. ¿Es el joven que está hablando con Dorotea?

PABLO. Sí, están sentados en la primera fila.   ¿No le conoces todavía?

CARLOS. Todavía no.   ¿De dónde es?

PABLO. Es colombiano.   Se llama Luis Sierra.   Su padre es un médico muy distinguido de Bogotá.

CARLOS. Ya sé quién[2] es.   Su padre está casado con una norteamericana que estudió en esta universidad, ¿verdad?

PABLO. Exactamente.   Y ella escribe artículos sobre los problemas sociales y económicos de Colombia.   Se han publicado algunos en el periódico de la universidad.

CARLOS. Los recuerdo.   Son los artículos que discutimos en clase la semana pasada, ¿verdad?   Son interesantes y están muy bien escritos.

---

[1] Before a noun **nuevo** means *new* in the sense of *another, different*, and after the noun, *new, brand-new*.   [2] Note that an accent mark is written on interrogative words when used in indirect questions as well as in direct questions.

PABLO. Se dice que Luis es músico y que toca la guitarra maravillosamente.
CARLOS. Bueno, ya entra el profesor. Me lo presentarás después.
PABLO. Con mucho gusto. Espérame después de esta clase.

casado, -a (**con**) married (to)	**la fila** row
colombiano, -a (*also noun*) Colombian	**la llegada** arrival
discutir to discuss	**maravillosamente** marvelously
distinguido, -a distinguished	**el músico** musician
económico, -a economic	

A. Busquen en el diálogo las frases que correspondan a las siguientes:

1. a new foreign student. 2. before the instructor's arrival. 3. I thought you were ill! 4. I have had to accompany . . . 5. they are sitting (seated) in the first row. 6. Not yet. 7. Where is he from? 8. His name is . . . 9. His father is married to . . . 10. social and economic problems. 11. Some have been published. 12. they are very well written. 13. They say that . . . 14. You will introduce him to me.

B. Para contestar en español:

Preguntas sobre el diálogo[1]

1. ¿Dónde se encuentran Carlos y Pablo? 2. ¿Qué ha tenido que hacer Pablo? 3. ¿Quién está hablando con Dorotea? 4. ¿Dónde están sentados Luis y Dorotea? 5. ¿De dónde es Luis? 6. ¿Qué escribe la madre de Luis? 7. ¿Qué dice Carlos de los artículos? 8. ¿Por qué no continúan charlando Carlos y Pablo?

Aplicación del diálogo

1. ¿Dónde nos encontramos ahora? 2. ¿Cuántos estudiantes extranjeros hay en esta universidad? 3. ¿Hay estudiantes extranjeros en esta clase? 4. ¿De qué países son los estudiantes extranjeros de esta clase? 5. ¿En qué fila está sentado (sentada) Ud.? 6. ¿Se publican artículos sobre problemas sociales en el periódico de esta universidad? 7. ¿Se discuten los artículos en clase? 8. ¿Se necesitan libros de texto en esta clase?

PRONUNCIACIÓN

A. Diphthongs. Review, in Appendix A, page 296, the sounds of the diphthongs. A diphthong is a sequence of two vowels pronounced in one syllable. As the first element of a diphthong, unstressed **i** is pronounced like a weak English *y* in *yes*, and

[1] Memorization of all or part of the dialogue in this lesson and hereafter is optional.

unstressed **u** is pronounced like *w* in *wet*. As the second element of a diphthong, unstressed **i** and **u** are glide sounds in the reverse direction: they start from the position of the preceding vowel and end in the position of Spanish **i** and **u**, respectively.

Remember that two adjacent strong vowels within a word do not combine in a single syllable, but form two separate syllables: **ve-o**. Likewise, when a weak vowel adjacent to a strong vowel has a written accent, it retains its syllabic value and forms a separate syllable: **dí-a**. An accent on a strong vowel merely indicates stress: **des-pués**.

Pronounce after your teacher:

1. estudiar	secretaria	alguien	comienza	cuando
cuaderno	nueve	puede	muy	Luis

2. traigo	vais	habéis	seis	oigo
soy	autor	la universidad	Europa	¿ve usted?
¿lo usamos?	¿jugó usted?	europeo	autobús	lo humano
leo	paseo	todavía	librería	señor Díaz
oímos	país	aprendió	adiós	también

B. Review Linking, in Appendix A, pages 297–298, and pronounce as one breath-group:

¿Cómo está usted?	¿Y usted?	¿Cuántos alumnos hay?
El que está hablando.	Está en su oficina.	En esta universidad.
Va a admitirle.	Y ella escribe.	Llega a las ocho y media.
¿Dónde has estado?	¿Diste un paseo?	Después de esta clase.

NOTAS GRAMATICALES

I. USOS DE «ESTAR» Y «SER»

A. **Estar** is used:

1. To express location (*i.e.*, to indicate where the subject is), whether temporary or permanent:

Ellos están en casa. They are at home.
¿Dónde has estado? Where have you been?
Monterrey está en México. Monterrey is in Mexico.

2. With an adjective to indicate the state or condition of the subject, when the state or condition is relatively temporary, accidental, or variable:

> **¿Está caliente[1] el café?**   Is the coffee hot?
> **Ellos han estado muy tristes.**   They have been very sad.
> **(Yo) creía que estabas enfermo.**   I thought (that) you were ill.

3. With the present participle to stress that an action is (was, has been, etc.) in progress at a given moment:[2]

> **Pablo está hablando con Dorotea.**   Paul is talking with Dorothy.
> **¿Qué estás haciendo ahora?**   What are you doing now?
> **Él estaba leyendo el periódico.**   He was reading the newspaper.
> **He estado trabajando toda la tarde.**   I have been working all afternoon.

4. With the past participle to describe a state or condition which results from a previous action (in this construction the past participle, which is used as an adjective rather than as a verb, agrees with the subject in gender and number):

> **Están sentados en la primera fila.**   They are seated in the first row.
> **Los artículos están muy bien escritos.**   The articles are very well written.
> **La ventana ya estaba cerrada.**   The window was already closed.

NOTE: Certain verbs, like **encontrarse**, **hallarse**, **verse**, **quedar(se)**, are often substituted for **estar**:

> **¿Dónde nos encontramos ahora?**   Where are we now?
> **La puerta ya se encontraba (se hallaba) cerrada.**   The door was already closed.
> **Ella quedó sorprendida al saber eso.**   She was surprised upon knowing (to know) that.

B. Ser is used:

1. To establish an identity between the subject and a noun or pronoun, and, less commonly, with adverbs, infinitives, or clauses used as nouns:

> **Él es músico.**   He is a musician.
> **Soy yo; es ella.**   It is I; it is she.

---

[1] Remember that in a question a predicate adjective normally follows the verb immediately.   [2] The progressive forms of **ir**, **salir**, and **venir** are rarely used.

> **Aquí es donde viven.**   Here is where they live.
> **Ver es creer.**   Seeing is believing.
> **Lo bueno es que él ya ha vuelto.**   What is good is that he has already returned.

2. With an adjective to express an essential quality or characteristic of the subject that is relatively permanent; this includes adjectives of color, size, shape, nationality, and the like, and those adjectives which describe personal qualities, including the adjectives **joven, viejo, rico, pobre, feliz**:

> **Luis es colombiano.**   Louis is a Colombian.
> **Los artículos son interesantes.**   The articles are interesting.
> **Estas casas son grandes (blancas).**   These houses are large (white).
> **No somos viejos.**   We are not old.
> **Aquel hombre no es rico (pobre).**   That man is not rich (poor).

3. With the preposition **de** to show origin, possession, or material, and with the preposition **para** to indicate for whom or for what a thing is intended:

> **¿De dónde es Luis?**   Where is Louis from?
> **¿Es de Roberto este coche?**   Is this car Robert's?
> **Estos relojes son de oro.**   These watches are (of) gold.
> **¿Para quién es el periódico?**   For whom is the newspaper?

4. In impersonal expressions:

> **Es necesario (mejor) esperar un rato.**   It is necessary (better) to wait a while.
> **No es fácil recordar eso.**   It is not easy to remember that.

5. To express time of day:

> **¿Qué hora es?**   What time is it?
> **Es la una y media.**   It is half past one.
> **Son las diez en punto.**   It is ten o'clock sharp.

NOTE: The verb is always plural in expressing time of day, except when followed by the hour *one o'clock*.

6. With the past participle to express the passive voice:

> **La carta fue escrita por Ana.**   The letter was written by Ann.
> **Él es estimado de todos.**   He is esteemed by all.
> **Los niños fueron vistos allí.**   The children were seen there.

In expressing the passive voice (*i.e.*, when the subject of the verb is acted upon by a person or thing) by means of **ser** and the past participle, the latter agrees with the subject in gender and number. The agent *by* is usually expressed by **por**; **de** is used, however, when the action represents a mental or emotional act (second example).

When a person receives the action of the verb (second and third examples), the third person plural active construction is replacing the passive construction, particularly in modern usage:

> **Todos le estiman.** All esteem him (He is esteemed by all).
> **Vieron a los niños allí.** They saw the children (The children were seen) there.

C. **Ser** and **estar** with certain adjectives

The meaning of some adjectives varies according to whether they are used with **ser** or **estar**. In general, **ser** indicates the normal or natural quality of the adjective, while **estar** indicates a temporary or subjective idea, often with the value of *look*, *feel*, *taste*, etc. A few examples which show the contrasts are:

With **ser**	With **estar**
Ana es buena. Ann is good. *(By nature)*	**Ana está buena.** Ann is well. *(In good health)*
José es malo. Joe is bad. *(By nature)*	**José está malo.** Joe is ill. *(In poor health)*
Él es enfermo. He is sickly. *(An invalid)*	**Él está enfermo.** He is sick. *(Temporarily)*
Ella es bonita. She is pretty. *(Naturally pretty)*	**¡Qué bonita está ella hoy!** How pretty she is (looks) today! *(Appearance)*
La nieve es fría. Snow is cold. *(Naturally cold)*	**El agua está fría.** The water is cold. *(Changeable, temporary)*
Marta es joven. Martha is young. *(Age regarded as characteristic)*	**Marta está joven hoy.** Martha is (looks) young today. *(Appearance)*
¿Es casado o soltero? Is he married (a married man) or single (a bachelor)?	**Está casado con una norteamericana.** He is married to an American woman.

NOTE: In the last example **casado** is considered a noun when used with **ser**, and an adjective, representing the result of an action (his marriage), when used with **estar**.

Ejercicios

A. Para contestar afirmativamente en español:

1. ¿Está abierta la ventana?
2. ¿Ha estado Pablo en México?
3. ¿Estarán Uds. listos a las tres?
4. ¿Están bien escritos todos los artículos?

5. ¿Has estado escuchando discos?
6. ¿Están Uds. sentados ahora?
7. ¿Estaba contenta la muchacha?
8. ¿Estuvo Carlos en México dos semanas?

B. Para contestar negativamente:

1. ¿Es profesor el padre de Luis?
2. ¿Es allí donde vive Carlos?
3. ¿Son largos los artículos?
4. ¿Son nuevas las dos guitarras?

5. ¿Es de Colombia aquel estudiante?
6. ¿Fue difícil aprender el diálogo?
7. ¿Eran las doce cuando llegó María?
8.. ¿Era para Dorotea el regalo?

C. Después de escuchar los dos grupos de palabras, combínenlos en una sola oración *(sentence)* por medio de la forma correcta de **ser** o **estar** en el presente de indicativo:

1. Nuestros amigos _____ jóvenes.
2. Esta revista _____ para Roberto.
3. La puerta no _____ cerrada ahora.
4. Uds. y yo _____ hablando en español.
5. Yo sé que _____ necesario practicar.

6. Luis Sierra _____ de Colombia.
7. El joven _____ muy simpático.
8. Esta agua no _____ muy fría.
9. Aquella casa nueva _____ de piedra.
10. La hermana de Juan _____ muy enferma hoy.

D. Para completar con la forma correcta de **estar** o **ser** en el presente de indicativo, menos en 9, 17 y 18:

1. ¿Qué _____ el tío de Juan? ¿_____ médico? 2. Enrique _____ de la Argentina; _____ argentino. 3. Lima, que _____ una ciudad grande, _____ en el Perú. 4. Aunque aquella señora _____ rica, nunca _____ contenta. 5. ¿Qué hora _____? —Creo que _____ las cinco y media. 6. Los Andes, que _____ montañas muy altas, siempre _____ cubiertos de nieve. 7. La novia de Carlos _____ rubia; se dice que _____ muy simpática. 8. El profesor Valdés no _____ en su oficina hoy porque _____ enfermo. 9. ¿Dónde has _____ tú? ¿_____ muy cansado? 10. No _____ difícil aprender el diálogo porque _____ bastante corto.

11. ¿Cuál _____ la fecha de hoy?   Y, ¿_____ martes o miércoles?   12. ¿Qué _____ haciendo tú en este momento?   —Yo _____ escuchando una cinta. 13. _____ mejor decir que nosotros no _____ ni ricos ni pobres.   14. ¿Para quién _____ estas cartas que _____ escritas en portugués?   15. Aquellos niños que _____ sentados en el patio _____ muy corteses.   16. Hoy _____ un día muy hermoso; por eso mi mamá _____ trabajando en su jardín.   17. Las ventanas _____ abiertas. ¿Por quién _____ (*pret.*) abiertas?   18. Este edificio _____ (*pret.*) construido por el señor Gómez.   _____ (*pres.*) bien construido.

II. LA CONSTRUCCIÓN REFLEXIVA PARA EXPRESAR EL SUJETO INDEFINIDO *ONE, THEY, YOU, WE, PEOPLE,* Y PARA EXPRESAR LA VOZ PASIVA

A. To express an indefinite subject, corresponding to English *one, people, we, you* (indefinite), Spanish uses **se** with the third person singular of the verb:

Se dice que Luis es músico.   They say (People say, One says, We say, It is said) that Louis is a musician.
No se puede entrar.   One (People, You) cannot enter.
Se trabaja mucho aquí.   One works (People, You work) hard here.

With a reflexive verb, and occasionally with other verbs, **uno** is used:

Uno se levanta tarde los domingos.   One gets up late on Sundays.
No se (Uno no) puede hacer eso.   One cannot do that (That cannot be done).

As in English, the third person plural may be used to indicate an indefinite subject:

Dicen que él volverá pronto.   They say (It is said) that he will return soon.

B. If the subject of a passive sentence is a thing and the doer of the action is not expressed, **se** is used to substitute for the passive voice.   In this case the verb is in the third person singular or plural, depending on whether the subject is singular or plural.   The reflexive verb normally precedes the subject in this construction.

Allí se habla español.   Spanish is spoken there.
Se cierran las tiendas a las cinco.   The stores are closed at five o'clock.
Se escribieron los artículos ayer.   The articles were written yesterday.
Se han publicado algunos en el periódico.   Some have been published in the newspaper.

When the subject is singular, as in **Allí se habla español,** the construction may be considered as an indefinite subject or as a passive sentence: *People (They) speak Spanish there,* or *Spanish is spoken there.*

Ejercicios

A. Después de escuchar cada frase, repitan la frase, cambiándola a la construcción reflexiva, según los modelos.

MODELOS: Cierran la puerta a las seis.   Se cierra la puerta a las seis.
                Aquí no compran libros.   Aquí no se compran libros.

1. En el Brasil hablan portugués.
2. Leen libros en la biblioteca.
3. No venden zapatos en la librería.
4. No conocen muy bien la música latinoamericana.
5. Cantan muchas canciones populares.
6. Ven un avión grande en el aeropuerto.
7. Aquí discuten problemas económicos.
8. No abren las oficinas hasta las diez.
9. Escriben muchos artículos buenos para este periódico.
10. Han publicado algunos de ellos.

B. Para expresar en español, usando **se** o **uno** como sujeto indefinido:

1. They say that it is going to rain.
2. How do they do that in Spain?
3. People know that she is in Mexico.
4. We cannot do that easily.
5. One enters through this door.
6. One dresses slowly at times.

III. LA «A» PERSONAL

When the direct object of the verb is a definite person (or persons), or a personified object, the personal or distinctive **a** (not translated in English) regularly introduces the object, except after **tener**:

> **Encontré a Juanito en el jardín.**   I found Johnny in the garden.
> **Vimos al señor Gómez.**   We saw Mr. Gómez.
> **Temen a la muerte.**   They fear death.
>
> BUT: **Tengo diez primos.**   I have ten cousins.

The personal **a** is also used when the direct object is **quien(es)**, *whom*, **¿quién(es)?** *whom?* or one of the indefinites or negatives[1] **alguien** and **nadie**, and **alguno, -a**, and **ninguno, -a**, when the latter two refer to persons:

> **¿Has visto a alguien?**   Have you seen anyone?
> **No he llamado a ninguno de ellos.**   I haven't called any (one) of them.

The distinctive **a** may also be used before geographical proper names, unless this name is preceded by the definite article, although in current usage **a** is being omitted more and more in such constructions:

[1] See Lección cuatro for discussion of the indefinites and negatives.

Visitaron (a) México.   They visited Mexico.
Desean ver el Cuzco.   They want to see Cuzco.

Because of the flexible word order in Spanish, the distinctive **a** is required occasionally to avoid ambiguity when both the subject and the direct object refer to things:

La paz sigue a la guerra.   Peace follows war.

Ejercicio

Lean en español, supliendo la **a** personal cuando se necesite *(it is needed)*:

1. Juan esperó _____ Bárbara.
2. ¿Han visto Uds. _____ sus tíos?
3. ¿_____ quién llamaste?
4. Luis conoce bien _____ Bogotá.
5. Yo conocí _____ la señora Sierra.

6. No he ayudado _____ nadie hoy.
7. Él quería visitar _____ la Argentina.
8. Ana tiene _____ muchos amigos allí.
9. ¿Acompañó Ud. _____ alguien ayer?
10. Él y yo saludamos _____ la profesora.

IV. «CONOCER» Y «SABER»

Conocer means *to know* in the sense of *to be acquainted with someone, to know (be familiar with) something, to meet* (for the first time), or *to recognize*.   The verb is followed by a clause only when it has the last meaning.

Yo conozco a la señorita.   I know the young lady.
El profesor conoce bien la ciudad.   The instructor knows the city well.

Saber means *to know* in the sense of *to have knowledge of, know facts*; followed by an infinitive it means *to know how to, can* (mental ability):

Ya sé quién es.   I already know who he is.
Sabíamos que él había llegado.   We knew that he had arrived.
Luis sabe tocar la guitarra.   Louis knows how to (can) play the guitar.

Ejercicio

Para leer en español, completando las frases con la forma correcta de **conocer** o **saber**:

1. Yo _____ que Luis es colombiano.
2. Voy a preguntarle si _____ a Marta.

3. Nosotros _____ a Miguel Valdés anoche.
4. ¿_____ Ud. dónde vive él?

5. ¿———— tú si nuestro profesor ———— bien el arte mexicano?
6. Los estudiantes ———— hablar español.

7. Todo el mundo ———— que yo no ———— bien el país.
8. Ana no ha ———— a mi amiga María.

RESUMEN

A. Usos de los verbos **estar** y **ser**. Lean en español, supliendo la forma correcta del verbo que se necesite:

1. Mi mamá ———— enferma hoy.
2. Esta comida ———— (*tastes*) muy rica.
3. ¿———— rico su amigo mexicano?
4. ¿Qué ———— tu padre?
5. Mi hermano quiere ———— abogado.
6. Nuestra hermana ———— contenta.

7. ¿De dónde ———— tú?
8. La puerta ———— (*pret.*) abierta por mí.
9. La puerta todavía ———— abierta.
10. ¿———— joven tu tía?
11. Yo ———— (*pres. perf.*) leyendo el libro.
12. ———— las nueve y cuarto.

B. Usos de la construcción reflexiva y de la voz pasiva. Para expresar en español:

1. How does one say that in Spanish?
2. People know that he is from Chile.
3. At what time is the door opened?
4. Books are not sold in this store.

5. One can learn this lesson easily.
6. The letter is written in Spanish.
7. These flowers were cut yesterday.
8. One sits down in order to rest.

9. Caroline made these dresses.
10. The dresses were made by Caroline.
11. The dresses are well made.

12. John closed the window.
13. The window was closed by John.
14. The window is closed now.

C. Usos de la **a** personal y de los verbos **conocer** y **saber**. Para expresar en español:

1. Whom did you (*fam. sing.*) call?
2. Paul and I saw Louis Morales.
3. Wait (*pl.*) for your friends.
4. Have you helped Jane today?

5. Do they know that we are here?
6. We know John's parents very well.
7. I know that they left last night.
8. Do you know anyone in Spain?

LECCIÓN DOS

Los pronombres personales.   Usos de los
pronombres personales que designan el sujeto.
Colocación del pronombre como objeto del verbo.   Las
formas preposicionales y la construcción redundante.
Los pronombres y verbos reflexivos.   Colocación respectiva
de dos pronombres, uno como objeto directo y otro como
objeto indirecto.   Repaso de los números cardinales

¿DÓNDE PASÓ USTED LAS VACACIONES?

(*La profesora habla con los estudiantes antes de comenzar la clase de español.*)

SRTA. FLORES.	Esta mañana ustedes han llegado muy temprano. Podemos charlar un poco antes de comenzar la lección.
CARLOS.	Señorita Flores, ¿por qué no nos cuenta usted lo que hizo durante el verano?
SRTA. FLORES.	Pasé el mes de julio en México, estudiando en la Universidad de Guadalajara. Me divertí mucho. Y usted, Carlos, ¿dónde pasó usted las vacaciones?
CARLOS.	Las pasé aquí, trabajando en una tienda. No puedo quejarme; me gustó mucho el trabajo.
SRTA. FLORES.	Me alegro de saber eso. ¿Qué va a hacer con el dinero que ha ganado?
CARLOS.	Lo estoy ahorrando para un viaje que pienso hacer el verano que viene.
SRTA. FLORES.	Se va a hacer rico, Carlos. Y usted, María, ¿qué hizo durante las vacaciones?

MARÍA.   Hicimos un viaje muy interesante por el sudoeste, visitando muchos
                 sitios en los estados de Nuevo México, Arizona y California.   En
                 ellos hay ríos, montañas y ciudades con nombres españoles.   Le
                 habría dado a usted gusto oírme pronunciarlos correctamente.

SRTA. FLORES.   Bueno, si quieren acercarse y sentarse, podremos comenzar la
                 lección de hoy.   Otro día hablaremos más de sus vacaciones.

ahorrar to save	**quejarse (de)** to complain (of)
correctamente correctly, accurately	**el trabajo** work

A. Busquen en el diálogo las frases que correspondan a las siguientes:

1. Where did you spend your vacation?   2. before beginning the Spanish class.
3. We can chat a little (while).   4. why don't you tell us what you did . . .?   5. I had
a very good time.   6. I spent it (*i.e.*, vacation) here.   7. I can't complain.   8. I
liked the work very much.   9. I am glad to know that.   10. I am saving it.   11. for
a trip that I am planning to take next summer.   12. You are going to become rich.
13. It would have pleased you very much.   14. to hear me pronounce them (*i.e.*, the
names) correctly.   15. if you will approach and be seated.   16. today's lesson.

B. Estudien las expresiones siguientes para emplear algunas de ellas en el
    diálogo citado, o para usarlas en un diálogo nuevo basado sobre el
    modelo:

comprar un coche (una bicicleta) to buy a car (a bicycle)	**seguir (i, i) trabajando** to continue working
costar (ue) mucho to cost a great deal	**tomar un curso** to take a course
la estación de gasolina service station	**visitar a mis abuelos** to visit my grandparents
practicar el español to practice Spanish	**vivir en el Canadá (la Florida)** to live in Canada (Florida)
quedarse aquí to stay here	**ya es la hora** the hour is over
los sábados Saturdays, on Saturdays	

PRONUNCIACIÓN

A. Spanish **p, t, c (qu, k)**.   In pronouncing these consonants, recall that the Spanish
sounds are pure stops, and not aspirated stops, as in English.   To avoid the aspiration,
or puff of air, that often follows the English sounds (*p*ʰen, *t*ʰen, *c*ʰan), the breath must

be held back during the articulation of the sound. The aspiration of the English sound is especially objectionable before **r** and before unstressed **i** and **u** in diphthongs; avoid **ᵗʰiene**, **ᵗʰres**. In the case of **t**, remember also that the Spanish sound is dental; that is, the tip of the tongue touches the back of the upper teeth, and not the ridge above the teeth, as in English. Pronounce after your teacher:

1. patio	pregunta	profesor	mapa	puse
2. tú	admitir	está	tengo	Tomás
3. canto	caso	saco	cuento	busqué
pequeño	aquí	quise	kilómetro	kilogramo
4. tiempo	tiene	quiero	puede	entrego

B. Review the observations on Spanish intonation, pages 17–18, 23–24, and Appendix A, pages 297–298, then read in Spanish, noting carefully the intonation patterns and the division into breath-groups. Why have certain syllables been underlined?

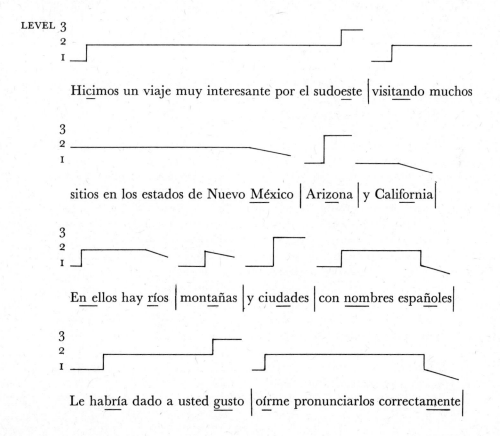

LEVEL 3

Hicimos un viaje muy interesante por el sudoeste │ visitando muchos

sitios en los estados de Nuevo México │ Arizona │ y California│

En ellos hay ríos │ montañas │ y ciudades │ con nombres españoles│

Le habría dado a usted gusto │ oírme pronunciarlos correctamente│

NOTAS GRAMATICALES

I. LOS PRONOMBRES PERSONALES

SINGULAR

Subject of Verb	*Object of a Preposition*	*Reflexive Object of a Preposition*
1. **yo** I	**mí** me	**mí** me, myself
2. **tú** you	**ti** you	**ti** you, yourself
3. **él** he **ella** she **usted** you	**él** him, it (*m.*) **ella** her, it (*f.*) **usted** you	**sí** himself, herself, yourself, itself

PLURAL

1. **nosotros, -as** we	**nosotros, -as** us	**nosotros, -as** us, ourselves
2. **vosotros, -as** you	**vosotros, -as** you	**vosotros, -as** you, yourselves
3. **ellos** they **ellas** they (*f.*) **ustedes** you	**ellos** them **ellas** them (*f.*) **ustedes** you	**sí** themselves, yourselves

II. USOS DE LOS PRONOMBRES PERSONALES QUE DESIGNAN EL SUJETO

The subject pronouns, except the polite forms for *you* (**usted** and **ustedes**, abbreviated to **Ud.** and **Uds.**, or **Vd.** and **Vds.**), are omitted unless needed for clearness or emphasis, or when two are combined as the subject. **Usted** and **ustedes**, which require the third person of the verb in Spanish, are regularly expressed, although excessive repetition should be avoided. The English subjects *it* and *they*, referring to things, are rarely expressed in Spanish, and the impersonal subject *it* is always omitted.

In general, the familiar forms **tú** and **vosotros, -as**, are used when the given name is used in English (in speaking to children, relatives, or close friends). In most of Spanish America **ustedes** is used for the plural of *you*, both familiar and polite. This practice is followed in the dialogues and exercises of this text.

Vamos al café ahora. We are going (Let's go) to the café now.
Ella lee un libro y él escribe una carta. She reads a book and he writes a letter.
Él y ella están en la biblioteca. He and she are in the library.
Ellas son felices. They (*f.*) are happy.
Usted habla bien el español. You speak Spanish well.
Tú hablas mejor que él. You speak better than he.

<table>
<tr><td colspan="3" align="center">SINGULAR</td></tr>
<tr><td>Direct Object of Verb</td><td>Indirect Object of Verb</td><td>Reflexive Object of Verb</td></tr>
</table>

me me	**me** (to) me	**me** (to) myself
te you	**te** (to) you	**te** (to) yourself
{**le, lo**[1] him		
{**lo** it (*m.*)		
la her, it (*f.*)	**le** (**se**) {(to) him, it	**se** {(to) himself, itself
{**le** you (*m.*)	{(to) her, it	{(to) herself, itself
{**la** you (*f.*)	{(to) you	{(to) yourself
lo it (*neuter*)		

PLURAL

nos us	**nos** (to) us	**nos** (to) ourselves
os you	**os** (to) you	**os** (to) yourselves
los, les[2] them		
las them (*f.*)	**les** (**se**) {(to) them	**se** {(to) themselves
{**los, les**[2] you	{(to) you	{(to) yourselves
{**las** you (*f.*)		

III. COLOCACIÓN DEL PRONOMBRE COMO OBJETO DEL VERBO

A. All object pronouns (direct, indirect, and reflexive) are regularly placed immediately before the verb, including the auxiliary verb **haber** in the compound tenses. Three major exceptions are explained in B, C, D, below.

Nos enviaron una tarjeta.   They sent us a card.
Ella no me llamó anoche.   She didn't call me last night.
Los he visto en la calle.   I have seen them in the street.

B. Object pronouns are placed after, and are attached to, affirmative commands.   (In commands the polite **usted**(**es**) is regularly expressed, but the familiar **tú** is used only for emphasis.)   Note that an accent must be written on the stressed syllable of a verb of more than one syllable when a pronoun is added:

Tráigalos usted en seguida.   Bring them at once.
Tómalo (tú), por favor.   Take it, please.

BUT: **Dame el periódico, por favor.**   Give me the newspaper, please.

[1] In Spanish America **lo** is more frequently used than **le**, meaning *him*.   [2] In Spain the form **les** is often used instead of **los** as direct object referring to masculine persons.

In negative commands, however, object pronouns precede the verb and are placed between the negative and the verb:

> **No les escriba usted hoy.**   Do not write to them today.
> **No me digas eso.**   Don't tell me that.
> **No te pongas el vestido nuevo.**   Don't put on the new dress.

C. Object pronouns are usually attached to an infinitive:

> **Empecé a leerlo.**   I began to read it.
> **Vamos a sentarnos ahora.**   We are going to (Let's) sit down now.

However, object pronouns may precede conjugated forms of certain verbs and verbal expressions, such as **ir a**, **haber de**, **querer**, **poder**, **saber**, followed by an infinitive:

> **Lo voy a hacer** *or* **Voy a hacerlo.**   I am going to do it.
> **Los he de traer** *or* **He de traerlos.**   I am to bring them.
> **La quieren ver** *or* **Quieren verla.**   They want to see her (it).
> **Usted se puede sentar** *or* **Usted puede sentarse.**   You may (can) sit down.
> **Se va a hacer** (*or* **Va a hacerse**) **rico, Carlos.**   You are going to become rich, Charles.

D. Object pronouns are attached to the present participle, except in the progressive forms of the tenses, in which case they may be attached to the participle or placed before the auxiliary. An accent must be written over the stressed syllable of the participle when a pronoun is attached:

> **Dándome la carta, Juan salió.**   Giving me the letter, John left.
> **Están leyéndola** *or* **La están leyendo.**   They are reading it.
> **Lo estoy ahorrando** *or* **Estoy ahorrándolo.**   I am saving it.

Ejercicios

A. Repitan cada frase y luego substituyan la frase en cursiva con el pronombre correspondiente, según el modelo.

MODELO: Carlos ahorró *el dinero.*   Carlos ahorró el dinero.   Carlos lo ahorró.

1. ¿Dónde pasó Ud. *las vacaciones?*
2. Visitamos *a nuestros abuelos.*
3. Mi hermano compró *la bicicleta.*
4. No he practicado mucho *el español.*
5. ¿No ha hecho Ud. *el trabajo?*
6. No pronuncian bien *los nombres.*

B. Para contestar empleando formas de mandato afirmativas y negativas, substituyendo el substantivo con el pronombre correspondiente.

MODELO: ¿Hago *el trabajo*?   Sí, hágalo Ud.   No, no lo haga Ud.

1. ¿Traigo *el dinero* ahora?   4. ¿Aprendo *los diálogos*?
2. ¿Compro *las flores*?   5. ¿Cierro *el libro*?
3. ¿Escribo *las frases*?   6. ¿Lavo *el coche* hoy?

C. Después de escuchar cada frase, repítanla dos veces, substituyendo el substantivo con el pronombre correspondiente, según el modelo.

MODELO: Estoy leyendo *el libro*.   Estoy leyéndolo.   Lo estoy leyendo.

1. Estoy ahorrando *el dinero*.   4. Yo estaba visitando *a María*.
2. Están pasando *las vacaciones* aquí.   5. Uds. no están mirando *el mapa*.
3. Estaban estudiando *la lección*.   6. No estás aprendiendo *los diálogos*.

D. Después de escuchar cada frase, repítanla dos veces, substituyendo el substantivo con el pronombre correspondiente.

MODELO: Voy a hacer *el viaje*.   Voy a hacerlo.   Lo voy a hacer.

1. ¿Vas a pasar *el verano* allí?   3. No quieren pronunciar *los nombres*.
2. Puedo traer *las revistas*.   4. No hemos de aprender *la canción*.

IV. LAS FORMAS PREPOSICIONALES Y LA CONSTRUCCIÓN REDUNDANTE

A. The prepositional forms are used only as objects of prepositions. They are the same as the subject pronouns, except for **mí** and **ti**:

> **Corrían hacia mí.**   They were running toward me.
> **Charlaré con él (ella).**   I shall chat with him (her).

When used with **con**, the forms **mí**, **ti**, and the reflexive **sí** (see section V, pages 50–51) become **conmigo**, **contigo**, **consigo**, respectively:

> **No van conmigo (contigo).**   They aren't going with me (with you).

B. The prepositional phrases **a mí, a ti, a él**, etc., are used in addition to the direct or indirect object pronoun for emphasis:

Yo la vi a ella, pero no a Juan.   I saw <u>her</u>, but not John.
A mí me gusta el cuadro.   <u>I</u> like the picture.

Since the indirect objects **le** or **les** have several meanings, the prepositional forms are often added for clearness.   They are added for courtesy when the direct object pronouns meaning *you* (polite) are used:

Yo le di a ella las flores.   I gave her the flowers.
Mucho gusto en conocerle(-la) a usted.   (I'm very) pleased to meet (know) you.

C. When a noun is expressed as the indirect object of the verb in Spanish, the corresponding indirect object pronoun is normally added.   With forms of **gustar**, the prepositional form must be used:

Le dimos a Felipe el dinero.   We gave Philip the money.
A Carlos le gusta (Le gusta a Carlos) la casa.   Charles likes the house.

The prepositional form must also be used when the verb is understood:

¿A quién viste?   ¿A él?   Whom did you see?   Him?
Les enseñé el reloj a ellos, pero no a ella.   I showed them the watch, but not her.

Ejercicio

Repitan cada frase y luego substituyan el substantivo con el pronombre correspondiente, según el modelo.

MODELO: Corrieron hasta *la esquina*.   Corrieron hasta la esquina.
                                          Corrieron hasta ella.

1. Fueron al río con *Ricardo*.
2. Charle Ud. un poco con *Marta*.
3. Estos regalos son para *mis padres*.
4. No hablen Uds. más de *las muchachas*.
5. Los niños corren hacia *la casa*.
6. El coche está enfrente de *ese edificio*.
7. Roberto trabaja en *aquella tienda*.
8. En *esos estados* hay varios parques.

V. LOS PRONOMBRES Y VERBOS REFLEXIVOS

A. Reflexive pronouns, which are used when the subject acts upon itself, may be direct or indirect objects:

Ricardo se sentó.   Richard sat down.
Voy a lavarme la cara.   I'm going to wash my face.
Levántense ustedes.   Get up.
Estamos desayunándonos.   We are eating breakfast.

The pronouns **mí, ti, nosotros, -as, vosotros, -as,** and **sí** (third person singular and plural) may be used reflexively: **para mí,** *for myself*; **para sí,** *for himself, herself, yourself* (polite), *itself, themselves* (*m.* and *f.*), *yourselves*; **Ella se lo llevó consigo,** *She took it with her* (*self*).

B. Reflexive verbs are much more frequent in Spanish than in English. A few verbs are always used reflexively in Spanish, while others may also be used as transitive or intransitive verbs, although usually with different meanings. Certain verbs and expressions which are regularly reflexive in Spanish are:

atreverse (a) *to dare* (*to*)	jactarse (de) *to boast* (*of*)
darse cuenta de *to realize*	quejarse (de) *to complain* (*of*)

Many intransitive verbs in English (that is, verbs that cannot take a direct object) are expressed in Spanish by using the reflexive pronoun with a transitive verb. Note the Spanish equivalents of some common English intransitive verbs:

acercar *to bring . . . near*	acercarse (a) *to approach, draw near*
acostar (ue) *to put to bed*	acostarse (ue) *to go to bed*
despertar (ie) *to awaken* (*somebody*)	despertarse (ie) *to wake up* (*oneself*)
divertir (ie, i) *to amuse*	divertirse (ie, i) *to have a good time*
lavar *to wash* (*something*)	lavarse *to wash* (*oneself*)
levantar *to raise, lift* (*up*)	levantarse *to get up, rise*
mudar *to change*	mudarse (de) *to change* (one's clothing, lodging, etc.)
sentar (ie) *to seat*	sentarse (ie) *to sit down*

In the case of certain verbs the reflexive translates *to become, get,* or *to be* plus an adjective. A few examples are:

alegrar *to make glad*	alegrarse (de) *to be glad* (*of, to*)
cansar *to tire* (*someone*)	cansarse *to become* (*get*) *tired*
vestir (i, i) *to dress* (*someone*)	vestirse (i, i) *to dress* (*oneself*), *get dressed*

Other common verbs whose meaning is changed when used reflexively are:

dormir (ue, u) *to sleep*	dormirse (ue, u) *to fall asleep*

hacer	*to do, make*	hacerse	*to become*
hallar	*to find*	hallarse	*to be found, be*
llamar	*to call*	llamarse	*to call oneself, be named*
poner	*to put, place*	ponerse	*to put on* (*oneself*); (+ adj.)
			to become

See Appendix E, pages 325–328, for other verbs of these types.

Ejercicio

Repitan cada frase; luego, al oír el sujeto nuevo, cambien la frase según el modelo.

MODELO: *Yo* me dormí en seguida.   Yo me dormí en seguida.
       (*José*)   José se durmió en seguida.

1. *Ana* se puso los guantes.   (*Ana y yo*)
2. *Yo* voy a sentarme cerca de ella.   (*Ricardo*)
3. *La niña* se vistió despacio.   (*Los niños*)
4. *Enrique* se divirtió mucho ayer.   (*Yo*)
5. *Tú* te levantaste tarde hoy.   (*Usted*)
6. *Jorge* está lavándose las manos.   (*Tú*)
7. *Juan y José* se alegraron de eso.   (*Luis y yo*)
8. *Pablo* se alegró de verlos.   (*Pablo y Carlos*)
9. *Yo* no me atreví a nadar en el río.   (*Nosotros*)
10. *Miguel y yo* nos mudamos de ropa hace media hora.   (*Yo*)
11. *Nosotros* no nos quejamos del profesor.   (*Roberto*)
12. *Tú* no te diste cuenta de eso.   (*Ustedes*)

VI. COLOCACIÓN RESPECTIVA DE DOS PRONOMBRES, UNO COMO OBJETO DIRECTO Y OTRO COMO OBJETO INDIRECTO

When two object pronouns are used together, the indirect object pronoun always precedes the direct. When both are in the third person, the indirect (**le, les**) becomes **se**. Since **se** may mean *to him, to her, to you* (polite), *to it*, or *to them*, the prepositional forms will often be required in addition to **se** for clarity. A reflexive pronoun precedes any other object pronoun.

    Él nos lo vendió.   He sold it to us.
    Lléveselo usted a ellos.   Take it to them.
    Ella empezó a leérmela.   She began to read it to me.
    No se lo escribas (**tú**) **a ella.**   Don't write it to her.

> **Dándomelos, Pablo salió.** Giving them to me, Paul left.
> **Luisa se lo puso.** Louise put it on.

Remember that an accent mark must be written on the stressed syllable of the verb when two object pronouns are attached to an infinitive, an affirmative command form, or present participle.

Ejercicio

Repitan cada frase; luego, substituyan los substantivos en cursiva con los pronombres correspondientes, según los modelos.

MODELOS: Juan le dio *las cosas a Marta.* Juan le dio las cosas a Marta.
Juan se las dio a ella.

José se lava *la cara.* José se lava la cara.
José se la lava.

1. Le llevé *el dinero a Felipe.*
2. No le escribí *la carta a Luis.*
3. Envíeles Ud. *los libros a sus amigos.*
4. No le vendan Uds. *a Ana el coche.*
5. No quieren traerme *las cosas* hoy.

6. No puedo leerles *el cuento a los niños.*
7. Él está explicándoles *los problemas.*
8. Ellos se están poniendo *los zapatos.*
9. Pónganse Uds. *el abrigo.*
10. No te laves *las manos* todavía.

VII. REPASO DE LOS NÚMEROS CARDINALES

A. Después de repasar los números cardinales y sus usos (Appendix C, pages 306–307), lean en español:

1. 18 muchachas. 2. 21 países. 3. 51 universidades. 4. 100 páginas. 5. 116 discos. 6. 200 preguntas. 7. 365 días. 8. 500 casas. 9. 1,000 empleados. 10. 1,000,000 de personas. 11. 5,000,000 de dólares. 12. 150,000 hombres.

B. Repasen el uso de los números para expresar fechas y los nombres de los meses (page 308); luego lean en español:

1. January 1, 1970. 2. May 2, 1972. 3. October 12, 1492. 4. September 29, 1547. 5. July 4, 1775. 6. February 22, 1789. 7. December 10, 1810. 8. November 11, 1812. 9. April 15, 1817. 10. March 31, 1827. 11. June 29, 1903. 12. August 14, 1809.

RESUMEN

A. Repitan cada frase; luego, substituyan el substantivo en cursiva con el pronombre correspondiente, colocándolo (*placing it*) correctamente:

1. Ellos comenzaron *el trabajo*.
2. Carlos visitó *a su abuelo*.
3. María compró *la bicicleta*.
4. Marta no hizo *los vestidos*.
5. Luis no leyó *las revistas*.

6. Traiga Ud. *las cintas*.
7. Lleven Uds. *sus cuadernos*.
8. Sirvan Uds. *los refrescos*.
9. No despierten Uds. *a Luisa*.
10. No pierdan Uds. *el autobús*.

11. Estamos terminando *las composiciones*.
12. Él y ella están leyendo *la novela*.
13. Mi mamá está visitando *a sus padres*.
14. Estaban practicando *el español*.

15. Vamos a leer *la lección*.
16. Han de llamar *a sus amigos*.
17. No querían lavar *el coche*.
18. Podían aprender *los diálogos*.

B. Repitan cada frase; luego, substituyan los substantivos en cursiva con los pronombres correspondientes:

1. Juan le envió *una tarjeta a Ana*.
2. Léales Ud. *la carta a los niños*.
3. No le vendas *el coche a Pablo*.
4. Ella está poniéndose *el vestido*.

5. Pónganse Uds. *los zapatos*.
6. No te pongas *el sombrero*.
7. Tengo que lavarme *las manos*.
8. Él ya se ha lavado *la cara*.

9. Los niños jugaban en *el parque*.
10. Marta está cerca de *sus padres*.

11. Ellos se quejaron de *las películas*.
12. Están sentados detrás de *su papá*.

C. Usos de los pronombres personales. Para expresar en español:

1. Tell me what she did yesterday.
2. Martha and he practice with me.

3. He and I work more than they.
4. <u>We</u> shall stay here this afternoon.

5. We saw Barbara; we saw her.
6. Did you call John? Did you call him?
7. They took the course; they took it.

8. Tom found his gloves; he found them.
9. My uncle Richard sold his house; he sold it.
10. I bought the cards; I bought them.

11. Write her a letter tomorrow.
12. Bring us the newspapers, please.
13. Take them this magazine tonight.

14. Do not send them the money yet.
15. Do not give Ann the flowers today.
16. Do not show them (*f.*) to her now.

D. Para expresar en español:

1. I put Johnny to bed; Johnny went to bed.
2. Jane amused the children; the children had a good time.
3. Robert's mother awakened him; Robert woke up early.
4. The teacher seated Mary in the first row; Mary sat down there.
5. Paul washed the car; then he washed his hands.
6. I realize that John became a doctor.

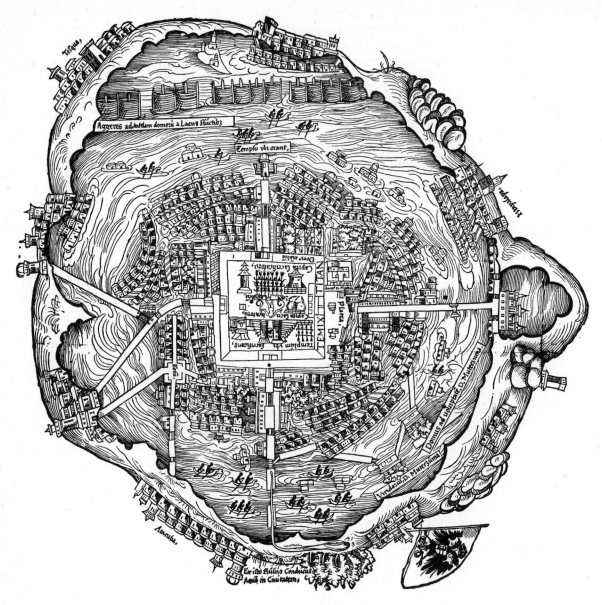

Mapa del lago y de la ciudad de México, 1524

LECTURA I

A. Estudio de palabras

Observations on Spanish cognates. The ability to recognize cognates is of enormous value in learning to read a foreign language. Only a few principles for recognizing cognates can be given here; other principles will be explained in the "Estudio de palabras" section of subsequent Lecturas. All examples listed below are taken from the reading selection of Lectura I.

1. Exact cognates. Many Spanish and English words are identical in form and meaning, although the pronunciation is different: anterior *(anterior, earlier)*, capital, civil, cruel, honor, labor, tropical, valor.

2. Approximate cognates. A few principles for recognizing approximate cognates are:

a. The Spanish word has a written accent and/or lacks a double consonant: América, Panamá, rebelión, región, religión.

b. Many English words lack Spanish final **-a, -e, -o** (and sometimes a written accent): azteca, marcha, persona, república; parte; océano, pacífico.

c. Certain Spanish nouns ending in **-cia** (also in **-cio**) end in *-ce* in English: abundancia, distancia, noticia, provincia, prudencia.

d. Certain Spanish nouns ending in **-ia** (**-ía**), **-io** end in *-y* in English: colonia, Epifanía (*Epiphany*), historia; territorio. (However, note the endings of Biblia, *Bible*, indio, *Indian*, and imperio, *empire*.)

e. Most Spanish nouns ending in **-ción** are feminine and end in *-tion* in English (sometimes the Spanish word lacks a double consonant): acusación, expedición, exploración, institución, nación, situación, vegetación.

f. Certain Spanish nouns ending in **-dad, -tad** end in *-ty* in English: crueldad, sinceridad; dificultad (*difficulty*), libertad.

g. Spanish adjectives ending in **-oso** end in *-ous* in English: maravilloso, religioso.

h. The Spanish ending **-ador, -edor, -idor**, applied to the stem of an infinitive, often indicates one who performs or participates in an action. *Compare:* conquistar, *to conquer, and* conquistador, *conqueror*; descubrir, *to discover, and* descubridor, *discoverer*; explorar, *to explore, and* explorador, *explorer*. Also note: emperador, *emperor*; gobernador, *governor*.

3. Less approximate cognates. Other words with miscellaneous differences which should be recognized easily, especially in context or when pronounced in Spanish are: bahía, *bay*; barril, *barrel*; cañón, *cannon*; capitán, *captain*; colono, *colonist*; conquista,

conquest; costa, *coast*; cristiano, *Christian*; desierto, *desert*; enemigo, *enemy*; enorme, *enormous*; época, *epoch*; espíritu, *spirit*; falso, *false*; fundación, *foundation, founding*; hostil, *hostile*; intérprete, *interpreter*; isla, *island*; istmo, *isthmus*; militar, *military*; oeste, *west*; permiso, *permission*; prisionero, *prisoner*; representante, *representative*; sudoeste, *southwest*; título, *title*; tribu, *tribe*; vano, *vain*; valle, *valley*.

B. Modismos *(Idioms)* y frases útiles

acabar de + *inf.* to have just + *p.p.*
acercarse a to approach, move toward
al año (día) siguiente (in, on) the following year (day)
al otro lado de on the other side of
al poco tiempo after (in) a short time
dar a to face
darse cuenta de to realize
de nuevo again, anew
dirigirse a to go (direct oneself) to
disfrutar de to enjoy
dos veces twice, two times
en busca de in search of
en ese momento at that moment

esto es that is
hay que + *inf.* one must, it is necessary to
llegar a ser to become
muchas veces many times, often
poco a poco little by little
por medio de by means of
tardar . . . en + *inf.* to take . . . to, delay . . . in
tener que + *inf.* to have to, must
tratar de + *inf.* to try to
tratar de + *obj.* to deal with
unirse a to join, unite with
unos (-as) cuantos (-as) a few, some (few)

C. Aspectos gramaticales[1]

1. **Al** plus an infinitive may be rendered into English by *on (in)*, *upon* plus a present participle, or by a finite verb introduced by *when*, as:

> **Al saber** Upon learning (finding out), When (he) learned (found out)
> **Al volver** On returning, When (he) returned

The infinitive may have a subject, in which case it follows the verb:

> **al estallar una rebelión** when a rebellion broke out
> **Al entrar Atahualpa en la plaza** When (As) Atahualpa entered the square

2. For a discussion of the passive voice and of the reflexive substitute for the passive in Spanish, see pages 35–36 and 38.

---

[1] The grammatical points explained in this section are marked in the Lectura with an asterisk, with few exceptions.

An additional use of the reflexive construction as a substitute for the passive occurs when **se** is used impersonally as the subject and the English noun subject is made the object of the Spanish verb.   The object pronoun **le** (*pl.* **les**) is used for a third person masculine object, direct or indirect:

Se le critica mucho a Cortés   Cortés is criticized (People criticize Cortés) a great deal

3. In Spanish when anything is taken away (bought, hidden, etc.) from anyone, the indirect object is used:

Para ocultar a los indios la muerte de ...
In order to hide from the Indians the death of ...

4. As explained on page 129, the infinitive is regularly used after the verbs **oír** and **ver**.   Note the use of the infinitive and the difference in meaning of the two expressions which follow:

los españoles oyeron decir que ... había un mar enorme ...
the Spaniards heard (it said) that ... there was an enormous sea ...
oyó hablar ... de tierras maravillosas ...
he heard (people talk) ... about marvelous lands ...

5. The definite and indefinite articles are discussed in some detail in Lección cuatro. In the following phrases used in this Lectura and listed separately here, note that the article is omitted in Spanish:

a manos de   at the hand(s) of
a poca distancia   at a short distance
en nombre de   in the name of

por orden de   at (by) the order of
por primera (tercera) vez   for the first (third) time

EXPLORADORES
Y CONQUISTADORES ESPAÑOLES

Durante la primera mitad del siglo XVI los españoles exploraron y conquistaron una gran[1] parte del Nuevo Mundo.   En un libro anterior[2] hemos hablado de exploradores, como Coronado, que visitaron por primera vez* los territorios que hoy forman parte del sudoeste de los Estados Unidos.   En esta Lectura vamos a tratar de algunos exploradores y conquistadores de otras partes de las dos Américas: Vasco Núñez de Balboa, Hernán Cortés, Francisco Pizarro y Hernando de Soto.

En el año 1510 Núñez de Balboa (1475–1517) guió la expedición de Martín Fernández de Enciso hasta la costa del istmo de Panamá, donde se fundó una colonia.   En la Española, hoy Santo Domingo, no le habían dado permiso para formar parte de la expedición, y Balboa había tenido que esconderse en uno de los barriles de provisiones.   Enciso le permitió continuar en la expedición al saber* que Balboa conocía bien las tierras adonde iban.

Al poco tiempo Balboa ganó la confianza[3] de los colonos y al estallar una rebelión*, llegó a ser el jefe de la nueva colonia.   Hablando con los indios, los españoles oyeron decir* que al otro lado de las montañas había un mar enorme, el Mar del Sur,[4] en el cual navegaban los barcos de una nación poderosa,[5] y que en esa nación podrían encontrar oro en abundancia.   Ésta fue la primera noticia que los españoles tuvieron del Océano Pacífico y del imperio de los incas.

En el mes de septiembre de 1513 Balboa, con 150 hombres, salió en busca del Mar del Sur.   Como tuvieron que atravesar una región de vegetación tropical y los indios eran hostiles, tardaron diez y nueve días en llegar a la cumbre[6] de las montañas, desde la cual Balboa vio por primera vez el gran océano.   En el lugar construyeron una cruz de madera,[7] con los brazos extendidos hacia los dos océanos.   Continuando hasta la costa, el 29 de septiembre Balboa entró en el agua y, en nombre del* rey de España, tomó posesión del Mar Pacífico y de todas sus costas y sus islas.

Al volver* a la colonia, Balboa encontró que sus enemigos habían lanzado[8] acusaciones falsas contra él y que el rey había nombrado a Pedrarias Dávila,

---

[1] **gran**, *great* (see page 111 for explanation).   [2] Turk and Espinosa: *Foundation Course in Spanish, Second Edition*, Heath, 1970.   [3] **confianza**, *confidence*.   [4] **Mar del Sur**, *Southern Sea*.   [5] **en el cual ... poderosa**, *in which the boats of a powerful nation sailed* (for a discussion of the long forms of relative pronouns, see pages 161–162).   [6] **cumbre**, *summit*.   [7] **cruz de madera**, *wooden cross*.   [8] **habían lanzado**, *had made (launched)*.

hombre cruel y codicioso,[1] gobernador de la colonia. Balboa se preparaba para emprender[2] un viaje de exploración al Perú cuando fue detenido por Pedrarias, que le condenó a muerte[3] en 1517. La república de Panamá ha honrado al descubridor dando su nombre a una ciudad y también a la moneda del país, que se llama *el balboa*.

Hernán Cortés (1485–1547) se embarcó para América a la edad de diez y nueve años. En la Española y en Cuba oyó hablar* muchas veces de tierras maravillosas que estaban al oeste, al otro lado del mar. Mandado por Diego Velázquez, gobernador de Cuba, a conquistar a México, resolvió emprender la conquista por cuenta propia.[4]

La expedición, que constaba de[5] unos 500 soldados, 12 naves, 16 caballos y unas cuantas armas de fuego,[6] llegó a la costa de México en el mes de abril de 1519. Después de fundar la ciudad de Veracruz, Cortés quemó[7] todas sus naves, menos una que mandó a España para anunciar la fundación de la nueva colonia. Con la ayuda de algunas tribus indígenas[8] que se convirtieron en aliados suyos,[9] Cortés y sus soldados invadieron el territorio de los aztecas. Al acercarse a Tenochtitlán, la capital de los aztecas, el emperador Moctezuma salió a recibirlos, y los españoles pudieron establecerse en la ciudad sin dificultad.

Comprendiendo que su pequeño ejército[10] estaba a la merced de los aztecas, los españoles se apoderaron de[11] la persona de Moctezuma y le obligaron a dar las órdenes que ellos le indicaban. Poco a poco los aztecas se dieron cuenta de la situación y se rebelaron contra los invasores.[12] Por orden de* los españoles Moctezuma salió a hablar con los indios, quienes le arrojaron una piedra que le causó la muerte.[13] Los españoles fueron obligados a salir de la ciudad la noche del 30 de junio de 1520. Aquella noche es conocida en la historia como «la Noche Triste»; en ella Cortés perdió unos 400 soldados. Al año siguiente, habiendo recibido nuevas fuerzas, Cortés pudo emprender de nuevo la conquista de Tenochtitlán.

Se le critica mucho a Cortés* por su crueldad, pero hay que reconocer que ningún conquistador le superó en valor, táctica militar, prudencia y sinceridad religiosa. Él mismo empezó la labor de establecer en la Nueva España,[14] esto es, en México, las instituciones que existían en su época en España.

---

[1] **codicioso,** *covetous, greedy.* [2] **emprender,** *(to) undertake.* [3] **le condenó a muerte,** *condemned him to death.* [4] **por cuenta propia,** *by himself, on his own (account).* [5] **constaba de,** *consisted of.* [6] **armas de fuego,** *firearms.* [7] **quemó,** *burned.* [8] **indígenas,** *native, Indian.* [9] **que ... suyos,** *who became (were converted into) allies of his* (see pages 201–202 for explanation of **suyos**). [10] **ejército,** *army.* [11] **se apoderaron de,** *took possession of, seized.* [12] **invasores,** *invaders.* [13] **le arrojaron ... muerte,** *they threw at him a stone which caused his death* (see pages 166–167 for explanation of the use of the indirect object). [14] New Spain, which was organized as a Viceroyalty in 1535, comprised all Spanish territory north of Panama; thus Mexico was called New Spain until its independence from the Mother country in 1821.

Talla en basalto de un Caballero Águila azteca

Uno de los compañeros de Núñez de Balboa, Francisco Pizarro (1475–1541), se asoció con[1] otro soldado, Diego de Almagro, y con el clérigo Hernando de Luque, para emprender la conquista del imperio de los incas.   Después de intentarlo[2] en vano dos veces, primero en 1524 y luego dos años después, Pizarro decidió volver a España, donde el rey, Carlos V, le nombró gobernador de las provincias del Perú.

En enero de 1531 Pizarro salió de Panamá por tercera vez.*   Llevaba 37 caballos y unos 180 soldados, entre ellos cuatro hermanos suyos.   Al llegar al norte del Perú, cruzaron montañas, ríos y desiertos en su marcha hacia Cajamarca, donde los esperaba Atahualpa, emperador de los incas.   En el camino se le unieron a Pizarro unos 130 hombres, entre ellos el capitán Hernando de Soto.

Atahualpa, que acababa de derrotar[3] a su hermano Huáscar en una guerra civil, creía que los incas podrían vencer fácilmente a los españoles.   En noviembre Pizarro ocupó la ciudad de Cajamarca, que los incas habían abandonado, y envió a un hermano suyo y a Hernando de Soto a decirle a Atahualpa que el representante de otro gran rey le invitaba a visitarle.   El inca, que estaba a poca distancia* de la ciudad, con un ejército de más de 30,000 hombres, les contestó que lo haría al día siguiente.

Pizarro escondió hombres, caballos y cañones en los edificios que daban a la plaza.   Al entrar Atahualpa en la plaza,* en una litera[4] ricamente adornada, le recibió un padre dominico, Vicente de Valverde.   Ofreciéndole al inca una Biblia, Valverde trató de explicarle, por medio de un intérprete, que debía aceptar[5] la religión cristiana y reconocer el poderío[6] del rey de España. Atahualpa arrojó la Biblia al suelo, contestando que ningún rey era más poderoso que él.   En ese momento los españoles que estaban escondidos atacaron a los indios, matando a muchos de ellos y prendiendo[7] a Atahualpa. Éste,[8] para obtener su libertad, ofreció llenar de oro el cuarto donde le tenían prisionero.   Aunque lo hizo, no le dieron la libertad que le habían prometido. Los españoles lanzaron acusaciones falsas contra él y le condenaron a muerte.

Continuando la conquista del imperio inca, los españoles marcharon al Cuzco, la capital del imperio.   Más tarde Pizarro se dirigió al valle del Rimac, donde, el seis de enero de 1535, en honor de la fiesta de la Epifanía, fundó la Ciudad de los Reyes, después llamada Lima.

Pizarro y Almagro no disfrutaron mucho tiempo de sus riquezas y conquistas.   Surgieron discordias entre los dos.[9]   Almagro fue vencido y

---

[1] **se asoció con**, *joined, formed a partnership with.*   [2] **intentar**, *to try.*   [3] **acababa de derrotar**, *had just defeated (routed).*   [4] **litera**, *litter.*   [5] **debía aceptar**, *he must(should) accept.*   [6] **poderío**, *power.*   [7] **prendiendo**, *seizing.*   [8] **Éste**, *The latter.*   [9] **Surgieron . . . los dos**, *Discord (Disagreements) arose between the two.*

«La captura de Atahualpa», según los De Bry,
famosos grabadores flamencos

Hernando de Soto

condenado a muerte por uno de los hermanos del conquistador.   Pizarro murió a manos de* un hijo de Almagro en 1541.

Hernando de Soto (1497–1542) había sido compañero de Pedrarias en Panamá y de Pizarro en el Perú antes de conseguir, en 1536, el título de gobernador de Cuba y de la Florida.   En 1539 partió de Cuba, con unos 600 hombres, para la Florida, donde esperaba hallar otra tierra tan rica como el Perú.   En el mes de mayo llegó a la bahía del Espíritu Santo, llamada ahora Tampa Bay.

Durante dos años de Soto exploró los bosques hacia el norte y hacia el oeste, sin hallar las riquezas que buscaba.   La marcha le llevó por las tierras que hoy forman los estados de la Florida, Georgia, las Carolinas, Alabama y Misisipí.   En la primavera del año de 1541 descubrió el río Misisipí.   Durante el año siguiente de Soto y sus compañeros continuaron sus exploraciones hacia el oeste, pasando por los estados de Misurí, Arkansas y Oklahoma.   Enfermo y desalentado,[1] de Soto murió el 21 de mayo de 1542.   Para ocultar a* los indios la muerte de su valiente jefe, sus compañeros envolvieron su cuerpo en una manta, lo llevaron al río y lo arrojaron en sus aguas.

[1] **desalentado**, *discouraged*.

65

PREGUNTAS

1. ¿En qué siglo exploraron y conquistaron los españoles una gran parte del Nuevo Mundo? 2. ¿Quién guió la expedición de Enciso hasta la costa del istmo de Panamá? 3. ¿Qué llegó a ser Balboa? 4. ¿Qué oyeron decir los españoles en Panamá? 5. ¿Por qué tardaron tantos días en llegar a la cumbre de las montañas? 6. ¿Qué vio Balboa desde la cumbre de las montañas? 7. ¿Qué hizo Balboa al llegar a la costa? 8. ¿Qué hicieron los enemigos de Balboa? 9. ¿Cómo murió Balboa? 10. ¿Qué ha hecho la república de Panamá para honrar al descubridor?

11. ¿Cuántos años tenía Cortés cuando se embarcó para el Nuevo Mundo? 12. ¿De qué oyó hablar muchas veces en la Española y en Cuba? 13. ¿Qué resolvió hacer cuando le mandó Diego Velázquez a conquistar a México? 14. ¿Qué nombre dieron a la ciudad que fundaron en la costa de México? 15. ¿Quemó Cortés todas sus naves? 16. Al acercarse los españoles a Tenochtitlán, ¿quién salió a recibirlos? 17. ¿Por qué se apoderaron los españoles de la persona de Moctezuma? 18. ¿Qué hicieron los indios cuando se dieron cuenta de la situación? 19. ¿Qué tuvieron que hacer los españoles la noche del 30 de junio de 1520? 20. ¿Cuándo pudo Cortés emprender de nuevo la conquista de la ciudad? 21. ¿En qué superó Cortés a los otros conquistadores españoles?

22. ¿A quién nombró el rey gobernador de las provincias del Perú? 23. ¿En qué año salió Pizarro de Panamá por tercera vez? 24. ¿Qué tuvieron que cruzar para llegar a Cajamarca? 25. ¿Qué pasó cuando Atahualpa entró en la plaza de Cajamarca? 26. ¿Qué ofreció hacer Atahualpa para obtener su libertad? 27. ¿Cómo y cuándo murió Pizarro?

28. ¿Qué esperaba hallar Hernando de Soto en la Florida? 29. ¿Qué descubrió en el año 1541? 30. ¿Qué tierras exploraron durante el año siguiente?

EJERCICIOS ESCRITOS

A. Uso de modismos y frases hechas *(fixed phrases)*

Escriban oraciones completas empleando las frases siguientes como elemento inicial:

1. La Lectura trata de . . .
2. Acabamos de leer . . .
3. Al saber Enciso que . . .
4. Como tuvieron que . . .
5. A la edad de diez y nueve años . . .
6. Cortés oyó hablar muchas veces . . .
7. En el mes de abril de 1519 . . .
8. Fueron obligados a salir de la ciudad de México . . .

B. Para expresar en español[1]

1. In the year 1510 Balboa arrived in (at) Panama, where, after a short time, he became the leader of the new colony which was founded there.   2. Talking with the Indians, the Spaniards heard that on the other side of the mountains there was an enormous sea.   3. It took Balboa and his men nineteen days to reach the summit, from which they saw the Pacific Ocean for the first time.   4. After taking possession of the great ocean and of all its coasts and its islands in the name of the king of Spain, Balboa returned to the colony, where Pedrarias condemned him to death.   5. When Cortés, who was in Cuba, heard about marvelous lands which were to the west, he resolved to undertake the conquest of that region.   6. He founded the city of Veracruz in 1519; then, he burned all his ships, except one which he sent to Spain.   7. He and his little army were able to settle in Tenochtitlán, but the Aztecs, after the death of their emperor, rebelled against the Spaniards.   8. Finally, Cortés conquered the Aztecs and, like other Spanish conquerors, began to establish the institutions which existed in Spain.   9. Upon reaching Peru on their third expedition, Pizarro and his soldiers had to cross mountains, rivers, and deserts in their march to Cajamarca. 10. Even though Atahualpa filled with gold the room where they held him prisoner, the Spaniards did not give him the freedom that they had promised him.   11. Continuing the conquest of the Inca empire, the invaders marched to Cuzco, and later, on January 6, 1535, Pizarro founded the City of the Kings, called Lima afterwards. 12. Hernando de Soto explored the forests toward the north and the west of Florida in search of a land as rich as Peru before discovering the Mississippi river in the spring of 1541.

C. Temas para un informe escrito

Escriban tres oraciones sobre cada uno de los temas siguientes:

1. Núñez de Balboa descubre el Océano Pacífico.
2. La conquista de Tenochtitlán.
3. Pizarro derrota y prende al emperador de los incas.

[1] In this and similar exercises the instructor may assign all or as few sentences as are considered necessary.

LECCIÓN TRES

Usos del pretérito de indicativo. Usos del
imperfecto de indicativo. Verbos con significados
especiales en el pretérito. La construcción reflexiva
para traducir *each other, one another*. Observaciones
sobre el uso de algunos verbos

HABLANDO POR TELÉFONO

(*Juan está estudiando; su compañero de cuarto, Miguel, regresa*[1] *de la biblioteca.*)

MIGUEL.	¡Hola, Juan! ¿Qué hay de nuevo?
JUAN.	¡Hombre! Acaba de llamarte Carlos.
MIGUEL.	¿Dejó algún recado?
JUAN.	No. Sólo dijo que quería hablar contigo. Me preguntó si yo quería ir al cine con él.
MIGUEL.	Le llamaré ahora mismo. (*Marca el número en el teléfono.*) 323-1647[2] . . . ¡Qué mala suerte! ¡La línea está ocupada! (*Cuelga el auricular. Al poco rato vuelve a levantar el auricular y marca el número otra vez. Contesta Carlos.*)
CARLOS.	¡Bueno![3]
MIGUEL.	¿Está Carlos? ¿Podría hablar con él?
CARLOS.	Habla Carlos. ¿Quién llama?
MIGUEL.	¡Ah! ¿Eres tú? Aquí habla Miguel.

[1] In Spanish America **regresar**, *to return, come back*, is widely used along with **volver**, which is more common in Spain.　　[2] Read: **tres dos tres—uno seis cuatro siete.**　　[3] Several Spanish expressions are used for the telephone greeting *Hello*: **Diga**, or **Dígame** (Spain); **Bueno** (Mexico); **Hola** (Argentina); **Aló** (in many other countries).

CARLOS. Hombre, te llamé hace unos minutos para preguntar por el diccionario que te presté.

MIGUEL. ¿No recuerdas que me lo pediste la semana pasada? Lo busqué pero no pude hallarlo. Creo que lo tiene Luisa. Si quieres, la llamaré.

CARLOS. No, no te preocupes. Ahora recuerdo que ella lo necesitaba para un informe que estaba preparando. Yo la llamaré.

MIGUEL. Muy bien. Pues, nos vemos en la biblioteca esta noche, ¿verdad?

CARLOS. ¡Cómo no! Hasta luego, Miguel.

al poco rato after a short while
el auricular receiver
¡bueno! hello! (*telephone*)
el diccionario dictionary
¿está Carlos? is Charles in?
habla (Carlos) this is (Charles), (Charles) is speaking
el informe report
la línea line
marcar el número to dial the number
preocuparse to worry, be concerned
el recado message
regresar to return, come back

A. Busquen en el diálogo las frases que correspondan a las siguientes:

1. What's new? 2. Charles has just called you. 3. Did he leave any message? 4. right away. 5. He dials the number. 6. What bad luck! 7. The line is busy! 8. He hangs up the receiver. 9. After a short while. 10. he takes up (lifts) the receiver again. 11. Is Charles in? 12. Is it you? 13. a few minutes ago. 14. to ask about the dictionary. 15. you asked me for it. 16. I couldn't find it. 17. don't worry. 18. we'll see each other. 19. Of course!

B. Preparen un diálogo original, de unas diez líneas, para recitar en clase, empleando las frases y preguntas siguientes como elemento inicial:

1. JUAN. ¿Está Luisa? ¿Podría hablar con ella?
   SRA. LÓPEZ. No está en casa en este momento. ¿Quiere dejar algún recado?

2. MIGUEL. ¿Eres tú, Carlos? Te llamo para preguntarte si te trajeron tus padres el regalo que te habían prometido.
   CARLOS. Sí, Miguel. Y ¡qué sorpresa! No puedes imaginarte lo que me trajeron.

3. LUIS. Estamos haciendo planes para una fiesta el sábado por la noche. ¿Podrás venir?
   DOROTEA. ¡Cómo no! Con mucho gusto. ¿Para qué hora nos invitas?

PRONUNCIACIÓN

The sounds of **r** and **rr**. Single **r**, except when initial in a word and when after **l**, **n**, or **s**, is a voiced, alveolar, single trill; that is, it is pronounced with a single tap produced by the tip of the tongue against the gums of the upper teeth. The sound is much like *dd* in *eddy* produced rapidly. When initial in a word, when after **l**, **n**, or **s**, and when doubled, the sound is a multiple trill, the tip of the tongue striking the gums in a series of very rapid vibrations. Pronounce after your teacher:

1. comeré   fueron   grabar   haré   eres
   iremos   Carlos   suerte   tres   auricular
   ahora   cuarto   hablar   llamaré   preguntar

2. rato   regalo   Ricardo   honra   guitarra
   alrededor   Enrique   querré   Israel   ferrocarril
   río   erre   carro   correr   recado

3. El perro de San Roque
   no tiene rabo
   porque Ramón Ramírez
   se lo ha cortado.

4. Erre con erre cigarro,
   erre con erre barril,
   rápidos corren los carros
   del ferrocarril.

NOTAS GRAMATICALES

I. USOS DEL PRETÉRITO DE INDICATIVO

The preterit tense, sometimes called the past definite, is a narrative tense. It expresses a single past action or state, the beginning or the end of a past action, or a series of acts when viewed as a complete unit in the past, regardless of the length of time involved. Duration is often defined by an adverb or adverbial expression; for example, **nunca** regularly requires the preterit.

¿Dejó algún recado? Did he leave any message?
Te llamé hace unos minutos. I called you a few minutes ago.
Pablo hizo tres viajes a México el año pasado. Paul made three trips to Mexico last year.
Los moros vivieron en España casi ocho siglos. The Moors lived in Spain almost eight centuries.
Empecé a tocar unos discos. I began to play some records.
Él nunca creyó lo que le dije. He never believed what I told him.

II. USOS DEL IMPERFECTO DE INDICATIVO

A. General use of the imperfect tense:

The imperfect indicative tense, frequently called the past descriptive, describes past actions, scenes, or conditions which were continuing for an indefinite time in the past. The speaker transfers himself mentally to a point of time in the past and views the action or situation as though it were taking place before him. There is no reference to the beginning or the end of the action or situation described.

Era un día frío del mes de febrero. El mar ofrecía un color azul obscuro. La madre y su hijo iban tristes y silenciosos por la playa. Cuando se hallaban a mitad del camino más o menos, vieron a lo lejos dos personas que venían hacia ellos.	It was a cold day in the month of February. The sea was a dark blue color. The mother and her son were going along the beach sad and silent. When they were more or less half way, they saw in the distance two persons who were coming toward them.

B. Specific uses of the imperfect tense are:

1. To describe what was happening at a certain time:

> **Marta leía (estaba leyendo) y María escribía (estaba escribiendo).** Martha was reading and Mary was writing.

2. To indicate that an action was customary or habitual, or indefinitely repeated, equivalent to English *used to, would,*[1] *was (were) accustomed to* plus an infinitive, and often to *was (were)* plus the present participle:

> **Iban a la iglesia todos los domingos.** They went (used to go, would go) to church every Sunday.

3. To describe the background or setting in which an action took place, or to indicate that an action was in progress when something happened (the preterit indicates what happened under the particular circumstances described):

> **Juan estudiaba cuando yo regresé de la biblioteca.** John was studying when I returned from the library.
> **Llovía mucho cuando Ana volvió a casa.** It was raining hard when Ann returned home.

[1] Do not confuse *would* meaning an habitual action, with *would* used as a conditional: **¿Podría (yo) hablar con él?** *Could I (Would I be able to) talk with him?* (See Lección seis.)

4. To describe a mental, emotional, or physical state in the past; thus, Spanish verbs used for English *believe, know, wish, feel, be able,* etc., are often in the imperfect rather than the preterit (see section III below):

> **Yo creía que estabas enferma.**   I believed that you were ill.
> **Ella quería ir al cine con él.**   She wanted to go to the movie with him.

5. To express indirect discourse in the past:

> **Carlos dijo que quería hablar contigo.**   Charles said he wanted to talk with you.
> **Ana me preguntó si yo podía ir con ella.**   Ann asked me if (whether) I could go with her.

6. To express time of day in the past:

> **¿Qué hora era cuando saliste?   —Eran las ocho.**   What time was it when you went out?   —It was eight o'clock.

III. VERBOS CON SIGNIFICADOS (*MEANINGS*) ESPECIALES EN EL PRETÉRITO

Certain common verbs, such as **saber, conocer, tener, querer, poder,** often have special meanings when used in the preterit.   In general, the use of the imperfect tense indicates existing desire, ability, etc., while the preterit indicates that the act was or was not accomplished.   Contrastive examples are:

Sabíamos que Pablo estaba en Chile.   We knew that Paul was in Chile.   (*Mental state*)
Supimos anoche que él estaba allí.   We found out (learned) last night that he was there.

Yo conocía[1] bien a Marta.   I knew Martha well.
Yo la conocí el año pasado.   I met her (made her acquaintance) last year.

Tomás quería llamar a Inés.   Tom wanted to call Inez.
Tomás quiso llamarla.   Tom tried to call her.

Ella no quería quedarse en casa.   She didn't want (was not wanting) to stay at home.
Ella no quiso quedarse allí.   She refused to (would not) stay there.

Ana tenía una carta cuando la vi.   Ann had a letter when I saw her.
Ana tuvo tres cartas esta mañana.   Ann received (got) three letters this morning.

---

[1] **Conocer** may be used in all tenses to mean *to recognize.*

Le dije que podía buscar el libro.   I told him that I could look for the book (*i.e.*, I was able to look, capable of looking, for the book).

Lo busqué pero no pude hallarlo.   I looked for it but couldn't find it (*i.e.*, I did not succeed in finding it).

Ejercicios

A. Repitan cada frase; luego, cambien el tiempo del verbo al pretérito de indicativo:

1. Miguel regresa de la biblioteca.
2. Habla por teléfono con Carlos.
3. Marca el número en el teléfono.
4. Vuelve a levantar el auricular.
5. Carlos quiere hablar con Miguel.
6. Le pregunta a Ana por un buen diccionario.
7. Miguel no puede hallarlo.
8. Carlos no quiere llamar a Dorotea.
9. Yo empiezo a preparar el informe.
10. El amigo de Juan no hace nada.
11. ¿Quiénes te traen regalos?
12. ¿Quién viene contigo?
13. ¿Van Uds. a la fiesta el sábado por la noche?
14. Yo busco un regalo para Carolina.

B. Repitan cada frase; luego, cambien el tiempo del verbo al imperfecto de indicativo:

1. Ella quiere charlar un rato contigo.
2. La línea está ocupada.
3. Dorotea necesita el diccionario de español.
4. Son las diez de la noche.
5. Pablo y yo no sabemos eso.
6. Vamos a la biblioteca todos los días.
7. Nos vemos allí a menudo.
8. ¿Puedes hablar con Ana María a veces?
9. Hay varias personas en la calle.
10. Hacemos planes para la fiesta.

C. Repitan cada frase; luego, cambien el primer verbo al pretérito y el segundo al imperfecto de indicativo:

1. Carlos dice que quiere hablar con Miguel.
2. Él me pregunta si yo voy a la biblioteca con él.
3. Cuando marca el número, la línea está ocupada.
4. ¿Ves a la muchacha que necesita el diccionario?
5. Elena nos escribe que puede visitarnos pronto.
6. Yo veo que hay muchos estudiantes en el teatro.

D. Lean cada frase en español, supliendo la forma correcta de cada infinitivo en cursiva:

1. Juan no *hablar* por teléfono cuando yo *entrar* en su cuarto.
2. Él *estudiar* su lección cuando yo *abrir* la puerta.
3. Juan me *decir* que *querer* enseñarme una composición que había escrito.
4. Él me *preguntar* si yo *tener* tiempo para leerla.
5. Al leerla, yo *ver* que *estar* bien escrita y que *ser* muy interesante.
6. Mientras yo *estar* leyéndola, *sonar* el teléfono.
7. Juan *levantar* el auricular y *contestar* en español.
8. Los dos *charlar* unos minutos y luego Juan *colgar* el auricular.
9. Su amigo *querer* saber si Juan *poder* ir al teatro el sábado.
10. Al poco rato yo *mirar* el reloj; *ser* las ocho y yo *tener* que irme en seguida.

IV. LA CONSTRUCCIÓN REFLEXIVA PARA TRADUCIR *EACH OTHER, ONE ANOTHER*

The plural reflexive pronouns **nos, os, se** may express a mutual or reciprocal action (one subject acting upon another):

> **Nos escribíamos a menudo.**   We wrote to each other often.
> **Se saludan cuando se ven.**   They greet one another when they see one another.

The redundant construction **uno (-a) a otro (-a), el uno al otro, unos a otros (unas a otras),** etc., may be added for clarity or emphasis. With prepositions other than **a**, the redundant form is added regularly:

> **Se burlan uno de otro.**   They make fun of each other (one another).
> **Ellos se gritaron el uno al otro.**   They shouted to each other (one another).

Ejercicio

Para contestar afirmativamente en español:

1. ¿Se escriben Uds. a menudo?
2. ¿Se verán Uds. mañana?
3. ¿Se miraron ellos tristemente?
4. ¿Van a ayudarse uno a otro?
5. ¿Se quejaban uno de otro?
6. ¿Se saludaron Ana y Pablo?

Repitan el ejercicio contestando negativamente en español.

V. OBSERVACIONES SOBRE EL USO DE ALGUNOS VERBOS

A. **Preguntar** and **pedir**

Preguntar means *to ask* (a question); **preguntar por** means *to ask for (about)*, *inquire about*:

> **Él me preguntó si yo quería ir.**   He asked me if (whether) I wanted to go.
> **Te llamé para preguntar por el libro.**   I called you to ask about the book.

Pedir means *to ask* (a favor), *ask for* (something), *to request* (something of someone). Later the use of **pedir**, *to ask* or *request someone to do something*, will be discussed.

> **Le pedí a Miguel el diccionario.**   I asked Michael for the dictionary.
> **Ellas no nos pidieron nada.**   They didn't ask us for anything.

With both these verbs (also with **decir** and a few other verbs), the person of whom something is asked is the indirect object.   The neuter pronoun **lo** is used to complete the sentence if a direct object is not expressed:

> **¿Pueden ir también?   —Se lo preguntaré (a ellos).**
>   Can they go too?   —I shall ask them (*lit.*, ask it of them).
> **¿Le pidió usted eso a Felipe?   —Sí, se lo pedí.**
>   Did you ask that of Philip?   —Yes, I asked him (it).

B. **Tomar, llevar,** and other verbs meaning *to take*

Tomar means *to take* in the sense of *to take* (in one's hand), *to take* (meals, food, beverages, etc.):

> **José, toma el libro, por favor.**   Joe, take the book, please.
> **Tomaron el avión de las dos.**   They took the two-o'clock plane.

Llevar means *to take* (*along*), *carry* (to some place):

> **Tomás llevó a su novia al baile.**   Tom took his girl friend to the dance.
> **Yo tomé la maleta en la mano y la llevé al coche.**   I took the suitcase in
>   my hand and took (carried) it to the car.

Llevarse means *to take* (*carry*) *away* (often *with oneself*):

> **Ella compró una blusa y se la llevó.**   She bought a blouse and took it
>   with her.

Quitar means *to take away* (*off*), *remove from*; **quitarse** means *to take off* (from oneself):

>**Ella quitó el libro de la mesa.**   She took (removed) the book from the table.
>**Ellos se quitaron los zapatos.**   They took off their shoes.

Sacar means *to take out, take* (photos):

>**Ella sacó muchas cosas de la bolsa.**   She took many things from her purse.
>**Yo saqué varias fotos en el parque.**   I took several photos in the park.

A few idiomatic expressions which include other uses of the English verb *to take* are:

bañarse   to take a bath, go swimming
dar un paseo (**una vuelta**)   to take a walk *or* stroll
desayunarse   to take (eat) breakfast
despedirse (**i, i**) (**de**)   to take leave (of)

dormir (**ue, u**) **la siesta**   to take a nap
hacer un viaje (**una excursión**)   to take a trip (excursion)
tardar (**mucho**) **en**   to take (long) to, be (long) in, delay (long) in

C. **Gustar** and **querer** (**a**)

The English verb *to like*, usually referring to things, is regularly expressed in Spanish by **gustar**, meaning *to please, be pleasing* (*to*).   The English subject (*I, he, you*, etc.) becomes the indirect object in Spanish, and the English object becomes the subject of the Spanish verb; *e.g.*, instead of *She likes the hat*, turn the sentence into *The hat is pleasing to her*: **Le gusta a ella el sombrero.**   This means that normally only the third person singular and plural forms of **gustar** are used.   English *it* and *them* are not expressed, and the Spanish subject, when expressed, usually follows the verb.

>**Me** (**Nos**) **gusta la foto.**   I (We) like the photo.
>**¿No le gusta a usted?**   Don't you like it?
>**Le gustaban a ella los regalos.**   She liked the gifts.

Remember that when a noun is the indirect object of **gustar**, the indirect object pronoun must also be used (see Lección dos, page 50):

>**A Carlos le gustan** (**Le gustan a Carlos**) **los discos.**   Charles likes the records.

Querer (**a**) means *to like, love, feel affection for*, a person:

>**Queremos mucho a Juanita.**   We like Jane very much (We are very fond of Jane).
>**Felipe y Ana se quieren mucho.**   Philip and Ann love each other a great deal.

Ejercicio

Contesten afirmativamente en español:

1. ¿Diste un paseo anoche?
2. ¿Dormiste la siesta ayer?
3. ¿Tomaste el autobús de las dos?
4. ¿Llevó Jorge a María al cine?
5. ¿Llevaron Uds. las cosas a casa?
6. ¿Hizo Ud. una excursión ayer?
7. ¿Se quitó Ud. el abrigo?
8. ¿Se bañó Ud. anoche?
9. ¿Se desayunó Ud. temprano?
10. ¿Tardó Ana mucho en llegar?
11. ¿Le pediste el libro a Marta?
12. ¿Les preguntó Ud. por el curso?
13. ¿Tomaron Uds. un refresco?
14. ¿Se despidieron Uds. de ellos?
15. ¿Hicieron Ud. y él un viaje a México?
16. ¿Sacó Ud. muchas fotos en el campo?
17. ¿Quiere Juan a María?
18. ¿Se quieren Marta y Jorge?

Repitan el ejercicio, preguntas 10 a 18, contestando negativamente en español.

RESUMEN

A. Lean en español, cambiando cada infinitivo en cursiva al pretérito o al imperfecto de indicativo:

1. *Ser* las nueve cuando yo *volver* del aeropuerto.
2. Cuando yo *ver* a María, la *invitar* a almorzar conmigo.
3. Pablo le *preguntar* a Carolina si ella *poder* ir al cine con él.
4. Miguel *marcar* el número de María, pero ella no *estar* en casa.
5. Él *querer* hablar con ella acerca de un informe que *estar* preparando.
6. Al poco rato él *ir* al café, pero no *poder* hallarla.
7. Los estudiantes *charlar* cuando el profesor *entrar* en la sala de clase.
8. Ellos *saber* que él *ir* a darles un examen.
9. Jorge *andar* despacio por la calle cuando yo le *ver*.
10. Yo le *decir* que *querer* devolverle su libro de español.

B. Usos del verbo *to take*. Para expresar en español:

1. Thomas took Martha to the dance.
2. Did Paul take the ten-o'clock bus?
3. Will you take a trip to Mexico?
4. Why didn't he take a walk with her?
5. They took coffee at seven.
6. Ask him whether he took a nap.
7. I took several photos in the park.
8. He took off his hat; he took it off.
9. Take the watch in your hand, please.
10. We took all the things from the car.

C. Usos del pronombre reflexivo **se** y de los verbos **gustar** y **querer**.   Para expresar en español:

1. We see each other every day.
2. Raymond and I help each other.
3. They were making fun of each other.
4. Do you visit one another often?
5. I like this gold watch.
6. Do you like it?

7. We like George's guitar.
8. They do not like this picture.
9. Mary likes to write articles.
10. Do you like to talk on the telephone?
11. Charles likes Helen very much.
12. I know that the two love each other.

LECCIÓN CUATRO

Usos del artículo definido.   Usos del artículo
indefinido.   El género y el número de los substantivos.
Usos de las palabras indefinidas y negativas

EL ALMUERZO ENTRE AMIGAS

(*Elena se encuentra en el apartamento de Luisa.   Están discutiendo los planes para la próxima reunión del Club Español.*)

ELENA.   ¡Hemos tenido mucha suerte!   El profesor Navarro acepta nuestra invitación.

LUISA.   ¿Hablará sobre la poesía contemporánea?

ELENA.   Sí, y como él también es poeta, dice que tendrá mucho gusto en leer algunos poemas suyos.

LUISA.   ¡Magnífico!   La profesora Valdés dará la bienvenida a todos y luego presentará al conferenciante.

ELENA.   (*Mirando su reloj de pulsera.*)   Pero, ¿sabes que ya son las doce y media? Si no me doy prisa, voy a llegar tarde para el almuerzo.

LUISA.   ¿Por qué no te quedas a almorzar conmigo?   Veré si queda algo en la nevera . . . (*Abre la nevera.*)   Hay leche, queso, jamón, lechuga y tomates.

ELENA.   Nunca tomo mucho al mediodía.   Si me permites ayudarte, me quedaré.

LUISA.   Bueno; puedes poner la mesa mientras yo preparo unos emparedados.   Yo también me conformo con cualquier cosa.   (*Al poco rato.*)   Bueno, no es ningún banquete, pero estarás[1] muerta de hambre.

ELENA.   Como dice el refrán español, «A buen hambre[2] no hay pan duro, ni falta salsa a ninguno[3]».

el banquete banquet
el conferenciante lecturer, speaker
  conformarse (**con**) to be satisfied (with)
  contemporáneo, -a contemporary
  cualquier(**a**) any (anyone) (*at all*)
  cualquier cosa anything (*at all*)
  dar la bienvenida a to welcome
  duro, -a hard
la invitación (*pl.* **invitaciones**) invitation

la lechuga lettuce
  muerto, -a de hambre starving (to death)
la nevera refrigerator
el poema poem
la poesía poetry
el poeta poet
  poner la mesa to set the table
  próximo, -a next
el reloj de pulsera wrist watch
la reunión (*pl.* **reuniones**) meeting

A. Busquen en el diálogo las frases que correspondan a las siguientes:

1. the plans for the next meeting. 2. We have been very lucky! 3. he also is a poet. 4. he will be very glad (pleased) to read. 5. some poems of his. 6. (she) will welcome everyone. 7. Looking at her wrist watch. 8. If I don't hurry. 9. I'll be late for lunch. 10. I'll see if there is anything left. 11. I never eat much at noon. 12. If you will let me (allow me to) help you. 13. I'll stay. 14. you can set the table. 15. I am satisfied with anything. 16. it is no banquet. 17. you must be starving.

B. Para contestar en español:

Preguntas sobre el diálogo

1. ¿Dónde se encuentra Elena? 2. ¿Qué están discutiendo las dos amigas? 3. ¿Por qué dice Elena que han tenido mucha suerte? 4. ¿Sobre qué hablará el profesor Navarro? 5. ¿Quién presentará al conferenciante? 6. ¿Se queda a almorzar Elena con Luisa? 7. ¿Qué hay en la nevera? 8. ¿Qué prepara Luisa para el almuerzo?

---

[1] **estarás**, *you must be* (*probably are*). For a discussion of the use of the future tense for conjecture or probability in the present, see Lección seis, page 127. [2] **A buen hambre**, *When hunger is great*. Apocopated feminine forms of adjectives, such as **buen, mal, primer, tercer, postrer, algún**, and **ningún**, although frequent in Golden Age Spanish, are no longer considered standard forms. They are still found in proverbs, fixed phrases, and rural speech. [3] **ni . . . ninguno**, *nor is anyone in need of sauce*. Compare the English, "Hunger is the best sauce."

Aplicación del diálogo

1. ¿Hay un Club Español en esta Universidad?   2. ¿Asisten muchos estudiantes a
las reuniones del Club Español?   3. ¿Son interesantes las reuniones del Club
Español?   4. ¿Vive usted en una Residencia de Estudiantes o en un apartamento?
5. ¿Por qué les gusta a algunos estudiantes vivir en un apartamento?   6. ¿Le gustan a usted las comidas en las Residencias de Estudiantes?   7. ¿A qué hora toma
usted el almuerzo generalmente?   8. ¿De qué refrán español se acuerda usted?

PRONUNCIACIÓN

Review the observations on Spanish intonation (pages 17–18, 23–24, and 45); then
write the first three exchanges of the dialogue of this lesson, dividing them into
breath-groups and into syllables, and outline the intonation patterns. Read the
exchanges, paying close attention to the intonation patterns.

NOTAS GRAMATICALES

I. USOS DEL ARTÍCULO DEFINIDO

The definite article **el** (*pl.* **los**) or **la** (*pl.* **las**) is used in Spanish, as in English, to
denote a specific noun.   In addition, the definite article in Spanish has a number of
other important functions.   A few of the special uses in Spanish are:

1. With abstract nouns and with nouns used in a general sense, indicating a whole
class:

> **¿Quién no admira la belleza?**   Who doesn't admire beauty?
> **¿Hablará sobre la poesía contemporánea?**   Will he talk about contem-
>   porary poetry?
> **Me gusta mucho el arte mexicano.**   I like Mexican art very much.

2. With titles (except before **don, doña, san, santo,** and **santa**) when speaking
about, but not directly to, a person:

> **El profesor Navarro acepta nuestra invitación.**   Professor Navarro
>   accepts our invitation.

> BUT: **Buenos días, señora Valdés.**   Good morning, Mrs. Valdés.
>   **Don Carlos López dio una conferencia.**   Don Carlos López gave a
>   lecture.

3. With days of the week and seasons of the year, except after **ser**, and with dates, meals, hours of the day, and with expressions of time modified:

> **Vendrán el sábado.**   They will come (on) Saturday.
> **Voy a llegar tarde para el almuerzo.**   I'll be (arrive) late for lunch.
> **Ya son las doce y media.**   It is already twelve-thirty.
> **Los vi la semana pasada.**   I saw them last week.
>
> BUT: **Hoy es lunes.**   Today is Monday.
>   **Es otoño.**   It is autumn.

4. With parts of the body, articles of clothing, and other things closely associated with a person, when the reference is clear, in place of the possessive adjective:

> **Marta se lavó las manos.**   Martha washed her hands.
> **Nos quitamos los zapatos.**   We took off our shoes.
> **Yo he perdido el reloj.**   I have lost my watch.
> **Ella tiene el pelo rubio.**   She has blond hair (Her hair is blond).

5. With the name of a language, except after **de** and **en**, and immediately after **hablar** (and sometimes after such verbs as **aprender, comprender, escribir, estudiar, leer, saber**):

> **El español no es fácil.**   Spanish is not easy.
> **Ana habla bien[1] el francés.**   Ann speaks French well.
>
> BUT: **¿Habla usted portugués?**   Do you speak Portuguese?
>   **Éste es un libro de español.**   This is a Spanish book.
>   **La carta está escrita en inglés.**   The letter is written in English.

6. With nouns of rate, weight, measure (English regularly uses the indefinite article):

> **Cuestan treinta dólares el par.**   They cost thirty dollars a pair.
> **Pagué ochenta centavos la docena.**   I paid eighty cents a dozen.

7. With names of rivers and mountains, with proper names and names of places when modified, and with the names of certain countries and cities:

> **El Amazonas está en el Brasil.**   The Amazon (River) is in Brazil.
> **Conocemos la España moderna.**   We know modern Spain.

---

[1] When any word other than the subject pronoun comes between forms of **hablar** and the name of a language, the article is used.

Some commonly used names of countries and cities which are preceded by the definite article in conservative literary usage (but which are often used without the article in journalistic and colloquial use) are:

(**el**) **Canadá**	(**el**) **Brasil**	(**el**) **Perú**	(**el**) **Callao**
(**los**) **Estados Unidos**	(**el**) **Ecuador**	(**el**) **Paraguay**	(**el**) **Cuzco**
(**la**) **Argentina**	(**la**) **Florida**	(**el**) **Uruguay**	(**la**) **Habana**

The article is seldom omitted in the case of **El Salvador**, which means *The Savior.*

NOTES. Special use of the definite article **el.** Feminine nouns which begin with stressed **a-** or **ha-** require **el** in the singular, instead of **la**, when the article immediately precedes: **el agua**, *the water*, **el hambre**, *hunger*; but **las aguas**, *the waters*, **la altura**, *the height.*

Recall the two contractions in Spanish of the masculine singular definite article: **a + el = al; de + el = del**. Examples: **Vamos al cine**, *We are going (Let's go) to the movie*; **Entro en el cuarto del muchacho**, *I enter the boy's room.*

II. USOS DEL ARTÍCULO INDEFINIDO

The indefinite article **un** (*m.*) and **una** (*f.*), *a, an*, is regularly repeated before each noun:

Ella tiene un reloj y una pulsera. She has a watch and bracelet.

The plural form **unos**, **unas** means *some, any, a few, several, about* (in the sense of approximately). Normally *some* and *any* are expressed in Spanish only when emphasized:

Ayer vi unas blusas bonitas. Yesterday I saw some (a few) pretty blouses.
El señor Díaz tiene unos sesenta años. Mr. Díaz is about sixty years old.

BUT: **¿Tiene usted dinero?** Do you have any money?
No tenemos que tomar notas. We don't have to take (any) notes.

In Spanish the indefinite article is omitted in certain cases in which it is regularly used in English:

1. After **ser**, with an unmodified noun of profession, occupation, religion, nationality, rank, or political affiliation, or in answer to the English *What is (he)?*

El padre de Juanita es médico. Jane's father is a doctor.
¿Qué es él? —Es profesor. What is he? —He is a teacher.

The indefinite article is used, however, when a person's identity is stressed, and when these nouns are modified:

> **Ella es una buena profesora.**   She is a good teacher.
> **¿Quién es ella?   —Es una profesora.**   Who is she?   —She is a teacher.

2. Often before nouns, particularly in interrogative and negative sentences, after prepositions, and after certain verbs (such as **tener** and **buscar**), when the numerical concept of *a, an (one)* is not emphasized:

> **¿Busca usted casa ahora?**   Are you looking for a house now?
> **Marta no tiene reloj.**   Martha doesn't have a (has no) watch.
> **José salió sin sombrero.**   Joseph went out without a hat.

3. With adjectives such as **otro, -a,** *another,* **tal,** *such a,* **cien(to),** *a (one) hundred,* **mil,** *a (one) thousand,* **cierto, -a,** *a certain,* **medio, -a,** *a half,* and with **¡qué!** *what a!* in exclamations:

> **Tráigame usted otro disco.**   Bring me another record.
> **Cierta muchacha me dijo eso.**   A certain girl told me that.
> **¡Qué hombre!**   What a man!

Ejercicio

Lean en español, supliendo el artículo—definido o indefinido—cuando sea necesario:

1. Buenos días, _____ señor López.   _____ señor Díaz no ha llegado todavía.
2. Hoy es _____ miércoles.   Siempre tengo tres clases _____ miércoles.
3. Ellos hablan _____ español.   Dicen que _____ español es difícil.
4. Piensan ir a _____ España.   Quieren conocer bien _____ España contemporánea.
5. El tío de Ana es _____ autor.   Es _____ autor distinguido.
6. ¿Qué es _____ don Carlos?   —Creo que es _____ músico.
7. ¿Quién es _____ doña Inés?   —Se dice que es _____ secretaria.
8. Felipe no tiene _____ reloj.   Vamos a regalarle _____ reloj de oro.
9. ¿Busca Ud. _____ abrigo hoy?   —Sí, busco _____ abrigo hecho en España.
10. A ella le gustan _____ rosas.   Su novio le manda _____ flores cada semana.
11. María habla bien _____ portugués.   No habla _____ francés.
12. Carlos siempre toma _____ café aquí.   No le gusta _____ café frío.

III. EL GÉNERO (*GENDER*) Y EL NÚMERO DE LOS SUBSTANTIVOS

A. Nouns referring to male beings, most nouns ending in **-o**, days of the week, the names of languages, certain nouns ending in **-ma**, **-pa**, **-ta**, and infinitives used as nouns, are masculine:

> **el jueves** Thursday　**el español** Spanish　**el mapa** map
>
> BUT: **la mano**, hand, **la radio**, radio (*as a means of communication*), **la foto** (*abbreviation of* **fotografía**), photo.

Nouns referring to female beings, and most nouns ending in **-a** (except those ending in **-ma**, **-pa**, **-ta**), or in **-(c)ión**, **-dad**, **-tad**, **-tud**, **-umbre**, **-ie** are feminine:

> **la invitación** invitation　**la reunión** meeting　**la verdad** truth

Exceptions are: **el día**, *day*, **el avión**, (*air*)*plane*, and nouns ending in **-ma**, **-pa**, **-ta** (see above).　Some nouns ending in **-a**, particularly in **-ista**, are either masculine or feminine: **el** (**la**) **artista**, *artist* (man or woman).

The gender of other nouns must be learned by observation:

> **el plan** plan　**el jamón** ham　**la suerte** luck　**la leche** milk

Many nouns ending in **-o**, particularly those of relationship, change **o** to **a** for the feminine: **el hijo**, *son*, **la hija**, *daughter*.

B. In general, to form the plural of nouns add **-s** to those ending in an unaccented vowel and **-es** to those ending in a consonant, including **y**.　Nouns ending in unaccented **-as**, **-es**, **-is**, and most family names, do not change in the plural: **el** (**los**) **parabrisas**, *windshield*(*s*), **el** (**los**) **lunes**, *Monday*(*s*); **Gómez** (family name), **los Gómez**, *the Gómez family*.　**Los señores Gómez** means *Mr. and Mrs. Gómez*.

SINGULAR	PLURAL
el emparedado sandwich	**los emparedados** sandwiches
el refrán proverb	**los refranes** proverbs
el joven young man	**los jóvenes** young men
el examen examination	**los exámenes** examinations

Note that the accent is not written on the plural **refranes**, and that it is added on the plurals **jóvenes** and **exámenes**, in order to keep the stress on the same syllable as in the singular.　Nouns ending in **-z** change the **z** to **c** before **-es**, and those in **-ión** drop the accent in the plural: **el lápiz**, **los lápices**; **la lección**, **las lecciones**.

Certain nouns denoting rank or relationship may be used in the masculine plural to refer to individuals of both sexes: **los reyes**, *the kings, the king(s) and queen(s)*; **los hermanos**, *the brothers, the brother(s) and sister(s)*.

Ejercicios

A. Repitan cada oración; luego, repítanla otra vez, cambiando los substantivos al plural y haciendo los otros cambios necesarios.

MODELO: El amigo de ella trae su libro.   El amigo de ella trae su libro.
                                                              Los amigos de ellas traen sus libros.

1. La niña tiene el lápiz en la mano.
2. El profesor le explica la lección al estudiante.
3. El poeta va a leer ese poema suyo a la clase.
4. La mujer siempre pasa por la calle los lunes.
5. La profesora de francés no sabe el refrán.
6. El artista nos enseña el cuadro español.
7. La muchacha habla del plan para la próxima reunión.
8. El joven no puede aceptar nuestra invitación.
9. El conferenciante hablará sobre un problema social.
10. El estudiante mira la foto del parque nacional.

B. Para contestar negativamente:

1. ¿Trabajas todo el día en casa?
2. ¿Es profesora la señorita Navarro?
3. ¿Es artista la señora Valdés?
4. ¿Conoces bien las costumbres peruanas?
5. ¿Tiene jardín la casa del señor Díaz?
6. ¿Tienes clase los sábados?
7. ¿Son interesantes los refranes?
8. ¿Aceptas la invitación para el almuerzo?

C. Después de oír el substantivo, repítanlo empleando el artículo definido; luego, repitan la frase en el plural.

MODELO: mapa   el mapa   los mapas

1. hijo.   2. profesora.   3. parque.   4. mano.   5. reunión.   6. universidad.   7. mes.   8. ciudad.   9. viaje.   10. jardín.   11. librería.   12. país.   13. máquina.   14. avión.   15. noche.   16. viernes.   17. flor.   18. rey.   19. alma.   20. examen.

IV. USOS DE LAS PALABRAS INDEFINIDAS Y NEGATIVAS

PRONOUNS

algo   something, anything
alguien   someone, somebody,
   anybody, anyone

nada   nothing, (not) . . . anything
nadie   no one, nobody, (not) . . .
   anybody (anyone)

PRONOUN OR ADJECTIVE

alguno   some(one), any; (*pl.*) some
cualquier(**a**)   any *or* anyone (*at all*)

ninguno   no, no one, none, (not) . . .
   any (anybody)

ADVERBS

siempre   always

también   also, too

nunca }
jamás }   never, (not) . . . ever

tampoco   neither, (not *or* nor) . . . either

CONJUNCTIONS

o   or
o . . . **o**   either . . . or

ni   nor, (not) . . . or
ni . . . **ni**   neither . . . nor, (not) . . .
   either . . . or

A. Simple negation is expressed by placing **no** immediately before the verb (or the auxiliary in the compound tenses and in the progressive forms of the tenses.)

If negatives such as **nada**, **nadie**, etc., follow the verb, **no** or some other negative word must precede the verb; if they precede the verb or stand alone, **no** is not used. If a negative precedes the verb, all the expressions in the Spanish sentence are negative, rather than indefinite, as in English.   After **que**, *than*, the negatives are used.

> **Miguel tiene algo.**   Michael has something.
> **No tiene nada** *or* **Nada tiene.**   He has nothing (He doesn't have anything).
> **Él nunca (jamás) trajo nada.**   He never brought anything.
> **Ana salió sin decir nada.**   Ann left without saying anything.
> **No lo hice tampoco** *or* **Tampoco lo hice.**   I didn't do it either (Neither did I do it).
> **¿Qué sabes? —Nada de particular.**   What do you know? —Nothing special.
> **Carlota lee más que nadie (nunca).**   Charlotte reads more than anyone (ever).
> **No veo ni a Juan ni a Marta.**   I don't see either John or Martha (I see neither John nor Martha).

If the verb is not expressed, **no** follows pronouns and adverbs: **Yo no,** *Not I*; **todavía no,** *not yet.*

B. The pronouns **alguien** and **nadie** refer only to persons, unknown or not mentioned before, and the personal **a** is required when they are used as objects of the verb:

> **¿Vio usted a alguien?** Did you see anyone?
> **Nadie me llamó, ni yo llamé a nadie.** No one called me, nor did I call anybody.

C. **Alguno** and **ninguno**, used as adjectives or pronouns, refer to *someone* or *none* of a group of persons or things already thought of or mentioned. The plural **algunos, -as**, means *some, any, several*. Before a masculine singular noun **alguno** is shortened to **algún**, and **ninguno** to **ningún**. **Ninguno, -a**, is used only in the singular.

> **Alguno de los niños lo dejó aquí.** Someone of the children left it here.
> **Ellos pasarán por aquí algún día.** They will come by here some day.
> **¿Conoces a algunas de las señoritas?** Do you know any of the young ladies?
> **Ninguna de ellas lo[1] sabe todo.** None of them knows everything.
> **Ningún hombre hará eso.** No man will do that.
> **No es ningún banquete.** It isn't any banquet.

D. Both **nunca** and **jamás** mean *never*, but in a question **jamás** means *ever* and a negative answer is expected. When neither an affirmative nor negative answer is implied, **alguna vez**, *ever, sometime, (at) any time*, is used.

> **Tomás nunca (jamás) me llama.** Tom never calls me.
> **¿Has visto jamás tal cosa? —No, nunca.** Have you ever seen such a thing? —No, never.
> **¿Ha estado usted alguna vez en México?** Have you ever (at any time) been in Mexico?

E. The plural **algunos, -as**, means *some, several, a few*; **unos, -as**, with the same meanings is more indefinite and expresses indifference as to the exact number. In some cases **unos, -as**, corresponds to *a pair of, two*; its place is taken by **algunos, -as**, in a **de**-phrase.

> **Hay algunos cuadros en la pared.** There are some pictures on the wall.
> **Él leerá algunos poemas suyos.** He will read some poems of his.
> **Unos niños están jugando en el jardín.** Some children are playing in the garden.
> **Marta tiene unos ojos bonitos.** Martha has two (a pair of) pretty eyes.

---

[1] When **todo**, *everything*, is the direct object of a verb, the direct object pronoun **lo** is also used.

Remember that unemphatic *some*, *any*, are not regularly expressed in Spanish:

> **¿Tiene usted dinero en el bolsillo?** Do you have some (any) money in your pocket?

A very emphatic way to express *any* (*at all*) is to place **alguno, -a**, after the noun:

> **Él hizo eso sin razón alguna.** He did that without any reason at all.

F. **Cualquiera** (*pl.* **cualesquiera**), which may drop the final **a** before a noun, means *any* in the sense of *any at all*:

> **Me conformo con cualquier cosa.** I'm satisfied with anything (at all).
> **Cualquier persona puede hacer eso.** Any person (at all) can do that.
> **Cualquiera de ellos me conoce bien.** Anyone of them knows me well.

G. **Algo** and **nada** are sometimes used as adverbs, meaning *somewhat*, *rather*, and (*not*) *at all*, respectively:

> **A menudo Juan llega algo tarde.** Often John arrives rather late.
> **Ese libro no es nada interesante.** That book isn't at all interesting.

Ejercicios

A. Repitan la frase; luego, cámbienla a la forma negativa.

MODELO: Ramón tiene algo.   Ramón tiene algo.   Ramón no tiene nada.

1. Veo algo sobre la mesa.
2. Juan le dio algo a su profesor de español.
3. Había algo en la nevera.

4. Alguien ha llamado a Miguel.
5. Hemos visto a alguien en el jardín de María.
6. Hay alguien en la cocina.

7. Alguno de los niños ha gritado mucho.
8. Algún hombre hará el trabajo.

9. Mi mamá ha invitado a alguno de los niños.
10. ¿Viene alguna de las muchachas?

11. ¿Siempre dices algo a alguien?
12. Alguna de ellas irá también.

13. Han visto a Juan o a Pablo.
14. El cuento es algo interesante.

B. Para contestar negativamente:

1. ¿Llamó alguien anoche?
2. ¿Almorzó contigo alguno de ellos?
3. ¿Nos ayudará algún muchacho?
4. ¿Has comprado alguna cosa hoy?
5. ¿Ha estado Ud. jamás en la ciudad de México?

6. ¿Siempre toma Ud. mucho al mediodía?
7. ¿Fueron Uds. al cine con alguien?
8. ¿Queda algo en la nevera?
9. ¿Buscó Ud. a alguna de las niñas?
10. ¿Discutes los planes con alguien?

C. Para completar empleando el equivalente de las palabras inglesas *some* o *any*:

1. _____ día pasaré por tu casa.   2. _____ estudiantes fueron al Club Español.
3. ¿Compró usted _____ zapatos en esta tienda?   4. El profesor Valdés va a leer _____ poemas suyos.   5. Nos conformaremos con _____ cosa.   6. No conozco _____ libro más interesante.   7. _____ mujeres acaban de entrar.   8. ¿Puede quedarse aquí _____ de las muchachas?   9. _____ de ellas puede poner la mesa.
10. Juan no tiene cuadro _____ en su cuarto.   11. Elena tiene _____ zapatos nuevos.   12. Mi mamá quiere preparar _____ emparedados para la reunión del club.   13. ¿Hay _____ tomates en la nevera?   14. No, y no hay _____ jamón tampoco.

RESUMEN

A. Lean en español, supliendo el artículo indefinido cuando sea necesario:

1. Luis no tiene _____ tocadiscos.
2. ¿Busca Ud. _____ coche ahora?
3. Mi abuelo dice que no necesita _____ coche en esa ciudad.
4. ¿Toman Uds. _____ café aquí?
5. Marta no quiere _____ bolsa nueva.

6. No puedo escribir sin _____ lápiz.
7. La mujer es _____ argentina rica.
8. ¿Qué es ella?   —Es _____ profesora.
9. ¿Quién es él?   —Es _____ médico.
10. Elena y _____ otra joven pasaron _____ media hora en la tienda.

B. Usos del artículo definido.   Para expresar en español:

1. Mr. Navarro is not at home today.
2. We go to church on Sundays.
3. Ann, wash (*fam.*) your hands.
4. Johnny, (*fam.*) put on your shoes.
5. Professor Valdés will leave for Argentina next month.

6. Today is Wednesday, isn't it?
7. The water was not cold (hot).
8. Does she like horses?
9. You like Spanish, don't you?
10. The lecturer will talk about contemporary poetry.

C. Usos de las palabras indefinidas y negativas.   Para expresar en español:

1. Do you have anything in your hand?
2. I haven't anything (I have nothing).
3. Jane invited someone for lunch.
4. Mary did not see anyone downtown.
5. Some girl lost her wrist watch.
6. None of the boys could find it.
7. We never buy anything in this store.
8. Martha sings better than anyone.
9. Have you ever (at any time) been in California?
10. Any man (at all) can help us.
11. That novel is not at all bad.
12. That woman never gives any money to anyone.

D. Formen oraciones originales, empleando las frases o palabras siguientes:

1. el arte español
2. el agua
3. el pelo negro
4. otra estudiante
5. unos discos
6. de español
7. mexicano
8. ¡qué!

«La Batalla de Araure», por Tito Salas
Simón Bolívar derrotó a los españoles en Araure,
Venezuela

LECTURA II

A. Estudio de palabras

Observations on Spanish cognates (Continued). Review the "Estudio de palabras" section of Lectura I, pages 57-58. A number of principles listed there are involved in the observations given below, and, naturally, many words fit more than one category. Also, the student is cautioned against assuming that all Spanish words having the sounds and forms mentioned can be turned into English by the corresponding changes indicated. An occasional word used in Lectura I and also used in this Lectura appears below.

1. Verb cognates

a. The ending of the Spanish infinitive is lacking in English: formar, permitir, representar, resultar.

b. The ending of the Spanish infinitive is -*e* in English: aspirar, continuar, decidir, declarar, invadir, organizar, realizar, retirar.

c. Certain infinitives ending in **-ar** end in -*ate* in English: celebrar, educar, elevar, separar, terminar, venerar.

d. Infinitives with additional differences are: aceptar, *to accept*; concebir (i, i), *to conceive*; distinguir, *to distinguish*; gobernar, *to govern*; iniciar, *to initiate*; ocurrir, *to occur*; proclamar, *to proclaim*; revelar, *to reveal*; sufrir, *to suffer*.

Often it is helpful to think of a similar meaning in English: encontrar (ue), *to encounter, find*; convocar, *to convoke, call*; elevar, *to elevate, raise*; terminar, *to terminate, end*; unir, *to unite, join*.

2. Approximate cognates (comparison of Spanish and English sounds)

a. Spanish initial **e** before a consonant group beginning with **s** (or **x**) = the English consonant group without the initial *e*: España, español, estado, estudio, estudiar.

b. The Spanish **k** sound (**qu** before **e** and **i**, but **c** in other cases, with a few exceptions in which the letter **k** appears) = English *ch* or (*c*)*k*: convocar, *to convoke*; kilómetro, *kilometer*; monarquía, *monarchy*; atacar, *to attack*.

c. Spanish **f** = English *ph*: triunfante, *triumphant*; triunfo, *triumph*.

d. Spanish **t** = English *th*: autoridad, *authority*; teoría, *theory*; trono, *throne*.

e. Spanish **u** = English *ou*: fundación, *foundation, founding*; fundar, *to found*; grupo, *group*.

3. Less approximate cognates. Other words with miscellaneous differences which should be recognized easily, especially in context or when pronounced in Spanish

are: bandera, *banner*; batalla, *battle*; carrera, *career*; congreso, *congress*; progreso, *progress*; imagen, *image*; nacional, *national*; norteamericano, *North American*; panamericano, *Pan American*; proyecto, *project*; puesto, *post*; razón, *reason*; Virgen, *Virgin*; voluntario, *volunteer*.

4. Keeping in mind the principles stated concerning certain endings of words in the "Estudio de palabras" section of Lectura I, give the meanings of: libertad; conspirador, dictador, libertador; misterioso; conferencia, injusticia, independencia, servicio; familia, revolucionario, victoria.

5. Deceptive cognates. From the outset the student should beware of a number of important cases in which the meaning of the Spanish cognate is quite different from the meaning that might be expected in English. The following examples appear in this Lectura: actual, *present, present-day*; la capital, *capital* (city), which must be distinguished from **el capital**, *capital* (money); la conferencia, *conference*, and *lecture*; la desgracia, *misfortune*; papel, *role*, and *paper*; realizar, *to realize*, in the sense of *to carry out*.

B. Modismos y frases útiles

a caballo   on horseback
a fines de   towards (at) the end of
a principios de   at the beginning of
a través de   across, through
atreverse a   to dare to
dar gritos   to cry out, shout
en poder de   in the hands (power) of
en seguida   at once, immediately
es decir   that is, that is to say
junto con   along with
negarse (ie) a   to refuse to
otra vez   again
poco después   shortly afterwards

poner fin a   to put an end to
ponerse en marcha   to set out, start out
por desgracia   unfortunately
por eso   therefore, for that reason, that's why
por fin   finally, at last
representar el mismo papel que   to play the same role as
sobre todo   especially, above all
tener lugar   to take place
tocarle a uno   to fall to one's lot, be one's turn

C. Aspectos gramaticales

1. The past participle may be used absolutely to express *time, manner, means,* and the like (see page 244):

Conseguida la independencia peruana . . .   Peruvian independence attained (After *or* When Peruvian independence was attained) . . .
Terminada la obra militar . . .   The military work ended (After the military work was ended) . . .

2. Word order in Spanish.   Contrary to the normal order of subject, verb, object (predicate noun, adjective, etc.) in a declarative sentence, the subject often follows the verb in Spanish.   In general, there is a tendency to avoid ending a Spanish sentence with a verb.   Some typical inversions found in this Lectura are:

a. When the subject is long or followed by a clause, or in relative and adverbial clauses when the verb does not have a noun object expressed:

> **ocurrieron ciertas injusticias . . . que no permitían el progreso . . .** certain . . . injustices which did not permit the progress . . . occurred
> **decidieron que había llegado el momento de sublevarse y gobernarse a sí mismas.** (they) decided that the moment to rebel and to govern themselves had arrived.

b. When an adverbial expression, prepositional phrase, or other types of incidental expressions begin the sentence:

> **Poco después tuvo lugar la misteriosa entrevista de . . . , donde por primera vez se encontraron Bolívar y San Martín.** Shortly afterwards the mysterious interview of (at) . . . , where Bolívar and San Martín met for the first time, took place.

c. When the reflexive construction is used as a substitute for the passive (see page 59):

> **En esta entrevista se discutieron los planes . . .** In this interview the plans . . . were discussed
> **se le considera a Hidalgo** Hidalgo is considered
> **se celebra la fiesta nacional de la república . . .** the national holiday of the republic is celebrated . . .

At times, however, the subject precedes the verb in the impersonal reflexive construction:

> **A este primer acto de la sublevación se le llama . . .** This first act of revolt is called . . . (They call this first act of revolt . . .)

3. Even though the article is regularly repeated before nouns in a series, when the nouns are closely related in meaning, the article may be omitted in polished style before all but the first noun:

> **los ideales y sueños** the ideals and dreams
> **los indios y campesinos** the Indians and countryfolk
> **un mayor énfasis y apreciación** a greater emphasis and appreciation

LOS LIBERTADORES

Durante los tres siglos de la dominación española ocurrieron ciertas injusticias económicas y políticas que no permitían el progreso de las colonias.*   A fines del siglo XVIII el ejemplo de la revolución norteamericana (1775) y de la revolución francesa (1789), y las nuevas ideas sobre la libertad y los derechos del hombre dieron esperanzas a los que aspiraban a separarse de la madre patria.[1]   Desde el siglo XVII la monarquía española había perdido poco a poco su poderío.   Cuando Napoleón invadió a España en 1808 y puso en el trono a su hermano José, las colonias decidieron que había llegado el momento de sublevarse y gobernarse a sí mismas.*   En la América española la lucha por[2] la independencia comenzó, por fin, en el año 1810.

Los tres grandes héroes de la independencia de la América española fueron Simón Bolívar, José de San Martín y el padre Miguel Hidalgo.

Simón Bolívar, el libertador del norte de la América del Sur, nació en Caracas, Venezuela, en 1783.   De familia distinguida, fue educado en España.   En 1810 volvió a Venezuela para tomar parte en la rebelión de la colonia contra la dominación española.   Después de varios años de lucha, logró expulsar[3] a los españoles de Venezuela.   En 1819 pasó a Nueva Granada,[4] donde fundó la república de la Gran Colombia, formada por las actuales[5] de Colombia, Panamá, Venezuela y el Ecuador.   En 1823 entró triunfante en Lima, y al año siguiente su ejército ganó la famosa victoria de Ayacucho, poniendo fin a la dominación española en la América del Sur. Conseguida la independencia peruana,* fundó la república del Alto Perú (hoy Bolivia).

Terminada la obra militar,* Bolívar trató de realizar el sueño de su vida: la creación de una gran república hispanoamericana comparable a la de[6] los Estados Unidos de Norteamérica.   Para realizarlo, propuso la formación de la Gran Confederación de los Andes, es decir, la unión de los países del norte del continente bajo la autoridad del mismo Bolívar.   En 1826 convocó en Panamá el primer Congreso Panamericano, pero, por desgracia, las nuevas naciones se negaron a aceptar el plan.   Hasta su muerte, en 1830, Bolívar siguió luchando en vano por lograr la unificación.   La Organización de los Estados Americanos, que recibió su nombre actual en la conferencia panamericana celebrada en Bogotá, Colombia, en 1948, es el resultado de más de un siglo de lucha por realizar los ideales y sueños* de Bolívar.

[1] **madre patria**, *mother country*.   [2] **Para** and **por** are used a number of times in this Lectura; see pages 241–243 for their uses.   [3] **logró expulsar**, *he succeeded in expelling* (*driving out*).   [4] Spain first created the viceroyalty of New Granada in northwestern South America in 1718.   [5] **las actuales**, *the present ones* (= republics).   [6] **la de**, *that of*.   (For explanation of **la**, see page 200.)

José de San Martín fue el libertador del sur del continente. Hijo de un capitán español que vivía en la Argentina, José fue enviado a España para estudiar la carrera militar. Pasó unos veinte años en el ejército español, donde se distinguió como soldado, sobre todo en la guerra contra Napoleón. En 1812 volvió a la Argentina para ofrecer sus servicios a las fuerzas revolucionarias y durante unos diez años representó en el sur del continente el mismo papel que Bolívar en el norte. Su marcha a través de los Andes, a principios del año 1817, es una de las hazañas[1] más notables de la historia militar.

El doce de febrero de 1817, con la ayuda del general Bernardo O'Higgins y sus tropas chilenas, San Martín sorprendió a los españoles y los derrotó en la sangrienta[2] batalla de Chacabuco. Se negó a aceptar el puesto de dictador de Chile y continuó con sus planes para la conquista del Perú. En 1821 ocupó a Lima, donde se proclamó «Protector del Perú». Poco después tuvo lugar la misteriosa entrevista de Guayaquil, Ecuador, donde por primera vez se encontraron Bolívar y San Martín.* En esta entrevista se discutieron los planes* para terminar la guerra de la independencia. Por razones desconocidas San Martín se retiró de la lucha, y en 1824 le tocó a Bolívar dar el golpe de muerte[3] a las fuerzas españolas en el Perú.

El resto de la vida de San Martín es un relato triste. Cuando volvió a la Argentina, no quisieron recibirle. Como Bolívar, había gastado su fortuna luchando por la libertad y por los ideales democráticos. Su esposa había muerto. Pobre y desilusionado, partió con su hija para Europa, donde murió unos treinta años después.

En México, es decir, en la Nueva España, la revolución contra los españoles no fue iniciada por militares, sino por el padre Miguel Hidalgo, cura[4] del pequeño pueblo de Dolores, en el estado de Guanajuato. Hacía muchos años que el padre Hidalgo trabajaba[5] por los derechos de los indios y por el mejoramiento del gobierno. Se había dedicado al cultivo de la tierra y a la enseñanza de artes y oficios.[6] El estudio del francés le había permitido conocer las nuevas teorías políticas. Junto con un grupo de amigos, había concebido el proyecto de realizar la independencia de la Nueva España.

Hidalgo y sus amigos revolucionarios no aspiraban precisamente a la fundación de una república; sólo deseaban establecer un gobierno formado por hombres nacidos en el país. Pensaban declarar la independencia en el mes de diciembre de 1810, pero un traidor reveló el plan a las autoridades

---

[1] **hazañas**, *deeds.*   [2] **sangrienta**, *bloody.*   [3] **le tocó . . . muerte**, *it fell to the lot of Bolívar to give the death blow.*   [4] **cura**, *priest.*   [5] **Hacía . . . trabajaba**, *For many years Father Hidalgo had been working.* (For use of **hacer**, see pages 232–233.)   [6] **enseñanza de artes y oficios**, *teaching of arts (crafts) and trades.*

Bernardo O'Higgins

José de San Martín

«La Batalla de Chacabuco», por J. L. A. T. Géricault

«El Paso de los Andes», por E. Lo Evy

españolas.   La noche del 15 de septiembre uno de los conspiradores descubrió
la traición y corrió unos veinte kilómetros a caballo para avisar a Hidalgo.

El día siguiente era domingo, y el cura llamó a misa[1] a los indios y
campesinos* del pueblo.   Después de hablar de los abusos y de las injusticias
que habían sufrido, los animó a sublevarse contra los españoles.   En un
momento de inspiración elevó la imagen de la Virgen de Guadalupe, muy
venerada por los indios, y en seguida todos empezaron a dar gritos por la
independencia.   A este primer acto de la sublevación se le llama* en la
historia de México «el Grito de Dolores».   Seguido de[2] miles de hombres y
mujeres indígenas, armados de palos, navajas[3] y machetes, y con la imagen
de la Virgen de Guadalupe como bandera oficial, Hidalgo se puso en marcha
hacia la ciudad de México.

En el camino miles de voluntarios se unieron a sus fuerzas, pero, por
razones desconocidas, Hidalgo no se atrevió a atacar la capital inmediatamente.   Cuando por fin decidió atacar la ciudad, fue rechazado[4] por los
españoles, y tuvo que retirarse a Guadalajara, donde organizó un nuevo
gobierno.   Unos meses después fue derrotado otra vez.   Él y varios compañeros suyos cayeron en poder de las tropas españolas y todos fueron
fusilados.[5]

Aunque Hidalgo fracasó,[6] otros patriotas mexicanos continuaron la lucha
hasta conseguir[7] el triunfo final.   Por eso se le considera a Hidalgo* como
el padre de la independencia mexicana, y se celebra la fiesta nacional de la
república* el 16 de septiembre.   En muchas ciudades y pueblos mexicanos
hay calles llamadas «Hidalgo» y «Diez y Seis de Septiembre», y uno de los
estados de México lleva su nombre.

---

[1] **misa,** *Mass.*   [2] **Seguido de,** *Followed by.*   (For use of **de,** see page 244.)   [3] **palos, navajas,**
sticks (clubs), knives.   [4] **fue rechazado,** *he was repulsed (driven back).*   [5] **fueron fusilados,** *were
shot.*   [6] **fracasó,** *failed.*   [7] **continuaron . . . conseguir,** *(they) continued the struggle until they
attained.*   (For use of a preposition plus an infinitive to replace a clause in Spanish, see page 191.)

«Independencia», (detalle de una pintura mural) por
Juan O'Gorman
El padre Miguel Hidalgo y sus seguidores

PRÁCTICAS ORALES

A. Diálogo. «En la clase de español»

(*El profesor inicia la discusión de la Lectura*, «Los libertadores.»)

PROFESOR.   Hoy comenzamos el estudio de las luchas por la independencia en la América española. ¿Quiénes fueron los tres grandes héroes de la independencia en Hispanoamérica?

ESTUDIANTE.   Si recuerdo bien, fueron Simón Bolívar, José de San Martín y el padre Miguel Hidalgo.

PROFESOR.   ¿Qué nuevas ideas daban esperanzas a los que aspiraban a separarse de España?

ESTUDIANTE.   Las nuevas ideas sobre la libertad y los derechos del hombre daban esperanzas a los que aspiraban a separarse de España.

PROFESOR.   ¿Dónde nació Bolívar y dónde fue educado?

ESTUDIANTE.   Bolívar nació en Caracas, Venezuela, y fue educado en España.

PROFESOR.   ¿Qué hizo Bolívar en 1810?

ESTUDIANTE.   En 1810 Bolívar volvió a Venezuela para tomar parte en la rebelión de la colonia contra la dominación española.

PROFESOR.   ¿Qué importancia tuvo la victoria de Ayacucho, en 1824?

ESTUDIANTE.   La victoria de Ayacucho puso fin a la dominación española en la América del Sur.

PROFESOR.   ¿Cuál fue el gran sueño de Bolívar?

ESTUDIANTE.   Su gran sueño fue la creación de una república hispanoamericana comparable a la de los Estados Unidos en Norteamérica.

PROFESOR.   ¿Quién representó en el sur del continente el mismo papel que Bolívar en el norte?

ESTUDIANTE.   José de San Martín representó en el sur del continente el mismo papel que Bolívar en el norte.

PROFESOR.   ¡Muy bien! Pero basta por ahora. Tenemos que pasar a otra parte de la lección.

B. Para formular preguntas en español

Formúlense[1] preguntas para las siguientes contestaciones:

1. El padre Miguel Hidalgo inició la revolución contra los españoles en la Nueva España. 2. Había concebido el proyecto de realizar la independencia de la Nueva España. 3. Hidalgo y sus amigos revolucionarios no aspiraban precisamente a la fundación de una república. 4. La noche del 15 de septiembre uno de los conspiradores descubrió la traición y corrió unos veinte kilómetros a caballo para avisar a Hidalgo. 5. Al día siguiente el cura Hidalgo llamó a misa a los indios y campesinos

---

[1] **Formulen** (subjunctive) + **se** (reflexive), *Formulate.* The reflexive form of the third person of the present subjunctive is often used in giving directions, or to express an action that is to be done. This construction is usually found in written instructions.

del pueblo.   6. Habló de los abusos y de las injusticias que habían sufrido y los animó a sublevarse contra los españoles.

7. Al elevar la imagen de la Virgen de Guadalupe, todos empezaron a dar grtios por la independencia.   8. A este primer acto de la sublevación se le llama «el Grito de Dolores».   9. Seguido de miles de hombres y mujeres indígenas, Hidalgo se puso en marcha hacia la ciudad de México.   10. Fue rechazado por los españoles, y tuvo que retirarse a Guadalajara.   11. Él y varios compañeros suyos cayeron en poder de los españoles y todos fueron fusilados.   12. Otros patriotas mexicanos continuaron la lucha hasta conseguir el triunfo final.

EJERCICIOS ESCRITOS

A. Uso de modismos y frases hechas

Escríbanse oraciones completas empleando las frases siguientes:

a fines de	atreverse a	negarse a	por eso
a través de	es decir	por desgracia	tener lugar

B. Para expresar en español

1. In Spanish America the three great heroes in the struggle for independence were Bolívar, San Martín, and Father Hidalgo.   2. Bolívar, who was born in Caracas and was educated in Spain, returned to Venezuela in 1810 to take part in the rebellion against the mother country.   3. After establishing several republics, he succeeded in giving the death blow to the Spanish forces in the famous battle of Ayacucho. 4. His military work ended, he tried in vain to carry out his dream of the union of all the countries of the north of South America.   5. San Martín, who was sent to Spain to study a (the) military career, spent some twenty years in the Spanish army. 6. After returning to Argentina in 1812, San Martín played the same role in the south of the continent as Bolívar in the north.   7. After defeating the Spaniards in Chile, San Martín refused to accept the post of dictator of the country.   8. He and his soldiers occupied Lima in 1821, but shortly afterwards he withdrew from the struggle.   9. Therefore, it fell to Bolívar's lot to end the war of independence. 10. The revolution in Mexico, that is, in New Spain, was initiated by Father Hidalgo, priest of the small town of Dolores.   11. He had dedicated himself to working for the rights of the Indians and peasants.   12. Even though Hidalgo could not establish a new government, today he is considered as the father of Mexican independence.

C. Dictado (*Dictation*)

The teacher will select lines from page 99 for dictation.   The following terms may be used by the teacher in giving a Dictado: coma, *comma*; punto, *period*; dos puntos, *colon*; punto y coma, *semi-colon*; punto y aparte, *new paragraph*.   For other punctuation marks, see page 304.

LECCIÓN CINCO

Las formas, la concordancia y la colocación
de los adjetivos. Expresiones con «hacer, haber» y «tener».
Palabras interrogativas y exclamaciones

LOS NUEVOS CAMPEONES

(El equipo en que juega Ramón acaba de ganar el campeonato de fútbol. Al volver a su cuarto Ramón se encuentra con su amigo Enrique.)

ENRIQUE.   ¡Enhorabuena, Ramón!   ¡Qué bien jugaron todos!

RAMÓN.   Gracias, Enrique.   Fue un partido muy reñido.   Los contrarios tenían unos defensas muy fuertes y muy rápidos.

ENRIQUE.   Casi perdimos las esperanzas cuando el tiro de Roberto pasó por encima de la portería.   Parecía un gol seguro.

RAMÓN.   Pero los delanteros volvieron a atacar con mayor furia y por fin ganamos el partido.

ENRIQUE.   No parece posible.   Sólo quedaba un minuto cuando Roberto marcó el gol.

RAMÓN.   Yo tenía mucho miedo.   Como llovía y había mucho lodo, era difícil pasar el fútbol.   Y no debemos olvidar que Arturo, el portero, jugó muy bien.   Hizo unas paradas extraordinarias.

ENRIQUE.   Es el primer campeonato que ha ganado nuestra universidad, ¿verdad?

RAMÓN.   Sí, pero no será el último.[1]   Ninguno de los jugadores se gradúa este año.

ENRIQUE.   ¿Echaron en la piscina al entrenador?

RAMÓN.   ¡Pobre hombre!   Nos dijo que llevaba un traje nuevo, pero no le permitimos mudarse de ropa.

ENRIQUE.   ¡Qué lástima!   Los jóvenes deben ser más corteses con los mayores.

---

[1] **Último, -a**, means *last* (in a series); **pasado, -a**, is used for *last* (just passed): **la semana pasada**, *last week*.

107

atacar to attack
el campeón (*pl.* **campeones**)
    champion
el campeonato championship
el contrario opposing player; *pl.* the
    other side, opposing players
el defensa back (*soccer*)
el delantero forward (*soccer*)
  echar (**en**) to throw *or* toss (into)
  ¡enhorabuena! congratulations!
el entrenador coach, trainer
el equipo team
la esperanza (*also pl.*) hope
  extraordinario, -a extraordinary

fuerte strong
la furia fury
el gol goal (*score*)
  graduarse (**ú**) (*like* **continuar**)
    to graduate
el lodo mud
  marcar to make (*a score*)
la parada stop
  por encima de over, above
la portería goal (*soccer*)
el portero goalkeeper (*soccer*)
  reñido, -a hard-fought
el tiro shot

A. Busquen en el diálogo las frases que correspondan a las siguientes:

1. (he) runs across his friend. 2. Congratulations! 3. a hard-fought game.
4. The other side. 5. We almost lost hope. 6. Robert's shot passed over the goal.
7. (they) attacked again. 8. with greater fury. 9. Only a minute was left.
10. Robert made the goal. 11. I was very (much) afraid. 12. it was very muddy.
13. Did you toss (throw) the coach into the pool? 14. he was wearing a new suit.
15. What a pity! 16. Young people should be more courteous with older people
(their elders).

B. Estudien las expresiones siguientes para emplear algunas de ellas en el
    diálogo citado, o para usarlas en un diálogo nuevo basado sobre el
    modelo:

calcular mal to misjudge
cero zero
defender (**ie**) to defend
desanimarse to become discouraged
empatar to tie (*in a game or in*
    elections)
errar[1] **el tiro** to miss (*a shot*)

felicitar to congratulate
hábil skillful
hacer una jugada prohibida
    (**contra**) to foul (*in a game*)
la liga league
el primer (**segundo**) **tiempo** the
    first (second) half (*of a game*)

PRONUNCIACIÓN

The sounds of Spanish **g** (**gu**) and **j** (**x**). At the beginning of a breath-group or
when after **n**, Spanish **g** (written **gu** before **e** or **i**) is a voiced velar stop, like a weak
English *g* in *go*. In all other cases, except before **e** or **i** in the groups **ge**, **gi**, Spanish **g**

---

[1] See footnote 1, page 322, for irregular forms of **errar** in the present indicative tense.

is a voiced velar continuant; that is, the breath is allowed to pass between the back of the tongue and the palate. (The diaeresis is used over **u** in the combinations **güe** and **güi** when the **u** is pronounced: **vergüenza**.)

Spanish **g** before **e** and **i**, and **j** in all positions, have no English equivalent. They are pronounced approximately like a strongly exaggerated *h* in *halt* (rather like the rasping German *ch* in *Buch*). Remember that the letter **x** in the words **México**, **mexicano**, and **Texas**, spelled **Méjico**, **mejicano**, and **Tejas** in Spain, is pronounced like Spanish **j**. Note, also, that the consonant **j** is silent in **reloj**, but pronounced in the plural **relojes**.

Pronounce after your teacher:

1.	ganamos	graduarse	guitarra	lengua
	distinguido	ninguno	con gusto	un gol
2.	la guitarra	es grande	Miguel	diálogo
	seguir	luego	dos goles	mucho gusto
3.	jefe	jamón	junio	extranjero
	dirigirse	generalmente	la Argentina	imaginarse
4.	Tengo un gato algo glotón.		Gané un reloj de pulsera.	
	El viaje de Jorge a Nuevo México.		Ningún jugador se quejó.	

NOTAS GRAMATICALES

I. LAS FORMAS, LA CONCORDANCIA (*AGREEMENT*) Y LA COLOCACIÓN DE LOS ADJETIVOS

A. Forms and agreement of adjectives

An adjective, which limits or describes a noun, must agree with the noun in gender and number, whether the adjective modifies the noun directly or is in the predicate. An adjective which modifies two or more singular nouns is put in the plural; if one noun is masculine and the other feminine, the adjective is regularly masculine plural. (The adjective should stand nearest the masculine noun.) Adjectives form their plurals in the same way as nouns (see Lección cuatro).

The feminine singular of adjectives ending in **-o** is formed by changing final **-o** to **-a**. Adjectives of nationality that end in a consonant, and adjectives that end in **-án, -ón, -or** (except the comparatives **mejor, peor, mayor, menor**, and such words as **interior, exterior, superior**, and a few others which were comparatives in Latin), add **-a** for the feminine. Other adjectives have the same form for the masculine and feminine.

SINGULAR		PLURAL	
Masculine	*Feminine*	*Masculine*	*Feminine*
nuevo	**nueva**	**nuevos**	**nuevas**
feliz	**feliz**	**felices**	**felices**

joven	joven	jóvenes	jóvenes
cortés	cortés	corteses	corteses
mexicano	mexicana	mexicanos	mexicanas
español	española	españoles	españolas
francés	francesa	franceses	francesas
hablador[1]	habladora	habladores	habladoras
mayor	mayor	mayores	mayores

Note the addition of the written accent: **joven-jóvenes**; the dropping of the accent: **cortés-corteses** and **francés-francesa, franceses, francesas**; and the change in spelling: **feliz-felices**.

B. Position of adjectives

Limiting adjectives (articles, unstressed possessives, demonstratives, numerals, indefinites, and other adjectives which show quantity) usually precede the noun.

Adjectives which distinguish or differentiate a noun from others of the same class (adjectives of color, size, shape, nationality, adjectives modified by adverbs, past participles used as adjectives, and the like) regularly follow the noun.

> **algunas muchachas mexicanas**   some Mexican girls
> **veinte estudiantes españoles**   twenty Spanish students
> **un niño muy feliz**   a very happy little boy
> **muchas cosas interesantes**   many interesting things
> **otra familia grande**   another large family
> **mis zapatos negros**   my black shoes
> **una pluma y un lápiz rojos**   a red pen and pencil

When two or more adjectives modify a noun, each occupies its normal position; if they follow the noun, the last two are regularly connected by **y**. Two or more singular adjectives may modify a plural noun:

> **el distinguido autor mexicano**   the distinguished Mexican author
> **el famoso héroe argentino**   the famous Argentine hero
> **las literaturas española y mexicana**   Spanish and Mexican literatures

Certain common adjectives (**bueno, mejor, mayor, malo, peor,** and less frequently **pequeño, joven, viejo,** and a few others) often precede the noun, but they may follow the noun to place more emphasis on the adjective than on the noun:

> **una buena muchacha** *or* **una muchacha buena**   a good girl
> **un joven poeta** *or* **un poeta joven**   a young poet

---

[1] **hablador, -ora,** *talkative.*

We have already observed that certain adjectives have a different meaning when they precede or follow a noun: for **nuevo, -a**, see page 31, fn. 1; for **mismo, -a**, and **propio, -a**, see sections 2 and 3, pages 136–137. In addition to **grande** (see section C, 2, below), two other examples are:

> **el hombre pobre**   the poor man (*not rich*)
> **el pobre hombre**   the poor man (*a man to be pitied*)
> **un amigo viejo**   an old friend (*elderly*)
> **un viejo amigo**   an old friend (*of long standing*)

For further treatment of the position of adjectives, see the explanation given on page 173.

C. Shortened forms of adjectives

1. A few adjectives drop the final **-o** when they precede a masculine singular noun: **bueno, malo, uno, primero, tercero, postrero** (*last*), **alguno, ninguno**.   **Alguno** and **ninguno** become **algún** and **ningún**, respectively.

> **el primer mes**   the first month   **ningún muchacho**   no boy
> **algún estudiante**   some student   **un buen coche**   a good car
>
> BUT: **los primeros días**   the first days
>   **una buena idea**   a good idea

2. Three common adjectives drop the last syllable under certain conditions.

a. **Grande** becomes **gran** before either a masculine or feminine singular noun, and usually means *great*:

> **un gran autor**   a great author   **una gran sorpresa**   a great surprise
>
> BUT: **dos grandes hombres**   two great men
>   **estas grandes obras**   these great works

When **grande** follows the noun, it regularly means *large, big*:

> **un país grande**   a large country   **estos coches grandes**   these large cars

b. **Santo** (not **Santa**) becomes **San** before all names of masculine saints, except those beginning with **Do-** or **To-**:

> **San Pablo** Saint Paul   **San Francisco**   St. Francis
>
> BUT: **Santo Tomás**   St. Thomas   **Santa María**   St. Mary
>   **Santo Domingo**   St. Dominic   **Santa Inés**   St. Agnes

c. **Ciento** becomes **cien** before all nouns, including **millones**, and before the adjective **mil**, but it is not shortened before numerals smaller than one hundred:

cien teléfonos	100 telephones	**cien mil personas**	100,000 persons
cien muchachas	100 girls	**ciento cincuenta hombres**	150 men

D. Use of prepositional phrases instead of adjectives

In Spanish a noun is rarely used as an adjective; instead, a prepositional phrase beginning with **de** or **para** is normally used. Such constructions may be considered compound nouns. A few examples are:

el campeonato de fútbol the football championship

el periódico de la universidad the university newspaper

el reloj de pulsera the wrist watch

estas tazas para café these coffee cups

un programa de televisión a TV program

un vaso para agua a water glass

Ejercicios

A. Repitan cada frase; luego, al oír un nuevo substantivo, formen otra frase haciendo los cambios necesarios.

MODELO: Es una canción mexicana.
       canciones

Es una canción mexicana.
Son canciones (*or* unas canciones) mexicanas.

1. Es un traje bonito.
    corbata
    sombreros
    blusas

2. Mi amigo es español.
    Mi amiga
    Los jugadores
    Las alumnas

3. ¿Es hablador el hombre?
    mujer?
    estudiantes?
    muchachas?

4. Es un día hermoso.
    noche
    árboles
    rosas

B. Repitan cada frase, y luego cámbienla al singular:

1. sus buenos amigos. 2. nuestras buenas amigas. 3. aquellos malos caminos. 4. aquellas niñas muy buenas. 5. otras revistas españolas. 6. nuestros hermanos

menores.   7. los primeros días buenos.   8. esas grandes oportunidades.   9. algunos
jugadores mexicanos.   10. aquellos grandes profesores.   11. estos pobres muchachos.
12. los nuevos campeones.   13. unos compañeros de clase.   14. estas tazas para
té.   15. aquellos programas de televisión.   16. unas paradas extraordinarias.

C. Primero oirán un substantivo; luego, oirán dos adjetivos, separados por
una pausa.   Combínenlos en una sola frase, según los modelos.

MODELOS: casa—una, nueva   una casa nueva
          edificio—aquel, tercer   aquel tercer edificio

1. hermano—nuestro, mayor   5. jugador—otro, buen
2. día—el, primer   6. ciudades—cuatro, españolas
3. señorita—aquella, simpática   7. autor—otro, gran
4. muchachos—varios, corteses   8. estudiante—algún, extranjero

II. EXPRESIONES CON «HACER, HABER» Y «TENER»

A. **Hacer** is used impersonally with certain nouns in Spanish in speaking of the
state of the weather and the temperature, while *to be* is used in English:

    ¿Qué tiempo hace hoy?   What kind of weather is it today?
    Hace buen (mal) tiempo.   It is good (bad) weather.
    Hizo (mucho) calor ayer.   It was (very) warm yesterday.
    Hará (mucho) fresco mañana.   It will be (very) cool tomorrow.
    Ha hecho (mucho) frío.   It has been (very) cold.
    Hacía (mucho) viento.   It was (very) windy.
    Hace mucho sol hoy.   It is very sunny (The sun is shining brightly) to-
        day.

Since **calor, fresco, frío, viento, sol** are nouns when used in these expressions, they
are modified by the adjective **mucho**, not the adverb **muy**.

B. **Haber**, used impersonally, also applies to certain natural phenomena, especially
those that are seen:

    Hay mucho sol.   It is very sunny.
    Hay luna esta noche.   The moon is shining (It is moonlight) tonight.
    Hay mucho lodo (polvo).   It is very muddy (dusty).
    Había niebla (neblina).   It was foggy (misty).

C. In speaking of a person, or anything living, **tener** is used with certain nouns:

> **Juan tiene (mucho) frío.**   John is *or* feels (very) cold.
> **Tenemos (mucho) calor.**   We are *or* feel (very) warm.

Compare the use of **estar** or **ser** with an adjective when referring to a changeable or inherent quality:

> **El agua estaba muy fría.**   The water was very cold.
> **El hielo es frío.**   Ice is cold.

Other common idiomatic expressions with **tener** are:

tener cuidado to be careful	**tener razón** to be right
tener hambre to be hungry	**no tener razón** to be wrong
tener sed to be thirsty	**tener sueño** to be sleepy
tener miedo to be afraid, frightened	**tener suerte** to be lucky, fortunate
tener prisa to be in a hurry	**tener vergüenza** to be ashamed

With all the above nouns, **mucho, -a,** translates English *very, (very) much*. **Mucha** is used with the feminine nouns **hambre, sed, prisa, razón, suerte, vergüenza.**

Some additional expressions with **tener** are:

> **¿Cuántos años tienes (tiene usted)?**   How old are you?
> **Tengo dieciocho años.**   I am eighteen (years old).
> **¿Qué tiene Carlos?**   What is the matter (What's wrong) with Charles?
> **Tienen ganas de ir a casa.**   They feel like going (are anxious to go) home.
> **Aquí tiene usted (el libro).**   Here is (the book).   (*Handing someone something.*)
> **Pablo tenía la culpa.**   Paul was at fault (to blame).
> **Tenemos que darnos prisa.**   We have to (must) hurry (up).

NOTE. **Tener prisa** means *to be in a hurry*, while **darse prisa** means *to hurry up*.

Ejercicios

A. Para contestar en español:

1. ¿Qué tiempo hace hoy?   2. ¿Qué tiempo hizo ayer?   3. ¿Qué tiempo ha hecho esta semana?   4. ¿En qué estación del año hace más calor?   5. ¿En cuál de las estaciones hace más frío?   6. ¿Qué tiempo hace en el otoño?   7. ¿Dónde hace frío todo el año?   8. ¿Qué tomamos cuando hace mucho calor?

9. ¿Hay sol hoy?   10. ¿Habrá luna esta noche?   11. ¿Hay mucho polvo ahora?
12. ¿Cuándo hay lodo?   13. ¿Hay niebla aquí a veces?

14. ¿Tiene usted frío en este momento?   15. ¿Qué hace usted cuando tiene hambre?   16. ¿Qué toma usted cuando tiene mucha sed?   17. ¿Tiene usted sueño en clase a veces?   18. ¿Tiene usted miedo de los animales?   19. ¿Tiene usted ganas de ir al cine esta noche?   20. ¿Cuántos años tiene usted?

B. Para expresar en español:

1. Are you (*pl.*) very sleepy?
2. The boys are in a hurry.
3. What's the matter with Paul?
4. How old is your (*fam. sing.*) sister?
5. Here is the football; take it.
6. We are not at fault.
7. I am hungry and thirsty.
8. He doesn't feel like studying.
9. Hurry up (*pl.*); it is late.
10. The children are not afraid.

III. PALABRAS INTERROGATIVAS Y EXCLAMACIONES

A. Interrogative words

1. **¿Quién?** (*pl.* **¿Quiénes?**) *Who? Whom?* refers only to persons; it requires the personal (or distinctive) **a** when used as the object of a verb:

> **¿Quién llamó?**   Who called?
> **¿A quiénes vio usted anoche?**   Whom did you see last night?

Whose? can only be expressed by **¿De quién(es)?** and the verb **ser**:

> **¿De quién es esta cinta?**   Whose tape is this?

All interrogatives bear the written accent in both direct and indirect questions:

> **No sé quién trajo los discos.**   I don't know who brought the records.

2. **¿Qué?** *What? Which?* is both a pronoun and an adjective; as an adjective it may mean *Which?*   For a definition, **¿Qué?** is used with **ser**:

> **¿Qué le enviaste a Marta?**   What did you send (to) Martha?
> **¿Qué cuadro le gusta a usted?**   Which picture do you like?
> **¿Qué es un examen?**   What is an examination?
> **¿Qué es Roberto?   —Es abogado.**   What is Robert?   —He is a lawyer.

3. **¿Cuál?** (*pl.* **¿Cuáles?**) *Which one (ones)? What?* asks for a selection and is regularly used only as a pronoun.   With **ser**, use **¿Cuál(es)?** for *What?* unless a definition or identification is asked for:

> **¿Cuál de los cuadros le gusta a usted?**   Which (one) of the pictures do you like?
> **¿Cuál es la capital de Chile?**   What (*i.e.*, Which city) is the capital of Chile?

4. Other interrogative words are:

¿cuánto, -a? how much?
¿cuántos, -as? how many?
¿dónde? where?
¿adónde? where? (*with verbs of motion*)
¿cómo? how? (in what way?)

¿cuándo? when?
¿por qué? why? (for what reason?)
¿para qué? why? (for what purpose?)
¿qué clase de . . . ? what kind of . . . ?
¿por dónde se va . . . ? how (*i.e.*, by what route) does one go?

¿Adónde iban ellos?   Where were they going?
¿Cuántas personas hay aquí?   How many persons are there here?
¿Cómo se puede hacer eso?   How can one do that?
¿Cómo te gusta el café?   ¿Con azúcar?   How do you like your coffee? With sugar?

The last sentence refers to one's taste.   *How do you like?* in the sense of *What do you think of?* is expressed by: **¿Qué te parece este coche?   —Me gusta mucho.**   *How do you like this car?   —I like it very much.*

B. Exclamations

1. **¡Qué** + a noun! means *What a (an) . . . !* When an adjective follows the noun, either **más** or **tan** must precede the adjective:

> **¡Qué obra más (tan) interesante!**   What an interesting work!
> **¡Qué lástima (sorpresa)!**   What a pity (surprise)!

When the adjective precedes the noun, **más** or **tan** is omitted; before plural nouns **¡qué!** means *what!*

> **¡Qué buena idea!**   What a good idea!
> **¡Qué hermosas flores!**   What beautiful flowers!

¡Qué! followed by an adjective or adverb means *how!*

¡**Qué guapo es!**   How handsome he is!
¡**Qué bien canta María!**   How well Mary sings!
¡**Qué suerte has tenido!**   How lucky (fortunate) you have been!

NOTE. In the last example, **suerte** is a noun in Spanish, but an adjective in English; the expression means literally: *What luck you have had!*

2. All interrogatives may be used in exclamations if the sense permits:

¡**Quién haría eso!**   Who would do that!
¡**Cuántas flores tiene ella!**   How many flowers she has!

With verbs, ¡**cuánto!** means *how*!

¡**Cuánto me alegro de saber eso!**   How glad I am to know that!
¡**Cuánto lo sentimos!**   How we regret it (sorry we are)!

Ejercicios

A. Para leer en español supliendo ¿**qué**? o ¿**cuál(es)**?:

1. ¿_____ pasó en el partido?
2. ¿A _____ hora terminó él?
3. ¿_____ jugadores jugaron mejor?
4. ¿_____ de ellos se gradúan este año?
5. ¿_____ otro deporte le gusta a Ud.?
6. ¿_____ clases tiene Ud. hoy?

7. Allí vienen dos jóvenes extranjeros.
   ¿_____ es Luis Sierra?
8. ¿_____ es el señor Martínez, abogado o médico?
9. ¿A _____ de los cafés prefieres ir?
10. ¿_____ de tus amigos te acompañan?

B. Escuchen cada frase; luego, cámbienla a una exclamación, usando ¡**qué**! o ¡**cuánto**!

MODELOS: Las flores son hermosas.
          La noche es muy bonita.
          Siento mucho no saberlo.

¡Qué hermosas son las flores!
¡Qué noche más (tan) bonita!
¡Cuánto siento no saberlo!

1. El día es malo.
2. Juan tiene buena suerte.
3. Hace buen tiempo.
4. Luis es guapo.
5. Es una sorpresa muy agradable.
6. Doña Marta es simpática.

7. Ramón jugó bien.
8. El jardín es bonito.
9. La muchacha está triste.
10. Me alegro de estar aquí.
11. Gritamos cuando él hizo el gol.
12. Nos divertimos allí.

RESUMEN

A. La colocación de los adjetivos. Para expresar en español:

1. My older brother has several good Mexican friends.
2. They like to go to football games.
3. Our players are the new champions this year.
4. It is the first championship that our team has won.
5. It was a very hard-fought game.
6. Our backs were very strong and fast.
7. Arthur is an excellent goalkeeper.
8. He made some extraordinary stops.
9. None of the good players graduates this year.
10. The coach was wearing a new suit.
11. They threw the poor man into the pool.
12. Young people should be more courteous with older people (their elders).

B. Para leer en español, supliendo la forma correcta de **estar**, **haber**, **hacer**, **ser** o **tener**. Usen el tiempo presente si no se indica otro tiempo:

1. ¿Qué tiempo _____ hoy?
2. _____ fresco y mucho viento.
3. Nosotros _____ mucho calor en este edificio.
4. No _____ (*pres. perf.*) mucho frío aquí este otoño.
5. A veces _____ mucho polvo.
6. No _____ (*future*) luna esta noche.
7. _____ (*fam. sing. command*) mucho cuidado y no _____ miedo.
8. Usted _____ razón; parece que él siempre _____ mucho frío.
9. _____ (*imp.*) niebla cuando salimos de casa.
10. El hielo _____ frío, pero a menudo el agua _____ caliente.

C. Usos de las palabras interrogativas y las exclamaciones. Para expresar en español:

1. Whom did you call this morning?
2. Which (ones) of the boys are going to the game?
3. Who are the good players?
4. Which one of them is the best goalkeeper?
5. What universities are in our league?
6. Which team will win the championship?
7. How well Raymond and Arthur played today!
8. What a fast game!
9. How fortunate our team is!
10. What a great surprise!
11. How glad the students are to have a good team!
12. Why didn't the coach change clothes?

D. Repitan cada frase; luego, al oír un nuevo substantivo, formen otra frase haciendo los cambios necesarios:

1. un día hermoso.   (noche)
2. un pueblo español.   (ciudad)
3. aquel niño cortés.   (niños)
4. su hermano mayor.   (hermanas)

5. mi amigo feliz.   (amigas)
6. el cuento francés.   (cuentos)
7. un hombre hablador.   (mujer)
8. ese camino largo.   (calles)

LECCIÓN SEIS

El tiempo futuro.   El tiempo condicional.
El futuro y el condicional para expresar probabilidad.
Uso del infinitivo después de una preposición.
Verbos seguidos del infinitivo sin preposición.   Verbos
que necesitan preposición ante un infinitivo

EL PERIÓDICO DE LA UNIVERSIDAD

(*Luis y Carlos están revisando los materiales que han de aparecer en el número del día siguiente.*)

LUIS.   ¿Dónde estará Ricardo?   Dijo que estaría aquí a las nueve, ¿verdad?

CARLOS.   Cuando estábamos para salir, le mandó llamar el profesor.   Como tardaba mucho en aparecer, decidí no esperarle más.

LUIS.   ¿Habrá terminado el artículo que nos prometió?   Es importante.   Ha de aparecer en la página editorial.   Y, ¿qué me dices de la primera plana? ¿Falta algo?

CARLOS.   Me parece que no.   Tenemos dos artículos sobre las elecciones, con fotos de los candidatos, y una extensa sección de noticias.

LUIS.   ¿Cuál será el tema del artículo de Ricardo?

CARLOS.   Se queja de la apatía de los estudiantes respecto de la reforma universitaria. Sólo una docena de estudiantes asistieron a la reunión de ayer.

LUIS.   ¿Habrá espacio para las críticas de los estrenos en el cine y en el teatro? Y, ¿dónde pondremos el artículo sobre la exposición de dibujos que se abrió en estos últimos días?

CARLOS.   ¿No sería bastante reservar un par de columnas en la última página?

Luis.   Está bien.   En la sección de deportes tendremos que poner una noticia
sobre el partido de ayer.   Los jugadores se quejan de que no les damos
bastante publicidad.

Carlos.   ¡Bah!   No se puede satisfacer a todos.   Pero oigo entrar a Ricardo.

aparecer   to appear, show up
la apatía   apathy
el candidato   candidate
la columna   column
la crítica   review
el dibujo   drawing
editorial *adj.* editorial
la elección (*pl.* **elecciones**)   election
en estos últimos días   during
these last few days
el estreno   première, first performance
la exposición (*pl.* **exposiciones**)
exhibition
extenso, -a   extensive, large
faltar   to be lacking (missing), need

los materiales   materials, copy
(*printing*)
me parece que no   I think (believe)
not
la noticia   news, news item
la plana   page (*printing*)
la publicidad   publicity
la reforma   reform
respecto de   in regard to, concerning
revisar   to check
satisfacer (*like* **hacer**)   to satisfy
el tema   subject, theme, topic
universitario, -a *adj.*   university
un par de   a couple (pair) of

A. Busquen en el diálogo las frases que correspondan a las siguientes:

1. (they) are checking the copy which is (the materials which are) to appear.
2. Where do you suppose Richard is?   3. When we were about to leave.   4. the
teacher had him called.   5. Since he delayed a long time in appearing (it took him a
long time to appear).   6. I decided not to wait for him (any) longer.   7. Do you
suppose he has finished . . .?   8. the first page.   9. Is there anything lacking (missing)?
10. an extensive news section.   11. What do you suppose is the subject . . .?
12. He complains about the apathy.   13. a dozen students attended yesterday's
meeting.   14. Do you suppose there is space . . .?   15. a couple of columns.
16. That's fine (All right).   17. The players complain that . . .   18. I hear Richard
coming in.

B. Preparen un diálogo original, de unas diez líneas, para recitar en clase,
empleando las frases y preguntas siguientes como elemento inicial:

1. Miguel.   ¿Has visto la foto que aparece en la primera plana del periódico?
   Juan.   Será una broma (*joke*); pero ¿tú crees que merece (*it merits* or *deserves*)
todo este espacio en la primera plana?

2. MARÍA.   Acabo de leer la crítica del estreno de anoche. Me parece claro que el autor no comprendió la comedia.

    DOROTEA.   ¿Quién escribiría la crítica? ¿Sería Ricardo?

3. ARTURO.   Parece que se anuncia una reunión general de los estudiantes para esta tarde.

    LUIS.   No he visto el periódico todavía. ¿De qué se quejan los estudiantes?

PRONUNCIACIÓN

A. The sounds of **s**. Spanish **s** is a voiceless, alveolar continuant, somewhat like the English hissed *s* in *sent*. Before the voiced **b, d, g, l, ll, m, n, r, v**, and **y**, however, Spanish **s** becomes voiced and is pronounced like English *s* in *rose*. Pronounce after your teacher:

1. desayuno	José	residencia	visitar	has estado
2. antes de	buenos días	es grande	las listas	las muchachas

B. The sounds of the letter **x**. Historically **x** is equivalent to English *ks* and it is so pronounced sometimes in affected pronunciation. In normal usage, however, it is pronounced the following ways:

1. Before a consonant it is pronounced *s*: **expresar**.
2. Between vowels it is pronounced *gs*: **examinar** (**eg-sa-mi-nar**)
3. In a few words, **x** may be pronounced *s*, even between vowels, as in **exacto** and **auxiliar** (*auxiliary*) and in words built on these words. Pronounce after your teacher:

1. explicar	excursión	extranjero	texto	exactamente
2. examen	existencia	éxito	exhibir	taxi

C. Silent consonants. A few consonants are dropped in Spanish pronunciation.

1. As stated earlier, the consonant **j** is silent in **reloj**, but is pronounced in the plural **relojes**.
2. The consonant **p** is silent in **septiembre**
3. The consonant **t** is silent in **istmo**.
4. Spanish **d** tends to fall in the ending **-ado**, and final **d** is regularly dropped, in familiar speech, in the word **usted**.
5. The letter **h** is silent in modern Spanish: **ahora**.

NOTAS GRAMATICALES

I. EL TIEMPO FUTURO

A. Meaning

In general, the future tense in Spanish corresponds to the English future tense, translated by *shall* or *will*:

> **Ana dice que esperará aquí.**   Ann says (that) she will wait here.
> **¿Dónde pondremos el artículo?**   Where shall we put the article?

B. Substitutes for the future

1. The present indicative tense is often substituted for the future (particularly if an expression of time is included) to make the statement more vivid, or to imply greater certainty that the action will take place, and in questions, when immediate future time is involved.

> **El partido empezará a las dos.**   The game will begin at two.
> **El partido empieza a las dos.**   The game begins at two.
> **¿Escuchamos un disco ahora?**   Shall we listen to a record now?
> **Vuelvo en seguida.**   I'll return at once (be right back).

2. **Ir a** plus an infinitive is used in the present indicative tense to refer to the near future.   (The imperfect **iba a, ibas a**, etc., is similarly used to replace the conditional, especially in Spanish America).

> **Van a llegar a la ciudad mañana.**   They are going to arrive at the city tomorrow.
> **Él dijo que iba a venir hoy.**   He said that he would (was going to) come today.

3. **Haber de** plus an infinitive, which denotes what *is*, or *is supposed*, *to* (happen), is sometimes the equivalent of the future tense, often with a sense of obligation.   (In the imperfect this expression may be used to represent the conditional.)

> **Ha de aparecer en la página editorial.**   It is to appear on the editorial page.
> **¿Qué he de hacer?**   What am I to do (shall I do)?   (What am I supposed to do?)
> **Yo sabía que él no había de pagar** (= **pagaría**).   I knew that he wouldn't pay.

4. In **si**-clauses the present indicative tense is used in Spanish, as in English, even though the action is to be completed in the future:

> **Si él vuelve mañana, me llamará.**   If he returns tomorrow, he will call me.

SPECIAL NOTE.   Do not confuse the use of **querer** plus an infinitive in asking a favor, which corresponds to English *will, be willing to*, with the true future.   Similarly, **no querer** plus an infinitive may express *be unwilling to, will not*.

> **¿Quiere usted abrir la ventana?**   Will you open the window?
> **¿Quieres ir al cine conmigo?**   Will you (Are you willing to) go to the movie with me?
> **Ellos no quieren esperar.**   They won't (are unwilling to) wait.

The future must be used, however, in cases such as:

> **¿Estarás en casa esta noche?**   Will you be at home tonight?

II. EL TIEMPO CONDICIONAL

A. Meaning

The conditional tense expresses a future action from the standpoint of the past and is translated in English by *should* or *would*.   (Its use in conditional sentences will be discussed in Lección nueve.)

> **Él dijo que estaría aquí pronto.**   He said that he would be here soon.

Remember that English *would (used to)* is often used to express repeated action in the past, in which case the imperfect indicative tense is used, as explained in Lección tres:

> **A veces dábamos paseos por el campo.**   At times we would take walks in the country.

In the preterit, **no querer** plus an infinitive may express *would not (refused to), was unwilling to*:

> **Ricardo no quiso decir nada de las críticas.**   Richard would not (refused to) say anything about the reviews.

B. The conditional may be used to express a polite or softened future statement:

Me gustaría acompañarlos. I should like to accompany them.

¿No sería bastante reservar un par de columnas en la última página del periódico? Wouldn't it be sufficient to reserve a couple of columns on the last page of the newspaper?

Ejercicios

A. Repitan cada frase; luego, empiecen la frase con **Luis dice que,** cambiando el verbo en cursiva al futuro:

1. *Puede* escribir un artículo.
2. *Hay* espacio para las críticas.
3. *Tiene* que poner una noticia.
4. *Sale* después de comer.
5. No se *queja* de los estudiantes.
6. No *ha* terminado el informe.

B. Repitan cada frase; luego, al oír otra forma del verbo, formen una nueva frase, según el modelo.

MODELO: Yo *sé* que Juan lo hará.   Yo sé que Juan lo hará.
  sabía   Yo sabía que Juan lo haría.

1. Yo *creo* que él sabrá revisar los materiales.   (*creía*)
2. Carlos *sabe* que habrá espacio para la noticia.   (*sabía*)
3. Luis *dice* que será bastante reservar un par de columnas.   (*dijo*)
4. *Creemos* que ella se quejará de la apatía de los estudiantes.   (*Creíamos*)
5. *Sabemos* que tendremos que escribir algo sobre el partido de ayer.   (*Sabíamos*)
6. Él *está* seguro de que ellos harán el trabajo esta noche.   (*estaba*)

C. Repitan la frase; luego, repítanla empleando el futuro, según los modelos.

MODELOS: Van a salir mañana.   Van a salir mañana.   Saldrán mañana.
  Ana ha de cantar hoy.   Ana ha de cantar hoy.   Ana cantará hoy.

1. He de poner algo en esta sección.
2. Hemos de tener un artículo sobre el partido.
3. Ha de aparecer en la sección de deportes.
4. ¿Qué van a decir de la primera plana?
5. ¿De qué van a quejarse ahora los estudiantes?
6. ¿Cuál va a ser el tema del artículo de Roberto?

D. Después de oír la pregunta, contesten empleando formas de mandato afirmativas y negativas, y substituyendo el substantivo con el pronombre correspondiente.

MODELO: ¿Pongo *el artículo* aquí? Sí, póngalo Ud. allí.
No, no lo ponga allí.

1. ¿Espero más *a Carlos*?
2. ¿Reviso *los materiales* ahora?
3. ¿Escribo *la crítica* hoy?

4. ¿Empiezo a escribir *la noticia*?
5. ¿Hago *el trabajo* esta tarde?
6. ¿Busco *las fotos* esta noche?

III. EL FUTURO Y EL CONDICIONAL PARA EXPRESAR PROBABILIDAD

The future is often used to indicate probability, supposition, or conjecture concerning an action or state in the present time:

¿Dónde estará Ricardo? I wonder where Richard is. (Where do you suppose Richard is?)
Estará en casa. He is probably (must be) at home.
¿Cuál será el tema del artículo? What do you suppose is the subject of the article? (What can the subject . . . be?)

Similarly, the conditional indicates probability or conjecture with reference to the past:

¿Quién escribiría la crítica? Who probably (do you suppose) wrote the review?
¿Sería Ricardo? Do you suppose it was Richard? (I wonder if it was Richard.)
Serían las dos cuando salieron de aquí. It was probably two o'clock when they left here.

Probability or conjecture may also be expressed by the future perfect tense, and occasionally by the conditional perfect:

¿Adónde habrá ido Carlos? Where can Charles have gone? (Where has Charles probably gone? Where do you suppose Charles has gone?)
¿Habrá terminado el trabajo ya? Do you suppose he has finished the work already?
¿Qué habría hecho él? What could he have done?

Ejercicios

A. Repitan; luego, cambien el verbo al futuro para expresar probabilidad:

1. ¿Quién es aquel hombre?
2. ¿Dónde está Ricardo?
3. ¿Adónde van los estudiantes tan tarde?
4. ¿Quién tiene el periódico de la mañana?
5. Los niños están jugando en el parque.
6. Hay mucha gente en el teatro.

Cambien el verbo al condicional:

7. ¿Qué hora era?
8. Eran las diez y media de la noche.
9. ¿Adónde iban los dos niños?
10. ¿Dónde estaban Ana y María el domingo pasado?

Cambien el verbo al futuro perfecto:

11. Ya han llegado a la reunión.
12. Él ha vuelto de la excursión a la sierra.
13. ¿Ha estado Juan en el campo?
14. ¿Han terminado el artículo sobre el partido de ayer?

B. Para expresar en español:

1. What time can it be? 2. Paul probably has many friends there. 3. Do you suppose Jane is ill? 4. I wonder who has the photos. 5. The students have probably written the news items. 6. Who do you suppose wrote this review? 7. Where did they probably go? 8. John probably returned home early.

IV. USO DEL INFINITIVO DESPUÉS DE UNA PREPOSICIÓN

In Spanish the infinitive is used after a preposition; in English the present participle is often used. **Al** plus an infinitive is the Spanish equivalent of English *Upon* (*On*) plus the present participle, or occasionally of a clause beginning with *When*. The infinitive may have a subject (which follows the infinitive), an object, or both.

Ricardo salió sin verme.   Richard left without seeing me.
Al saberlo yo, **le escribí.**   Upon finding it out (When I found it out), I wrote to him.
Después de leer el artículo, **lo revisó.**   After reading the article, he checked it.
Además de hacer eso, **escribió una crítica.**   Besides doing that, he wrote a review.

V. VERBOS SEGUIDOS DEL INFINITIVO SIN PREPOSICIÓN

A. Verbs that do not require a preposition before an infinitive

A few of the many verbs which do not require a preposition before an infinitive when there is no change in subject are: **decidir, desear, esperar, necesitar, pensar (ie)** (when it means *to intend, plan*), **poder, preferir (ie, i), prometer, querer, saber, sentir (ie, i)** *(to be sorry, regret)*, **temer.**

> **No se puede satisfacer a todos.** One cannot satisfy everybody.
> **Siento no poder ir con ustedes.** I'm sorry I cannot go (I am sorry not to be able to go) with you.

The infinitive follows impersonal expressions without a preposition:

> **Es bueno (posible) asistir a la reunión.** It is well (possible) to attend the meeting.

See Appendix E, pages 325–328, for a more complete list of verbs of the types mentioned in this section and in section VI following.

B. Some special uses of the infinitive follow

1. After **oír** and **ver** the infinitive is regularly used in Spanish, while the present participle is often used in English. Note the word order in the first example.

> **Oigo entrar a Ricardo.** I hear Richard coming in (enter).
> **Los vimos salir.** We saw them leave (leaving).

2. **Dejar, hacer, mandar,** and **permitir** are usually followed by the infinitive when the subject of the verb which follows is a pronoun. (Some exceptions to this usage will be discussed later.)

> **Déjeme (Permítame) usted llamarle.** Let me (Permit me to) call him.
> **Le mandé escribir un artículo.** I ordered him to (had him) write an article.

While usage varies, with **dejar** and **hacer** personal objects are usually direct; with other verbs they are usually indirect.

Often the infinitive is translated by the passive voice, especially when its subject is a thing:

> **Él hizo facturar la maleta.** He had the suitcase checked.
> **Las mandé (hice) poner en el coche.** I ordered *or* had them put in the car.

> **Él le mandó llamar.**   He had him called.
> **Hice revisar el artículo.**   I had the article checked.

VI. VERBOS QUE NECESITAN PREPOSICIÓN ANTE UN INFINITIVO

A. Verbs which take **a** before an infinitive

All verbs expressing motion or movement to a place, the verbs meaning *to begin*, and certain others such as **atreverse**, *to dare*, **aprender**, *to learn*, **enseñar**, *to teach, show*, **ayudar**, *to help, aid*, and **obligar**, *to oblige*, require **a** before an infinitive.   The last three verbs have the subject of the infinitive expressed.

> **Fueron (Corrieron) a ver el coche.**   They went (ran) to see the car.
> **Él aprendió (empezó) a cantar la canción.**   He learned (began) to sing the song.
> **Él me enseñó (ayudó) a hacer eso.**   He taught (helped) me to do that.

Volver a plus an infinitive means (*to do*) *again*:

> **Vuelva usted a leer la noticia.**   Read the news item again.

B. Verbs which take **de** before an infinitive

Three common verbs which require **de** are **acordarse** (**ue**) (**de**), *to remember*, **alegrarse** (**de**), *to be glad* (*to*), and **olvidarse** (**de**), *to forget* (*to*).   (**Olvidar** plus an infinitive also means *to forget* [*to*].)

> **Nos alegramos de verte.**   We are glad to see you.
> **Juan se olvidó de llamar a Juanita.**   John forgot to call Jane.

Dejar de plus an infinitive means *to stop, fail to*.   **Tratar de** means *to try to*, and **tratarse de** means *to be a question of*.   **Acabar de** (used in present and imperfect) means *have just, had just*.

> **Dejaron de tocar la guitarra.**   They stopped playing the guitar.
> **No dejes de volver temprano.**   Don't fail to return early.
> **No se trata de aprender eso.**   It is not a question of learning that.
> **Ramón acaba (acababa) de entrar.**   Raymond has (had) just entered.

Some verbs followed by an adjective or noun require **de** before an infinitive, as well as before a noun or noun clause.

Tengo miedo de esperar aquí. I'm afraid to wait here.
Estamos seguros de que él nos ayudará. We are sure that he will help us.
Estamos seguros de poder ayudarlos. We are sure of being able to help them.
Los muchachos están cansados de trabajar. The boys are tired of working.

C. Verbs which take **en** before an infinitive

Common verbs are: **consentir (ie, i) en**, *to consent to, agree to,* **insistir en**, *to insist on,* **pensar (ie) en**, *to think of,* **tardar en**, *to delay in, take long to.*

    Él tardaba en aparecer. It was taking him long to appear (He delayed in appearing).

Ejercicios

A. Repitan la frase; luego, cámbienla a una forma de mandato con **usted** como sujeto:

1. Roberto nos enseña a bailar la rumba.
2. Ana comienza a leer la comedia.
3. Elena aprende a tocar la canción.
4. No dejan de revisar el artículo.
5. María le ayuda a lavar el coche.
6. No se olvidan de hacer el trabajo a tiempo.
7. No tratan de jugar en la calle.
8. No tardan mucho en llegar.

B. Lean en español, supliendo la preposición correcta cuando sea necesario:

1. Hemos _____ poner estos artículos en la primera plana. 2. Ayúdame tú _____ revisar esta crítica. 3. Trata tú _____ darles más publicidad a los jugadores. 4. No es necesario _____ dejar más espacio en esta página. 5. Juan nos obligó _____ esperar una hora. 6. Pensamos _____ ver la exposición de dibujos hoy. 7. No podemos _____ pasar mucho tiempo allí. 8. Mucho gusto _____ conocerle a usted. 9. Mi hermana no consentirá _____ asistir a la reunión. 10. Ella dice que se trata _____ terminar una composición para mañana. 11. Vuelva usted _____ leer esta sección de deportes. 12. Estoy seguro _____ poder hacerlo pronto. 13. ¿Sabes si Tomás prefiere _____ quedarse aquí? 14. ¿Están cansados _____ aprender tantas palabras? 15. Mi mamá tardó _____ salir de la tienda. 16. Esperamos _____ divertirnos mucho esta noche. 17. Pablo insiste _____ pagar la cuenta. 18. Juan acaba _____ llamar a Carolina.

RESUMEN

A. Usos de verbos para expresar el futuro.   Para expresar en español:

1. Where shall I put this long article?
2. Does (Will) today's game begin at two o'clock?
3. Will you be able to check the news item right away?
4. I believe that it is to appear in the sports section.
5. Shall I leave this photo on the first page?
6. Won't you write a column for the last page?
7. What are we to do now?   Is there anything lacking?
8. Shall we wait longer for Richard?
9. We are supposed to see whether there is an article on the elections.
10. There is probably space for the exhibition of drawings.

B. Repitan la frase; luego, repítanla otra vez, cambiando el verbo al tiempo correspondiente para expresar probabilidad.

MODELOS: ¿Quién es?   ¿Quién es?   ¿Quién será?
        ¿Dónde han estado?   ¿Dónde han estado?   ¿Dónde habrán estado?
        Eran las cinco.   Eran las cinco.   Serían las cinco.

1. ¿Qué tiene Felipe?
2. Los jóvenes van al partido.

3. ¿Cuál es el tema del artículo?
4. ¿Hay espacio para esta crítica?

5. ¿Ha ido Carlos al centro?
6. ¿Dónde han puesto las fotos?

7. Felipe ya ha vuelto.
8. Han visto el estreno en el teatro.

9. ¿Qué hora era?
10. ¿Adónde fueron sus amigos?

11. ¿Eran españolas las dos señoritas?
12. Estuvieron en casa anoche.

C. Usos del infinitivo.   Para expresar en español:

1. Let me drive the car this afternoon, please.
2. My father had (made) me wash it this morning.
3. Mother, I shall have the dress cleaned tomorrow.
4. Have him write a review of the film he saw last night.
5. We heard Mary singing in Spanish.
6. Paul has just bought a new suit.
7. Don't fail to come to visit me often.
8. Have you seen them walking through the park?

9. Upon seeing her, I handed her the two drawings.
10. Besides doing that, I chatted with her about the art exhibition.

D. Formen frases en español usando un infinitivo después de las expresiones siguientes:

1. olvidarse de   3. volver a   5. enseñar a   7. consentir en
2. dejar de   4. tardar en   6. tratar de   8. atreverse a

La Laguna del Inca, Portillo, Chile

LECTURA III

PRESENTACIÓN

A. Estudio de palabras

1. Approximate cognates (comparative endings of Spanish and English words)

a. Endings of many Spanish nouns

(1) Spanish **-ismo** = English *-ism*: modernismo, realismo, romanticismo.

(2) Spanish **-ista** = English *-ist*: ensayista (*essayist*), modernista, novelista, protagonista. *Compare* cuento, *short story, and* cuentista, *short story writer*; periódico, *newspaper, and* periodista, *journalist.*

(3) Spanish **-mento, -miento** = English *-ment*: mejoramiento, *betterment, improvement*; movimiento, *movement.*

(Nouns ending in **-ismo, -mento, -miento** are usually masculine; those ending in **-ista** can be masculine or feminine.)

b. Certain Spanish adjectives ending in **-ico, -a** = English *-ic, -ical*: histórico, *historic(al)*; novelístico, *novelistic*; político, *political*; patológico, *pathological*; técnico, *technical*; típico, *typical.*

c. The Spanish adverbial ending **-mente** = English *-ly*: directamente, fielmente (*faithfully*), principalmente.

d. The Spanish infinitive ending **-izar** = English *-ize, -yze*: analizar, *to analyze*; simbolizar, *to symbolize.*

2. Less approximate cognates. Pronounce and note the English meaning of: aislado, *isolated*; análisis, *analysis*; barbarie, *barbarism, lack of culture*; brillante, *brilliant*; civilizador, *civilizing*; corriente, *current*; enérgico, *energetic*; frontera, *frontier*; ilustre, *illustrious*; intrínseco, *intrinsic*; símbolo, *symbol*; víctima, *victim*; demostrar (ue), *to demonstrate, show*; destruir, *to destroy*; explotar, *to exploit*; mencionar, *to mention*; reinar, *to reign.*

3. *Compare the meanings of the following pairs of words:* educar *and* educador; ensayo *and* ensayista; gaucho, *gaucho* (*cowboy*), *and* gauchesco, *gaucho, of* (*pertaining to*) *the gaucho*; llanura, *plain, and* llanero, *plainsman*; país *and* paisaje, *countryside*; pensar *and* pensador; reflejar, *to reflect, and* reflejo, *reflection*; relatar, *to relate, and* relato, *story, tale.*

4. Deceptive cognates. As in the English cognate, Spanish **diversión** is used in the sense of *amusement* more commonly than in that of *deflection*. Similarly, Spanish **visión** may mean *view* as well as *vision.*

5. In this Lectura find as many words as you can which illustrate each of the following principles: Spanish **-cia** = English *-ce*; **-ia, -io** = *-y*; **-ción** = *-tion*; the verb ending **-ar** = *-ate.*

135

B. Modismos y frases útiles

a menudo   often, frequently
además de   besides, in addition to
al lado de   beside, at (on) the side of
así como   just as
en conjunto   as a whole
en tiempo de   at (in) the time of
en vez de   instead of, in place of
fijarse en   to notice, turn one's
   attention to
frente a   opposite, in the face of

la mayor parte de   most of, the
   greater part of
por lo tanto   therefore
por último   finally, ultimately
servir (i, i) de   to serve as
sin duda   doubtless, without a doubt
soñar (ue) con   to dream of (about)
tener en cuenta   to bear in mind
venir a ser   to become, come to be
volverse (ue)   to become

C. Aspectos gramaticales

1. Additional omissions of the indefinite article not explained on pages 85–86 are:

a. With nouns in apposition if the information is explanatory and not stressed:

> **Facundo Quiroga, gaucho malo de la ancha pampa, . . .**   Facundo
> Quiroga, a bad gaucho of the broad pampa (plain), . . .
> **El gaucho, hombre independiente, soberbio y enérgico, . . .**   The gaucho,
> an independent, proud, and energetic man, . . .
> **en los Estados Unidos—país que . . .**   in the United States—a country
> which . . .

b. Before a form of **ser**, at the beginning of a sentence, or a clause, to add terseness
to the style:

> **Obra clásica . . . es**   A classic work . . . is
> **Gran parte de las novelas contemporáneas son . . .**   A great part of the
> contemporary novels are . . .
> **Buen ejemplo . . . es**   A good example . . . is

c. After **como** or **de**, meaning *as*:

> **sirvió de tema**   (he) served as a theme (subject)
> **como reflejo**   as a reflection

d. With a predicate noun after **volverse**, *to become*:

> **se vuelve llanero**   he becomes a plainsman

2. The meanings and uses of **mismo, -a**

a. The adjective **mismo, -a**, when used before a noun, usually means *(the) same*:

> **la prosa del mismo período**   the prose of the same period

b. Used after a noun, a subject pronoun, or prepositional form of a personal pronoun, **mismo, -a**, emphasizes the word or phrase it modifies, and means *myself, yourself, itself*, etc., and sometimes *very, very same, even*:

> **la naturaleza misma**   nature itself, the very same nature
> **la llanura misma**   the plain itself, the very same plain
>
> ALSO: **ellos mismos**   they themselves

c. **El mismo (la misma**, etc.) . . . **que** means *the same . . . as*:

> **los mismos movimientos literarios que**   the same literary movements as

d. After adverbs of time and place, the adverb **mismo** means *this (that) very, right (away, now)*, and sometimes the word cannot be translated into English. We have already used the expression **ahora mismo**, *right away (now)*. Other examples are: **hoy mismo**, *this very day*; **allí mismo**, *that very place*; **mañana mismo**, *tomorrow* (with emphasis on **mañana**).

3. The meanings and uses of **propio, -a**

a. The adjective **propio, -a**, *proper, suitable*, also has the meaning *own, (of) one's own*:

> **No es propio de María llegar tarde.**   It is not proper of Mary to arrive late.
> **han llegado a tener una vida propia**   (they) have come to have a life of their own (their own life)
> **comenzó a tener una vida propia**   (it) began to have a life of its own (its own life)

b. Like **mismo, -a**, it may be used to emphasize the word it modifies. After a possessive adjective, it is translated *own*; following a noun or a personal pronoun, it is interchangeable with **mismo, -a**, although less widely used. Examples are: **en su propia casa**, *in his own house*; **ellos propios (mismos)**, *they themselves*.

4. The neuter article **lo** is used with masculine singular adjectives to form an expression almost equivalent to an abstract noun. The translation varies according to the context. See pages 247–248 for further explanation. Similar uses of the neuter article will appear in subsequent Lecturas.

> **Lo extraño y lo patológico atraían siempre a Quiroga . . .**   The unusual (What was unusual *or* strange) and the pathological (what was pathological) always attracted Quiroga . . .

CORRIENTES CULTURALES DE LA
AMÉRICA ESPAÑOLA

En esta Lectura y en las dos siguientes ensayaremos una visión de conjunto[1] sobre las corrientes culturales de la América española. No podremos analizar en unas cuantas páginas la vida cultural de cada uno de los diez y ocho países desde la época de la independencia. Nos limitaremos a mencionar los géneros[2] literarios más importantes y a algunos de los escritores, pintores y músicos que se han distinguido en los últimos dos siglos.

Fijándonos primero en la historia literaria, hay que tener en cuenta que la literatura hispanoamericana se desarrolló[3] durante el siglo XIX bajo la influencia de la española y de la europea, en general. Hallamos, por lo tanto, en la América española los mismos movimientos literarios que* en España: el romanticismo, el costumbrismo,[4] el realismo y el modernismo.

La poesía y el ensayo fueron los géneros más cultivados en el siglo XIX. En el siglo XX la novela y el cuento han llegado a tener una vida propia,* al lado de los dos géneros citados. Nunca se ha cultivado mucho el teatro en la América española.

El escritor más importante del siglo XIX fue, sin duda, Domingo Faustino Sarmiento (1811–1888), quien ha sido considerado como el representante más ilustre de la cultura sudamericana de su época. Aunque nació en un ambiente[5] pobre y humilde, dedicó la mayor parte de su vida al mejoramiento cultural y político de la Argentina. Fue soldado, periodista, político, educador y, por último, presidente de su país. En su obra maestra,[6] *Facundo, o civilización y barbarie* (1845), Sarmiento presenta un análisis magnífico del gaucho, de su vida, de sus vicios y de sus diversiones. Facundo Quiroga, gaucho* malo de la ancha pampa, simboliza la barbarie frente a la civilización, representada por la ciudad y el gobierno de Buenos Aires.

El gaucho, hombre* independiente, soberbio y enérgico, que vivía aislado y libre de las influencias de la civilización y del gobierno, sirvió de tema* para numerosos poemas, novelas, cuentos y dramas. Esta literatura gauchesca, en conjunto, fue una de las contribuciones más originales de la literatura hispanoamericana del siglo XIX. Obra clásica* de la literatura de América y el mejor poema gauchesco es *Martín Fierro* (1872), escrito por José Hernández.

---

[1] **ensayaremos . . . conjunto,** *we shall attempt (to give) a general view.* [2] **género,** *genre, (literary) type.* [3] **se desarrolló,** *(was) developed.* [4] **costumbrismo,** *literature of customs and manners.* [5] **ambiente,** *atmosphere, environment.* [6] **obra maestra,** *masterpiece.*

La pampa

Martín Fierro
Personificación del actor Alfredo Alcón

Mientras toca la guitarra, el payador[1] relata la historia triste de su vida: los días felices que había pasado en las estancias[2] de la pampa, sus penalidades[3] en el ejército y su vida de fugitivo, que termina con su fuga[4] a la frontera para unirse a los indios.

El peruano Ricardo Palma (1833–1919) desarrolló otro género interesante. Su obra maestra, *Tradiciones peruanas*, contiene anécdotas, cuentos y leyendas de carácter histórico e imaginario, en que Palma no sólo evoca la vida y el espíritu del Perú en tiempo de los virreyes[5] españoles, sino que[6] también presenta un panorama de la vida peruana en la época moderna.   Aunque ha tenido muchos imitadores, ninguno ha logrado aproximarse al estilo personal y a la perfección técnica de este gran escritor peruano.

Ya hemos hablado, en otro libro,[7] del movimiento modernista, que surgió en la América española a fines del siglo XIX.   Como sabemos, fue una de las contribuciones más importantes de América a la literatura del mundo.   Así como Rubén Darío (1867–1916) fue el maestro reconocido de la poesía modernista, el ensayista y pensador José Enrique Rodó (1872–1917) se destacó[8] en la prosa del mismo período.*   En su libro *Ariel* (1900), escrito en un estilo claro y puro, el pensador uruguayo habla a la juventud de América sobre sus anhelos[9] por la unidad espiritual del continente, con la que Simón Bolívar había soñado en vano hacía casi un siglo.[10]   En su análisis de los elementos buenos y malos de la democracia en los Estados Unidos—país* que él no conocía directamente, pues no lo había visitado—, presenta los contrastes entre la cultura norteamericana y la de Hispanoamérica.

En el siglo XIX la novela en la América española siguió principalmente los movimientos europeos y sólo en el siglo XX comenzó a tener una vida propia.*   En la época contemporánea ha llegado a ser el género más importante, no sólo por su valor intrínseco, sino como reflejo* de la cultura hispanoamericana de nuestro tiempo.   Gran parte* de las novelas contemporáneas son realistas, es decir, los autores tratan de interpretar la vida que los rodea.   En muchos casos presentan al hombre en lucha[11] con la naturaleza, y a menudo el paisaje o la naturaleza misma* viene a ser el protagonista de la novela.   La interpretación de las fuerzas de la naturaleza y su influencia sobre el hombre han sido temas típicos de las obras novelísticas desde fines del siglo pasado.

---

[1] **payador**, *gaucho singer.*   [2] **estancias**, *ranches.*   [3] **penalidades**, *'roubles, hardships.*   [4] **fuga**, *flight.*   [5] **virreyes**, *viceroys.*   [6] For the explanation of the use of **sino que**, *but*, see page 247.   [7] see footnote 2, page 60.   [8] **se destacó**, *stood out.*   [9] **anhelos**, *yearnings, longing.*   [10] **con la que . . . siglo**, *of which Simón Bolívar had dreamed in vain almost more than a century before.*   [11] **en lucha**, *in a (his) struggle.*

Rómulo Gallegos

Buen ejemplo* de la novela de este tipo es *Doña Bárbara* (1929), del novelista venezolano Rómulo Gallegos. El tema de la novela es la vida de las llanuras de Venezuela, donde reina la fuerza en vez de la ley. En unos cuadros impresionantes demuestra que los hombres son los productos y las víctimas de la llanura misma.* Doña Bárbara, que simboliza la barbarie de la llanura, lucha en vano contra Santos Luzardo, símbolo del espíritu civilizador de la ciudad, el cual sólo logra triunfar cuando se vuelve llanero* y adquiere bastante fuerza para dominar a sus enemigos.

Otra obra semejante es *La vorágine*[1] (1924), del escritor colombiano José Eustasio Rivera (1889–1928). En esta novela el verdadero protagonista es la selva,[2] que, con su fuerza y su violencia, destruye a los seres[3] humanos que tratan de explotarla.

Además de la novela, se ha cultivado mucho el cuento en la América española. Los temas son abundantes y variados y, en conjunto, reflejan fielmente la vida de todas las clases sociales. Entre los centenares[4] de cuentistas de todos los países sudamericanos, se destaca el brillante escritor Horacio Quiroga (1878–1937), uno de los mejores cuentistas del mundo hispanoparlante.[5] Aunque nació en el Uruguay, pasó muchos años en las selvas del norte de la Argentina, donde encontró temas para muchos de sus cuentos. Como en las novelas que hemos descrito,[6] la naturaleza, es decir, el calor tropical, las lluvias, la vegetación, los ríos y los animales, determina la vida del hombre que trata de vivir en la selva. Lo extraño y lo patológico* atraían siempre a Quiroga, y en algunos de sus relatos los protagonistas son los animales de la selva.

---

[1] **La vorágine**, *The Vortex*.　　[2] **selva**, *forest, jungle.*　　[3] **seres**, *beings.*　　[4] **centenares**, *hundreds.*
[5] **hispanoparlante**, *Spanish-speaking.*　　[6] **descrito**, *p.p.* of **describir**, *to describe.*

PREGUNTAS

1. ¿Qué se discute en esta Lectura?   2. ¿En qué nos fijaremos primero?   3. ¿Cómo es que hallamos en la América española los mismos movimientos literarios que en España?   4. ¿Qué géneros literarios se cultivaron más en el siglo XIX?   5. ¿En el siglo XX?

6. ¿Quién ha sido considerado como el escritor más importante del siglo XIX? 7. ¿A qué dedicó la mayor parte de su vida?   8. ¿Qué presenta Sarmiento en su obra maestra?   9. ¿Qué representa Facundo Quiroga?   10. ¿Cómo vivía el gaucho?   11. ¿Cuál fue una de las contribuciones más originales de la literatura hispanoamericana del siglo XIX?   12. ¿Cuál es el mejor poema gauchesco? 13. ¿Qué relata el payador?

14. ¿Cuál es la obra maestra de Ricardo Palma?   15. ¿Qué evoca Palma en esta obra?   16. ¿Qué escritor se destacó en la prosa modernista?   17. ¿Qué trata de presentar Rodó en *Ariel*?

18. ¿Qué puede decirse acerca de la novela en la época contemporánea? 19. ¿Qué tratan de interpretar los autores?   20. ¿Cuáles son algunos temas típicos de las obras novelísticas modernas?   21. ¿Cuál es el tema de la novela, *Doña Bárbara*?   22. ¿Contra quién lucha Doña Bárbara?   23. ¿Cuándo logra triunfar Santos Luzardo?

24. ¿Quién escribió *La vorágine*?   25. ¿Qué trata de demostrar el autor en esta obra?   26. ¿Quién es uno de los mejores cuentistas del mundo hispanoparlante? 27. ¿Dónde encontró temas para muchos de sus cuentos?

EJERCICIOS ESCRITOS

A. Uso de modismos y frases hechas

Escriban oraciones completas y originales empleando las frases siguientes como elemento inicial:

1. En vez de ensayar una visión de conjunto . . .
2. Fijándome primero en la historia política de . . .
3. Además de interpretar la vida que le rodea . . .
4. A menudo el autor trata de . . .
5. No sólo escribe novelas sino que . . .
6. Usted debe tener en cuenta . . .
7. Por último llegó a ser . . .
8. Yo sueño en vano con . . .

B. Para expresar en español:

1. One must bear in mind that in Spanish America we find the same literary movements as in Spain.   2. Poetry and the essay were the most important types in the nineteenth century.   3. Besides these two types, in the present century the novel and the short story have also come to have a life of their own.   4. Sarmiento, the great educator, journalist, and president of Argentina, has been considered the most famous representative of South American culture of the past century.   5. In his masterpiece, *Facundo*, barbarism is represented by the bad gaucho, and civilization, by the city and government of Buenos Aires.   6. The gaucho literature, the works of Ricardo Palma, and the modernist movement represent the most original contributions of Spanish America to the literature of the world.   7. Just as Simón Bolívar dreamed of the political unity of the South American continent, the great essayist and thinker Rodó worked for the spiritual unity of all Spanish America.   8. A great part of the contemporary novels present man in his struggle with nature, and often nature or the landscape becomes the real protagonist of the works.   9. The theme of *Doña Bárbara*, by the Venezuelan novelist Gallegos, is the life of the plains of that country, where force reigns instead of law.   10. Doña Bárbara, who represents the barbarism of the plain, struggles in vain against Santos Luzardo, a symbol of the civilizing[1] force of the city.   11. Santos only succeeds in triumphing over his enemy when, finally, he becomes a plainsman.   12. The brilliant short story writer Quiroga describes faithfully the forests of the north of Argentina, where nature determines the life of the man who tries to live there.

C. Temas para un informe escrito

Escriban tres oraciones sobre cada uno de los temas siguientes:

1. La vida y obra de Domingo Faustino Sarmiento.
2. La literatura gauchesca.
3. Temas típicos de las obras novelísticas desde fines del siglo XIX.

[1] Use **civilizadora.**   (See pages 109–110 for the feminine form of certain adjectives.)

LECCIÓN SIETE

Teoría del modo subjuntivo.   Las formas del
presente de subjuntivo.   El subjuntivo en cláusulas
substantivas.   Otras formas de mandato

UNA EXCURSIÓN A LA SIERRA

(*Los padres de Ana tienen una casa de campo en un lugar hermoso de la sierra.   Ana ha invitado a
Elena a pasar las vacaciones con ella.*)

ANA.   ¿Has llamado a tus padres, Elena?   ¿Te permiten ir a la sierra con
nosotros?

ELENA.   Acabo de hablar con ellos.   No tienen otros planes.   Me piden que te
dé las gracias por la invitación.

ANA.   De nada, Elena.   ¡Cuánto me alegro de que puedas acompañarnos!
Dudo que haya un sitio más hermoso en la sierra.

ELENA.   Habrá mucha nieve en esta estación del año, ¿verdad?

ANA.   ¡Ya lo creo!   Y como sé que te gustan los deportes de invierno, te aconsejo
que lleves tus esquíes.   Y no dejes de llevar tus patines.   Es posible que
podamos patinar también.

ELENA.   Sólo siento no poder quedarme durante las dos semanas.   Mis padres
quieren que pase unos días en casa de mis abuelos.

ANA.   No te había dicho que mi padre vendrá a buscarnos.   Yo prefiero que él
conduzca cuando hay nieve y hielo en la carretera.

ELENA.   ¿A qué hora quiere tu padre que salgamos?

ANA.   Insiste en que estemos listas a las seis.

ELENA.   No creo que haya[1] ninguna dificultad en salir a esa hora.   Que esté aquí
         a las seis.   Estaré lista, Ana.

ANA.   Pues acostémonos en seguida.   ¡Que descanses mucho, Elena!   Hasta
         mañana.

buscar a uno to come (go) for one, pick one up	**el esquí** (*pl.* **esquíes**) ski
dar las gracias a to thank	**esquiar**[2] (**í**) to ski
la dificultad difficulty	**el patín** (*pl.* **patines**) skate
	patinar to skate

A. Busquen en el diálogo las frases que correspondan a las siguientes:

1. Will they let you go (permit you to go) . . . with us?   2. I have just spoken with
them.   3. They ask me to thank you.   4. for the invitation.   5. Don't mention
it.   6. I doubt that there is . . .   7. There is probably much snow.   8. I should
say so!   9. don't fail to take . . .   10. I'm sorry I can't stay.   11. my father will
come to pick us up.   12. He insists that we be ready.   13. I don't believe there will
be any difficulty.   14. Let him be here at six.   15. let's go to bed at once.   16. I
hope you will (May you) rest!

B. Para contestar en español:

Preguntas sobre el diálogo

1. ¿De qué hablan Ana y Elena en este diálogo?   2. ¿Con quiénes acaba de hablar
Elena?   3. ¿Qué le piden a Elena sus padres?   4. ¿De qué se alegra Ana?   5. ¿Qué
dice Ana del sitio adonde piensan ir?   6. ¿Qué le aconseja Ana a Elena?   7. ¿Qué
siente Elena?   8. ¿A qué hora quiere que salgan el padre de Ana?

Aplicación del diálogo

1. ¿Le gustan a usted los deportes de invierno?   2. ¿En qué estación del año hay
nieve y hielo en esta parte del país?   3. ¿Qué tiempo hace hoy?   4. ¿Es agradable
conducir cuando hay hielo en la carretera?   5. ¿Sabe usted patinar?   6. ¿Se puede
esquiar por aquí?   7. ¿Piensa usted hacer una excursión a la sierra?   8. ¿Le
gusta a usted ir a la sierra en el[3] verano o en el invierno?

---

[1] Note that the present subjunctive of the impersonal form of **haber,** corresponding to the present indicative
hay, is **haya,** *there is* (*are*), *there may be.*   [2] Conjugated like **enviar** (**í**), page 321.   [3] The definite article
is often omitted with the seasons in prepositional phrases: **en verano, en invierno**; **un día de primavera,**
a spring day.

PRONUNCIACIÓN

The pronunciation of **y**, *and*.   Recall that, within a breath-group, the conjunction **y** (phonetically an unstressed **i**) combines with a preceding vowel or consonant, or with a following vowel to form one syllable.   The principles that govern the pronunciation of **y** are the following:

1. When initial in a breath-group before a consonant, or when between consonants, it is pronounced like the Spanish vowel **i**: **Y se marchó (Y-se-mar-chó)**, **tres y tres (tre-s y-tres)**.

2. When initial in a breath-group before a vowel, or when between vowels, it is pronounced like Spanish **y**: **¿y usted? (¿y us-ted?)**, **éste y aquél (és-te-y a-quél)**.

3. Between **d**, **s**, or **z** and a vowel within a breath-group, it is also pronounced like Spanish **y**: **usted y ella (us-ted-y e-lla)**, **éstos y aquéllos (és-tos-y a-qué-llos)**.

4. Between **l**, **n**, or **r** and a vowel within a breath-group, it is pronounced as the first element of a diphthong, with the preceding consonant, the **y**, and the following vowel in a single syllable: **aquél y éste (a-qué-l y és-te)**, **hablan y escriben (ha-bla-n y es-cri-ben)**, **entrar y esperar (en-tra-r y es-pe-rar)**.

5. Between a vowel and a consonant, it forms a diphthong with the vowel that precedes it: **Marta y Juan (Mar-ta y-Juan)**.

Apply the above principles in the following exercises:

1. Write the following phrases and sentences, dividing them into syllables and underlining the stressed syllables:

Son las tres y cuarto.	Y se fue.
Es rica y elegante.	Y escribe bien.
Son blancos y amarillos.	¿Van Carlos y Arturo?
El español y el francés.	Treinta y seis.

2. Read the following phrases and sentences as single breath-groups:

Lean y traduzcan esta frase.	Iremos Carlos y yo.
Busco un lápiz y una pluma.	Sabe el inglés y el francés.
Saben leer y escribir.	Miren y escuchen.
Es fácil y agradable.	Usted y Arturo van.
Blanco y negro.	Y útiles y honrados.

NOTAS GRAMATICALES

I. TEORÍA DEL MODO SUBJUNTIVO

The word *subjunctive* means *subjoined* and, except for its use in main clauses to express commands, the subjunctive mood is regularly used in subordinate or dependent clauses. The indicative mood expresses *facts*, makes *assertions*, states *certainties*, or asks direct questions. In general, the subjunctive is dependent upon an *attitude*, a *wish*, a *feeling*, or some *uncertainty* in the mind of the speaker, expressed or implied in the main clause. The reference in the dependent clause is to an unaccomplished act or state.

In the case of a dependent clause the student must observe whether the idea expressed in the principal clause is one which requires the subjunctive in Spanish, then whether the subject of the dependent clause is <u>different</u> from that of the main verb. If this is true in both cases, the subjunctive will generally be used.

The subjunctive is more widely used in English than many persons realize because its forms differ from the indicative mood only in the third person singular and in some irregular verbs. In this and later lessons the subjunctive will be discussed according to its use in noun, adjective, and adverbial clauses. In the examples which follow note, in the noun clauses, the various English equivalents of the Spanish subjunctive forms: English present tense, the future, use of the modal auxiliary *may*, and the infinitive:

> **Yo no creo que ella esté aquí.** I do not believe that she is (will be) here.
> **Esperamos que lo hagan.** We hope that they may (will) do it.
> **Yo no quiero que él venga.** I do not wish that he come (I don't want him to come).

II. LAS FORMAS DEL PRESENTE DE SUBJUNTIVO

Recall that in the present subjunctive tense the endings of **-ar** verbs begin with **-e**, while those of **-er** and **-ir** verbs begin with **-a**:

tomar:	tome	tomes	tome	tomemos	toméis	tomen
comer:	coma	comas	coma	comamos	comáis	coman
abrir:	abra	abras	abra	abramos	abráis	abran

In earlier lessons we have used the third person singular and plural and the second person singular forms of the present subjunctive in commands. See Cuarta lección preliminar, pages 25–27, for uses of these forms, and Appendix D, pages 311–324, for the present subjunctive forms of all types of verbs. Remember that the stem of the present subjunctive of all but six verbs (**dar, estar, haber, ir, saber,** and **ser**) is formed by dropping the ending **-o** of the first person singular of the present indicative.

Ejercicio

Para contestar, empleando una forma de mandato con **Ud.** o **Uds.** como sujeto.

MODELOS: ¿Busco el libro?   Sí, búsquelo Ud.
           ¿Le pedimos algo?   Sí, pídanle Uds. algo.

1. ¿Abro las ventanas?   6. ¿Vamos al centro hoy?
2. ¿Toco el disco ahora?   7. ¿Volvemos antes de las cinco?
3. ¿Me siento en la primera fila?   8. ¿Seguimos leyendo la novela?
4. ¿Pongo la mesa ahora mismo?   9. ¿Servimos refrescos esta noche?
5. ¿Escojo un vestido en esta tienda?   10. ¿Comenzamos a cantar?

III. EL SUBJUNTIVO EN CLÁUSULAS SUBSTANTIVAS

The subjunctive is regularly used in a noun clause (*i.e.*, a clause used as the subject or object of a verb) when the verb in the main clause expresses or implies ideas of the speaker such as those of *wish, advice, request, command, permission, approval, cause, suggestion, preference, insistence*, and the like, as well as their negatives. Remember that in English the infinitive is most commonly used after such verbs, but in Spanish a noun clause, usually introduced by **que**, is regularly used if the subject of the dependent clause is <u>different</u> from that of the main clause.

> **Ella quiere ir al campo.**   She wants to go to the country.   (*Subjects the same*)
> **Ella quiere que yo vaya también.**   She wants me to go too. (*Subjects different*)
> **José prefiere conducir.**   Joseph prefers to drive.   (*Subjects the same*)
> **José prefiere que yo conduzca.**   Joseph prefers that I drive. (*Subjects different*)
> **Insiste en que estemos listas a las seis.**   He insists that we be ready at six.

With certain verbs, *e.g.*, **decir, pedir, aconsejar**, and others·which require the indirect object of a person, the subject of the infinitive in English is expressed as the indirect object of the main verb and understood as the subject of the subjunctive verb in the dependent clause. In the case of a sentence like *Ask him to come*, think of it as, *Ask of (to) him that he come.*

> **Pídale usted a ella que espere un rato.**   Ask her to wait a while.
> **Te aconsejo que lleves tus esquíes.**   I advise you to take your skis.
> **No le digas que me ayude.**   Don't tell him to help me.
> **Le permitiré a Juan que juegue hoy.**   I shall permit John to play today.

In Lección seis we found that **dejar, hacer, mandar,** and **permitir** are usually followed by the infinitive when the subject of a dependent verb is a pronoun. The subjunctive is also used after these verbs, particularly when the dependent verb has a noun subject (last example, page 149). One also says: **Permitiremos que lleven sus patines,** *We shall permit that they take their skates.*

Ejercicios

A. Repitan la oración; luego, al oír la frase con la conjunción (*conjunction*) **que,** formen una nueva oración, según el modelo.

MODELO: Prefiero hacer eso.   Prefiero hacer eso.
         que Ud.   Prefiero que Ud. haga eso.

1. Quiero ir a la sierra.   (que Uds.)
2. Preferimos pasar todo el día allí.   (que ellos)
3. ¿Quieres ir a esquiar?   (que nosotros)
4. ¿Desea Ud. hacer la excursión mañana?   (que yo)
5. No quieren volver antes de las cuatro.   (que tú)
6. ¿A qué hora quiere ella salir?   (que Juan y yo)
7. ¿Deseas pasar unos días en el campo?   (que tus hermanos)
8. Insistirán en comprar una casa de campo.   (en que yo)

B. Después de oír una frase, oirán una oración incompleta; formen una nueva oración introducida por la oración incompleta, según el modelo.

MODELO: ir a casa.   (Dígales Ud. que)   Dígales Ud. que vayan a casa.

1. darle las gracias.   (Quiero que ellos)
2. estar listos a las ocho.   (Pídales Ud. que)
3. llevar los patines.   (Le aconsejo a Juan que)
4. venir a buscarnos.   (¿Prefieres que ellos . . . ?)
5. no olvidarse de los esquíes.   (Les diré que)
6. conducir el coche.   (No le permitiré a Carlos que)

IV. EL SUBJUNTIVO EN CLÁUSULAS SUBSTANTIVAS (CONTINUACIÓN)

The subjunctive is used in noun clauses dependent upon verbs or expressions of emotion or feeling, such as *joy, sorrow, fear, hope, pity, surprise,* and the like, as well as their opposites, provided that there is a change in subject from that of the main verb. Some common expressions of emotion are:

alegrarse (**de que**)   to be glad (that)   **temer**   to fear
esperar   to hope   **tener miedo** (**de que**)   to be afraid
sentir (**ie, i**)   to regret, be sorry   (that)
ser lástima   to be a pity (too bad)

Me alegro de verte.   I am glad to see you.   (*Subjects the same*)
¡Cuánto me alegro de que vayas!   How glad I am that you will go!   (*Subjects different*)
Siento no poder quedarme.   I'm sorry I cannot (I'm sorry not to be able to) stay.
Sienten que no podamos esperar.   They are sorry (that) we cannot wait.
Tenemos miedo de que Ana no venga.   We are afraid that Ann will not come.
Es lástima que ella no sepa patinar.   It is a pity that she cannot (doesn't know how to) skate.

Ejercicio

Repitan la oración; luego, al oír la frase con la conjunción **que**, úsenla para formar una nueva oración, siguiendo el modelo.

MODELO: Espero divertirme mucho allí.   Espero divertirme mucho allí.
         que tú   Espero que tú te diviertas mucho allí.

1. Me alegro de poder ir contigo.   (de que Elena)
2. Temen tener que trabajar mañana.   (que Roberto)
3. Es lástima no saber esquiar.   (que Inés)
4. Esperamos encontrar una casa de campo.   (que los señores Díaz)
5. ¿Sienten Uds. no llegar a tiempo?   (que sus padres)
6. ¿Tienes miedo de patinar allí?   (que nosotros)

V. EL SUBJUNTIVO EN CLÁUSULAS SUBSTANTIVAS (CONTINUACIÓN)

The subjunctive is used in noun clauses after expressions of *doubt, uncertainty, belief expressed negatively*, and *denial*. Common verbs of this type are:

no creer   not to believe   **no estar seguro de que**   not to be sure that
dudar   to doubt   **negar** (**ie**)   to deny

Creemos que habrá nieve.   We believe (think) there will be snow.   (*Certainty*)
No creo que haya ninguna dificultad.   I don't believe that there is (will be) any difficulty.   (*Uncertainty*)

Dudo que haya un sitio más hermoso.   I doubt that there is a more beautiful place.

Niegan que yo comprenda eso.   They deny that I understand that.

No estamos seguros de que vayan.   We aren't sure that they are going (will go).

Note that **creer** and **estar seguro, -a, de que** express certainty and that they are followed by the indicative in a clause, while **no creer que** and **no estar seguro, -a, de que** express uncertainty or doubt and they require the subjunctive in a clause.

When **creer** is used in questions, the speaker may imply doubt on the action in the dependent clause, in which case the subjunctive is used. If no implication of doubt is made, the indicative is used. **No creer que** in a question implies certainty.

¿Cree Ud. que vuelvan hoy?   Do you believe they will return today?   (*Doubt in mind of the speaker*)

¿Cree Ud. que habrá nieve?   Do you believe there will be snow?   (*The speaker has no opinion*)

¿No crees que podemos esquiar?   Don't you believe (think) we can ski?

Ejercicio

Para expresar en español:

1. I believe that John's father will buy a country house.   2. Helen doesn't believe that Mary knows how to skate.   3. We are sure that the boys will take their skis.   4. Ann is not sure that they will be ready at six.   5. John doesn't believe that there is much snow in the mountains.   6. My friends deny that there is ice on the highway.   7. Do you believe that they will come to pick us up? (*Certainty implied*)   8. I doubt that they will arrive before noon.

VI. EL SUBJUNTIVO EN CLÁUSULAS SUBSTANTIVAS (FIN)

Impersonal expressions that contain ideas of *possibility, necessity, uncertainty, probability, strangeness, doubt,* and the like, require the subjunctive in the dependent clause provided that a subject is mentioned. Impersonal expressions of fact and certainty, such as **Es cierto (verdad, evidente)**, *It is certain (true, evident)*, require the indicative; when no subject is expressed, the infinitive is used:

Es preciso (mejor) llamarlos.   It is necessary (better) to call them.

Es posible (probable) que patinemos.   It is possible (probable) that we shall skate.

Puede (ser) que Ana se quede en casa.   It may be that Ann will stay at home.
Será fácil que aprendas eso.   It will be easy for you to learn that.
No es cierto (verdad) que haya nieve en la sierra.   It isn't certain (true) that there is snow in the mountains.

Some common impersonal expressions which often require the subjunctive are:

basta it is sufficient (enough)		**es lástima** it is a pity (too bad)	
conviene it is fitting (advisable)		**es mejor** it is better	
es bueno it is well		**es necesario** it is necessary	
es difícil it is difficult		**es posible** it is possible	
es dudoso it is doubtful		**es preciso** it is necessary	
es extraño it is strange		**es probable** it is probable	
es fácil it is easy		**importa** it is important, it matters	
es importante it is important		**puede (ser)** it may be	
es imposible it is impossible		**más vale (vale más)** it is better	

These expressions really fall under sections III, IV, and V, pages 149–152, but they are treated separately for convenience and clarity.

The infinitive <u>may</u> be used after most impersonal expressions if the subject of the dependent verb is a <u>personal pronoun</u>, not a noun.   In this case the subject of the dependent verb is the indirect object of the main verb.

Me (les) es mejor ir hoy.   It is better for me (them) to go today.

BUT: **Es extraño que Ana no esté aquí.**   It is strange for Ann not to be here.

Ejercicios

A. Repitan cada oración; luego, formen una nueva oración empleando el infinitivo, como en el modelo.

MODELO: Vale más que Juan vuelva hoy.   Vale más que Juan vuelva hoy.
                                                                 Vale más volver hoy.

1. Es preciso que patinemos hoy.
2. Importa que Ud. no olvide eso.
3. Es posible que lleven los esquíes.
4. No basta que Ud. aprenda el diálogo.
5. Será mejor que busques otro sitio más hermoso.
6. Conviene que hagan planes para el viaje.
7. Puede que sea verdad.
8. No es fácil que aprendas la canción.
9. No es preciso que se muden de ropa.
10. Es bueno que Uds. tengan cuidado si hay hielo en la carretera.

B. Repitan la frase; luego, al oír una expresión impersonal, formen otra frase cambiando la original, según los modelos.

MODELOS: Juan podrá esquiar hoy.   Juan podrá esquiar hoy.
            Es posible que   Es posible que Juan pueda esquiar hoy.
            Es cierto que   Es cierto que Juan podrá esquiar hoy.

1. Ellos tienen otros planes.   (Es lástima que)
2. Ana aprenderá a conducir fácilmente.   (Es probable que)
3. Yo llamaré a Dorotea ahora mismo.   (Será mejor que)
4. Mis abuelos no están aquí.   (Es extraño que)
5. Ellos se quedarán varios días en la sierra.   (Es verdad que)
6. El señor López comprará una casa de campo.   (No es cierto que)
7. Mis padres volverán esta noche.   (No es posible que)
8. Tú te divertirás mucho en la excursión.   (Es evidente que)
9. Juan vendrá a buscarnos pronto.   (Importa que)
10. Estaremos listos a las cinco y media.   (Es cierto que)

VII. OTRAS FORMAS DE MANDATO

A. The first person plural of the present subjunctive, and sometimes **vamos a** plus the infinitive, express commands equal to *let's* or *let us* plus a verb. **A ver** is regularly used for *Let's see.*

Remember that object pronouns are attached to affirmative commands and to infinitives, but they precede the verb in negative commands:

> **Llamemos a Elena.**   Let's call Helen.
> **Abrámosla.** ⎫
> **Vamos a abrirla.** ⎬ Let's open it.
> **No los dejemos allí.**   Let's not leave them there.

NOTE. **Vamos** is used for the affirmative *Let's* (*Let us*) *go.* **No vamos a casa** can only mean *We are not going home.* The subjunctive **No vayamos** must be used for *Let's not go*: **No vayamos todavía**, *Let's not go yet.*

When the reflexive **nos** is added to this command form, the final **-s** is dropped from the verb:

> **Vámonos.**   Let's be going, Let's go.
> **Levantémonos** (**Vamos a levantarnos**).   Let's get up.
> **No nos sentemos.**   Let's not sit down.

B. **Que**, equivalent to the English *have*, *let*, *may*, *I wish*, or *I hope*, introduces indirect commands, except in the first person. In such cases object pronouns precede the verb, and a noun subject often follows the verb. This construction is really a clause dependent upon a verb of *wishing*, *hoping*, *permitting*, etc., with the main verb understood, but not expressed.

> **Que esté aquí a las seis.** Let him be here at six.
> **Que los traiga Juan.** Have (Let, May) John bring them.
> **¡Que te diviertas mucho!** May you (I want you to, I hope you) have a very good time!

Remember that when *let* means *allow* or *permit*, it is translated by **dejar** or **permitir**: **Déjele (Permítale) usted a Pablo que vaya a esquiar,** *Let Paul (Allow* or *Permit Paul to) go skiing.*

Ejercicios

A. Para contestar dos veces, primero afirmativa, y luego negativamente, según el modelo.

MODELO: ¿Escribimos la frase?   Sí, escribámosla.   No, no la escribamos.

1. ¿Llevamos los patines?   3. ¿Buscamos a Elena?
2. ¿Seguimos el coche?   4. ¿Devolvemos los esquíes?

MODELO: ¿Nos acostamos?   Sí, acostémonos.   No, no nos acostemos.

5. ¿Nos levantamos?   7. ¿Nos vamos?
6. ¿Nos sentamos?   8. ¿Nos vestimos?

B. Después de oír un mandato, formen otra frase de mandato precedida de la frase **Yo no puedo** o **Nosotros no podemos**, siguiendo los modelos.

MODELOS: Lleve Ud. la comida.   Yo no puedo, que la lleve él.
         Cierren Uds. las ventanas. Nosotros no podemos, que las cierren ellos.

1. Traiga Ud. los paquetes.   5. Escojan Uds. el sitio.
2. Sirva Ud. el café.   6. Toquen Uds. los discos.
3. Pague Ud. la cuenta.   7. Váyanse Uds.
4. Siéntese Ud.   8. Acérquense Uds.

RESUMEN

A. Repitan la oración; luego, al oír el comienzo (*beginning*) de otra oración, complétenla, según los modelos.

MODELOS: Habrá nieve allí.   Habrá nieve allí.
        Creo que   Creo que habrá nieve allí.
        No creo que   No creo que haya nieve allí.

1. Mi padre vendrá a buscarnos.   (Yo estoy seguro de que)
2. Ana podrá acompañarnos.   (No estamos seguros de que)
3. Podremos patinar mañana.   (Nuestros amigos creen que)
4. Tú comprarás un par de esquíes.   (Ellos no creen que)
5. Hay hielo en la carretera.   (Dudamos que)
6. Mi hermano irá a la sierra esta tarde.   (Mi mamá niega que)
7. Estaremos listos a las siete.   (¿No crees que . . . ?)
8. Elena se quedará en casa de sus abuelos toda la semana.   (Marta cree que)

B. Usos del subjuntivo en cláusulas substantivas. Para expresar en español:

1. I want you (*fam. sing.*) to invite Ann to spend her (the) vacation with us.
2. And I advise you to call her now, because she is probably at home.
3. John insists that I go to the meeting with him today.
4. Ask them to be here before eight o'clock.
5. We are sorry that Robert will not return until tomorrow.
6. How glad I am that he can stay here all week!
7. They are afraid that you (*fam. sing.*) cannot accompany them!
8. We hope that Paul will thank them for the gift right away.
9. We are not sure that Richard will drive his car today.
10. It is important to do that; it will be easy for Henry to do it.
11. It is true that there is snow in the mountains; it is not certain that there is much ice.
12. It is impossible for me to leave at six (*two ways*).

C. Para contestar, usando la forma de mandato con **usted:**

1. ¿Empiezo a leer la carta?
2. ¿Sigo aprendiendo la canción?
3. ¿Le llevo algo al niño?
4. ¿Les doy las gracias ahora?
5. ¿Me siento en esta silla?
6. ¿Me quedo aquí hasta la una?
7. ¿Le digo que vuelva hoy?
8. ¿Me acerco al señor Díaz?

D. Otras formas de mandato.   Para expresar en español:

1. Have John wash it.
2. May you (*fam. sing.*) be happy!
3. Have Jane wait a few moments.
4. May you (*pl.*) have a good time!

5. Let's take the skis to them (*two ways*).
6. Let's sit down now (*two ways*).
7. Let's not go to the park yet.
8. Let's not put on our hats.

LECCIÓN OCHO

El (presente) perfecto de subjuntivo. Las
cláusulas adjetivas y los pronombres relativos. El
subjuntivo en cláusulas adjetivas. Usos especiales
del objeto indirecto

CARLOS SE ENCUENTRA UN POCO ENFERMO

(Durante el desayuno en la Residencia de Estudiantes uno de los diez o doce amigos que se reúnen todos los días a desayunarse en la misma mesa advierte la ausencia de uno de ellos. Juan le pregunta a un compañero por el que falta.)

JUAN. ¿Has visto a Carlos? No ha bajado a desayunarse, lo cual me parece muy extraño.

LUIS. No se siente bien esta mañana. Dudo mucho que se haya levantado.

JUAN. ¿Qué le pasa?

LUIS. Dice que le duele la garganta.

JUAN. ¿Tiene fiebre?

LUIS. Le tomé la temperatura y parece que tiene un grado y medio. Me preguntó si conocemos a algún médico que hable español.

JUAN. El médico con quien hablamos en casa del profesor Valdés es mexicano. Nos dijo que tiene su oficina en un edificio grande a unas tres cuadras de aquí.

LUIS. Es el edificio en cuyo piso bajo se encuentra una farmacia, ¿verdad?

JUAN. Creo que sí. ¿Hay alguien que pueda llevarle a la oficina del médico?

LUIS. Yo le llevaré. Hoy no tengo clases por la mañana.

JUAN. Espero que no sea más que un resfriado. Si es algo grave, tendremos que llamar a la madre de Carlos, la cual vive en San Agustín.

LUIS. Ya veremos. De todos modos habrá que hacer lo que diga el médico.

159

advertir (**ie, i**) to notice
Agustín Augustine
la **ausencia** absence
la **cuadra** (city) block
la **farmacia** drugstore, pharmacy
la **fiebre** fever
la **garganta** throat

el **grado** degree
grave serious, grave
¿qué le pasa? what's the matter
  with him (her, you)?
reunirse (**ú**) to meet, gather
la **temperatura** temperature
ya soon, presently

A. Busquen en el diálogo las frases que correspondan a las siguientes:

1. twelve friends who meet every day. 2. John asks . . . about the one who is missing. 3. which (fact) seems very strange to me. 4. He doesn't feel well. 5. What's the matter with him? 6. his throat hurts. 7. I took his temperature. 8. some doctor who speaks (may speak) Spanish. 9. The doctor with whom we spoke. 10. (at) some three blocks from here. 11. on the first floor of which. 12. I believe so. 13. I hope it's only a cold. 14. If it is something serious. 15. We'll soon see. 16. At any rate. 17. it will be necessary (we *or* one will have) to do. 18. whatever the doctor says (may say).

B. Estudien las expresiones siguientes para emplear algunas de ellas en el
   diálogo citado, o para usarlas en un diálogo nuevo basado sobre el
   modelo.

la **cama** bed
el **doctor** doctor (*title*)
el **dolor** ache, pain
la **enfermedad** sickness
  estar ausente to be absent
  guardar cama to stay in bed
la **medicina** medicine
  mejorarse to improve, get better

no es nada grave it is nothing (not
  at all) serious
la **píldora** pill
el **pulso** pulse
¿qué tiene él (ella)? what's the matter with him (her)?
tener dolor de cabeza to have a
  headache

PRONUNCIACIÓN

A. Review the observations on Spanish intonation (pages 17–18, 23–24, and 45); then read the first six exchanges of the diàlogue of this lesson, paying close attention to the intonation patterns.

B. **Dictado.** The teacher will select four exchanges of the dialogue of this or of the preceding lesson as an exercise in dictation.

NOTAS GRAMATICALES

I. EL (PRESENTE) PERFECTO DE SUBJUNTIVO

The present perfect subjunctive tense is formed by the present subjunctive of **haber** with the past participle. After verbs in the main clause which require the subjunctive in the dependent clause, Spanish uses the present perfect subjunctive tense to translate English *have* (*has*) plus the past participle.

SINGULAR		PLURAL	
haya		**hayamos**	
hayas	tomado, comido, vivido	**hayáis**	tomado, comido, vivido
haya		**hayan**	

Dudo mucho que él se haya levantado.   I doubt very much that he has gotten up.

Siento mucho que no hayan llegado.   I'm very sorry they haven't arrived.

Es posible que Ana haya estado enferma.   It's possible that Ann has been ill.

Ejercicio

Repitan la oración; luego, repítanla otra vez, cambiando el verbo de la cláusula subordinada al perfecto de subjuntivo.

MODELO: Yo dudo que él esté aquí.   Yo dudo que él esté aquí.
Yo dudo que él haya estado aquí.

1. Espero que Juan baje a comer.
2. Es lástima que él no se sienta bien.
3. No creo que él tenga un resfriado.
4. Me alegro de que tú abras todas las ventanas.
5. Él duda que Uds. lean el cuento.
6. Sentimos mucho que ella no se ponga los guantes.
7. Tengo miedo de que ellos no lleven sus patines.
8. Me parece extraño que Uds. no vayan a la sierra.

II. LAS CLÁUSULAS ADJETIVAS Y LOS PRONOMBRES RELATIVOS

An adjective clause modifies a noun or pronoun and is introduced by a relative pronoun.   In the sentence *I know a boy who can help us*, the adjective clause *who can help us* modifies *boy*.   *Who* is a relative pronoun and *boy* is the antecedent of the clause.

A. Simple relative pronouns

1. **Que**, *that*, *which*, *who*, and, when used as direct object of a verb, *whom*, is invariable and refers to persons or things. Used as the object of a preposition, **que** refers only to things. The relative pronoun is sometimes omitted in English when used as the object of a verb, but not in Spanish.

> **la casa que compró**   the house (that) he bought
> **los amigos que se reúnen**   the friends who meet (gather)
> **el artículo de que hablaban**   the article of (about) which they were talking
> **los jóvenes que vimos**   the young men (whom) we saw

2. **Quien** (*pl.* **quienes**), *who*, *whom*, refers only to persons. It is used mainly as the object of a preposition, always meaning *whom*, and sometimes instead of **que** when the relative pronoun *who* is separated from the antecedent by a comma. The personal **a** is required when **quien(es)** is the direct object of a verb.

> **el médico con quien hablamos**   the doctor with whom we talked
> **el señor Díaz, quien me llamó, quiere . . .**   Mr. Díaz, who called me,
>   wishes . . .
> **los hombres a quienes vimos ayer**   the men (whom) we saw yesterday

In the last sentence **que** may replace **a quienes**, and in conversation is more widely used.

3. **El cual** (**la cual, los cuales, las cuales**), *that*, *which*, *who*, *whom*, is used to clarify which one of two possible antecedents the clause modifies, and after prepositions such as **sin**, **por**, and those of more than one syllable. Be sure that the long relative agrees with its antecedent. (These long relatives are much more widely used in literary style than in everyday conversation. Watch for their uses in the Lecturas.)

> **la madre de Carlos, la cual vive en . . .**   Charles' mother, who lives in . . .
> **el coche cerca del cual están jugando**   the car near which they are playing

El que (**la que, los que, las que**) may be substituted for forms of **el cual**, particularly after prepositions, as in the second example.

4. **Lo cual** (sometimes **lo que**), *which* (*fact*), a neuter form, is used to refer back to an idea, statement, or situation, but not to a specific noun:

> **No ha bajado a desayunarse, lo cual me parece extraño.**
> He hasn't come down for breakfast, which (fact) seems strange to me.

B. Compound relative pronouns

1. **El** (**la**) **que,** *he* (*she*) *who, the one who* (*that, which*), and **los** (**las**) **que,** *those* or *the ones who* (*that, which*), may refer to persons or things. These forms are often called compound relatives because the definite article (which originated from the Latin demonstrative) serves as the antecedent of the **que**-clause. (Do <u>not</u> use forms of **el cual** in this construction.)

> **Juan pregunta por el que falta.** John asks about the one who is missing.
> **Estas muchachas y las que vienen . . .** These girls and the ones (those) who come . . .
> **Los que se reúnen aquí . . .** Those who meet here . . .

Quien (*pl.* **quienes**), which refers only to persons, sometimes means *he* (*those*) *who, the one*(*s*) *who,* particularly in proverbs:

> **Quien mucho duerme, poco aprende.** He who sleeps much, learns little.

2. **Lo que,** *what, that which,* a neuter form, refers only to an idea or statement:

> **Lo que dice Juan es verdad.** What (That which) John says is true.
> **Yo sé lo que ustedes quieren hacer.** I know what you want to do.

3. **Cuyo, -a, -os, -as,** *whose, of whom, of which,* is a relative possessive adjective. It agrees with the noun it modifies in gender and number:

> **el edificio en cuyo piso bajo** the building on the first floor of which (on whose first floor)
> **la mujer cuyos hijos** the woman whose children (the children of whom)

Remember that **¿De quién(es)?** expresses *Whose?* in a question: **¿De quién es esta casa?** *Whose house is this?* (*lit.,* Of whom is this house?)

Ejercicios

A. Después de oír las dos frases, combínenlas, usando el pronombre relativo **que**, según el modelo.

MODELO: Ella tenía un libro.   Era nuevo.   El libro que ella tenía era nuevo.

1. Ana compró un vestido.   Es muy bonito.
2. Juanita sirvió unos refrescos.   Eran excelentes.

3. Vimos a los niños.   Estaban en el parque.
4. Conocimos al hombre ayer.   Es médico.
5. Varios jóvenes se reúnen aquí.   Son estudiantes.

Combinen las dos frases, usando el pronombre relativo **quien**, según el modelo.

MODELO: Vimos al joven.   Es mexicano.   Vimos al joven, quien es mexicano.
El joven a quien vimos es mexicano.

6. Saludé a la joven.   Es española.
7. Hablamos con la muchacha.   Es estudiante de esta universidad.
8. Charlamos con aquel señor.   Trabaja en esta tienda.
9. Llamé a aquella niña.   Está jugando en el patio.
10. Conocimos a aquella señorita anoche.   Es profesora de inglés.

Combinen las dos frases, usando **el cual** o una de sus formas, según el modelo.

MODELO: La madre de Carlos vive en San Agustín.   Vendrá a visitarle pronto.
La madre de Carlos, la cual vive en San Agustín, vendrá a visitarle pronto.

11. Los amigos de Marta estudian en la biblioteca.   Tienen un examen mañana.
12. La tía de Miguel viaja por México.   Le envió una carta.
13. El abuelo de Inés ha escrito libros sobre México.   Vive en San Antonio.
14. Las hijas de la señora Díaz corren hacia el parque.   Son muy simpáticas.

B. Lean en español, supliendo el pronombre relativo:

1. La casa de campo _____ compraron es hermosa.   2. Los patines _____ tengo son de Roberto.   3. El niño _____ (*two ways*) vieron ustedes es mi hermanito. 4. El señor Navarro, _____ (*two ways*) es español, dio la conferencia.   5. El edificio de _____ hablan es muy grande.   6. Las señoras con _____ charla mi mamá son mexicanas.   7. Me gusta la casa cerca de _____ juegan los muchachos.   8. Los amigos de Juan, _____ se reúnen aquí, son estudiantes de esta universidad. 9. ¿Hiciste _____ dijo el médico?   10. Los jóvenes no han vuelto, _____ nos parece extraño.   11. Estos esquíes y _____ tiene Ana son nuevos.   12. Esta tarjeta y _____ recibí la semana pasada son de mis padres.   13. Mi tío construyó este edificio y _____ está en la esquina.   14. _____ busca, halla.

III. EL SUBJUNTIVO EN CLÁUSULAS ADJETIVAS

When the antecedent of an adjective clause is <u>indefinite</u> or <u>negative</u>, that is, when the adjective clause refers back to someone or something that is uncertain, unknown, indefinite, or nonexistent, the subjunctive is used in it.   In general, if *any, whatever,* or *whoever* can be applied to the antecedent, the subjunctive is required.   The idea of futurity is often involved.

The indicative is used, however, when the antecedent refers back to someone or something that is certain or definite.   This includes an action that occurs as a general rule.

¿Hay alguien que pueda llevarle a la oficina del médico?   Is there anyone who can take him to the doctor's office?

¿Tiene ella un amigo que haya estado en México?   Does she have a friend who has been in Mexico?

Queremos una casa que sea más grande.   We want a (any) house that is larger.

Haremos lo que diga el médico.   We shall do what(ever) the doctor says (may say).

No hay nadie que haya jugado mejor.   There is no one who has played better.

Ana no ve nada que le guste.   Ann doesn't see anything (sees nothing) that she likes.

BUT: **Ana encuentra algo que le gusta mucho.**   Ann finds something that she likes a great deal.

Yo siempre hago lo que me piden.   I always do what (that which) they ask of me.

Ricardo tiene un tío rico que vive en San Agustín.   Richard has a rich uncle who lives in St. Augustine.

In adjective clauses the personal **a** is omitted when a noun does not refer to a specific person (first example below).   It is used, however, before the pronouns **alguien** and **nadie**, and before forms of **alguno** and **ninguno** when referring to a person and when used as direct objects.

Necesito un hombre que me ayude mañana.   I need a man who will (may) help me tomorrow.

¿Conoce usted a algún médico que hable español?   Do you know a (any) doctor who speaks Spanish?

No conozco a nadie que diga eso.   I don't know anyone who says (will say) that.

Ejercicios

A. Repitan cada frase; luego, al oír el comienzo de otra frase, completen la nueva frase, según el modelo.

MODELO: Tiene un traje que le gusta.   Tiene un traje que le gusta.
          Quiere un traje   Quiere un traje que le guste.

1. Buscamos al joven que habla bien el español.
   Buscamos un joven
2. Tienen una casa que tiene ocho cuartos.
   Necesitan una casa
3. Cerca de aquí hay un sitio que es más hermoso.
   Cerca de aquí no hay ningún sitio
4. Deseamos reunirnos en el café donde sirven comidas mexicanas.
   Deseamos reunirnos en algún café
5. Quiero encontrar a la señorita que ha vivido en México.
   Quiero encontrar una señorita
6. Espero ver al niño que ha estado en el museo.
   Espero ver un niño

B. Para expresar en español:

1. I see some of the boys who meet here every day.
2. We believe that there is someone who can take him to the doctor's office.
3. We are looking for a secretary who writes Spanish.
4. Do you know anyone who speaks the language well?
5. We prefer a girl who has lived in Mexico or Chile.
6. Mr. Martínez needs a man who can work in his store.
7. Is there any boy who wants to go to the drugstore now?
8. We do not see anyone who has time (in order) to do it.
9. The girls want to find some dresses that they like.
10. The children will do what(ever) their mother may say.

IV. USOS ESPECIALES DEL OBJETO INDIRECTO

A. If an action is performed on one person by another, the corresponding indirect object pronoun is used with the verb. This construction most often involves parts of the body, articles of clothing, or things closely related to the person. Note that the definite article replaces the possessive adjective.

Le tomé la temperatura. I took his temperature (*lit.*, I took to him the temperature).

La madre les lavó las manos. The mother washed their hands.

Remember that the reflexive pronoun is used when the subject acts upon itself:

Mi madre se tomó la temperatura. My mother took her (own) temperature.

Juanito se lavó las manos. Johnny washed his hands.

B. The verb **doler**, *to ache, hurt*, has as its subject a noun expressing a part of the body, and the person is the indirect object:

Le (Me) duele la garganta. His (My) throat aches (hurts).

A ella le duele (Le duele a ella) la cabeza. Her head aches.

Ejercicio

Repitan la frase; luego, al oír un nuevo sujeto, formen otra frase, según el modelo.

MODELO: Ana se tomó la temperatura. Ana se tomó la temperatura.
      Mi hermana Mi hermana le tomó a Ana la temperatura.

1. Juanito se lavó las manos. (Yo)
2. Pablo se quitó los zapatos. (Ella)
3. Ana se compró un reloj. (Su papá)
4. Marta se puso la ropa. (Su mamá)
5. Juan se sirvió café. (Carolina)
6. Luisa se cortó la mano. (Yo no)

RESUMEN

A. Repitan cada pregunta; luego, contéstenla negativamente, haciendo los cambios necesarios en la cláusula adjetiva.

MODELO: ¿Ve Ud. algo que sea mejor? ¿Ve Ud. algo que sea mejor?
      No veo nada que sea mejor.

1. ¿Ve Ud. a alguien que pueda llevar la maleta?
2. ¿Hay alguien que tenga un resfriado hoy?

3. ¿Conoce Ud. a algún médico que hable español?
4. ¿Ves algo que Marta pueda comprar?
5. ¿Hay alguna cosa aquí que le guste a él?
6. ¿Hay alguien que conozca a aquel señor?
7. ¿Conoces a alguien que haya ido a la sierra?
8. ¿Ha leído Ud. algo que haya sido más interesante?

B. Usos de los pronombres relativos.   Para expresar en español:

1. The young lady whom (*two ways*) we met yesterday is from Colombia.
2. John's sister, who has just arrived, is studying at another university.
3. This is the building on whose first floor the lawyer has his office.
4. Ask George what he did with the book of which we were talking.
5. Our cousins have not returned yet, which (fact) surprises me.
6. These women and the one who is near the car are friends of my mother.
7. It can be said that those who (*two ways*) practice much, learn rapidly.
8. These two articles and the one which Helen read are well written.

C. Usos del objeto indirecto.   Para expresar en español:

1. The children washed their hands.
2. Their mother washed their hands.
3. Ann didn't take off her shoes.
4. Her sister took her shoes off her.
5. The doctor took her temperature.
6. Did you take your temperature?
7. Did Jane put on her new hat?
8. I put her hat on her.
9. My head aches (*two ways*).
10. Does your throat hurt?

D. Repaso.   Repitan cada oración; luego, repítanla otra vez, cambiando el verbo al pretérito de indicativo:

1. Carolina va a la sierra con algunos amigos. 2. José y yo no podemos acompañarlos. 3. El señor Díaz hace un viaje a México. 4. Los jóvenes nos traen varios regalos. 5. María se sienta en la primera fila. 6. Mi mamá no duerme la siesta. 7. Los muchachos nunca me piden nada. 8. Oyen cantar a María. 9. Roberto sigue leyendo la novela. 10. ¿Qué te dicen tus amigos? 11. ¿Cuáles de los estudiantes vienen a la reunión? 12. ¿Es fácil aprender el diálogo? 13. Les doy las gracias por la invitación. 14. Mi mamá se pone el vestido nuevo. 15. Arturo no se acuerda de eso. 16. Todos se divierten mucho en la excursión. 17. Mi papá conduce el coche al aeropuerto. 18. Nuestro tío construye una casa de campo.

19. Los estudiantes advierten la ausencia de Carlos. 20. María no quiere dar un paseo con Pablo. 21. Yo llego a la universidad a las nueve. 22. Él no sabe nada de particular. 23. Bárbara tiene que escribir una carta a un amigo mexicano. 24. Roberto y Carolina andan despacio por la calle. 25. Ella y yo volvemos a casa a las cinco de la tarde.

PROSAS PROFANAS

POR

RUBÉN DARÍO

ILUSTRACIONES

DE

ENRIQUE OCHOA

Volumen II de las obras completas. Administración: Editorial MUNDO LATINO
MADRID
SPAIN

LECTURA IV

PRESENTACIÓN

A. Estudio de palabras

1. Approximate cognates

a. As we have seen in Lectura III, Spanish nouns ending in **-ista** end in *-ist* in English: novelista, *novelist*.   Just as the corresponding adjectival ending in Spanish varies between **-ista** and **-ístico, -a**, the English equivalent may end in *-ist* or *-istic*: naturalista, *naturalist* (noun), and *naturalistic*; humanista, *humanist*, but humanístico, *humanistic*.   The adjective realista means *realistic*, while indianista means *Indianist*.

b. We have also seen in Lectura III that often the Spanish adjectival ending in **-ico, -a,** = English *-ic, -ical*, as in these new words which occur in this Lectura: anatómico, artístico, auténtico, filosófico, ideológico, lírico, médico (*medical*), poético, psicológico.   Notice, however, utópico, *Utopian*, and the nouns lógica, *logic*, and trópico, *tropic(s)*, *tropical region*.

c. Give the English cognates for the following words and point out the variations in spelling and/or ending: acentuar, acumular, atención, apreciación, atractivo, colaborar, exageración, futilidad, imparcialidad, intelectual, silencio, vacuidad.

d. Find as many verbs as you can in this Lectura which illustrate each of the following principles: 1) the ending of the Spanish infinitive is lacking in English; 2) the ending of the Spanish infinitive is *-e* in English.

e. List the words in the Lectura whose English cognates lack Spanish final **-a, -e, -o**.

2. Less approximate cognates.   Pronounce the following words and note the English meaning: apropiado, *appropriate*; asfixiar, *to asphyxiate, suffocate*; detalle, *detail*; énfasis, *emphasis*; explotación, *exploitation*; habitante, *inhabitant*; humilde, *humble*; huracán, *hurricane*; maestría, *mastery, skill*; materia, *matter*; párrafo, *paragraph*; ritmo, *rhythm*; seudónimo, *pseudonym*; simpatía, *sympathy*; sintaxis, *syntax*; valioso, *valuable*.

3. *Compare the meanings of the following words:* amigo *and* amistad, *friendship*; cultivar *and* cultivador, *cultivator*; cultura, cultural *and* culto, *cultured, learned*; escribir, escritor, escritora, *and* describir, *to describe*; espíritu, espiritual *and* espiritualidad; fuerte, fuerza, *strength, force*, esfuerzo, *effort, and* reforzar, *to reinforce*; historia *and* historiador, *historian*; humano, *human, and* humanidad, *humanity*; morir, muerte, *and* moribundo, *moribund, dying person*; persona, personal, personalidad *and* personaje, *personage, character* (in a literary work); poesía, poeta, poético, poetisa, *poetess, and* poetizar, *to poetize, make poetic*; popular, pueblo, *town, village,* and *people, populace, and* pueblecito, *small town, village*; representar, representante (*noun*), *and* representativo (*adjective*); sentir, *to feel, and* sentido, *sense, meaning*; vergüenza, *shame, and* vergonzoso, *shameful*.

4. Deceptive cognates.   The following examples (one of which has been mentioned in the preceding paragraph and another in Lectura I) occur in the reading selection: **intentar**, *to attempt*, *try* and, only rarely, *to intend*; **personaje**, *personage*, and also *character* (in a literary work); **preocupación**, *concern*, *worry*, as well as *preoccupation*; **sensibilidad**, *sensitivity*, more often than *sensibility*; **valor**, *value*, as well as *valor*, *courage*.

B. Modismos y frases útiles

a lo largo de   throughout
a veces   at times
con el tiempo   in (in the course of) time
en (por lo) general   in general, generally
figurar entre   to appear among, be
hoy día   nowadays, today
llamar la atención (a uno)   to attract (one's) attention
no sólo . . . sino (también)   not only . . . but (also)

poco después de   shortly after
por ejemplo   for example
¡por supuesto!   of course! certainly!
referirse (ie, i) a   to refer to
relacionar (con)   to relate (to)
reunirse con   to join
tal vez   perhaps
tanto . . . como   both . . . and, as much . . . as
volver (ue) las espaldas a   to turn one's back on, reject

C. Aspectos gramaticales

1. Observations on the gender of nouns

a. The gender of the masculine nouns **problema** and **tema** often causes students trouble.   They tend to think of them as feminine nouns.   Why is this so?

b. The nouns **persona** and **figura**, used in this Lectura, as well as **víctima**, in the preceding Lectura, are feminine in gender; articles and adjectives used with them must be put in the feminine form, even when the nouns refer to male beings: **La figura central es un campesino**, *The central figure is a peasant.*

2. Nouns and adjectives of nationality.   Several suffixes are used to form nouns and adjectives of nationality.

a. Give in Spanish the names of the Spanish American countries from which the following nouns and adjectives are derived: colombiano, dominicano, mexicano, peruano; argentino; chileno; uruguayo; guatemalteco; nicaragüense.

b. Other examples, not used in the Lectura, are: boliviano, cubano, ecuatoriano, venezolano; paraguayo; brasileño, hondureño, panameño, portorriqueño (puertorriqueño); costarricense.

3. Observations on the position of adjectives

In the preceding grammar lessons we have followed the general principle that limiting adjectives precede the noun, and that descriptive adjectives, which single out or distinguish one noun from another of the same class, follow the noun.   We have also found: 1) that a few adjectives (such as **bueno, -a, malo, -a,** etc.) usually precede the noun, although they may follow to distinguish qualities of the noun, and 2) that certain adjectives assume different meanings when used before or after the noun (see Lección cinco).

Descriptive adjectives may also precede the noun when they are used figuratively, or when they express a quality that is generally known or not essential to the recognition of the noun.   In such cases there is no desire to single out or to differentiate. Also, when a certain quality has been established with reference to the noun, the adjective often precedes the noun.

Examples taken from the following Lectura are:

> **la fuerte personalidad de Rubén Darío**   the strong personality of Rubén Darío
> **son escritores de exquisita sensibilidad**   they are writers of exquisite sensitivity
> **estas breves notas**   these brief notes
> **la total destrucción**   the total destruction
> **el abominable carácter de Cruz**   the abominable character of Cruz
> **erudito de sólida formación humanística**   (a) scholar of solid humanistic formation (training)

Other examples (not included in this Lectura) are:

> **los altos Andes**   the high Andes   **las hermosas flores**   beautiful flowers
> **la blanca nieve**   white snow   **el famoso autor**   the famous author

Whenever an adjective is changed from its normal position, the speaker or writer gives a subjective or personal interpretation of the noun.   An adjective placed before the noun loses much of its force and expresses its quality as belonging to the noun as a matter of course.   When it follows, it indicates a distinguishing quality and it assumes the chief importance.   In English this result is attained by a slight pause and the stress of voice.

4. Uses of the prepositional form of object pronouns

When the direct object of a verb is a pronoun used reflexively, and the indirect object is any other personal pronoun, the latter is expressed by the prepositional form:

> **el hombre que se entrega a ella . . .**   the man who abandons himself
> (surrenders) to it . . .

Similarly, when **a** is used after verbs of motion, it is a true preposition and is followed
by the prepositional form of the pronoun:

> **Me acerqué a ella.**   I approached her *or* it (*f.*).
> **La carta no ha llegado a mí.**   The letter has not reached me.

5. **Todos, -as,** may either precede or follow a plural personal pronoun: **todos
ellos** *or* **ellos todos,** *all of them, they all.*   Note that when English *all of* precedes
the pronoun, the word *of* is not translated in Spanish.   Other examples are:
nosotros todos, *we all, all of us*; **ellas todas,** *all of them* (*f.*), *they all.*

Also, **todos, -as,** may stand for a noun in the plural:

> **No todos quedaron fieles . . .**   Not all (*or* all of them) remained faithful . . .
> **todos contribuyeron . . .**   all (of them) contributed . . .

«Gabriela Mistral», por José López Mezquita

Jorge Luis Borges

Alfonso Reyes

CORRIENTES CULTURALES DE LA AMÉRICA
ESPAÑOLA (*continuación*)

Como hemos indicado en la Lectura anterior, los géneros literarios más cultivados en Hispanoamérica durante el siglo XX han sido la poesía, la novela y el cuento, y el ensayo.

La obra y la fuerte* personalidad del nicaragüense Rubén Darío determinaron la evolución de la poesía hispanoamericana en los primeros años del siglo actual. Entre los poetas jóvenes que se aprestaron a[1] colaborar con él en la transformación de la poesía había varios de primer orden,[2] como el argentino Leopoldo Lugones (1874–1938), el colombiano Guillermo Valencia (1873–1943), el uruguayo Julio Herrera y Reissig (1875–1910) y el mexicano Amado Nervo (1870–1919). No todos* quedaron fieles a las tendencias del modernismo; pero todos* contribuyeron elementos valiosos a la poesía nueva del continente.

Poco después de 1920 los poetas volvieron las espaldas al modernismo. A través del ultraísmo y del surrealismo[3] se acercaron a las múltiples tendencias de la poesía actual. Las preocupaciones políticas y sociales absorbieron a veces el interés de los poetas; otras veces lo regional y lo popular les llamaron la atención.[4] La rebelión social y política era acompañada de la rebelión poética; el poeta se rebelaba no sólo contra los metros y los ritmos, sino también contra la sintaxis y hasta[5] contra la lógica. El peruano César Vallejo (1892–1938) y el chileno Pablo Neruda (1904–   ) son representantes típicos de estas tendencias. En la literatura actual el argentino Jorge Luis Borges (1899–   ) y el mexicano Octavio Paz (1914–   ) son escritores de exquisita* sensibilidad que continúan buscando nuevas maneras de expresión tanto en la poesía como en la prosa.

Al concluir estas breves* notas sobre la poesía contemporánea, hay que dedicar algunas palabras a una escritora chilena que se distinguió no sólo en la poesía, sino también en la enseñanza y en la vida intelectual en general. Gabriela Mistral, seudónimo de Lucila Godoy (1889–1957), es tal vez la escritora más distinguida de la América del siglo XX. Ganó fama internacional como poetisa y en 1945 recibió el Premio Nobel de Literatura. Sus poesías, que muestran una espiritualidad muy elevada, son un reflejo de su vida de dolores y de sus esfuerzos contra las injusticias del mundo.

[1] **se aprestaron a**, *prepared themselves to.*   [2] **varios de primer orden**, *several excellent (first-rate) ones.*   [3] **ultraísmo**, *ultraism*; **surrealismo**, *surrealism.* (Two of several literary "isms" or generations of the period.)   [4] **les llamaron la atención**, *attracted their attention* (lit., *attracted the attention to them*).   [5] **hasta**, *even.*

En sus viajes por las Américas y por Europa y al representar a Chile como cónsul en varios países, siempre demostró una simpatía profunda por la humanidad y por la amistad internacional. Su vida ha servido de ejemplo del nuevo puesto que ocupan hoy día muchas mujeres en la América española.

La novela representativa del modernismo es *La gloria de don Ramiro*, publicada en 1908 por el argentino Enrique Larreta (1875–1961). Como novela histórica es excelente y se basa en informes sólidos sobre la España del siglo dieciséis. Pero su tema no era apropiado al momento;[1] se preparaba ya[2] un cambio de dirección en la prosa, que resultaría en un mayor énfasis y apreciación[3] de lo americano. Ejemplos típicos de la nueva dirección regional son *El inglés de los güesos*[4] (1924), del argentino Benito Lynch (1885–1951), y la obra maestra del género, *Don Segundo Sombra* (1926), de Ricardo Güiraldes (1886–1927). Agregando elementos artísticos y cultos a la técnica aprendida en el naturalismo, Güiraldes transformó la realidad en materia poética. Agrandó[5] y poetizó la figura del gaucho. Se considera su obra como una de las expresiones literarias de mayor valor en la literatura hispanoamericana.

La Revolución de 1910 en México, con todos sus problemas políticos y sociales, ha servido de base para una multitud de obras literarias de diversas formas. La novela más célebre del período es *Los de abajo*[6] (1916), de Mariano Azuela (1873–1952). El autor, que era médico en uno de los ejércitos revolucionarios, analiza con vigor y realismo el horror, la confusión y la futilidad de la conflagración. Según uno de los personajes de la obra, «La revolución es el huracán y el hombre que se entrega a ella* no es ya el hombre, es la miserable hoja seca arrebatada por el vendaval.[7]» La figura central es un campesino, Demetrio Macías, que coge su fusil, abandona su casa y huye a la sierra, donde se reúne con algunos amigos que le siguen. Llega a ser general de unas fuerzas revolucionarias; pero con el tiempo es traicionado y muere, sin haber conseguido nada, en la misma sierra donde había ganado su primera victoria.

En todos los países que tienen habitantes indios ha aparecido lo que se llama la novela indianista. En ésta, por lo general, los autores protestan contra el abuso y la explotación de los indios. Otro escritor mexicano, Gregorio López y Fuentes (1897–   ), en su novela *El indio* (1935), da una

---

[1] **apropiado al momento,** *appropriate at the moment, suitable for that period (time).*   [2] **se preparaba ya,** *was already being prepared, was getting under way then.*   [3] For the omission of the article, see page 97. [4] **El inglés de los güesos,** *The Englishman of the Bones (i.e., The Archaeologist).* (Colloquially, initial **b, h,** or **v** followed by **ue** becomes **g**; thus, **güesos** is used for **huesos** in popular speech.) [5] **Agrandó,** *He exalted.*   [6] **Los de abajo,** *The Underdogs.*   [7] **hoja . . . vendaval,** *dry leaf carried away by the windstorm.*

VILLA EN LA SILLA PRESIDENCIAL

Pancho Villa sentado en la silla presidencial
La época de Pancho Villa es tema de *Los de abajo*

imagen fiel de los problemas del pueblo indígena en su patria. Considerada por muchos como la mejor novela indianista es *El mundo es ancho y ajeno*[1] (1941), del peruano Ciro Alegría (1909–   ). Con gran maestría el autor describe la vida miserable y la total* destrucción de un pueblo humilde de los Andes.

Junto con la preocupación por los problemas sociales se nota, en los últimos años, una tendencia hacia la novela psicológica y filosófica. El chileno Eduardo Barrios (1884–1963) se ha distinguido en este tipo de novela. Su obra maestra es *El hermano asno*[2] (1922), que trata de los tormentos del alma de un fraile franciscano. Otros hábiles narradores que aspiran a destacar[3] lo que el hombre de hoy día siente, piensa y es, son Manuel Rojas (1896–   ), que, nacido en la Argentina, escribe en Chile, y el argentino Eduardo Mallea (1903–   ), autor de *La bahía de silencio* (1940), en que cada personaje intenta descubrir su propia personalidad. En *Historia de una pasión argentina* (1935), Mallea censura duramente las clases poderosas que asfixian la vida auténtica del pueblo. La protesta social anima también las obras del poeta y novelista guatemalteco Miguel Ángel Asturias (1899–   ), que en 1967 recibió el Premio Nobel de Literatura. En su novela más conocida, *El señor presidente* (1941), describe con amargura[4] la vida vergonzosa de un país hispanoamericano dominado por el despotismo (sin indicar cuál es).

La novela mexicana entra en una fase nueva con una obra importante de Agustín Yáñez (1904–   ), *Al filo del agua*[5] (1947). La novela describe la vida atrasada de un pueblecito de Jalisco, apartado de las rutas culturales y comerciales, en los años en que germina la revolución mexicana. Se plantea el conflicto[6] de la novela en el antagonismo entre las personas que se amparan[7] en la tradición, en la iglesia y en las convenciones, y las que representan las fuerzas nuevas. La imparcialidad con que se documenta el ambiente político e ideológico de aquellos años es notable. La técnica naturalista de Yáñez se halla reforzada con procedimientos modernos, como el sueño, el monólogo interior y párrafos de tensión lírica. Como en Asturias, no falta la tendencia a la exageración y a la caricatura.

Se acentúan las tendencias mencionadas en las obras de novelistas mexicanos más jóvenes, como Juan José Arreola (1918–   ), Juan Rulfo (1918–   ) y Carlos Fuentes (1929–   ). Obra típica es *La muerte de Artemio Cruz* (1962), de Fuentes, en que el autor censura la vida del hombre

---

[1] **El mundo es ancho y ajeno**, *Broad and Alien is the World.*   [2] **El hermano asno**, *Brother Ass.* (This title was taken from the term St. Francis of Assisi, 1182–1226, founder of the Franciscan Order, used for his weak body.)   [3] **destacar**, *emphasize, make stand out.*   [4] **con amargura**, *bitterly, with bitterness.*   [5] **Al filo del agua**, *The Edge of the Storm.*   [6] **Se plantea el conflicto**, *The conflict . . . is posed (set up).*   [7] **se amparan**, *seek protection (help).*

de negocios moderno, que, desprovisto[1] de sentido moral, acumula grandes fortunas pensando solamente en su medro[2] personal.   La estructura de la obra es muy moderna.   El relato de la agonía de Cruz, que se extiende a lo largo de la novela, con gran alarde[3] de detalles médicos y anatómicos, es interrumpido repetidamente por los recuerdos del moribundo.   Estos recuerdos, que se refieren a momentos dispersos de su vida, subrayan[4] el abominable* carácter de Cruz y la vacuidad de su existencia.

El ensayo sigue siendo uno de los géneros más populares e[5] interesantes de la literatura hispanoamericana de nuestro tiempo.   El dominicano Pedro Henríquez Ureña (1884–1946), los mexicanos José Vasconcelos (1882–1959) y Alfonso Reyes (1889–1959), y el colombiano Germán Arciniegas (1900–   ) figuran entre los cultivadores más brillantes de este género.   La influencia del idealismo y del optimismo de Rodó[6] es evidente en todos ellos.*

José Vasconcelos, abogado, historiador, educador y político, que llegó a ser candidato a la presidencia de México, es una de las figuras más atractivas de la historia social y cultural de su país.   Su obra más discutida es *La raza cósmica* (1925), en la que expone la teoría de una quinta raza, que regiría el destino humano y tendría su centro en el trópico.   El escritor más distinguido del grupo es Alfonso Reyes, erudito de sólida* formación humanística.   En una serie de trabajos esbozó[7] una política utópica para las Américas, basada en la concordia intercontinental y en un sentido social y democrático de la cultura.

---

[1] **desprovisto**, *devoid.*   [2] **medro**, *advancement.*   [3] **alarde**, *display.*   [4] **subrayan**, *underline, emphasize.*   [5] For explanation, see page 247.   [6] See page 140.   [7] **esbozó**, *he sketched, outlined.*

José Vasconcelos

PRÁCTICAS ORALES

A. Diálogo.   «En el comedor de la Residencia de Señoritas»

(Dos estudiantes están almorzando juntas.   Charlan sobre la lección de la clase de español.)

ESTUDIANTE 1ª[1]   ¿Has leído la lección para mañana?   No sé si podré recordar los nombres de tantos escritores.

ESTUDIANTE 2ª   Yo trato de comprender los diferentes movimientos y tendencias y luego relaciono con ellos la obra de algún escritor importante.

ESTUDIANTE 1ª   ¿Qué cambios en la poesía pueden observarse después del modernismo?

ESTUDIANTE 2ª   Después de 1920 comienzan las múltiples tendencias de la poesía actual.   Las preocupaciones políticas y sociales, por ejemplo, absorben a veces el interés de los poetas.

ESTUDIANTE 1ª   El peruano César Vallejo y el chileno Pablo Neruda son representantes típicos de las tendencias nuevas, ¿verdad?

ESTUDIANTE 2ª   Sí, tienes razón . . .   Pero parece que el argentino Borges y el mexicano Paz son los escritores más representativos de la literatura actual.

---

[1] 1ª = **primera**, and 2ª = **segunda**.   Similarly, 1º = **primero**, and 2º = **segundo**.

ESTUDIANTE 1ª   La vida de Gabriela Mistral me ha interesado mucho. Parece
                   que puede servir de ejemplo del nuevo puesto que ocupa la mujer
                   hoy día en la América española.

ESTUDIANTE 2ª   Como sabes, ganó fama internacional como poetisa y en 1945
                   recibió el Premio Nobel de Literatura.

ESTUDIANTE 1ª   La novela también ha tenido muchos cultivadores durante el siglo
                   XX. ¿Has leído *La gloria de don Ramiro*?

ESTUDIANTE 2ª   Todavía no; pero pienso sacarla de la biblioteca—como también
                   El inglés de los güesos y *Don Segundo Sombra*.

ESTUDIANTE 1ª   Me parece de gran interés la novela de la Revolución mexicana.
                   Tú has leído *Los de abajo*, ¿verdad?

ESTUDIANTE 2ª   ¡Por supuesto! Es una obra magnífica. Azuela analiza con
                   vigor y con realismo el ambiente de aquellos años.

ESTUDIANTE 1ª   Recuerdo con horror las palabras de uno de los personajes de la
                   novela, «La revolución es el huracán y el hombre . . . es la miserable
                   hoja seca arrebatada por el vendaval.»

ESTUDIANTE 2ª   La discusión de mañana será muy interesante. Veremos lo que
                   nos dice el profesor.

B. Para formular preguntas en español

Los estudiantes formularán una o más preguntas para cada una de las siguientes
contestaciones:

1. En la novela indianista los autores, por lo general, protestan contra el abuso y la
explotación de los indios.   2. La obra de Ciro Alegría, *El mundo es ancho y ajeno*, es
considerada como la mejor novela indianista.   3. El chileno Eduardo Barrios se ha
distinguido en la novela psicológica y filosófica.   4. Manuel Rojas y Eduardo Mallea
aspiran a destacar lo que el hombre de hoy día siente, piensa y es.   5. En su novela
Historia de una pasión argentina, Mallea censura duramente las clases poderosas que
asfixian la vida auténtica del pueblo.   6. En *El señor presidente*, Asturias describe con
amargura la vida vergonzosa de un país hispanoamericano dominado por el
despotismo.

7. La novela de Agustín Yáñez, *Al filo del agua*, inicia una nueva fase en la novela
mexicana.   8. Algunos procedimientos modernos que se notan en la técnica de
Yáñez son el sueño, el monólogo interior y el uso de párrafos de tensión lírica.
9. Se acentúan las tendencias mencionadas en las obras de Juan José Arreola, Juan
Rulfo y Carlos Fuentes.   10. En *La muerte de Artemio Cruz*, Fuentes censura la vida
del hombre de negocios moderno, que, desprovisto de sentido moral, acumula grandes
fortunas pensando solamente en su medro personal.   11. Henríquez Ureña, Vasconcelos, Reyes y Arciniegas figuran entre los ensayistas más brillantes de la literatura
hispanoamericana de nuestro tiempo.   12. Alfonso Reyes basa sus ideas sobre una
política utópica para las Américas en la concordia intercontinental y en un sentido
social y democrático de la cultura.

EJERCICIOS ESCRITOS

A. Uso de modismos y frases hechas

Usen los modismos y frases siguientes en oraciones completas:

á lo largo de   referirse a
llamar la atención (a uno)   reunirse con
no sólo . . . sino (también)   volver las espaldas a

B. Para expresar en español

1. Several first-rate poets collaborated with Rubén Darío in the new Spanish American poetry, called *modernismo*. 2. Shortly after 1920 many writers turned their backs on modernism, and they began to look for new ways of expression both in poetry and in prose. 3. Gabriela Mistral, the most distinguished poetess of the present century, always demonstrated a deep sympathy for humanity and for international friendship. 4. *Don Segundo Sombra*, the masterpiece of Güiraldes, in which he poeticized the figure of the Argentine gaucho, is one of the novels of greatest value in Spanish American literature. 5. The most famous novel of the Revolution of 1910 in Mexico is *The Underdogs*, written by Azuela, who was a doctor in one of the revolutionary armies. 6. The author analyzes with great realism the horror, confusion, and futility of the Revolution, with all its social and political problems. 7. Demetrio Macías abandons his home and flees to the mountains, where he joins some friends; he soon becomes a general, but in time he is betrayed and he dies without having attained anything. 8. The Indianist novel, in which the novelists protested against the abuse and exploitation of the Indians, has appeared in all the countries which have many Indian inhabitants. 9. Just as López y Fuentes gives a faithful picture of the problems of the native people of Mexico, the Peruvian Ciro Alegría describes with great skill the miserable life of a humble town of the Andes. 10. In the contemporary novel, along with the tendency towards the psychological and philosophical novel, one observes the concern with (**por**) social protest. 11. The essay continues to be (being) not only one of the most popular literary types of today (our time), but also one of the most interesting. 12. Perhaps the most distinguished essayist is the scholar, Alfonso Reyes, who, in a series of works, sketched a Utopian policy for the Americas.

C. Dictado

The teacher will select lines from page 177 for dictation.

LECCIÓN NUEVE

Formas del imperfecto de subjuntivo. El
pluscuamperfecto de subjuntivo. Usos de los tiempos
del subjuntivo. El subjuntivo en cláusulas adverbiales.
El subjuntivo en frases condicionales

UNA CÁMARA PARA EL VIAJE A MÉXICO

(Son las diez de la noche. Roberto acaba de regresar a su cuarto. Ha ido de compras con su padre y han cenado en el centro. Entra su amigo Jorge.)

JORGE. ¡Hola, Roberto! Aunque sea tarde, he venido a ver si encontraste la cámara que deseabas.

ROBERTO. Pasa, Jorge. Me ha regalado mi papá una cámara de treinta y cinco milímetros. Quiero que la veas.

JORGE. ¡Hombre! ¿Por qué no me llamaste para que te ayudara a escoger entre tantas marcas buenas? *(Le enseña Roberto la cámara.)* Pero, ¡ésta es magnífica!

ROBERTO. Pasé por tu cuarto a eso de las tres, pero habías salido antes de que yo llegara.

JORGE. ¡Gastas el dinero como si fueras millonario! Te gustaría aumentar tu colección de transparencias,[1] ¿verdad? Con la pantalla y el proyector que te regalaron para tu cumpleaños, ya no te falta nada.

ROBERTO. Pienso sacar muchas fotografías cuando vaya a México este verano.

JORGE. También llevarás tu cámara de cine, ¿verdad?

ROBERTO. Habrá ocasiones en que podré usar las dos. Cuando haya bailes o fiestas populares, será mejor usar la cámara de cine.

[1] For *slide, transparency*, **la diapositiva** is also used.

185

JORGE.   ¿Por qué no metes un rollo de película en la cámara para probarla?

ROBERTO.   Es una buena idea, aunque me será difícil hacerla revelar antes que me marche.

JORGE.   Si tuviera dinero, haría el viaje contigo.   Si fuésemos juntos, nos divertiríamos mucho.

ROBERTO.   Si no hubieras ido a Nueva York para las Navidades, tus ahorros no habrían bajado tanto . . .   Pero si sigues trabajando en la biblioteca, podrás reunir el dinero fácilmente.   ¿Qué te parece la idea?

JORGE.   ¡Me parece magnífica! Prometo acompañarte con tal que consiga el dinero.

el ahorro economy; *pl.* savings	**el millonario** millionaire
aumentar to increase, augment	**las Navidades** Christmas time
bajar to decline	**la pantalla** screen (*movie*)
la cámara (**de cine**) (movie) camera	**probar** (**ue**) to try out, test
gastar to spend (*money*), waste, use (up)	**el proyector** projector
juntos, -as together	**reunir** (**ú**) to collect, get (together)
la marca brand, make, kind	**revelar** to reveal, develop (*film*)
meter to put (in)	**el rollo** roll (*of film*)
el milímetro millimeter	**la transparencia** slide, transparency

A. Busquen en el diálogo las frases que correspondan a las siguientes:

1. He has gone shopping. 2. Even though it is (may be) late. 3. a thirty-five millimeter camera. 4. I want you to see it. 5. so that I might help you. 6. at about three o'clock. 7. before I arrived. 8. as if you were a millionaire. 9. you no longer lack anything. 10. When there are (may be) popular dances or festivals. 11. it will be difficult for me to have it developed. 12. If I had some (the) money. 13. I would take the trip with you. 14. If we should (were to) go together. 15. If you hadn't gone to New York. 16. your savings wouldn't have declined so much. 17. if you continue working. 18. How do you like the idea? 19. I think it's wonderful! 20. provided that I get the money.

B. Preparen un diálogo original, de unas diez líneas, para recitar en clase, empleando las frases y preguntas siguientes como elemento inicial:[1]

1. LUIS.   ¿Dónde has estado, Roberto?   No te vi en el comedor.
   ROBERTO.   He estado en el centro con Jorge.   Buscábamos un proyector nuevo para mi padre.

---

[1] Review of dialogues on pages 8, 22, 43, and 145–146 will be helpful to the student in preparing the new dialogues.

2. ROBERTO.   Esta noche vamos a mirar las transparencias que traje de mi viaje
                por Yucatán.
   MIGUEL.   ¿Quieres que te preste la pantalla nueva que me han regalado?

3. LUISA.   ¿Por qué no hacemos una excursión a la sierra durante las vacaciones?
   ELENA.   Pero, Luisa, ¿dónde podría conseguir el dinero?

NOTAS GRAMATICALES

I. FORMAS DEL IMPERFECTO DE SUBJUNTIVO

The imperfect subjunctive tense in Spanish has two forms, often referred to as the
-ra and **-se** forms, and the same two sets of endings are used for the three conjugations. To form the imperfect subjunctive of <u>all</u> verbs, regular and irregular, drop
-ron of the third person plural preterit indicative and add **-ra, -ras, -ra, -ramos,
-rais, -ran** or **-se, -ses, -se, -semos, -seis, -sen.** Only the first person plural
form has a written accent. Remember that the **-er** and **-ir** verbs have the same
endings in all tenses except in the present indicative. The two imperfect subjunctive
tenses are interchangeable in Spanish, except in conditional sentences (section V of
this lesson) and in softened statements (Lección diez).

tomar:	tomara	tomaras	tomara	tomáramos	tomarais	tomaran
	tomase	tomases	tomase	tomásemos	tomaseis	tomasen
comer:	comiera	comieras	comiera	comiéramos	comierais	comieran
vivir:	viviese	vivieses	viviese	viviésemos	vivieseis	viviesen

See Appendix D, pages 315–324, for the imperfect subjunctive forms of irregular and
stem-changing verbs. For easy reference, the infinitive, third person plural preterit,
and the first person singular imperfect subjunctive forms of some common irregular
verbs are listed here.

Inf.	*3rd Pl. Pret.*	*Imp. Subj.*	*Inf.*	*3rd Pl. Pret.*	*Imp. Subj.*
andar	**anduvieron**	**anduviera, -se**	estar	**estuvieron**	**estuviera, -se**
caer	**cayeron**	**cayera, -se**	haber	**hubieron**[1]	**hubiera, -se**
conducir	**condujeron**	**condujera, -se**	hacer	**hicieron**	**hiciera, -se**
construir	**construyeron**	**construyera, -se**	ir	**fueron**	**fuera, -se**
creer	**creyeron**	**creyera, -se**	oír	**oyeron**	**oyera, -se**
dar	**dieron**	**diera, -se**	poder	**pudieron**	**pudiera, -se**
decir	**dijeron**	**dijera, -se**	poner	**pusieron**	**pusiera, -se**

[1] See page 245 for the preterit forms of **haber.**

querer	**quisieron**	**quisiera, -se**	t⟨ ⟩	**tuvieron**	**tuviera, -se**
saber	**supieron**	**supiera, -se**	traer	**trajeron**	**trajera, -se**
ser	**fueron**	**fuera, -se**	ver	vieron	viera, -se

Stem-changing verbs, Class I (which end in **-ar** and **-er**), have no stem change in the imperfect subjunctive. In Class II verbs (**sentir, dormir**) the stem vowel **e** becomes **i**, and **o** becomes **u** in the third person singular and plural of the preterit, and in the entire imperfect subjunctive. In Class III verbs (**pedir, reír**) the stem vowel **e** becomes **i** in the same forms.

sentir (ie, i)	**sintieron**	**sintiera, -se**	pedir (i, i)	**pidieron**	**pidiera, -se**
dormir (ue, u)	**durmieron**	**durmiera, -se**	reír (i, i)	**rieron**	**riera, -se**

II. EL PLUSCUAMPERFECTO DE SUBJUNTIVO

The pluperfect subjunctive is formed by using either the **-ra** or **-se** imperfect subjunctive form of **haber** plus the past participle.

hubiera	**hubiese**	
hubieras	**hubieses**	
hubiera	**hubiese**	tomado, comido, vivido
hubiéramos	**hubiésemos**	
hubierais	**hubieseis**	
hubieran	**hubiesen**	

Yo sentía mucho que él ya hubiera (hubiese) comido.   I was very sorry that he had already eaten.

III. USOS DE LOS TIEMPOS DEL SUBJUNTIVO

When the main verb in a sentence which requires the subjunctive in a dependent clause is in the present, future, or present perfect tense, or is a command, the verb in the dependent clause is regularly in the <u>present</u> or <u>present perfect</u> subjunctive tense:

Quiero que veas la cámara.   I want you to see the camera.
Le diré (he dicho) que vuelva pronto.   I shall tell (have told) him to return soon.
Pídales usted que nos enseñen la pantalla.   Ask them to show us the screen.
Es posible que se hayan marchado.   It is possible that they have left.

When the main verb is in the preterit, imperfect, conditional, or pluperfect tense, the verb in the dependent clause is usually in the <u>imperfect</u> subjunctive, unless the English past perfect tense is used in the dependent clause, in which case the pluperfect subjunctive is used in Spanish:

> **Le pedí** (**pedía**) **que me lo diera.**   I asked (was asking) him to give it to me.
> **No había nadie que pudiese ayudarnos.**   There was no one who could help us.
> **Yo dudaría que Ana hubiese ido de compras.**   I would doubt that Ann had gone shopping.

Contrary to the above statements, the imperfect subjunctive may follow the present, future, or present perfect tense when, as in English, the action of the dependent clause took place in the past:

> **No creo que Juan regresara anoche.**   I don't believe John returned last night.

Ejercicios

A. Lean en español, supliendo la forma correcta del verbo entre paréntesis; usen las dos formas del imperfecto de subjuntivo cuando sea necesario este tiempo:

1. Carolina insiste en que yo (ir) de compras con ella.   2. Ella insistió en que yo (estar) en su casa a las dos.   3. Mi hermano quiere que yo le (comprar) un rollo de película.   4. Yo quería que él lo (meter) en su cámara nueva para probarla. 5. Carolina busca un regalo que le (gustar) a su mamá.   6. Ella deseaba encontrar algo que no (costar) demasiado.   7. No creo que Ricardo (haber) ido a clase hoy. 8. Yo no creía que él se (haber) marchado.

B. Repitan cada oración; luego, al oír una nueva frase inicial, completen la oración, haciendo los cambios necesarios:

1. Yo no quiero que se marchen todavía.   (Yo no quería)
2. Les pediré que vuelvan a reunirse pronto.   (Les pediría)
3. Desean buscar una casa que sea más cómoda.   (Deseaban)
4. No hay nadie que se dé cuenta de eso.   (No había nadie)
5. Es posible que Juan pueda reunir el dinero.   (Era posible)
6. José duda que Jorge siga trabajando en la biblioteca.   (José dudaba)
7. Será mejor que Roberto escoja la cámara para su cumpleaños.   (Sería mejor)
8. No estamos seguros de que hayan hecho el viaje.   (No estábamos seguros de)

IV. EL SUBJUNTIVO EN CLÁUSULAS ADVERBIALES

An adverbial clause, which modifies a verb and indicates *time, purpose, concession, condition, result, negative result,* and the like, is introduced by a conjunction, often a compound with **que** as the last element. If the action has taken place or is an accepted fact, the indicative mood is used; if the action may take place but has not actually been accomplished, the subjunctive is normally used in the clause.

A. Time clauses:

The subjunctive is used after conjunctions of time if the action in the dependent clause has not been completed at the time indicated by the main clause; that is, when the time referred to in the clause is <u>indefinite</u> and <u>future</u>, and therefore <u>uncertain</u>, from the standpoint of the time expressed in the main clause. **Antes (de) que,** *before,* always requires the subjunctive since the action indicated in the clause cannot have taken place.

When the time clause expresses an accomplished fact in the present or past time, or expresses a customary occurrence, the indicative is used.

Common conjunctions which introduce time clauses are:

antes (de) que　before	**después (de) que**　after
así que　as soon as	**hasta que**　until
cuando　when	**luego que**　as soon as
en cuanto　as soon as	**mientras (que)**　while, as long as

Yo estudié hasta que regresó Felipe.　I studied until Philip returned.
Cuando yo veo a Juan, le saludo.　When I see John, I greet him.
En cuanto yo le vea, le saludaré.　As soon as I see him, I shall greet him.
Cuando haya bailes, será mejor usar la cámara de cine.　When there are dances, it will be better to use the movie camera.
Tú habías salido antes de que yo llegara.　You had left before I arrived.
Ana quería leer hasta que Pablo la llamara.　Ann wanted to read until Paul called (should call) her.

B. Concessive and result clauses:

Aunque, *although, even though, even if,* is followed by the subjunctive mood unless the speaker wishes to express a statement as a certainty, or is indicating an accomplished fact, in both of which cases the indicative mood is used:

Aunque sea tarde, he venido a verte.　Even though it may be late, I have come to see you.
Aunque es tarde, he venido a verte.　Although it is late, I have come to see you. (*Certainty implied*)
Aunque yo estaba cansado, fui con él.　Although I was tired, I went with him. (*A fact*)

Two other conjunctions, **de manera que** and **de modo que**, both meaning *so that*, may express result, in which case they are followed by the indicative mood. They may also express purpose, in which case the subjunctive is used. Compare the following sentences (also see section C below):

Juan habló de manera (modo) que le entendimos. John spoke so that (in such a way that) we understood (did understand) him.

Hable usted de manera (modo) que le entendamos. Speak so that we may understand you. (*No certainty that we will*)

NOTE. In certain adverbial constructions if there is no change in subject, the corresponding preposition plus the infinitive is used instead of a clause with the subjunctive:

¿Por qué no metes un rollo en la cámara para probarla? Why don't you put a roll in the camera to (in order that you may) try it?

Aprendan el diálogo de memoria para poder repetirlo. Learn the dialogue by heart in order to be able to (so that you can) repeat it.

C. Purpose, proviso, conditional, negative result clauses:

Certain conjunctions denoting *purpose, proviso, condition, negative result,* and the like, always require the subjunctive because they cannot introduce a statement of fact. By their very meaning they indicate that the action in the clause is uncertain or that the action may not, or did not, actually take place. In addition to **de manera que** and **de modo que,** *so that* (see section B), some other conjunctions of these types are:

a fin de que	in order that	**para que**	in order that
a menos que	unless	**siempre que**	provided that
con tal (de) que	provided that	**sin que**	without

¿Por qué no me llamaste para que te ayudara? Why didn't you call me in order that I might help you?

Prometo acompañarte con tal que consiga el dinero. I promise to go with you provided that I get (obtain) the money.

Los niños salieron sin que los oyera su mamá. The children went out without their mother's hearing them.

Ejercicios

A. Para leer en español, supliendo la forma correcta del verbo entre paréntesis:

1. Siempre empieza la clase en cuanto (entrar) el profesor.
2. Eran las diez de la noche cuando Roberto (regresar) a su cuarto.
3. Vamos a enseñarles la cámara en cuanto (llegar) ellos.

4. La compré aunque me (costar) demasiado.
5. Aunque (llover) esta noche, tendremos que ir al teatro.
6. Dijeron que se marcharían mañana aunque (hacer) mal tiempo.
7. Quédense ustedes en casa hasta que (volver) yo del mercado.
8. No llegarán a tiempo a menos que (darse) prisa.
9. Hable usted de modo que le (oír) bien todos los estudiantes.
10. Traeré el proyector para que usted lo (ver).
11. Mi papá me lo compró para que yo (poder) mirar las películas.
12. Tráigame usted café con tal que (estar) caliente.
13. Habíamos comido antes de que ellos (haber) vuelto a casa.
14. Juan no podrá ir con ustedes sin que yo le (dar) el dinero.
15. No ganará mucho mientras que (trabajar) en esta tienda.

B. Repitan cada pregunta; luego, contéstenla afirmativamente, agregando
   (*adding*) una cláusula introducida por la frase **aunque Pablo**, según el
   modelo.

MODELO: ¿Hará Ud. el viaje?   ¿Hará Ud. el viaje?   Sí, aunque Pablo lo
                                        haga.

1. ¿Escogerá Ud. una cámara?   4. ¿Mirará Ud. las transparencias?
2. ¿Buscará Ud. una pantalla?   5. ¿Irá Ud. de compras hoy?
3. ¿Sacará Ud. muchas fotografías? 6. ¿Seguirá Ud. trabajando allí?

C. Para expresar en español:

1. When I take a trip, I take many photographs.   2. As soon as I have time, I
shall buy two or three rolls of film.   3. Mary's aunt will stay with Jane while her
parents are (may be) in Mexico.   4. It will be better to use the movie camera when
there are (may be) popular dances.   5. Before you leave, I want you to put a roll
of film in the camera in order to try it.   6. I waited for Helen in order that she
might help me to select a dress.   7. Robert said he would come to my room provided
that I should show him some slides.   8. Richard promised to accompany us unless
he should have to work in his father's store.

V. EL SUBJUNTIVO EN FRASES CONDICIONALES

In earlier lessons we have used simple conditions in which the present indicative is
used in the English *if*-clause and the same tense in the Spanish **si**-clause (see Lección
seis):

   Si Juan está en su cuarto,   **está estudiando.**
   If John is in his room,   he is studying.

Si ellos tienen dinero,	**harán el viaje.**
If they have (the) money,	they will take the trip.

Simple conditions are also expressed in past time:

Si Ana recibió (ha recibido) el cheque,	**compró el vestido.**
If Ann received (has received) the check,	she bought the dress.

In a **si**-clause which implies that a statement is contrary to fact (*i.e.*, not true) in the present, Spanish uses either form of the imperfect subjunctive. A contrary-to-fact sentence may also be expressed in the past, in which case the pluperfect subjunctive is used in the **si**-clause (see the second example below).

The conclusion or main clause of a conditional sentence is usually expressed by the conditional (or conditional perfect), as in English. (In reading you will also find the **-ra** form of the imperfect or pluperfect subjunctive in the main, or result, clause; in the exercises of this text only the conditional or conditional perfect will be used.)

Si yo tuviera (tuviese) dinero,	**haría el viaje.**
If I had (the) money (*but I don't*),	I would take the trip.
Si Pablo hubiese (hubiera) venido,	**me habría llamado.**
If Paul had come (*but he didn't*),	he would have called me.

Como si, *as if*, also expresses a contrary-to-fact condition, in which case the conclusion, or main clause, is understood:

> **¡Gastas el dinero como si fueras millonario!** You spend money as if you were a millionaire!

Similarly, either form of the imperfect subjunctive is used in the **si**-clause to express a condition that may (might) not be fulfilled in the future. Whenever the English sentence has *should, were to*, in the *if*-clause, the imperfect subjunctive is used in Spanish:

Si fuésemos (fuéramos) juntos,	**nos divertiríamos mucho.**
If we should (were to) go together,	we would have a very good time.
Si vinieran (viniesen) mañana,	**harían el trabajo.**
If they should (were to) come tomorrow,	they would do the work.

NOTE. The future and conditional indicative and the present subjunctive tenses are not used after **si** meaning *if*. When **si** means *whether*, the indicative must be used: **No sé si podrán venir**, *I do not know whether they will be able to come.*

Ejercicios

A. Repitan cada frase; luego, al oír otra cláusula con **si**, completen la frase:

1. Si Carlos tiene dinero, comprará un traje.
   Si Carlos tuviera dinero,
   Si Carlos hubiera tenido dinero,
2. Si ella ve a Marta, le dará la cámara.
   Si ella viese a Marta,
   Si ella hubiese visto a Marta,
3. Si vamos juntos, nos divertiremos.
   Si fuéramos juntos,
   Si hubiéramos ido juntos,

B. Repitan la frase; luego, cambien la forma de los verbos, según el modelo.

MODELO: Si tienen tiempo, irán de   Si tienen tiempo, irán de compras.
         compras.   Si tuvieran tiempo, irían de compras.

1. Si José vuelve a casa, nos llamará.
2. Si María está en su cuarto, escribirá la composición.
3. Si vamos a México, sacaremos muchas fotografías.
4. Si no es tarde, charlaré con usted un rato.

MODELO: Si la compras, podrás usarla.   Si la compras, podrás usarla.
                                    Si la comprases, podrías usarla.

5. Si metes un rollo de película, podrás probar la cámara.
6. Si lo llevas mañana, lo revelarán pronto.
7. Si traen el proyector, veremos las transparencias.
8. Si sigo trabajando, reuniré bastante dinero para el viaje.

MODELO: Si han venido, le habrán visto.   Si han venido, le habrán visto.
                                    Si hubieran venido, le habrían visto.

9. Si ella ha ido de compras, habrá comprado muchas cosas.
10. Si han encontrado algo, se lo habrán enviado a su mamá.

RESUMEN

A. Repitan cada frase; luego, al oír una nueva conjunción, substitúyanla en la frase:

1. *En cuanto* yo tenga tiempo, voy a escoger un proyector. (*Cuando*)
2. *Después que* llegue Miguel, nos marcharemos. (*Antes de que*)

3. No podré acompañarte *a menos que* él me preste el dinero.   (*sin que*)
4. Todos se reunirán aquí *con tal que* vengan los otros.   (*después que*)
5. Yo traje la cámara *para que* usted la viera.   (*de modo que*)
6. Decidieron ir al campo *aunque* lloviese.   (*a menos que*)
7. Ellos querían quedarse aquí *hasta que* llegase el médico.   (*aunque*)
8. Se lo di a Luisa *de manera que* pudiera comprar un regalo.   (*para que*)

B. Lean en español; luego, repitan cada frase, comenzando con las palabras entre paréntesis y cambiando el verbo de la cláusula subordinada a la forma del imperfecto de subjuntivo que termina en **-ra**:

1. Queremos que ellos *vayan* de compras con nosotros.   (Queríamos)
2. Yo no creo que Felipe *haya* podido hacer el viaje.   (Yo no creía)
3. Pídale usted al señor Díaz que *traiga* su proyector.   (Jorge le pidió)
4. No será posible que *vuelvan* antes del mes de mayo.   (No sería)
5. No vemos a nadie que *tenga* cámara de cine.   (No vimos)
6. ¿Hay alguien que *conozca* a aquel señor?   (¿Había alguien . . . ?)
7. Ella dice que saldrá en cuanto *vuelvan* los niños.   (Ella dijo que saldría)
8. Yo le llamaré para que te *ayude* a escoger una maleta.   (Yo le llamé)
9. Creen que él irá a verlos aunque *sea* tarde.   (Creían que él iría)
10. Ana quiere esperar hasta que *lleguen* sus amigas.   (Ana quería esperar)

C. Usos del subjuntivo en frases condicionales.   Para expresar en español:

1. If Robert has the money, he will buy a camera.
2. If Robert were to go to Mexico, he would take many photographs.
3. If he had had time, he would have tried out the camera.
4. If Charles arrives before six o'clock, we shall eat supper downtown.
5. If he should come earlier, we would look at some slides.
6. If I had seen a good projector, I would have bought it.
7. Raymond talks as if he had a cold.
8. I know that if he stayed in bed, he was ill.

D. Repaso de algunas expresiones usadas en las Lecciones siete, ocho y nueve.   Para expresar en español:

1. You are welcome.
2. I should say so!
3. He thanked me for the gift.
4. Pick us up at five, please.
5. What's the matter with him?
6. Jane doesn't feel well.
7. She is absent today.
8. Martha only has a cold.
9. It is nothing serious.
10. I believe so.
11. At any rate.
12. He left at about four o'clock.
13. How do you like the idea?
14. I think it is wonderful!

LECCIÓN DIEZ

Repaso de los adjetivos y de los pronombres
demostrativos.   Los adjetivos posesivos.   Los
pronombres posesivos.   Otros usos del subjuntivo.
Usos de los adjetivos como substantivos.
Los diminutivos

COMPRANDO UN RADIO[1]

(*Ricardo y Tomás entran en una tienda donde venden aparatos de radio.   Se acerca un dependiente.*)

DEPENDIENTE.	Buenos días, señores. ¿En qué puedo servirles?
RICARDO.	Busco un radio de onda corta. ¿Quiere enseñarme algunos modelos de este año, por favor?
DEPENDIENTE.	¿Le interesa a usted un aparato con tocadiscos o uno de radio solo?
RICARDO.	No me interesa el tocadiscos; nuestro televisor tiene uno.
DEPENDIENTE.	Pues aquí hay dos de la misma marca. Éste tiene doce tubos, y ése, ocho. ¿Quiere usted que yo ponga éste o ése?
RICARDO.	Ponga usted el más pequeño, por favor.·
DEPENDIENTE.	A ver si puedo sintonizar una emisora mexicana. A esta hora es difícil a causa de la estática . . . No se oye bien . . . Trataré de sintonizar una emisora de Nueva York. ¡Ah, sí! ¿Qué les parece?
TOMÁS.	(*Dirigiéndose a Ricardo.*) El tono es maravilloso. Me recuerda el mío.
RICARDO.	Es como el de mi hermanita; no he oído el tuyo . . . (*Al dependiente.*) Pues antes de decidirme, quisiera escuchar el otro. (*El dependiente lo pone y escuchan unos momentos.*)

[1] For *radio* (*set*), **el radio** is used; for *radio* as a means of communication, **la radio** is used.

TOMÁS.   No me gusta tanto como el otro.

DEPENDIENTE.   Ni a mí[1] tampoco.   Como ustedes pueden ver, tenemos modelos de
                otras marcas.   Ése tiene frecuencia modulada.   Voy a ponerlo . . .

TOMÁS.   (*A Ricardo*.)   Los de esa marca son excelentes.   Un amigo mío tiene
                uno y está encantado con él.

RICARDO.   (*Al dependiente*.)   Este último me parece el mejor.   ¿Cuánto cuesta?

DEPENDIENTE.   Ochenta dólares.   Y a ese precio es una ganga.

RICARDO.   ¡Dios mío!   Tal vez usted tenga razón; pero antes de comprarlo
                quisiera consultarlo con mi padre.

DEPENDIENTE.   Como usted quiera;[2] pero no debiera esperar mucho.   Es un modelo
                muy popular.

a causa de because of	**la ganga** bargain
el aparato (de radio) (radio) set	**maravilloso, -a** marvelous
consultar to discuss, consult	**recordar (ue)** to remind (one of)
decidirse to make up one's mind	**sintonizar** to tune in
la emisora broadcasting station	**el televisor** television set
la estática static	**el tocadiscos** record player
la frecuencia frequency	**el tono** tone
frecuencia modulada FM	**el tubo** tube

A. Busquen en el diálogo las frases que correspondan a las siguientes:

1. where they sell radio sets.   2. What can I do for you?   3. a short-wave radio.
4. Will you show me . . .?   5. Do you want me to turn on this one?   6. Let's see
whether I can tune in . . .   7. because of the static.   8. I shall try to tune in . . .
9. How do you like it?   10. Addressing Richard.   11. It reminds me of mine.
12. It's like my little sister's.   13. Before making up my mind.   14. I should (would)
like to hear.   15. I don't like it so much as the other (one).   16. The ones (Those) of
that brand.   17. This last one.   18. I should like to discuss it.   19. As you like
(may wish).   20. you shouldn't wait long.

B. Para contestar en español:

Preguntas sobre el diálogo

1. ¿Qué les pregunta el dependiente a Ricardo y a Tomás?   2. ¿Qué contesta
Ricardo?   3. ¿Le interesa a Ricardo un aparato con tocadiscos?   4. ¿Cuál de los
dos radios escuchan primero?   5. ¿Por qué no se oye bien la emisora mexicana?
6. ¿Qué dice Tomás del tono del aparato?   7. ¿Qué aparato pone por fin el
dependiente?   8. ¿Por qué no lo compra Ricardo?

[1] **Ni a mí tampoco,** *Neither do I.*   Remember that the prepositional form must be used when the verb (**gustar**
here) is understood.   [2] Note the use of the subjunctive here after the conjunction **como,** *as,* expressing
indefiniteness.

Aplicación del diálogo

1. ¿Cuántos aparatos de radio tiene usted? 2. ¿Tiene usted un radio de onda corta? 3. ¿Tiene frecuencia modulada? 4. ¿Qué programas extranjeros ha escuchado usted? 5. ¿Tiene usted televisor en su cuarto? 6. ¿Qué programas de televisión le gustan a usted? 7. ¿Tiene usted tocadiscos? 8. ¿Se oyen emisoras mexicanas desde esta parte del país?

NOTAS GRAMATICALES

I. REPASO DE LOS ADJETIVOS Y DE LOS PRONOMBRES DEMOSTRATIVOS

A. A demonstrative adjective agrees in gender and number with the noun it modifies and, in Spanish, is repeated before nouns in a series. **Este** points out persons or things near the speaker; **ese**, persons or things near to, or associated with, the person addressed; **aquel**, persons or things distant from the speaker or person addressed, or unrelated to either. (Do not confuse the demonstrative, which points out the noun to which it refers, with the relative pronoun **que**, *that*.)

M. Sing.	*F. Sing.*		*M. Pl.*	*F. Pl.*	
este	**esta**	this	**estos**	**estas**	these
ese	**esa**	that (*nearby*)	**esos**	**esas**	those (*nearby*)
aquel	**aquella**	that (*distant*)	**aquellos**	**aquellas**	those (*distant*)

    este hombre y esta mujer   this man and woman
    esos aparatos cerca de usted   those sets near you
    aquella joven allí   that young lady there (*distant*)

B. The demonstrative pronouns are formed by placing an accent on the stressed syllable of the adjectives: **éste, ése, aquél**, etc. The use of the pronouns corresponds to that of the adjectives, except that singular forms often mean *this* (*one*), *that* (*one*). They may be used as subject or object of the verb, or they may stand alone.

    There are three neuter pronouns (**esto**, *this*, **eso**, *that*, **aquello**, *that*) which are used when the antecedent is a statement, a general idea, or something which has not been identified. Since there are no neuter adjectives, an accent is not required on these three forms.

    Me gustan ese radio y éste.   I like that radio (set) and this one.
    ¿Quiere usted que yo ponga éste o ése?   Do you want me to turn on this
       one or that one?
    Este modelo y aquéllos son nuevos.   This model and those (*yonder*) are new.

¿Cuál de las marcas prefieres? ¿Ésta? Which one of the brands do you prefer? This one?
¿Qué es esto? What is this?
Eso no es muy interesante. That isn't very interesting.

C. The demonstrative pronoun **éste** is used to indicate *the latter* (that is, the nearer), and **aquél**, *the former*. Contrary to English usage, in Spanish, when both are used, *the latter* always comes first:

Ana y Marta no vienen porque ésta no se siente bien. Ann and Martha aren't coming because the latter doesn't feel well.
Ricardo y su hermana van de compras; ésta busca un radio y aquél, un tocadiscos. Richard and his sister go shopping; the former is looking for a record player and the latter, a radio.

D. We found in Lección ocho that the Spanish definite article replaces the demonstrative before **que.** Similarly, it replaces the demonstrative before **de. El (la, los, las) de** means *that (those) of, the one(s) of (with, in)*; sometimes in English this construction is expressed by a possessive (first two examples):

mi abrigo y el de Felipe my topcoat and Philip's (that of Philip)
estas blusas y las de Ana these blouses and Ann's (those of Ann)
las del pelo rubio the ones (girls) with (the) blond hair
la del sombrero rojo the one with (in) the red hat

The neuter article **lo** followed by **de** means *that (matter, affair) of*:

Lo de su amigo me interesa. That (affair) of your friend interests me.

Ejercicios

A. Para contestar afirmativamente, empleando el pronombre demostrativo correspondiente.

MODELOS: ¿Quiere Ud. este traje?   Sí, quiero ése.
          ¿Es barata esta marca?   Sí, ésa es barata.

1. ¿Le gusta a Ud. este radio?   3. ¿Tiene buen tono esa marca?
2. ¿Le interesan a Ud. estos aparatos? 4. ¿Escuchas aquellas canciones?

5. ¿Son caras esas cámaras?   7. ¿Prefieres aquel radio de onda corta?
6. ¿Son mexicanos esos discos?   8. ¿Sintoniza Ud. aquella emisora?

B. Para expresar en español:

1. This building and that one (*distant*) are new.   2. Those radios and these have a
marvelous tone.   3. I prefer this small set to that one (*nearby*).   4. Shall I turn on
this television set or that one (*distant*)?   5. Here are two brands; this one has ten
tubes, and that one, eight.   6. The clerk says it is a bargain, but I do not believe
that.   7. John and Mary entered the store; the latter was looking for a record player.
8. Jane's dress and Helen's are very pretty.   9. Who is that boy, the one with red
hair?   10. That girl (*distant*) and the one in the green hat are cousins of Paul.

II. LOS ADJETIVOS POSESIVOS

Possessive adjectives agree in gender and number with the thing possessed (that is,
with the noun modified), not with the possessor, as in English.   The short, or unstressed, forms precede the nouns, and they are repeated before nouns in a series in
Spanish.

SINGULAR	PLURAL	
mi	**mis**	my
tu	**tus**	your (*fam.*)
su	**sus**	his, her, its, your (*polite*)
nuestro, -a	**nuestros, -as**	our
vuestro, -a	**vuestros, -as**	your (*fam.*)
su	**sus**	their, your

The long, or stressed, forms follow the noun.   They are used for clearness and
emphasis, in direct address, to translate *of mine, of his,* etc., after the verb **ser**, and in a
few set phrases.   These forms are:

mío, mía	**míos, mías**	my, of mine
tuyo, tuya	**tuyos, tuyas**	your (*fam.*), of yours
suyo, suya	**suyos, suyas**	his, her, your (*polite*), its, of his, of hers, of yours, of its
nuestro, nuestra	**nuestros, nuestras**	our, of ours
vuestro, vuestra	**vuestros, vuestras**	your (*fam. pl.*), of yours
suyo, suya	**suyos, suyas**	their, your (*pl.*), of theirs, of yours

¿Traes tus libros?   Are you bringing your books?
Ana tiene dos libros míos.   Ann has two books of mine.
Bárbara y una amiga suya vienen.   Barbara and a friend of hers are coming.
Carlos, ¿son suyas estas cosas?   Charles, are these things yours?
Ellos son buenos amigos míos (nuestros).   They are good friends of mine (ours).
Querida (amiga) mía: My dear (friend):
¡Dios mío!   Heavens!

Since **su(s)** and **suyo** (-a, -os, -as) have several meanings, the forms **de él, de ella,** etc., may be substituted to make the meaning clear.   (The prepositional form is not used for any long possessive other than **suyo, -a, -os, -as**).

> **Me gusta su casa.**   I like his (her, your, their) house.
> **Me gusta la casa de él (de ella, de usted).**   I like his (her, your) house.
> **¿Es de ellos este coche?**   —**No, es de él.**   Is this car theirs?   —No, it is his.

Ejercicios

A. Repitan cada frase; luego, repítanla otra vez empleando una frase con una forma de **suyo**, según el modelo.

MODELO: Carlos y una amiga *de él*   Carlos y una amiga de él
                                            Carlos y una amiga suya

1. este traje *de él*   5. aquel tocadiscos *de ellos*
2. ese radio *de ella*   6. esta cámara *de él*
3. aquellas transparencias *de ellos*   7. esas películas *de ustedes*
4. esos discos *de usted*   8. varias fotografías *de ella*

B. Repitan cada pregunta; luego, contéstenla afirmativamente, según los modelos.

MODELOS: ¿Es nuestra esta cámara?   ¿Es nuestra esta cámara?
                                            Sí, es nuestra.

         ¿Son míos (suyos) esos libros?   ¿Son míos (suyos) esos libros?
                                            Sí, son suyos (míos).

1. ¿Es nuestro aquel disco?   5. ¿Es nuestra aquella guitarra?
2. ¿Son míos estos lápices?   6. ¿Son nuestros aquellos dibujos?
3. ¿Son suyas estas transparencias?   7. ¿Es tuyo ese televisor?
4. ¿Es suyo este radio?   8. ¿Son mías esas revistas?

III. LOS PRONOMBRES POSESIVOS

The possessive pronouns are formed by using the definite article with the long forms of the possessive adjectives. Remember that after **ser** the article is usually omitted.

el mío	**la mía**	**los míos**	**las mías**	mine
el tuyo	**la tuya**	**los tuyos**	**las tuyas**	yours (*fam.*)
el suyo	**la suya**	**los suyos**	**las suyas**	his, hers, its, yours (*polite*)
el nuestro	**la nuestra**	**los nuestros**	**las nuestras**	ours
el vuestro	**la vuestra**	**los vuestros**	**las vuestras**	yours (*fam.*)
el suyo	**la suya**	**los suyos**	**las suyas**	theirs, yours

mi radio; el mío, el nuestro   my radio; mine, ours
nuestra casa; la mía, la nuestra   our house; mine, ours
Ana, yo tengo los libros míos y los tuyos.   Ann, I have my books and yours.
Señor López, ¿tiene usted los suyos?   Mr. López, do you have yours?
Juan tiene la pluma suya y las mías.   John has his pen and mine.

Since **el suyo** (**la suya, los suyos, las suyas**) may mean *his, hers, its, yours* (polite), *theirs,* these pronouns may be clarified by using **el de él, el de ella,** etc. The article agrees with the thing possessed:

> **Carlos mira el suyo.**   Charles looks at his (hers, yours, theirs).
> **El coche de ellos y el de ustedes están aquí.**   Their car and yours are here.
> **Nuestros padres y los de ella vienen.**   Our parents and hers are coming.

Ejercicios

A. Repitan cada frase; luego, repítanla otra vez, substituyendo el substantivo con el pronombre posesivo, o con la frase **el (la) de él (de ella)**, etcétera.

MODELOS: Lleva *su equipaje.*   Lleva su equipaje.   Lleva el suyo.
Tengo la *maleta de Juan.*   Tengo la maleta de Juan.   Tengo la de él.

1. Ana tiene *su blusa.*
2. Vamos a *nuestra casa.*
3. ¿Tiene ella *su bolsa?*
4. Pablo lleva *mis cámaras.*
5. El *jardín de mi mamá* es bonito.
6. Las *flores de Inés* son hermosas.
7. ¿Quieres ver *nuestras películas?*
8. Juan, no conduzcas *tu coche* hoy.

B. Para contestar afirmativamente, según los modelos.

MODELOS: ¿Tienes tu cámara?   Sí, tengo la mía.
         ¿Quieren ellos sus fotos?   Sí, quieren las suyas.

1. ¿Ve Ud. su coche?   5. ¿Mira Ana su televisor?
2. ¿Escuchan Uds. su tocadiscos?   6. ¿Tiene Carlos sus compras?
3. ¿Traen Uds. sus composiciones?   7. ¿Desean ellas sus regalos?
4. ¿Buscas tus guantes?   8. ¿Lleva él su maleta?

C. Para expresar en español:

1. I want you to bring your camera and mine. 2. Tell them to take their skates and yours. 3. John doubts that his sister and mine will go to the movie. 4. Wait a moment in order that I may give you her composition and his. 5. Let me bring my skis and hers tomorrow morning. 6. Whose records are these? —Do you (*fam. sing.*) have mine?

IV. OTROS USOS DEL SUBJUNTIVO

Uses of the subjunctive as the main verb in a sentence, other than in polite commands and in negative familiar commands (see Cuarta lección preliminar), are:

A. After **tal vez** and **quizá(s)**, and less commonly **acaso**, all meaning *perhaps*, when doubt or uncertainty is implied:

     Quizás él ha llegado.   Perhaps he has arrived.   (*Certainty implied*)
     Tal vez tenga usted razón.   Perhaps you may be right.   (*Uncertainty implied*)

B. To make a statement or question milder or more polite (sometimes called a softened statement or question), the **-ra** imperfect subjunctive forms of **deber**, **querer**, and sometimes **poder**, are used:

     Debo ayudar a mi mamá.   I must (ought to) help my mother.   (*Strong obligation*)
     Yo debiera llamarla.   I should call her.   (*Milder obligation*)
     Quiero ir al cine.   I want to go to the movie.   (*Strong wish*)
     Yo quisiera ir contigo.   I should like to go with you.   (*More polite*)
     ¿Pudieras esperar un momento?   Could you wait a moment?   (*Polite question*)

NOTE.   Remember that the conditional of **gustar** also means *should (would) like* and may be used instead of **quisiera**, etc.: **Nos (Me) gustaría verlos**, *We (I) should like to see them.*

C. After **¡Ojalá!**, with or without **que**, *Would that! I wish that!* The present subjunctive is used in an exclamatory wish which refers to something which may happen in the future.   The imperfect subjunctive is used to express a wish concerning something that is contrary to fact in the present, and the pluperfect subjunctive to express a wish concerning something that was contrary to fact in the past.

> **¡Ojalá (que) ella me llame!**   Would that she call me!
> **¡Ojalá que supiesen eso!**   Would that they knew that!
> **¡Ojalá hubieran vuelto antes!**   (How) I wish they had returned before!

Ejercicios

A. Para contestar negativamente, agregando una frase introducida por **pero quisiera**, y substituyendo el objeto del verbo con el pronombre correspondiente.

MODELO: ¿Has visto el radio de él?   No, pero quisiera verlo.

1. ¿Has llamado a tu hermana?   3. ¿Has oído mis discos?
2. ¿Has comprado el televisor?   4. ¿Has sintonizado aquella emisora?

B. Para cambiar al imperfecto de subjuntivo, según los modelos.

MODELOS: Quiero probar la cámara.   Quisiera probar la cámara.
Quiero que tú saques la foto.   Quisiera que tú sacaras la foto.
Debo llamar a mi mamá.   Debiera llamar a mi mamá.

1. Quiero enseñarle este modelo.   5. Queremos que Uds. oigan aquél.
2. Queremos escuchar el otro.   6. Debo consultar eso con mi padre.
3. Quieren comprar el más grande.   7. Debemos ayudar a aquel señor.
4. ¿Quieres que yo ponga ése?   8. No deben esperar mucho.

C. Para contestar con una oración introducida por **tal vez (quizás)**.

MODELO: ¿Volverán ellos esta noche?   Tal vez (Quizás) vuelvan esta noche.

1. ¿Vendrá ella mañana?   3. ¿Les interesará el tocadiscos?
2. ¿Encontrarán una ganga allí?   4. ¿Escogerán otra marca?

D. Para cambiar al presente de subjuntivo después de **¡Ojalá que!**

MODELO: ¿Leerán la novela?   ¡Ojalá que lean la novela!

1. ¿Llegarán esta noche?   3. ¿Se divertirán en la fiesta?
2. ¿Podrá ella visitarnos?   4. ¿Buscará él otra casa?

Para cambiar al imperfecto y al pluscuamperfecto de subjuntivo después de **¡Ojalá que!**, siguiendo los modelos.

MODELOS: No creen lo que él dijo.   ¡Ojalá que creyeran lo que él dijo!
        No han llegado a tiempo.   ¡Ojalá que hubieran llegado a tiempo!

5. No están en casa.   8. No van a Nueva York.
6. Ella no sabe la canción.   9. No han vuelto del viaje.
7. No pueden pasar por aquí.   10. Él no ha visto la exposición.

V. USOS DE LOS ADJETIVOS COMO SUBSTANTIVOS

Many adjectives may be used with the definite article, demonstratives, numerals, and other limiting adjectives, to form nouns. In this case the adjective agrees in gender and number with the noun understood. Remember that adjectives of nationality are also used as nouns: **Luis es mexicano,** *Louis is (a) Mexican.*

Este último me parece el mejor. This last one seems to me (to be) the best (one).
No me gusta tanto como el otro. I don't like it so much as the other one.
Ponga usted el más pequeño. Turn on the smaller one.
Una joven compró las blancas. A young lady bought the white ones (*f.*).

Ejercicio

Repitan cada frase; luego, repítanla otra vez, empleando el adjetivo como substantivo.

MODELO: ¿Te gusta la blusa roja?   ¿Te gusta la blusa roja?   ¿Te gusta la roja?

1. La casa amarilla es del señor Díaz. 2. Me gusta este televisor grande.
3. Quieren buscar una casa más grande. 4. Prefiero ver unos zapatos negros.

5. Esta última blusa es muy bonita. 6. ¿Puede usted sintonizar una emisora mexicana? 7. ¿Cuánto cuesta la otra marca? 8. Miramos varios aparatos nuevos. 9. Yo quisiera escuchar algunos discos españoles. 10. ¿Qué les parece a ustedes este radio pequeño?

VI. LOS DIMINUTIVOS

In Spanish diminutive endings are often used to express not only small size, but affection, pity, scorn, ridicule, and the like. The most common endings are: **-ito, -a**; **-illo, -a**; **-(e)cito, -a**; **-(e)cillo, -a**. Frequently, the use of these suffixes with nouns precludes the need for adjectives. For the choice of ending rely upon observation. A final vowel is often dropped before adding the ending.

hermana	sister	**hermanita**	little sister
hermano	brother	**hermanito**	little brother
Juan	John	**Juanito**	Johnny
pueblo	town	**pueblecito**	small town, village
señora	lady, woman	**señorita**	young lady (woman)
ventana	window	**ventanilla**	ticket window

Applied to baptismal names these endings indicate affection, with no implication of size: **Juanita**, *Jane*; **Anita**,[1] *Annie*; **Tomasito**, *Tommy*. Sometimes a change in spelling is necessary to preserve the sound of a consonant when a final vowel is dropped: **Diego**, *James*, and **Dieguito**, *Jimmie*. Similarly, note the change in spelling in the adverb **poco**, *little* (quantity), and **poquito**, *very little*; also, in the noun **taza**, *cup*, and **tacita**, *small (tiny) cup*.

Give the base word to which each diminutive suffix has been added:

casita	small house, cottage	**mesita**	small table, stand
cosilla	small thing, trifle	**momentito**	(short) moment
florecita	small (tiny) flower	**mujercita**	pleasant little woman
golpecito	slight blow, tap	**pequeñito, -a**	very small, tiny
hijito	(dear) son	**piedrecita**	small stone, pebble
hombrecito	nice little man	**pobrecito**	poor boy (man, thing)
jovencito	nice young fellow (man)	**regalito**	small gift

---

[1] The diminutives given in the rest of this section are not listed in the end vocabulary since they are not used elsewhere in this text. Watch for similar and other uses of diminutives in reading.

RESUMEN

A. Repitan la frase; luego, repítanla otra vez, siguiendo el modelo.

MODELO: mi casa y la casa de Ana   mi casa y la casa de Ana
                                          mi casa y la de Ana

1. estos jardines y el jardín de mi madre.
2. estas mujeres y la mujer del vestido amarillo.
3. este edificio y el edificio de piedra.
4. esta señorita y la señorita del pelo negro.
5. este radio y el radio de mi hermano.
6. aquellos discos y los discos de música mexicana.
7. este lugar y el lugar que visitó él.
8. estas dos marcas y la marca que nos ha enseñado usted.
9. estos modelos y los modelos que él me mostró.
10. aquella emisora de Nueva York y las emisoras que oímos ayer.

B. Escuchen la pregunta; luego, contéstenla afirmativamente empleando el pronombre posesivo, siguiendo los modelos.

MODELOS: ¿Es tuya esta bolsa?   Sí, es mía.
         ¿Son de ella estos zapatos?   Sí, son suyos.

1. ¿Es tuyo este tocadiscos?   5. ¿Son de él estos guantes?
2. ¿Es mío este paquete?   6. ¿Son de ustedes esas flores?
3. ¿Es de usted ese proyector?   7. ¿Son tuyas esas revistas?
4. ¿Es nuestra esa cámara?   8. ¿Son de María estos discos?

C. Otros usos del subjuntivo y usos de los adjetivos como substantivos.   Para expresar en español:

1. I should like to buy the white blouse, not the green one.
2. You ought to look at this red hat, not the blue one.
3. Would that she liked this one as much as the other one!
4. Perhaps he may prefer small cars to larger ones.
5. Would you like to take her those yellow roses instead of the red ones?
6. Which of the brands do you like, this one or the other one?

D. Usos de los adjetivos y pronombres posesivos.   Para expresar en español:

1. Is he a friend of yours?   —Yes, he is a friend of mine.
2. Is this camera ours?   —Yes, it is ours, not hers.

3. This composition is not mine.   Is it yours (*two ways*)?
4. They listen to their radio, and we listen to ours.
5. These rolls of film are mine, and that one is yours (*fam.*).
6. This hat is Jane's; it is not yours.
7. Heavens!   I have put on your gloves, not mine.
8. Mary and several (girl) friends of hers are going to the meeting.

Interior y púlpito de la iglesia de la Compañía,
Quito, Ecuador

Iglesia de San Agustín Acolman, México

LA PINTURA EN LA AMÉRICA ESPAÑOLA

CABEZA DE JAGUAR (detalle)
Mosaico de plumas, hecho en el Perú, hace novecientos años
Cortesía, The Brooklyn Museum
The A. Augustus Healy Fund
Fotografía de Andreas Feininger

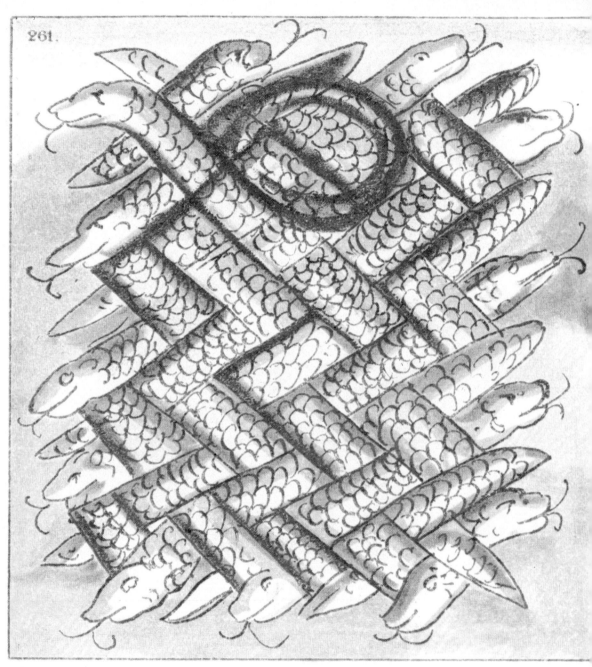

PINTURA AZTECA
Obra de un artista de la época prehispana
Cortesía, Biblioteca, Museo Nacional de Antropología e Historia, México, D. F.
Fotografía de Bradley Smith, New York

LA ORACIÓN EN EL HUERTO
Cortesía, Museo de San Carlos
Colección, Instituto Nacional de
Bellas Artes, México, D. F.

CABRERA

LA VIRGEN Y EL NIÑO CORONADOS, 1762
Cortesía, Philadelphia Museum of Art
Dr. Robert H. Lamborn Collection
Fotografía de Alfred J. Wyatt

Anónimo EL NACIMIENTO DE CRISTO
Cortesía, Instituto Nacional de Bellas Artes, México, D. F.

RIVERA

COMPOSICIÓN CON RELOJ, 1926-27
*Cortesía, Museo Nacional de Bellas Artes,
Buenos Aires, Argentina*

REVOLUCIÓN, GERMINACIÓN (mural), 1926-27
*Cortesía, Escuela Nacional de Agricultura, Chapingo, México
Fotografía de Bradley Smith, New York*

OROZCO

LAS SOLDADERAS, ca. 1930
Cortesía, Museo Nacional de Arte Moderno, Chapultepec, I.N.B.A., México, D. F.
Fotografía de Bradley Smith, New York

ECO DE UN GRITO, 1937
Collection, The Museum of Modern Art, New York. Gift of Edward M. M. Warburg

TAMAYO

VENDEDORAS DE FRUTAS, 1952
Cortesía, Albright-Knox Art Gallery,
Buffalo, New York
Gift of Seymour H. Knox

LA LLAMADA DE LA REVOLUCIÓN, 1935
Colección de Pascual Gutiérrez Roldán
Fotografía de Bradley Smith, New York

José Sabogal AGUADORAS (Water Bearers), 1951
Cortesía, San Francisco Museum of Art
Gift of Mr. and Mrs. Garfield Warner

MÉRIDA

EL PRESENTE ETERNO, 1944
Cortesia, Museum of Art, Rhode Island School of Design, Providence, R. I.

TORRES GARCÍA

ARTE CONSTRUCTIVO, 1942
*Cortesía, Museo Nacional de Bellas Artes,
Buenos Aires, Argentina*

1943 AMÉRICA, 1943
*Cortesía, Museum of Art, Rhode Island
School of Design, Providence, R. I.*

VERGARA GREZ

EL SOL EN LA LUNA, 1964
*Cortesía, R. Vergara Grez y Antonio R. Romera,
Santiago, Chile*

SIMETRÍA DINÁMICA
*Cortesía, R. Vergara Grez y Antonio R. Romera,
Santiago, Chile*

SOTO

CURVAS INMATERIALES VERDES Y NEGRAS, 1966
(madera y metal)
Cortesía, Museum of Art, Rhode Island School of Design, Providence, R. I.

MAC ENTYRE

EN VIOLETA, 1966
Cortesía, Museum of Art, Rhode Island School of Design, Providence, R. I.

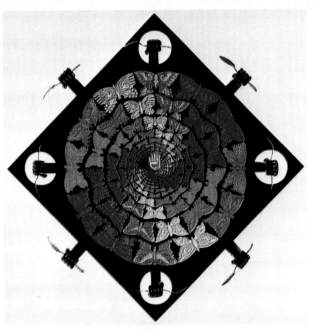

FRIEDEBERG

CONFESIONES DE UN ERIZO ICONOCLASTA
*Cortesía, Consejo Nacional de Turismo de México y
Galería Antonio Souza, México, D. F.*

CUEVAS

AUTORRETRATO
Cortesía, José Luis Cuevas y Galería de Arte Mexicano

LECTURA V

PRESENTACIÓN

A. Estudio de palabras

1. Approximate cognates.   Pronounce and note the English meaning of each word: aptitud, *aptitude*; arcaico, *archaic*; cerámica, *ceramics, pottery*; claustro, *cloister*; ecuestre, *equestrian*; esencia, *essence*; ético, *ethical*; gótico, *Gothic*; inmenso, *immense*; majestuoso, *majestic*; orquesta, *orchestra*; principio, *principle*; régimen,[1] *regime, rule*; sinfónico, *symphonic, symphony*; asegurar, *to assure*; florecer, *to flourish*; manifestarse, *to be manifest*; prevalecer, *to prevail*.

Pronounce and give the English meaning of the following Spanish words which begin with e- before a consonant group, but which lack the initial *e* in English: escena, escuela, escultura, espacio, especial, espontáneo, estado, estatua, estilo.

2. Compare the meanings of the following groups of related words: arquitecto, arquitectura, arquitectónico; arte, artista, artístico; carácter, característica (*noun*), característico (*adj.*); colonia, colonial, colonizador; composición, compositor, componer; escultor, escultura, escultórico; extraño, extranjero; importante, importancia, importar, *to be important* (but see below, under deceptive cognates); invención, inventivo; mural (*noun and adj.*), muralista, muralismo; música, músico (*noun*), musical; origen, original; pintar, pintor, pintura; pueblo, poblador, población; rey, reino, virreinato, *viceroyalty*; técnica (*noun*), tecnológico (*adj.*); tinte (*noun*), *dye*, *dyeing*, tintóreo (*adj.*), *dyeing, tinctorial*.

Find in this Lectura the Spanish adjectives formed from the following names of places: Cuba, Chile, el Ecuador, Guatemala, la América hispana, la Argentina, Lima, México, el Uruguay, Valencia, Venezuela.

3. Give the English cognates for the following verbs and point out the variations in spelling and/or ending: considerar, diferir, exceder, experimentar, expresar, interesar, interpretar, pintar, representar; adquirir, aspirar, citar, combinar, describir, determinar, introducir, observar, producir, reproducir, surgir; asimilar, crear, cultivar, dedicar, decorar, dominar, educar, emigrar.

4. Deceptive cognates.   The verb **importar**, mentioned above, may mean *to import*, as well as *to be important*.   The noun **oración**, which we know as *sentence*, may also mean *prayer*, and, although rarely, *oration*.   The verb **apreciar** means *to esteem*, as well as *to appreciate*.

B. Modismos y frases útiles

acabar con   to put an end to   así como   as well as

---

[1] The plural of **régimen** is **regímenes**.   As in the case of **carácter** (*pl.* **caracteres**), the stress shifts one syllable in the plural.

de (en) nuestros días   (of) today, of (in) our time
dejar de + *inf.*   to stop, cease + *pres. part.*; cease to + *inf.*
dentro de   in, within
desde . . . hasta   from . . . (up) to
en cambio   on the other hand
en cuanto a   as for, in regard to
en gran parte   largely, in large measure

en relación con   in relation to
esforzarse (ue) por   to strive for, make an effort to
incorporarse a   to be incorporated into
interesarse por   to become interested in
los (las) demás   the other (rest of the)
llegar a + *inf.*   to go so far as to + *inf.*; succeed in + *pres. part.*
para fines de   towards the end of

C. Aspectos gramaticales

1. Gender of certain nouns.   **Arte** is normally masculine when used in the singular: **la nota característica del arte**, *the characteristic note of art*; **el arte plateresco**, *Plateresque art*.   In the plural it is regularly feminine: **las bellas artes**, *(the) fine arts*; **las artes**, *arts* (in general); **las artes visuales**, *the visual arts*.

The noun **mar** is normally masculine, as in this Lectura: **el Mar Caribe**, *the Caribbean Sea*.   In later reading you may encounter its use as a feminine noun, especially in fixed phrases, such as **alta mar**, *high seas*; **baja mar**, *ebb (low) tide*; **la mar de cosas**, *lots of things*.

2. Adjectives (also certain nouns) ending in **-ista**, and occasionally in **-na**.   Such words have only one form for the masculine and feminine; examples from this Lectura (not marked with asterisks) are: el arte vanguardista, el elemento indígena, elementos indígenas, un enfoque racionalista, la gran escuela muralista, la influencia indígena, el movimiento expresionista, un movimiento indígena, la pintura surrealista, una tendencia vanguardista, los tipos indígenas.

3. Use of prepositions.   We are familiar with the normal meaning of the common Spanish prepositions: **a**, *to*, *at*; **con**, *with*; **de**, *of*; **en**, *in*, *on*; **por**, *for*; watch, however, for constructions in which these prepositions have other meanings.   In addition to those listed in section B above, note the following: **el amor por**, *the love of* (*for*); **la incorporación . . . a**, *the incorporation . . . in*(*to*); **la preocupación por**, *the concern with*; and an expression which has been used earlier, **ha servido de base**, *(it) has served as a basis*.

D. Notas sobre ciertos estilos arquitectónicos en la América española

Given Spain's long history and the influences from without and from within the country, it is natural that there was a gradual blending or fusion in the architectural types which developed through the centuries, and which were taken to the New World. For examples of some of the styles which are discussed briefly here, see the illustrations on pages 210 and 214.

1. Gothic architecture in Europe is characterized, in general, by pointed arches, ribbed vaulting, vertical lines, solid walls, and flying buttresses. In the New World, particularly in Mexico, most of the buttresses were built against the walls, and the monastic churches often served a double purpose of religious and military monument, as evidenced in their towers and battlements. Because of changes from early Gothic and the fusion with other styles, the term "decadent" Gothic came to be used. The monastery of San Agustín Acolman offers one of the best examples of the fortress-type monastery and church, built under Spanish direction, but with Indian laborers and craftsmen. The entrance is of fine Plateresque character.

2. The Plateresque style, characteristically Spanish and prevalent in Spain in the early sixteenth century, was called thus because its delicate, exquisite, and rich ornamentation resembled the work of the plateros *(silversmiths). It emphasized surface decoration or ornamentation, rather than anything structural, and straight horizontal lines predominate. The ornamentation was concentrated at the entrance or portal of a building. While religious buildings dominated the early architecture in the Americas, as time passed, palaces and public buildings of similar styles appeared.*

3. The Mudéjar *(Spanish Moorish) type resulted from the work of the* mudéjares *(Moslems) who were allowed to keep their own religion in Spain after their conquest by the Christians. This type is characterized by lace-like geometrical decoration of walls and archways, largely of brick and plaster, and often by use of colorful glazed tiles. The use of Indian workmen accounts for certain indigenous elements found in American architectural designs, particularly in Mexico, Peru, and Ecuador.*

4. Baroque architecture is characterized by heavy, lavish, often excessive, ornamentation, with an emphasis on the curved and broken line and on crowded swirls. This type, transplanted into Spanish America in the seventeenth century, at a time when the wealth of the colonies was growing rapidly, became its most characteristic art form. Because of the abundance of stone for construction and the long native tradition of ornamentation, which existed before the arrival of the Spaniards, it was natural that this style should take hold in the Americas. The façade of the Jesuit church of la Compañía *in Quito, one of the examples mentioned in the Lectura, is so intricately carved that it resembles filigree, and its interior is decorated in gold leaf and red Plateresque.*

5. Churrigueresque architecture, developed in Spain by José Churriguera (1650–1723), is sometimes called Ultra-Baroque because of the exaggerated and highly involved, often overly-rich and excessively complicated, decorative details. Evolving from the luxuriant Baroque, the Churrigueresque in Mexico, for example, became in the eighteenth century what is frequently called the first indigenous architectural style in America.

Iglesia de San Sebastián y Santa Prisca, Taxco, México

CORRIENTES CULTURALES DE LA
AMÉRICA ESPAÑOLA (*fin*)

Al introducir en América la civilización europea, los colonizadores españoles dieron una importancia especial a las bellas artes.* Como veremos en las páginas que siguen, la nota característica del arte* en la América hispana es la incorporación de elementos americanos a* los estilos importados de Europa.

En la arquitectura los pobladores españoles reproducen los estilos que entonces prevalecían en España. En el siglo XVI, por ejemplo, la iglesia de San Agustín Acolman, al norte de la ciudad de México, muestra el estilo gótico[1] decadente de la época, combinado con el plateresco; el claustro de la iglesia de San Francisco de Lima combina el arte* plateresco con elementos del mudéjar. En el siglo XVII y en la primera parte del siglo siguiente, los edificios son de estilo barroco, sobre todo en su variedad churrigueresca, que en América muestra una fuerte influencia de corrientes indígenas. Es una época de riqueza arquitectónica en que se construyen en América algunos de los ejemplos más bellos del arte barroco del mundo, entre ellos el Sagrario Metropolitano de la catedral de México, la iglesia de San Sebastián y Santa Prisca en Taxco, la catedral de Zacatecas, la iglesia de Santo Domingo en Oaxaca, la iglesia de Tepotzotlán—todos en México—, y el templo de la Compañía, en Quito.

La pintura y la escultura se cultivan tan intensamente como en Europa. Los focos[2] más importantes de actividad artística son los virreinatos de la Nueva España (México) y del Perú y la región ecuatoriana. El pintor Baltasar de Echave, de origen vasco, que emigró a México hacia 1590, es considerado como el fundador de la escuela mexicana. Su mejor obra existente es quizás la *Oración en el huerto*.[3]

Gregorio Vázquez (1638–1711), nacido en Santa Fe de Bogotá,[4] representa la pintura en el Nuevo Reino de Granada en el siglo XVII. El limeño Miguel de Santiago disputa con Vázquez el primer lugar[5] entre los pintores coloniales; su cuadro más notable es *La Regla*,[6] que pintó en 1656 para el convento de San Agustín de Quito. La región ecuatoriana es el centro

---

[1] For explanation of this style and others used in this Lectura, see Notas, pages 212–213. [2] **focos**, *centers, focuses.* [3] **Oración en el huerto,** *Christ in the Garden* (lit., *Prayer in the Garden*). [4] **Santa Fe de Bogotá,** *Holy Faith of Bogotá.* (The name the Spaniards gave to the town, founded in 1538, which became the capital of the colony called the New Kingdom of Granada; later the name was shortened to Bogotá.) [5] **disputa ... lugar,** *contends with Vázquez for first place.* [6] **La Regla,** *The Order* (*i.e.*, the Augustinian Order).

más importante de actividad escultórica en la época colonial, con escultores
como el célebre Padre Carlos (1620–1680) y los indios, Olmos y Manuel
Chili, autores de muchas producciones admirables.

En el siglo XVIII se destacan los pintores mexicanos José María Ibarra
(1688–1756), llamado el Murillo de la Nueva España, autor de *La Purísima*,[1]
La samaritana,[2] y otros cuadros excelentes, y Miguel Cabrera (1695–1768),
nacido en Oaxaca. Cabrera es el más popular de todos los pintores mexicanos; *La Virgen del Apocalipsis* (1760) es el ejemplo más notable de las obras
que de él quedan.

En el siglo XIX dos insignes arquitectos se distinguen también en la
escultura y en la pintura, el valenciano Manuel Tolsá (1757–1816), que
pasó a México en 1791, y el mexicano Francisco Eduardo Tresguerras
(1765–1833). Tolsá es el gran escultor de la época; como arquitecto terminó las obras de la catedral de México; como escultor fue el autor de la
magnífica estatua ecuestre de Carlos IV, en la ciudad de México. Tresguerras fue el último de los grandes arquitectos del régimen colonial. De
celebrada versatilidad, se distinguió también como escultor, pintor, músico
y poeta.

Para fines del siglo XIX los pintores hispanoamericanos ya muestran
tendencias nuevas: algunos siguen las escuelas francesas, dominantes en
Europa; pero otros buscan inspiración en los temas americanos. Ya dentro
del siglo actual, cuando el movimiento impresionista, de origen francés,
dominaba en los círculos artísticos del mundo, surgió la gran escuela muralista
de México, que, con Diego Rivera, José Clemente Orozco y David Alfaro
Siqueiros, ha florecido hasta nuestros días.

Como en el caso de la literatura, la preocupación por* los problemas
sociales determinó este cambio de dirección de la pintura de Hispanoamérica.
En México la Revolución de 1910 ha servido de base para la obra artística
de los pintores citados, que han producido una larga serie de pinturas murales
que decoran las paredes de muchos edificios públicos. Las artes,* las fiestas
populares, la vida de los indios y las nuevas ideas sociales les han proporcionado[3] una gran variedad de temas.

Las ideas sociales y políticas de Diego Rivera (1886–1957) le llevaron a
hacer de la pintura un medio de propaganda para educar al pueblo. La
inmensa composición que se halla en la escalera del Palacio Nacional, en la
ciudad de México, describe toda la historia del país—desde el período
prehispánico hasta el actual—y, también, la visión de un futuro ideal.

---

[1] **La Purísima**, *The Most Holy Virgin.*   [2] **La samaritana**, *The Samaritan Woman.*   [3] **les han**
proporcionado, *have furnished them.*

El hombre y el mundo contemporáneo son también el tema general de José Clemente Orozco (1883–1949), que se interesó especialmente por los aspectos más sórdidos y tristes de la vida mexicana. Se ha dicho que ningún otro pintor le ha superado en la expresión del aspecto eterno, humano y trágico de las luchas civiles de un país. Para ver sus mejores obras hay que ir a Guadalajara, México.

Los temas revolucionarios adquieren un vigor extraordinario en las obras de David Alfaro Siqueiros (1898–　), quien se ha esforzado por abrir nuevos caminos al muralismo. Ha experimentado con el uso de materiales nuevos, así como con la fusión de la pintura y la escultura. Entre sus murales más importantes figura el de la rectoría[1] de la Ciudad Universitaria de México.

El pintor mexicano Rufino Tamayo (1899–　) representa una forma moderada del muralismo de su país, expresado en términos de valores universales. Hay murales suyos en Smith College y en varios edificios públicos del estado de Texas.

Hacia 1920 empezó también en el Perú un movimiento indígena en el arte. Aunque se desarrolló bajo la influencia del muralismo mexicano, difiere de éste por su tono más moderado. José Sabogal (1888–1956), jefe de la nueva expresión artística de su país, ha buscado su inspiración en el paisaje, en los tipos indígenas y en las costumbres rurales del Perú, empleando como fondo los majestuosos Andes. Aunque también ha interpretado la vida por los ojos del indio, no se observa en sus obras la nota de propaganda, como en las de los artistas mexicanos.

Notables representantes de las corrientes artísticas de influencia europea son el pintor guatemalteco Carlos Mérida (1893–　), el cubano Wifredo Lam (1902–　), y el uruguayo Joaquín Torres García (1874–1948). Mérida ha sido uno de los exponentes más importantes de la pintura abstracta en América. Lam desarrolla su obra en relación con los principios del surrealismo. La contribución del pintor uruguayo ha sido la más importante en relación con las tendencias actuales. En 1928 llegó a crear un estilo nuevo, de formas rectangulares, basado en el principio de la acumulación de imágenes, por medio de las cuales aspiraba a expresar un simbolismo místico, de valor universal. De los pintores contemporáneos es el que ha ejercido mayor influencia en las generaciones jóvenes de la América española.

Hoy día el arte vanguardista es cultivado intensamente en muchos países de Hispanoamérica. En Chile, por ejemplo, el *Grupo Rectángulo*, fundado

---

[1] **rectoría**, *rector's (president's) office.*

en 1954, por Ramón Vergara Grez (1923–   ), ha rechazado[1] el *informalismo*
y las demás derivaciones de la pintura surrealista (las cuales aspiraban a
acabar con todas las normas en el arte) y se esfuerza por dar un enfoque[2]
racionalista y un valor ético al arte.   Desde 1963 el grupo se llama *Forma y
espacio* y hace concesiones al arte cinético.[3]   Tendencias semejantes se
encuentran en las producciones del venezolano Jesús Soto (1923–   ) y
del argentino Eduardo Mac Entyre (1929–   ).   Los dos buscan nuevas
formas de expresar aspectos positivos e imaginativos de nuestra época
tecnológica.

Dos notables pintores mexicanos pueden representar las tendencias van-
guardistas en su país: Pedro Friedeberg (1937–   ) y José Luis Cuevas
(1934–   ).   La precisión en la invención matemática, la nota de crítica
social y la preocupación por lo sobrenatural son elementos importantes de
su arte.

En nuestros días la vitalidad de las artes* visuales en Hispanoamérica es
extraordinaria.   El hecho más importante es que el arte hispanoamericano
ha dejado de ser nacional y se ha incorporado a la escena internacional.

La aptitud artística del hispanoamericano se manifiesta también en otras
artes más populares, como la cerámica, la orfebrería[4] y la producción de
tejidos.[5]   Aun antes de la llegada de los españoles, las civilizaciones indígenas
de América habían producido obras maravillosas de cerámica y de orfebrería
que el viajero puede admirar hoy en los museos.   En el arte del tinte los
pueblos indios excedían a los europeos, y muchas de sus materias tintóreas
fueron introducidas en Europa después de la conquista.   Hoy día es muy
apreciada la cerámica de Puebla y de Oaxaca, en México; son admirados los
tejidos de Guatemala y de otros países de gran población india; entre otros
lugares, las ciudades de Taxco (México) y Lima son famosas por la producción
de artículos de oro y plata, etcétera.

En cuanto a la música, puede decirse que el amor por* ella es una de las
características de la América latina.   Desde la época colonial ha habido[6]
dos corrientes distintas: la popular, que representa la expresión espontánea
del pueblo, y la culta, que muestra influencias europeas.   Las variedades de
la música popular son infinitas; cada país tiene una rica tradición musical,
con formas propias.   En algunos casos se han mezclado elementos indígenas
y extranjeros.   La música popular de México, por ejemplo, es en gran parte
de procedencia andaluza, y su estilo es arcaico, como en las danzas llamadas
jarabe[7] y zapateado.[8]   La rumba, la conga y otras formas de la música

---

[1] **ha rechazado,** *has rejected.*   [2] **enfoque,** *focus(ing).*   [3] **cinético,** *kinetic* (consisting in or
depending upon motion).   [4] **orfebrería,** *gold or silver work.*   [5] **tejidos,** *textiles, weaving(s).*
[6] **ha habido,** *there have been.*   [7] **jarabe,** a popular dance, such as the *Mexican Hat Dance.*
[8] **zapateado,** *clog (tap) dance.*

Músico indio de las montañas
bolivianas

Estudiantes de la Universidad del
Cuzco bailan danzas folklóricas

popular de Cuba y de las demás islas del Mar Caribe,* en cambio, muestran una fuerte influencia de la música negra.   En los países donde la población india es grande, la influencia indígena es muy notable.

En el siglo XX muchos compositores, como los argentinos Juan Carlos Paz y Juan José Castro, el cubano Ernesto Lecuona, el uruguayo Eduardo Fabini, y los mexicanos Manuel Ponce, Silvestre Revueltas y Carlos Chávez, han llegado a desarrollar una música de auténticos temas americanos.

Lecuona (1896–1963) se distinguió como pianista, compositor y director de orquesta.   Algunas de sus composiciones, como *Malagueña, Danza negra* y *Siboney,* de inspiración popular, llegaron a ser célebres tanto en Norteamérica como en Hispanoamérica.   Juan José Castro (1895–1968) compuso la música de escena[1] para *Bodas de sangre,*[2] de García Lorca, poeta y dramaturgo español.

Carlos Chávez (1899–   ) es el fundador de la Orquesta Sinfónica de México.   Convencido de que existe una música mexicana con un carácter y un vigor propios, Chávez se ha dedicado a integrar las diversas fuentes de la tradición nacional.   Aunque la esencia de su música es mexicana, sus temas son originales, y se ha asimilado completamente el elemento indígena. Su técnica y su genio inventivo le han asegurado un puesto muy alto en el mundo musical.

El chileno Claudio Arrau (1903–   ), uno de los grandes pianistas de nuestros días, es considerado como uno de los mejores intérpretes de la obra pianística de Beethoven.

Entre los compositores más jóvenes hay algunos muy notables, como el chileno Juan Antonio Orrego Salas (1919–   ), profesor del Conservatorio Nacional de Chile, y el argentino Alberto Ginastera (1916–   ), director del Conservatorio de Música de su país.   Entre las composiciones de Ginastera merecen citarse su poema sinfónico, *Ollantay*[3] (1948), y su ópera *Bomarzo,* estrenada en Washington en 1967.

---

[1] **música de escena,** *background music.*   [2] **Bodas de sangre,** *Blood Wedding.*   [3] **Ollantay,** originally a controversial drama of uncertain authorship and date, possibly written first in Quechua verse in pre-Hispanic days, was presented in Spanish in the eighteenth century.   The action, set in Cuzco, the ancient Inca capital, deals with the love of Ollantay, an Inca chieftain of humble birth, and the Inca princess Cusi Coyllur.

Juan Carlos Paz

PREGUNTAS

1. Al introducir en América la civilización europea, ¿a qué dieron una importancia especial los colonizadores españoles? 2. ¿Cuál es la nota característica del arte en la América hispana? 3. ¿Qué estilos muestran los edificios que se construyeron en el siglo XVI? 4. ¿Qué estilos muestran los edificios en el siglo XVII y en la primera mitad del siglo siguiente?

5. ¿Quién es considerado como el fundador de la escuela de pintura en México? 6. ¿Quién disputa con Gregorio Vázquez el primer lugar entre los pintores coloniales? 7. ¿Qué pintores mexicanos se destacan en el siglo XVIII? 8. ¿Qué ilustres arquitectos se distinguieron en México en el siglo XIX?

9. ¿Cuándo surgió la gran escuela muralista de México? 10. ¿Qué ha servido de base para la obra artística de los muralistas mexicanos? 11. ¿Qué describe la composición de Rivera que se halla en la escalera del Palacio Nacional, en la ciudad de México? 12. ¿Qué se ha dicho del pintor José Clemente Orozco? 13. ¿Cuáles son algunos caminos nuevos que Siqueiros ha tratado de abrir al muralismo? 14. ¿Dónde se encuentran en nuestro país pinturas murales de Rufino Tamayo? 15. ¿En qué ha buscado su inspiración el pintor José Sabogal?

16. ¿Qué corrientes artísticas representan los pintores Mérida, Lam y Torres García? 17. ¿Cuál de ellos ha ejercido mayor influencia en relación con las tendencias actuales? 18. ¿Qué aspira a expresar Torres García por medio de las imágenes que acumula en sus cuadros? 19. ¿Dónde se fundó el *Grupo Rectángulo* y cómo se llama el grupo ahora? 20. ¿Qué aspectos de nuestro tiempo tratan de expresar los pintores Jesús Soto y Eduardo Mac Entyre? 21. ¿Cuáles son algunos elementos importantes de las obras de Pedro Friedeberg y de José Luis Cuevas?

22. ¿Qué otras artes se han cultivado en Hispanoamérica? 23. ¿Qué ciudades son famosas por la producción de artículos de oro y plata?

24. ¿Qué puede decirse de la música de la América latina? 25. ¿Qué dos corrientes ha habido desde la época colonial? 26. ¿De qué procedencia es, en gran parte, la música popular de México? 27. ¿En qué regiones de América es muy importante la influencia de la música negra? 28. ¿Qué han llegado a desarrollar muchos compositores hispanoamericanos en el siglo XX? 29. ¿Quién fue el autor de las composiciones *Malagueña, Danza negra* y *Siboney*? 30. ¿Qué gran compositor se ha dedicado a integrar las diversas fuentes de la tradición nacional de México? 31. ¿De qué países son los compositores Orrego Salas y Alberto Ginastera? 32. ¿Qué obra de Ginastera fue estrenada en Washington en 1967?

EJERCICIOS ESCRITOS

A. Uso de modismos y frases hechas

Escriban oraciones completas empleando las frases siguientes como elemento inicial:

1. En cuanto a la arquitectura . . .
2. Entre los demás escultores . . .

3. Se encuentran iglesias barrocas desde . . .
4. Entre algunos círculos la pintura surrealista ha dejado de . . .
5. Los dos se esfuerzan por . . .
6. Fue Torres García quien . . .
7. Creo que esta composición llegará a ser . . .
8. El elemento indígena, en cambio, . . .

B. Para expresar en español:

1. The Spanish colonizers incorporated American elements into the different artistic styles which prevailed in Europe.   2. The most important centers of artistic activity in the colonial period were the viceroyalties of New Spain and of Peru, and the Ecuadorian region.   3. In architecture the Spaniards reproduced a variety of styles, as the Gothic, the Plateresque, the Spanish Moorish, and, especially, the Baroque. 4. Some of the most beautiful examples of these architectural styles can be seen today in Mexico City, Lima, Quito, and other cities which were important in the colonial period.   5. Painting and sculpture, largely of religious character during those centuries, were cultivated as intensely as in Europe.   6. By the end of the nineteenth century many Spanish American painters began to seek inspiration in American themes, and in the present century the great muralist movement appeared.   7. The Revolution of 1910 in Mexico, with all its social, political, and economic problems, has served as a basis for the mural paintings of Rivera, Orozco, Siqueiros, and other artists, which decorate the walls of many public buildings.   8. The Peruvian José Sabogal sought his inspiration in the landscape, in the native types, and in the rural customs of his country, interpreting life through the eyes of the Indian.   9. Nowadays, with the introduction of many new tendencies in the works of the painters of many countries, Spanish American art has ceased to be national and it has been incorporated into the international scene.   10. Even before the arrival of the Spaniards, the native civilizations of America had produced marvelous works of ceramics, gold and silver work, and textiles, and today the traveler can still admire these popular arts in many countries, especially in those which have a great Indian population.   11. The love for music is one of the characteristics of all Latin America, and there have been two distinct currents: the popular one, which represents the spontaneous expression of the people, and the learned one, which shows European influences.   12. Among the many notable composers who have come to develop a music of authentic American themes, Carlos Chávez, founder of the Symphony Orchestra of Mexico, stands out as one of the principal figures in (**de**) the musical world.

C. Temas para un informe escrito

Escriban un informe, de unas 120 palabras, sobre uno de los temas siguientes:

1. Las bellas artes en la época colonial.
2. El arte vanguardista en Hispanoamérica.
3. Elementos indígenas y extranjeros en la música contemporánea de Hispanoamérica.

LECCIÓN ONCE

Comparación de los adjetivos y de los adverbios.
Comparaciones de igualdad. «Hacer» en expresiones de
tiempo. La traducción de *must*

¿QUÉ PARTE DEL CONCIERTO TE HA GUSTADO MÁS?

(*María se encuentra con Antonio durante el intermedio de un concierto en el Teatro Universitario.*)

MARÍA. Antonio, ¡tú por aquí! Hace tiempo que no te veo en un concierto de música sinfónica.

ANTONIO. No exageres, María. ¿No nos vimos hace dos semanas en el concierto de la Orquesta Universitaria?

MARÍA. Tienes razón. Pues me parece que la mayor parte de los estudiantes de nuestra clase han venido al concierto.

ANTONIO. Nos dijo el profesor que no debiéramos perder el segundo número, de Carlos Chávez. Es el representante más ilustre de la música mexicana de nuestros días.

MARÍA. ¿Qué parte del concierto te ha gustado más?

ANTONIO. Pues la composición de Chávez me ha parecido muy impresionante. Es la primera vez que oigo una obra suya. Es diferente de lo que yo esperaba. Los ritmos son más definidos, y es más fácil percibir las melodías.

MARÍA. ¡Claro! Las fuentes de su música son más populares. Deben de relacionarse con tonadas tradicionales de México.

ANTONIO. Sí; según el profesor, Chávez se ha dedicado a desarrollar una música de auténticos temas americanos.

225

MARÍA.   Y no olvides que es un compositor más moderno que los otros.   Tal vez
por eso no hayan resultado los otros números tan interesantes como el
suyo.

ANTONIO.   Es posible . . .   Pero ya se apagan las luces, María.   A ver si la segunda
parte del programa nos gusta tanto como la primera.

Antonio Anthony
apagar to turn off, lower (*lights*)
auténtico, -a authentic
¡claro! clearly! certainly! of
course!
el compositor composer
el concierto concert
dedicarse a to dedicate (devote)
oneself to
definido, -a definite
desarrollar to develop
exagerar to exaggerate
la fuente fountain; source

ilustre illustrious, famous
impresionante impressive, moving
el intermedio intermission
la luz (*pl.* **luces**) light
la melodía melody
percibir to perceive, see
relacionarse (con) to be related (to)
el representante representative
resultar to result, turn out (to be)
el ritmo rhythm
según according to
la tonada air, song
tradicional traditional

A. Busquen en el diálogo las frases que correspondan a las siguientes:

1. What part . . . have you liked best (most)?   2. you here!   3. I haven't seen you for
a long time.   4. at a symphony concert.   5. Don't exaggerate.   6. Didn't we see each
other two weeks ago?   7. I believe (it seems to me) that most of the students in
(of) our class.   8. the teacher told us that we shouldn't miss the second number.
9. He is the most famous representative.   10. in our time (of today).   11. It is
the first time that I have heard a work of his.   12. It's different from what (than) I
expected.   13. it is easier to perceive.   14. They must be related to . . .   15. don't
forget that . . .   16. he is a more modern composer.   17. Perhaps that's why (for
that reason) the other numbers haven't turned out to be so interesting.   18. the
lights are being lowered.   19. Let's see whether we like the second part as much as
the first.

B. Estudien las expresiones siguientes para emplear algunas de ellas en el
diálogo citado, o para usarlas en un diálogo nuevo basado sobre el
modelo.

el argumento plot (*of music or
drama*)

el carácter (*pl.* **caracteres**)[1] character

---

[1] Normally the addition of **-s** or **-es** in forming the plural of nouns does not change the spoken stress of the
words.   One of the few exceptions is the plural form **caracteres**, with a shift of the stress one syllable toward
the end of the word.   See also footnote 1, page 211.

clásico, -a classic
el desenlace ending, denouement
el elemento element, part
la emoción (*pl.* emociones) emotion
emocionante exciting, thrilling
encantar to charm, delight
el espíritu spirit
la fuerza force, strength

impresionar to impress, move
indígena *m. and f. adj.* native
la inspiración (*pl.* inspiraciones)
 inspiration
la leyenda legend
producir to produce
sencillo, -a simple
típico, -a typical

NOTAS GRAMATICALES

I. COMPARACIÓN DE LOS ADJETIVOS Y DE LOS ADVERBIOS

A. When we make unequal comparisons in English we say *tall*, *taller*, *tallest*; *expensive*, *more (less) expensive*, *most (least) expensive*. In Spanish, place **más**, *more*, *most*, and **menos**, *less*, *least*, before the adjective. The definite article is used when *the* is a part of the meaning, and the adjective must agree with the noun in gender and number: **el más alto**, **la más alta**, **los más altos**, **las más altas**. Sometimes the possessive adjective (**mi**, **tu**, etc.) replaces the definite article.

One can tell from the context when an adjective in Spanish has comparative or superlative force; that is, whether **más** means *more* or *most*, and whether **menos** means *less* or *least*. Even though an adjective modified by **más** or **menos** usually follows the noun, as in the examples below, in reading you will note exceptions to this practice (also see NOTA, page 173). After a superlative, *in* is translated by **de**. *Than* is translated by **que** before a noun or pronoun. After **que**, *than*, the negatives **nadie**, **nunca**, **nada**, **ninguno, -a**, replace **alguien**, **siempre**, **algo**, and **alguno, -a**, respectively.

Los ritmos son más definidos. The rhythms are more definite.
Es un compositor más moderno que los otros. He is a more modern
 composer than the others.
Es el representante más ilustre de la música mexicana de nuestros
 días. He is the most famous representative of Mexican music in our time.
Ella habla más que nunca (nadie). She talks more than ever (anyone).

Than is translated by **de** before a numeral or numerical expression in an affirmative sentence; if the sentence is negative, either **que** or **de** may be used, the preference being for **que**. Theoretically, **no . . . más que** means *only* and **no . . . más de** means *not . . . more than*.

¿Has escrito más de diez composiciones? Have you written more than
 ten compositions?

No necesito más que cinco dólares.   I need only five dollars.
No necesito más de cinco dólares.   I do not need more than five dollars.
(*Five at the most*)

When *than* is followed by an inflected verb form, it is expressed by **de** + the definite article + **que**, that is, by **del que, de la que, de los que, de las que**, really meaning *than the one(s) who (which, that)*, if the point of comparison is a noun which is the object of the first verb and is elliptically omitted in the second member.

Él tiene más flores de las que vende.   He has more flowers than he sells.
Hace más frío hoy del que hizo ayer.   It is colder today than it was yesterday.
Yo escribo más cartas de las que recibo.   I write more letters than I receive.

When *than* is followed by an inflected verb form, but the second member is elliptical in such a way that the verb of the first member must be repeated in order to complete the idea, **que** is replaced by **de lo que**.   (In such sentences the verb which follows **de lo que** often expresses a mental state.)

Ella es más bonita de lo que crees.   She is prettier than (what) you believe (she is).
El concierto es mejor de lo que me imaginaba.   The concert is better than I imagined (it would be).
Es diferente de lo que yo esperaba.   It is different than (from what) I expected (it to be).

B. The comparative of adverbs is also regularly formed by placing **más** or **menos** before the adverb.   The article is not used in the superlative, except that the neuter form **lo** is used when an expression of possibility follows.

Es más fácil percibir las melodías.   It is easier to perceive the melodies.
Vuelvan ustedes del concierto lo más pronto posible.   Return from the concert the soonest possible (as soon as possible).

C. Six adjectives and four adverbs, most of which have already been used in this text, are compared irregularly:

ADJECTIVES

bueno	good	**(el) mejor**	(the) better, best
malo	bad	**(el) peor**	(the) worse, worst

grande large	⎰ (**el**) **más grande**	(the) larger, largest
	⎱ (**el**) **mayor**	(the) greater, older, greatest, oldest
pequeño small	⎰ (**el**) **más pequeño**	(the) smaller, smallest
	⎱ (**el**) **menor**	(the) smaller, younger, smallest, youngest

mucho(s) much (many)   **más** more, most
poco(s) little (few)   **menos** less, fewer

Mejor and **peor** precede the noun, just as **bueno, -a,** and **malo, -a,** regularly precede it, except when emphasized.   Used with the definite article, the forms are:

el mejor (**peor**)	**los mejores** (**peores**)
la mejor (**peor**)	**las mejores** (**peores**)

Grande and **pequeño, -a,** have regular forms which refer to size, while the irregular forms **mayor** (*m. and f.*) and **menor** (*m. and f.*) usually refer to persons and mean *older* and *younger*, respectively.

Most (of), The greater part of, is translated by **La mayor parte de**; the verb normally agrees with the noun following this expression: **La mayor parte de los estudiantes van a los conciertos**, *Most (of the) students go to the concerts.*

ADVERBS

bien well   **mejor** better, best   **mucho** much   **más** more, most
mal bad, badly   **peor** worse, worst   **poco** little   **menos** less, least

D. A high degree of quality, without any element of comparison (sometimes called the absolute superlative), is expressed by the use of **muy** before the adjective or adverb, or by adding the ending **-ísimo** (**-a, -os, -as**) to the adjective.   When **-ísimo** is added, a final vowel is dropped.   **Muchísimo**, rather than **muy mucho**, is used for the adjective or adverb *very much (many)*.

Ella es muy hermosa (**hermosísima**).   She is very beautiful.
Se divirtieron muchísimo.   They had a very good time.

Ejercicios

A. Completen las frases con la forma comparativa del adjetivo o del adverbio.

MODELO: Este concierto es bueno, pero el otro fue _____.
      Este concierto es bueno, pero el otro fue mejor.

   1. Este edificio es grande, pero aquél es _____.

2. Esta música es buena, pero la otra es _____.
3. Esta obra es larga, pero la última fue _____.
4. Aquella casa blanca es pequeña, pero la amarilla es _____.
5. Aquellas calles son cortas, pero ésta es _____.
6. Yo estoy cansado, pero mi mamá está _____.
7. José tiene dos años más que Pablo; éste es el _____.
8. Marta tiene un año menos que Ana; aquélla es la _____.
9. Carolina toca bien, pero su hermana toca _____.
10. Juan baila mal, pero Miguel baila _____.
11. A mí me interesa mucho la música, pero a él le interesa _____.
12. Ellos tienen poco tiempo, pero yo tengo _____.

B. Para contestar afirmativamente, siguiendo los modelos.

MODELOS: ¿Es grande el parque?   Sí, es más grande que éste.
         ¿Son difíciles las frases?   Sí, son más difíciles que éstas.

1. ¿Son hermosas las flores?   4. ¿Es mala la novela?
2. ¿Es larga la carretera?   5. ¿Está contenta la muchacha?
3. ¿Es bueno el hotel?   6. ¿Es popular la música?

MODELO: ¿Es bonita la casa?   Sí, es la casa más bonita de todas.

7. ¿Es sencillo el argumento?   9. ¿Es ilustre el compositor?
8. ¿Es típica la leyenda?   10. ¿Es interesante la obra?

MODELO: ¿Es hermosa Carolina?   Sí, es muy hermosa; es hermosísima.

11. ¿Son altos los árboles?   13. ¿Son malas las composiciones?
12. ¿Es guapo su novio?   14. ¿Es grande la emoción?

C. Lean en español, supliendo la palabra o frase equivalente a *than*:

1. Creo que hay más _____ mil estudiantes en el teatro.
2. Este concierto es mejor _____ el último.
3. Hay más fuentes en México _____ tenemos en este país.
4. Pablo tiene más amigos en la ciudad _____ tú crees.
5. Marta ha escrito más composiciones _____ me imaginaba.
6. Hoy ella tocará más números _____ tocó la semana pasada.
7. Esta música es diferente _____ yo esperaba.
8. No olvides que este compositor es más moderno _____ el otro.

II. COMPARACIONES DE IGUALDAD (*EQUALITY*)

Tan + an adjective or adverb + **como** means *as (so) . . . as*. **Tan** used without **como** means *so*, sometimes *as*.

Pablo es tan fuerte como Enrique. Paul is as strong as Henry.
¿Por qué está ella tan contenta? Why is she so happy?

Also, before an adjective **tan** is used instead of **tal** to mean *such (a)*:

¡Es un día tan hermoso! It is such a beautiful day!
Nunca he leído cuentos tan interesantes. I have never read such interesting stories.

BUT: **¿Has visto jamás tal cosa?** Have you ever seen such a thing?

Tanto, -a (**-os, -as**) + a noun + **como** means *as (so) much (many) . . . as*. **Tanto** is also used as a pronoun or adverb, with or without **como**, meaning *as (so) much (many) (. . . as)*.

No hay tantos conciertos como antes. There aren't so many concerts as before.
Ella tiene muchos discos; yo no tengo tantos. She has many records; I do not have so many.
Nos gusta la segunda parte tanto como la primera. We like the second part as much as the first.
Dígales usted a los niños que no corran tanto. Tell the children not to run so much.

Ejercicios

A. Repitan cada oración; luego, al oír un substantivo o un adjetivo, substitúyanlo en la oración original, haciendo los cambios necesarios:

1. Esta casa no es tan *vieja* como aquélla.
   (*nuevo, pequeño, grande, cómodo, bonito*)

2. Elena tiene tantas *blusas* como Luisa.
   (*sombreros, tiempo, amigos, ropa, vestidos*)

3. Ella recibe muchas *revistas*, pero yo no recibo tantas.
   (*periódicos, dinero, cartas, invitaciones, regalos*)

B. Oirán una frase, luego una o más palabras.   Formen una frase nueva empleando **tan . . . como**, según el modelo.

MODELO: Luis está ocupado.   (Carlos)   Luis está tan ocupado como Carlos.

1. La composición es impresionante.   (la otra)
2. Los temas son auténticos.   (los de Chávez)
3. Este concierto es emocionante.   (el de la música mexicana)
4. Las muchachas están contentas.   (la profesora)
5. El primer número fue maravilloso.   (el segundo)
6. Juan y yo estábamos cansados.   (Roberto)

Formen frases nuevas empleando **no . . . tanto, -a (-os, -as) . . . como**, según el modelo.

MODELO: Yo toco muchos números.   Yo no toco tantos números como Ana.

7. Bárbara escucha muchas orquestas.
8. Aquel compositor usa muchos ritmos.
9. Ricardo pasa mucho tiempo tocando.
10. Antonio ha escrito muchas composiciones.
11. Marta conocía muchos temas americanos.
12. Nosotros percibimos muchas melodías.

III. «HACER» EN EXPRESIONES DE TIEMPO

A. In Spanish, **hace** followed by a period of time (**minuto, hora, día, mes**, etc.) plus **que** and a verb in the present tense, or a present tense plus **desde hace** followed by a period of time, indicates that an action began in the past and that it is still going on in the present.   When **desde hace** is used, the word order in Spanish is the same as in English.   Note that in English the present perfect tense is used.

Hace una hora que estoy aquí *or* **Estoy aquí desde hace una hora.**
    I have been here for an hour (*lit.*, It makes an hour that I am here).
¿Cuánto tiempo hace que viven aquí?
    How long have they been living (*lit.*, How long does it make that they live) here?
Hace varios días que Ricardo busca un puesto.
    Richard has been looking for a position for several days.   (*Or* For several days Richard has been looking for a position.)
Hace tiempo que no te veo en un concierto.
    I haven't seen you at a concert for a long time.

Hacía followed by a period of time plus **que** and a verb in the imperfect tense, or the imperfect tense plus **desde hacía** followed by a period of time, indicates that an action had been going on for a certain period of time and was still continuing when something else happened.   The pluperfect tense is used in English.

Hacía un mes que yo vivía allí cuando la conocí *or* **Yo vivía allí desde hacía un mes cuando la conocí.**   I had been living there (for) a month when I met her (*lit.*, It made a month that I was living there . . .).

B. When **hace** is followed by a period of time after a verb in a past tense, it regularly means *ago*, or *since*. If the **hace**-clause comes first in the sentence, **que** usually (although not always) introduces the main clause.

Llegué hace una hora *or* **Hace una hora que llegué.**   I arrived an hour ago *or* It is an hour since I arrived.
Nos vimos hace dos semanas.   We saw each other two weeks ago.

Ejercicios

A. Después de oír una oración, oirán una expresión de tiempo; combinen los dos elementos en una nueva oración, siguiendo los modelos.

MODELO: Leo el libro.   (Hace una hora)   Hace una hora que leo el libro.

1. Viven en México.   (Hace cinco meses)
2. Estudio el español.   (Hace más de un año)
3. Estamos en el teatro.   (Hace una hora y media)
4. No te veo en la biblioteca.   (Hace tiempo)
5. No vamos al cine.   (Hace una semana)
6. Estoy esperando a Marta.   (Hace quince minutos)

B. Después de oír una pregunta, oirán una expresión de tiempo; úsenla para contestar la pregunta, según los modelos.

MODELO: ¿Cuánto tiempo hace que lees?   (una hora)   Leo desde hace una hora.

1. ¿Cuánto tiempo hace que vives aquí?   (seis meses)
2. ¿Cuánto tiempo hace que conoce Ud. a María?   (un mes y medio)
3. ¿Cuánto tiempo hace que tocas la guitarra?   (cuatro años)
4. ¿Cuánto tiempo hace que ella habla por teléfono?   (veinte minutos)

MODELO: ¿Cuándo salió ella?   (hace   Ella salió hace media hora.
           media hora)   Hace media hora que ella salió.

5. ¿Cuándo volviste a casa?   (hace tiempo)
6. ¿Cuándo fueron Uds. al centro?   (hace varios días)
7. ¿Cuándo llovió aquí?   (hace una semana)
8. ¿Cuándo viste a Carlota?   (hace un rato)
9. ¿Cuándo vino Miguel a este país?   (hace varios meses)
10. ¿Cuándo llegaste a la clase?   (hace diez minutos)

C. Para expresar en español:

1. The concert began fifteen minutes ago.   2. We have been here for an hour.
3. My sister has studied Spanish music for several years.   4. How long have you
been playing the guitar?   5. I began to play it three months ago.   6. Charles and I
attended a symphony concert three days ago.   7. We had been waiting for a long time
when they turned off the lights.   8. The orchestra has been playing in the University
Theater for many years.

IV. LA TRADUCCIÓN DE *MUST*

When *must* = *to have to* expresses a strong obligation or necessity, **tener que** + an
infinitive is used.   The impersonal form is **hay** (**había**, **habrá**, etc.) **que** + an
infinitive.

Ellos tienen que esperar.   They must (have to) wait.
Hay que hacer eso.   One must (It is necessary to) do that.

When *must* = *is (was) to, is (was) supposed to* expresses a mild obligation or commitment,
haber de + an infinitive is used:

Hemos de reunirnos esta noche.   We must (are to) meet tonight.
Habían de salir a las dos.   They were (supposed) to leave at two.

For a moral obligation, duty, customary action, etc., **deber** is used:

Ella debe llamar a su mamá.   She must (ought to) call her mother.

When *must* expresses probability in the present, it is indicated by the future (or future
perfect) of the verb (see Lección seis), or by **deber** (**de**) + an infinitive:

Estarán en el café.   They must be (probably are) at the café.
Deben de estar allí.   They must be there.
Juan habrá leído la novela.   John must have read the novel.
Debe de haberla leído.   He must have read it.
Deben de relacionarse con tonadas tradicionales.   They must be related
to traditional airs.

Ejercicio

Después de oír una pregunta, oirán un verbo o una frase; contesten afirmativamente, usando la forma correcta del verbo correspondiente.

MODELOS: *¿Son* las dos?   (*deber de*)   Sí, deben de ser las dos.
   ¿Has de ir tú ahora?   (*tener que*)   Sí, tengo que ir ahora.

1. ¿*Están* ellos en la biblioteca?   (*deber de*)
2. ¿*Es* la una?   (*deber de*)
3. ¿*Va* Juan *a* tocar la guitarra?   (*haber de*)
4. ¿*Iban a* reunirse temprano?   (*haber de*)
5. ¿*Es necesario* llegar a tiempo?   (*haber que*)
6. ¿*Será preciso* decidir eso pronto?   (*haber que*)
7. ¿*Debemos* ir al concierto esta noche?   (*tener que*)
8. ¿*Has de* apagar las luces?   (*tener que*)
9. ¿Creían que *podían* esperar un rato?   (*deber*)
10. ¿*Han de* pagar la cuenta ahora?   (*tener que*)

RESUMEN

A. Repitan cada oración; luego, formen otra oración, empleando **no . . .
tan . . . como**, siguiendo el modelo.

MODELO: Elena es más alta que Ana.   Elena es más alta que Ana.
                Ana no es tan alta como Elena.

1. Ella lee más despacio que yo.
2. Yo me levanté más tarde que
ellos.
3. Esta música es más clásica que ésa.
4. Él pronuncia más correctamente que
Ud.

Usen **no ... tanto, -a (-os, -as) ... como**, siguiendo el modelo.

MODELO: Yo tengo más flores que ella.   Yo tengo más flores que ella.
                                             Ella no tiene tantas flores como yo.

5. María lee más novelas que yo.   7. Allí hay más fuentes que aquí.
6. Ana escucha más música que   8. Esa obra tiene más melodías que
   Pablo.   ésta.

B. Usos de las formas comparativas de los adjetivos y de los adverbios.
   Para expresar en español:

1. This building is large; it is larger than that one (*distant*); it is the largest one in the
   state.
2. Our house is small; it is smaller than the yellow one; it is the smallest one in the
   block.
3. We ran across John's older brother and Mary's younger sister downtown
   yesterday.
4. There are more than one hundred foreign students here; there are more than I
   imagined.
5. John says that he has already written more compositions this semester than he
   wrote last year.
6. Most of the students in (of) our Spanish class speak better than you believe.

C. Comparaciones de igualdad.   Para expresar en español:

1. This concert is as exciting as the last one.
2. I have never heard such definite rhythms.
3. There aren't so many people here tonight as the last time.
4. Most people do not have so much interest in concerts as I.
5. Robert plays the guitar better than I, but I do not practice so much.
6. Let's see if the second part of the program is as interesting as the first.

D. Para traducir *must, to have to, to be to,* etc.   Para expresar en español:

1. They must be (*two ways*) at the movie now.
2. Jane and Paul must have arrived (*two ways*) late.
3. My parents are (supposed) to look for a television set today.
4. Henry says that I am to turn off the lights at eleven.

5. We must always greet our teacher in Spanish.
6. My roommate had to write a long composition last night.
7. One must remember that Chávez is a great composer.
8. The sources of his music must be related to traditional airs.

LECCIÓN DOCE

Resumen de los usos de «para» y «por». Usos del
participio pasado. El pretérito perfecto de indicativo.
Usos del participio presente. Las conjunciones
«e» y «u». Usos de «pero, sino» y «sino que». El artículo
neutro «lo». El pronombre neutro «lo». La formación de los
adverbios. Verbos auxiliares para expresar el modo

PLANES PARA LAS VACACIONES

(Dos estudiantes llegan temprano a la clase de arte y charlan mientras esperan al profesor.)

ROBERTO.   Estamos para terminar el semestre. ¿Qué planes tienes para las vacaciones, Luis?

LUIS.   ¡Hombre! No vas a creer lo que ha pasado. Mis abuelos me han ofrecido el dinero para hacer un viaje por Hispanoamérica.

ROBERTO.   Y lo has aceptado, por supuesto. ¿Qué países vas a visitar primero? Si yo estuviera en tu lugar, iría primero a Chile o a la Argentina.

LUIS.   Hay que creer en la telepatía. A mediados de junio parto para Buenos Aires, acompañado de mi hermano Juan. Concluida la visita allí, iremos en avión a Santiago, y luego continuaremos el viaje por la costa del Pacífico.

ROBERTO.   Estoy por pedirle a mi padre que me permita ir con ustedes. Como sabes, hace mucho tiempo que busco un puesto en algún país de la América del Sur.

LUIS.　　　No sólo has estudiado el español, sino que has tomado cursos de economía política.　¿Por qué no escribes a casas comerciales que tengan sucursales en la América española?

ROBERTO.　Es lo que pienso hacer.　Pero no te preocupes por mí.　¿Qué otros países vas a visitar?　Supongo que no dejarás de pasar unas semanas en México.

LUIS.　　　Naturalmente.　No hay mejor sitio para los que se interesan por la pintura.

ROBERTO.　Si puedo ausentarme de aquí por un mes, tal vez los visite allá.

LUIS.　　　¡Qué gusto nos daría verte en Taxco o en San Miguel de Allende![1]

ROBERTO.　Pues todo está arreglado.　Por falta de dinero no los acompañaré ahora, pero espero que nos veamos en México por agosto.

LUIS.　　　Pero, ¡hombre!　¡Qué mala memoria tengo!　He dejado en mi cuarto el informe que había de entregar hoy.

ROBERTO.　Todavía tienes más de diez minutos.　¿Por qué no vas por él?

LUIS.　　　No he traído mi coche hoy.　¿Puedes prestarme el tuyo?

ROBERTO.　¡Cómo no!　Es el de la capota amarilla.　Está estacionado detrás de la biblioteca.　Aquí tienes las llaves.

LUIS.　　　Gracias, sé cuál es.　Vuelvo en seguida.

a mediados de　about the middle of
allá　there (*often after verbs of motion*)
arreglar　to arrange, settle
ausentarse　to absent oneself, get away
la capota　top (*of automobile*)
la casa comercial　business firm
concluir (**y**)　to conclude, end, finish
la costa　coast
la economía política　political economy, economics
entregar　to turn in
estacionar　to park

estar por　to be inclined to, feel like
la falta　lack, want
Hispanoamérica　Spanish America
el informe　report; *pl.* information
interesarse por　to be interested in
la llave　key
naturalmente　naturally
ofrecer　to offer
la pintura　painting
por agosto　sometime in August
la sucursal　branch office
la telepatía　telepathy
la visita　visit

A.　Busquen en el diálogo las frases que correspondan a las siguientes:

1. We are about to finish.　2. of course.　3. If I were in your place.　4. I would go first to Chile.　5. It is necessary (One has) to believe in telepathy.　6. About

---

[1] Both Mexican cities are famous for their art schools and artist colonies.

the middle of June. 7. accompanied by my brother. 8. Once our visit there is ended. 9. by plane. 10. I feel like asking my father to . . . 11. I have been looking for a job for a long time. 12. You have not only studied Spanish. 13. but you have taken courses. 14. business firms which have branches. 15. don't worry about me. 16. I suppose you will not fail to spend. 17. There is no better place. 18. for those who are interested in painting. 19. If I can get away from here for a month. 20. perhaps I'll visit you. 21. For want (lack) of money. 22. sometime in August. 23. What a bad memory I have! 24. It's the one with the yellow top. 25. Here are the keys. 26. I'll be right back.

B. Preparen un diálogo original, de unas doce líneas, para recitar en clase, empleando las frases y preguntas siguientes como elemento inicial:[1]

1. Luis.
Siento mucho no haber podido pasar por tu casa hasta ahora. ¿Has decidido marcharte?

Carlos.
Sí, Luis. Salgo mañana en el avión de las dos. ¿Qué quieres que les diga a tus amigos en Buenos Aires?

2. Roberto.
¿Estás ocupado, Enrique? Si no tienes otros planes, quisiera invitarte a ir al centro conmigo.

Enrique.
¿Necesitas comprar algo?

3. Carlos.
Como usted sabe, me gustaría conseguir un puesto en algún país de la América española.

Sr. Navarro.
No me parece difícil. Pero primero quiero que me dé usted algunos informes sobre sus estudios universitarios.

NOTAS GRAMATICALES

I. RESUMEN DE LOS USOS DE «PARA» Y «POR»

A. **Para** is used:

1. To express the purpose, the use, the person, or the place for which persons or things are intended or destined:

> **Esta carta es para Miguel.** This letter is for Michael.
> **¿Qué planes tienes para las vacaciones?** What plans do you have for vacation?
> **Ya han partido para México.** They have already left for Mexico.

---

[1] Review of dialogues on pages 121–122, 185–186, and 197–198 will be helpful to the student in preparing the new dialogues.

2. To express a point or farthest limit of time in the future, often meaning *by*:

> **Este diálogo es para mañana.**   This dialogue is for tomorrow.
> **Que estés aquí para las cinco.**   May you be here by five.

3. With an infinitive to express purpose, meaning *to*, *in order to*:

> **Me ofreció el dinero para hacer el viaje.**   He offered me the money (in order) to make the trip.
> **Estamos para terminar el semestre.**   We are about to finish the semester.

4. To express *for* in a comparison that may be understood or stated:

> **Para ustedes, esto será fácil.**   For you, this will be easy.
> **Juanito habla bien para un niño.**   Johnny talks well for a child.

B. **Por** is used:

1. To express *for* in the sense of *because of, on account of, for the sake of, on behalf of, in exchange for, about, as*:

> **Por falta de dinero él no pudo ir.**   For lack of money he couldn't go.
> **¿Lo harás por mí?**   Will you do it for (because of) me?
> **Pagué diez dólares por la camisa.**   I paid ten dollars for the shirt.
> **No te preocupes por mí.**   Don't worry about me.
> **Le tomaron por español.**   They took him for (as) a Spaniard.

2. To express the space of time during which an action continues (*for, during*):

> **Me ausentaré por un mes.**   I'll get away for a month.
> **Ella saldrá mañana por la tarde.**   She will leave tomorrow afternoon.

3. To show *by what* or *by whom* something is done; also *through, along*:

> **El viaje fue arreglado por Luis.**   The trip was arranged by Louis.
> **Juan habló con ella por teléfono.**   John talked with her by telephone.
> **Han viajado por Hispanoamérica.**   They have traveled through Spanish America.

4. To indicate the object of an errand or search, *for,* after such verbs as **ir, enviar, mandar, preguntar, venir:**

> **Han enviado (venido, ido) por Ana.**   They have sent (come, gone) for Ann.
> **Preguntaron por ella.**   They asked for (about) her.

5. With an infinitive to express uncertain outcome (often to denote striving for something), or something yet to be done:

> **Luchaban por ganar la paz.**   They were struggling to win peace.
> **Estoy por pedirle eso.**   I feel like asking (am inclined to ask) him for that.
> **La carta todavía está por escribir.**   The letter is still to be written.

6. To form certain idiomatic expressions (some of which could be placed under the above headings):

por aquí (around, by) here	**por falta de** for lack of
por cierto certainly, for sure	**por favor** please
por desgracia unfortunately	**por fin** finally, at last
¡por Dios! for heaven's sake!	**por lo general** in general, generally
por encima de over, above	**por lo tanto** therefore
por eso because of that, therefore, that's why	**por primera vez** for the first time
por ejemplo for example	**por supuesto** of course, certainly
	por último finally, ultimately

¿Por qué? means *Why?   For what reason?*, while **¿para qué?** means *why? for what purpose?*

Ejercicio

Para leer en español, supliendo la preposición **para** o **por**:

1. ¿Cuándo partirán _____ la Argentina?   2. ¿Tiene usted muchos planes _____ el verano?   3. Yo le di las gracias a María _____ todo.   4. Arturo me dijo que vendría _____ mí a las ocho.   5. ¿Por qué se preocupa usted tanto _____ Ricardo?   6. Su mamá hizo el vestido _____ ella (*i.e., for her use*).   7. ¿_____ quién es este|billete?   —Es _____ mí.   8. Es _____ el concierto que van a presentar el sábado _____ la noche.   9. Estoy seguro de que está _____ llover pronto. 10. Tráeme tú una taza _____ té, _____ favor.   11. Los muchachos jugaron _____ dos horas.   12. Anduvieron despacio _____ la calle.   13. Escoja usted una tarjeta _____ Dorotea.   14. ¿Cuánto pagaste _____ ese reloj?   15. Parece que todo el mundo lucha _____ ganar más dinero.   16. ¿Es verdad que comemos _____ vivir?   17. ¿Crees que le tomaron _____ argentino?   18. _____ fin podemos hacer planes _____ la reunión.   19. Tendremos que darnos prisa _____

llegar a tiempo.   20. ¿_____ qué sirven los amigos?   21. Voy a enviar _____
Antonio _____ entregarle estas cartas.   22. Que vuelvan ustedes ___ el mediodía.
23. Este artículo, que fue escrito _____ Ana, es _____ el periódico de hoy.
24. _____ una persona que se siente muy bien, ella se queja mucho.

II. USOS DEL PARTICIPIO PASADO

A. The past participle is most commonly used with the appropriate tense of **haber**
to form the perfect tenses, in which case the participle always ends in **-o**.   It is also
frequently used as an adjective, including its use with **estar** and similar verbs to
express a state or condition which results from a previous action, and with **ser** to
form the passive voice.   In the latter two constructions, the past participle agrees
in gender and number with the noun or pronoun it modifies.

> **Hemos visto la película.**   We have seen the film.
> **La puerta estaba (se encontraba) abierta.**   The door was open.
> **Los vasos fueron rotos por Juanito.**   The glasses were broken by Johnny.

B. The past participle also may be used independently with a noun or pronoun to
express *time, manner, means,* and the like.   (This is sometimes called the absolute use
of the past participle.)   Used thus, the participle precedes the noun or pronoun it
modifies, and with which it agrees in gender and number.   The translation depends
on the context.

> **Concluida la visita allí, iremos a Chile.**   Once our visit there is ended
> (After the visit there is ended), we shall go to Chile.
> **Salido el avión, volví a casa.**   After the plane had left (The plane having
> left), I returned home.

NOTE.   **De** often replaces **por** with verbs other than **estar** or **ser** to introduce an
agent dependent upon a past participle: **Parto para Buenos Aires, acompañado
de mi hermano Juan**, *I'll leave for Buenos Aires, accompanied by my brother John.*
Compare the normal use of **por** in the passive voice (see pages 35–36).

III. EL PRETÉRITO PERFECTO DE INDICATIVO

The preterit perfect tense is formed with the preterit of **haber** and the past participle.
It is translated like the English past perfect tense, but is used only after conjunctions
such as **cuando, en cuanto, después que, apenas** (*scarcely, hardly*).   In the case

of **apenas,** the word *when* is carried over to the following clause in English; it is not expressed in Spanish.

SINGULAR		PLURAL	

hube ⎫
hubiste ⎬ hablado, comido, vivido
hubo ⎭

hubimos ⎫
hubisteis ⎬ hablado, comido, vivido
hubieron ⎭

> **En cuanto (Cuando) él hubo metido el rollo, cerró la cámara.** As soon as (When) he had put in the roll, he closed the camera.
> **Apenas él hubo regresado; me llamó.** Scarcely had he returned, when he called me.

In spoken Spanish the simple preterit often replaces the preterit perfect. The Spanish pluperfect is used to translate the English past perfect in other cases: **Habían vuelto,** *They had returned.*

IV. USOS DEL PARTICIPIO PRESENTE

The present participle, also called the gerund, has a number of important functions.

1. **Estar** is used with the present participle to express the progressive forms of the tenses, that is, to express the action of the verb as continuing at a given moment (see page 34):

> **Los niños están (estaban) gritando.** The children are (were) shouting.
> **¿Qué estás leyendo ahora?** What are you reading now?

2. Verbs of motion, particularly **ir, andar, venir,** are used with the present participle to give a more graphic representation of an action in progress. These verbs normally retain something of their literal meaning. **Seguir** and **continuar,** *to continue, keep on,* are followed by the present participle. (The progressive forms of **ir, salir, venir** are seldom used.)

> **Él iba (venía) andando despacio.** He was (going, coming) walking slowly.
> **Sigan (Continúen) ustedes charlando.** Continue *or* Keep on chatting.

Ir + a present participle is also equivalent to the English *to go on* or *keep* + present participle, *do something gradually* (*slowly, more and more*):

> **Ellos van aprendiendo a hablar bien.** They keep on learning (are gradually learning) to speak well.

La temperatura iba subiendo.   The temperature was rising (slowly, more and more).

3. Referring to the subject, expressed or understood, the present participle may be used to convey a variety of adverbial relationships:

Pasan mucho tiempo jugando en el parque.   They spend much time playing in the park.
Andando rápidamente, llegué a tiempo.   By walking rapidly, I arrived on time.

Ejercicios

A. Escuchen la oración; luego, repítanla, usando el participio pasado, como en el modelo.

MODELO: *Al escribir la carta*, Ana se la   Escrita la carta, Ana se la envió a
         envió a Marta.   Marta.

1. *Al cerrar la puerta*, la profesora empezó a hablar en español.
2. *Al concluir el dibujo*, Miguel lo vendió.
3. *Después de leer los artículos*, Luisa los revisó.
4. *Al comprar la maleta*, Roberto la metió en el coche.
5. *Después de hacer los planes*, los estudiantes los anunciaron.
6. *Al entregar el informe*, Carolina fue a la biblioteca.

B. Repitan cada oración; luego, al oír un verbo, substituyan la forma correcta del verbo seguida del participio presente, según los modelos.

MODELO: Luis mira un mapa.   (estar)   Luis mira un mapa.   Luis está
                                            mirando un mapa.

         Andaban despacio.   (ir)   Andaban despacio.   Iban andando
                                            despacio.

1. Roberto visita a sus abuelos.   (estar)
2. Luis hacía un viaje por Hispanoamérica.   (estar)
3. Los niños corren hacia nosotros.   (venir)
4. Ellos se acercaban al patio.   (ir)
5. Nosotros aprendemos la lengua poco a poco.   (ir)
6. Los precios suben mucho, ¿verdad?   (ir)

    7. Ella anda rápidamente por la calle.   (venir)
    8. En este momento Juan estaciona el coche.   (estar)
    9. Luis se interesa más por la pintura.   (ir)
  10. Lea usted hasta las cuatro.   (seguir)

V. LAS CONJUNCIONES «E» Y «U»

Before words beginning with **i-**, **hi-** (but not **hie-**), Spanish uses **e**, *and*, for **y**. Before words beginning with **o-**, or **ho-**, Spanish uses **u**, *or*, for **o**.

      Luis habla español e inglés.   Louis speaks Spanish and English.
      Juanita hizo eso siete u ocho veces.   Jane did that seven or eight times.

      BUT: **nieve y hielo**   snow and ice

VI. USOS DE «PERO, SINO» Y «SINO QUE»

The English conjunction *but* is usually expressed by **pero** in Spanish. When *but* means *on the contrary, but instead,* **sino** is used in place of **pero** in an affirmative statement which contradicts a preceding negative statement. Usually no verb—other than an infinitive—may be used after **sino**.

      Me probé el traje pero no lo compré.   I tried on the suit but did not buy it.
      No fueron en autobús, sino en avión.   They didn't go by bus, but by plane.
      No vimos a Roberto, sino a Jorge.   We didn't see Robert, but George.
      Yo no quiero jugar, sino descansar.   I don't want to play, but to rest.

If the sentence contains different clauses, **sino que** is used:

      No sólo has estudiado el español, sino que has tomado cursos de economía política.   You have not only studied Spanish, but you have taken courses in economics.

VII. EL ARTÍCULO NEUTRO «LO»

    1. The neuter article **lo** is used with masculine singular adjectives, with adverbs, and with past participles used as adjectives, to form an expression almost equivalent to an abstract noun. The translation of this abstract idea or concept varies according to context.

Lo malo es que no están aquí.   What is bad (The bad thing *or* part) is that
they aren't here.
Lea usted lo escrito.   Read what is (has been) written.

2. The neuter article **lo** used with an adjective or adverb followed by **que** translates
how:

¿Sabes lo contentas que están ellas?   Do you know how happy they are?

3. Remember the uses of the neuter article **lo** explained earlier: **lo que** meaning
what, that which; **lo de** meaning *that (matter, affair) of* (see Lección diez); **de lo que**,
than, in certain comparisons, and **lo (más pronto) posible**, *the soonest possible* (see
Lección once).

VIII. EL PRONOMBRE NEUTRO «LO»

In addition to its use as a pronoun object meaning *it* (**No lo creo**, *I don't believe it*),
the neuter pronoun **lo** is used:

1. To complete the sentence when no direct object is expressed, with verbs such as
advertir, decir, pedir, preguntar, saber, and the like (see page 76):

Como ellos no lo saben, yo se lo diré.   Since they don't know it, I'll tell
them.
¿Podrías ir?   Pregúntaselo a ella.   Could you go?   Ask her.

2. With certain verbs such as **ser** and **parecer**, in answer to a question, or to refer
back to a noun, adjective, or whole idea, sometimes with the meaning of *so*:

¿Es usted estudiante?   —Sí, lo soy.   Are you a student?   —Yes, I am.
Él estará cansado, pero no lo parece.   He must be tired, but he doesn't
seem so.

IX. LA FORMACIÓN DE LOS ADVERBIOS

In Spanish, adverbs of manner are formed by adding **-mente** (compare the English
suffix *-ly*) to the feminine singular of adjectives.   Adverbs may also be formed by
using **con** plus a noun.

claro	clear	**claramente**	clearly	**con cuidado**	carefully
fácil	easy	**fácilmente**	easily	**con frecuencia**	frequently

When two or more adverbs are used in a series, **-mente** is added only to the last one:

Ella habla rápida y correctamente.   She speaks rapidly and correctly.

Occasionally adjectives are used in Spanish as adverbs, particularly in the spoken language and regularly in poetry, with no change in form other than the usual agreement:

Ellos vivían felices.   They were living happily.
Todas iban muy contentas.   All (*f.*) were going very contentedly.

Ejercicios

A. Después de oír una oración, oirán una frase; substituyan la frase en la oración, según el modelo.

MODELO: *Lo malo* es que ya han salido.   (*Lo peor*)   Lo peor es que ya han salido.

1. *Lo bueno* es que Luis aceptó el puesto.   (*Lo mejor*)
2. *Lo importante* es hablar correctamente.   (*Lo necesario*)
3. Hay que recordar *lo dicho.*   (*lo hecho*)
4. No traten ustedes de hacer *lo difícil.*   (*lo imposible*)
5. Repitan ustedes *lo escrito.*   (*lo leído*)
6. Arregle usted *lo nuestro.*   (*lo suyo*)
7. Siempre andan *lo más despacio* posible.   (*lo más rápidamente*)
8. Parece que vuelven *lo más tarde* posible.   (*lo más pronto*)
9. Sabemos *lo contentos que* están ellos.   (*lo tristes que*)
10. No puedes imaginarte *lo largas que* son las lecciones.   (*lo difíciles que*)

B. Para contestar afirmativamente, usando el pronombre neutro **lo**.

MODELO: ¿Es profesora la señorita Gómez?   Sí, lo es.

1. ¿Es abogado el señor Díaz?   4. ¿Soy yo profesor (profesora)?
2. ¿Son norteamericanos sus padres?   5. ¿Parecen ellos estar contentos?
3. ¿Son Uds. estudiantes?   6. ¿Parece ser sencilla la obra?

C. Para leer en español, supliendo la conjunción **pero, sino** o **sino que**:

1. Traté de llamar a Felipe, _____ nadie contestó.
2. A Carlos le gusta la música clásica, _____ a mí no.

3. Estas melodías no son mexicanas, _____ argentinas.
4. El coche de Ricardo no tiene capota blanca, _____ negra.
5. Los niños no andaban despacio, _____ corrían rápidamente.
6. Mis amigos van a Taxco, _____ no pueden visitar San Miguel de Allende.
7. Inés dice que no quiere estudiar, _____ dormir la siesta.
8. He de quedarme aquí, _____ no se preocupen ustedes por mí.

D. Den los adverbios que correspondan a los adjetivos:

1. fuerte.   2. rico.   3. alegre.   4. sencillo.   5. triste.   6. típico.   7. cortés.
8. exacto.   9. social y económico.   10. claro y rápido.

X. VERBOS AUXILIARES PARA EXPRESAR EL MODO (*MODAL AUXILIARIES*)

A. Translation of *can* and *may*

If *can* expresses physical ability, the present tense of **poder** is used; **saber** indicates mental ability:

> **Yo dudo que él pueda ir allá.**   I doubt that he can go there.
> **¿Sabe usted jugar al golf?**   Can you (Do you know how to) play golf?

Some of the ways in which *may* is expressed are:

> **Puedes salir ahora si quieres.**   You may go out now if you wish.
> **Es posible que él lo concluya.**   He may (It is possible that he may) finish it.
> **Puede (ser) que se vayan hoy.**   They may (It may be that they will) leave today.
> **Aunque le vea yo, no se lo diré.**   Even though I may see him, I'll not tell him.
> **Que sean ustedes felices.**   May you be happy.
> **¿Se puede entrar?**   May I (we, one) come in?

B. Translation of *could* and *might*

Could, meaning *would be able to, might*, is translated by the imperfect, preterit, or conditional indicative, or by the imperfect subjunctive of **poder**:

> **Ella podía cantar bien.**   She could (was able to) sing well.
> **Pablo no pudo terminar el trabajo.**   Paul couldn't finish the work.
> **¿Podrías ayudarnos?**   Could you (Would you be able to) help us?

Dijeron que podrían esperar.   They said they could (might be able to) wait.
Era posible que vinieran (pudiesen venir).   It was possible that they
  might come.

C. Translation of *should (ought to)*, *should like*

Deber may be used in all tenses to express various degrees of obligation.   When
should indicates a mild obligation (less strong than that expressed by the present tense
of **deber**), the **-ra** imperfect subjunctive, the imperfect or conditional indicative
tenses of **deber** are used:

Usted debiera ir a verlos.   You should (ought to) go (to) see them.
Yo sabía que debía buscarle.   I knew that I should look for him.
Creíamos que Ana debía (debiera, debería) venir.   We thought Ann
  should come.

The preterit of **deber** expresses an obligation at a time previous to another past
action:

Usted debió aceptar el puesto.   You should (ought to) have accepted the
  position.

In a sentence that expresses a contrary-to-fact condition or an improbable condition
in the future (see Lección nueve), *should* is translated by the conditional indicative
tense in the main clause, and by the imperfect subjunctive tense in the **si**-clause:

Si yo tuviera tiempo, iría allá.   If I had (should have) time, I should (would)
  go there.

Should like may be translated by the **-ra** imperfect subjunctive forms of **querer**, or by
the conditional indicative of **gustar**:

Me gustaría (Yo quisiera) ir con él.   I should like to go with him.

Ejercicio

Para expresar en español:

1. Can you go to the office with me?   2. Jane can play the guitar well, but she
cannot play it today because she is ill.   3. What can I do for you?   4. You (*pl.*)

may sit down if you wish.   5. May they have a good time tonight.   6. You should look at several brands of radios if you should go to that store.   7. The clerk said last week that he could show you some new models.   8. Betty knows that she must call us today.   9. I should like (*two ways*) to drive your new car.   10. If I were in your place, I would park it near John's (that of John).

RESUMEN

A. Escuchen el modelo; luego, formen dos frases nuevas, una, empleando la voz pasiva, y la otra, empleando **estar** con el participio pasado, según el modelo.

MODELO: Juan escribió la carta.   La carta fue escrita por Juan.
                                       La carta está escrita.

1. Mi padre estacionó el coche.   4. Mi hermana puso la mesa.
2. Mi tía concluyó la visita.   5. El estudiante abrió las ventanas.
3. José arregló todo eso.   6. Yo pagué la cuenta.

B. Usos del participio pasado, del participio presente y del pretérito perfecto de indicativo.   Para expresar en español:

1. Continue (*pl.*) playing in the patio until I call you.
2. The students are (gradually) learning some Spanish songs.
3. Robert was walking (*progressive*) rapidly towards Jane's house.
4. As soon as they had returned home, they sent for us.
5. By working six or eight hours, I can finish this composition.
6. The composition written, I shall turn it in to the teacher.
7. The exercises finished, I listened to some Mexican records.
8. The trip of Louise and Inez was arranged by a business firm.
9. Someone had failed to open the door; therefore, it was still closed.
10. Richard, accompanied by some friends of his, was making (*progressive*) plans for (the) vacation (*pl.*) in South America.

C. Usos del artículo y del pronombre neutro **lo**.   Para expresar en español:

1. The best thing is to leave for Argentina next week.
2. That matter of Robert seems very strange to me.
3. Come to see us the soonest possible.

4. That is what Thomas and I intend to do.
5. Is Mr. López a musician?   —Yes, he is.
6. Is Mary an art student?   —No, she isn't.
7. Can you tell Barbara that?   —Yes, I shall tell her (it).
8. Did he turn in the report?   —I did not ask him (it).

D. Para contestar afirmativamente en español:

1. ¿Sabes jugar al golf?
2. ¿Puedes jugar conmigo hoy?
3. ¿Podrías llevarle a Ana la llave?
4. ¿Deben ustedes escribirles a sus padres?
5. ¿Debieran ustedes visitar a sus tíos?
6. ¿Quisieran ustedes ir a México este verano?
7. ¿Es posible que tu padre te ofrezca el dinero para ir allá?
8. ¿Sería posible que él te lo ofreciera?
9. ¿Puede ser que tú consigas el puesto que deseas?
10. ¿Podría ser que tú lo consiguieras?
11. ¿Irá usted a la sierra si alguien le (la) invita?
12. ¿Iría usted a México si alguien le (la) invitara?

Cúpula del Capitolio de Buenos Aires, Argentina

LECTURA VI

PRESENTACIÓN

A. Estudio de palabras

1. Approximate cognates.   Pronounce and note the English meaning of each word: burocrático, *bureaucratic*; descontento, *discontent*; equitativo, *equitable*; humanitario, *humanitarian*; injusto, *unjust*; miembro, *member*; objetivo, *objective*; obstáculo, *obstacle*; privilegio, *privilege*; sistema, *system*; sufrimiento, *suffering*; acelerar, *to accelerate*; asumir, *to assume*; garantizar, *to guarantee*; mantener, *to maintain*.

2. Compare the meanings of the following groups of related words: aumentar, *to augment, increase*, aumento, *increase*; comercio, comercial, comerciar, *to trade, have commercial relations*; común, *common*, comunidad, *community*; cooperar, *to cooperate*, cooperación, *cooperation*; débil, *weak*, debilidad, *weakness*; desarrollar, *to develop*, desarrollo, *development*, subdesarrollado, *underdeveloped*; discutir, *to discuss*, discusión; distribuir, *to distribute*, distribución; diverso, *diverse, different*, diversificar, *to diversify*; estructura, *structure, development*, estructuración, *building process*; evolución, *evolution*, evolutivo, *evolutionary*; imponer, *to impose*, oponer, *to oppose*, proponer, *to propose*; industria, industrial, industrializar, industrialización; mejor, mejora *and* mejoramiento, *betterment, improvement*; mundo, mundial, *world(-wide)*, *universal*; rápido, rapidez, *rapidity, speed*; producir, producción, producto, productora, *producer*; vivir, vivienda, *dwelling, house*.

3. The meaning of many Spanish words may be deduced in context by first associating the closest English cognate, then by thinking of one or more English words of approximately the same meaning.   Some examples in this Lectura are: ampliar, *to amplify—to enlarge, broaden*; efectuar, *to effect—to carry out*; elevar, *to elevate—to raise*; fomentar, *to foment—to promote, encourage, foster*; retardar, *to retard—to slow down*; activación, *activation—promotion*; disminución, *diminution—decrease*; disparidad, *disparity—inequality*; eficaz, *efficacious—effective*; entidad, *entity—body, organization*; índice, *index—rate*; jurídico, *juridical—legal*; organismo, *organism—organization, agency*; urbanización, *urbanization—city planning (growth)*.

4. Find in this Lectura Spanish nouns in **-o, -a**, and **-ado**, related to the following verbs: esforzarse, estimular, intentar, pasar, progresar; ayudar, buscar, practicar; resultar, tratar.

5. Deceptive cognates.   The noun **cifra** may mean *figure*, as well as *cipher*; **inversiones** means *investments* (and only rarely, *inversions*); **perjuicio**, *detriment, damage*, should not be confused with **prejuicio**, *prejudice, bias*; **recurso**, *recourse*, also means *resource*, and in the plural, *resources, means*.   Remember that **papel**, *paper*, is commonly used in the sense of *role*.

255

Note the use of **medio**, as a noun, for *way, means*; and as an adjective meaning *middle*: **la clase media**, *the middle class*.

The adjectives **exterior** and **interior** may be used in the sense of *foreign* and *domestic*, respectively. The adverb **desgraciadamente** means *unfortunately*, not *disgracefully*. Compare **por desgracia**, *unfortunately*, used earlier.

B. Modismos y frases útiles

a pesar de   in spite of, despite
al año   yearly, each year
al ritmo (actual)   at the (present) rate
los bienes de equipo   capital goods
el comercio exterior   foreign trade
dar un paso   to take a step
de manera ejemplar   in an exemplary way
deberse a   to be due to
la demanda interior   domestic demand
en perjuicio de   to the detriment of
la fuente de ingresos   source of income
llevar a cabo   to carry out

más adelante   later (farther) on
la mayoría de   the majority of, most (of)
el nivel de vida   standard of living
oponerse a   to oppose
pasar de   to exceed
por consiguiente   consequently, therefore
prestar atención (a)   to pay attention (to)
respecto de   with regard to, concerning
sin embargo   nevertheless

C. Aspectos gramaticales

1. Gender and number of certain nouns and adjectives.   **Agrícola**, *agricultural*, is another adjective ending in **-a** which has only one form for the masculine and feminine: **la producción agrícola**, *agricultural production*; **un país agrícola**, *an agricultural country*.

Masculine nouns in **-ma** which occur in this Lectura are: **problema**, **programa**, and **sistema**.

Latin terms used as nouns usually do not change in the plural; the article suffices to indicate the plural: **el déficit**, *the deficit*, **los déficit**, *the deficits*.

Occasionally a masculine noun in **-or** has a comparable feminine form in **-ora**: **el productor**, *producer*, **la productora**, *producer*.   Compare **profesor** and **profesora**.

2. We learned in Lección ocho that the Spanish definite article replaces the demonstrative pronoun before **que**.   When a preposition precedes **que**, the demonstrative pronoun is restored, but the accent mark is not used:

sobre todo en aquellos en que la población indígena . . .
above all in those in which the native population . . .

3. Notes on the use of the present participle. We are familiar with the use of the present participle with the verbs **estar** and **ir** to form progressive tenses:

se está emprendiendo un vasto programa social . . . ,
a vast social program is being undertaken . . . ,
van surgiendo diversos tipos de sociedades . . .
different types of societies are gradually appearing (are beginning to appear) . . .

The verbs **continuar** and **seguir** are similarly used to express that an action is continuing:

Si la población continúa creciendo . . .
If the population continues to grow (growing) . . .
el comercio exterior no sigue aumentando . . .
foreign trade does not continue increasing (to increase) . . .

Typically Spanish is the use of the present participle (as explained in Lección doce) to convey a variety of adverbial relationships. In English the preposition *by* frequently introduces the construction:

Se espera que el libre comercio . . . contribuya al desarrollo económico general, ampliando los mercados y estimulando . . .
It is hoped that free commerce (trade) . . . will contribute to the general economic development, by enlarging the markets and by stimulating . . .

Special care is required with the English adjective forms in *-ing*, which rarely, if ever, are translated by the Spanish present participle. Note, in this Lectura, **dominante**, *dominating*; **entrante**, *coming, next* (month, year, century). English nouns in *-ing* often show a suffix or an infinitive form in Spanish: **la financiación**, *financing*; **el bienestar**, *well-being* (*welfare*).

4. When the adverb **aún**, *still, yet*, follows (and sometimes when it precedes) the verb or word it modifies, it is pronounced and written as two syllables: **aún**.

No han llegado aún. They haven't arrived yet.

Aun (occasionally **aún**) also means *even*, in which case it precedes the word it modifies:

Aun antes de la llegada . . . Even before the arrival . . .
Un paso aún más importante . . . An even (still) more important step . . .

5. After reviewing the use of the subjunctive in adjective clauses (Lección ocho) explain why the four subjunctive forms are used in the sentence on page 262, lines 26–29.

HISPANOAMÉRICA EN EL ÚLTIMO
TERCIO DEL SIGLO XX

Los problemas económicos y sociales que los países hispanoamericanos tendrán que resolver durante las próximas décadas son sumamente graves. A pesar de los esfuerzos de los últimos años, la América latina no ha logrado progresar con la rapidez deseada. Los elementos de protesta y de crítica social y política que hemos observado al tratar de la literatura y del arte en las Lecturas anteriores reflejan el descontento y la frustración de muchos sectores de la sociedad. Aunque muchos de estos problemas son comunes a las regiones subdesarrolladas, será de interés tratar de ellos en su contexto hispanoamericano.

El problema más evidente es el de la debilidad económica y política de los países hispanoamericanos frente a la gran república norteamericana. En parte se debe al fraccionamiento[1] geográfico del territorio; pero también se debe a fuertes sentimientos nacionalistas que se han opuesto a los intentos de unificación propuestos desde la época de Bolívar. Como veremos más adelante, alguna forma de integración económica será necesaria para garantizar un futuro de paz y de bienestar para nuestros vecinos al sur del Río Grande.

Otro problema urgente es el de la injusta distribución de la riqueza y del poder. La disparidad entre las clases ricas y las masas es excesiva. Las clases ricas defienden sus privilegios desesperadamente y no se preocupan suficientemente con los sufrimientos de las clases bajas. En muy pocos países se practica la democracia, y para mantener el orden se ha acudido a[2] los gobiernos militares.

Para que puedan desarrollarse en Hispanoamérica las ideas democráticas habrá que dedicar atención especial a la educación de las masas. En los últimos años se han construido miles de escuelas; pero es penoso[3] observar que el índice de analfabetismo[4] todavía pasa del 50 por 100 en muchos países, sobre todo en aquellos en que* la población indígena es numerosa.

Otro problema gravísimo es el del rápido aumento de la población, el cual, entre otras dificultades, ha creado la necesidad de aumentar proporcionalmente la producción alimenticia.[5] Si la población continúa creciendo* al ritmo actual (aproximadamente el 3 por 100 al año), llegará a los seiscientos millones de habitantes en el siglo entrante. Hispano-

---

[1] **fraccionamiento,** *fractioning, division.* [2] **se ha acudido a,** *they have resorted to.* [3] **penoso,** *distressing.* [4] **analfabetismo,** *illiteracy.* [5] **alimenticia,** *(of) food.*

américa no tiene hoy día los recursos económicos para construir las escuelas
y las viviendas que se necesitan.   ¿Qué medios podrán encontrarse para
elevar el nivel de vida en el siglo XXI?

En general, se ha considerado la industrialización como el medio más
eficaz para elevar el nivel de vida en las zonas subdesarrolladas.   En la
América hispana, sin embargo, los obstáculos que encuentra la industrialización son muy graves.   Uno de los más importantes es la falta de recursos
económicos.   En la economía de los países hispanoamericanos el comercio
exterior ha sido una de las principales fuentes de ingresos,[1] por el estímulo
que constituye para las actividades industriales y comerciales.   Pues, a pesar
de los esfuerzos de los últimos años, el comercio exterior no sigue aumentando* con la suficiente rapidez. Desgraciadamente la exportación de
productos básicos—como el café o los minerales—no varía mucho de un
año a otro.   Además, en la nueva edad industrial y tecnológica en que
vivimos, la exportación de productos básicos no tiene la importancia que
tiene la de artículos manufacturados.   Los países industrializados, por consiguiente, comercian con países del mismo tipo, en perjuicio de los países
subdesarrollados.   En 1953 las exportaciones hispanoamericanas constituían
el 9.5[2] por ciento de las exportaciones del comercio mundial; diez años más
tarde la cifra había bajado al 5.5 por 100.   Es evidente que Hispanoamérica no puede continuar en el papel de productora de materias básicas.
Además de diversificar y de aumentar la producción agrícola, tendrá que
desarrollar la capacidad de competir en la producción de artículos manufacturados.

Para contrarrestar[3] la disminución de las exportaciones ha habido un
esfuerzo por aumentar la demanda interior, por la creación de mercados
nuevos.   Es claro que para efectuar una intensa activación del comercio
interior habrá que comenzar con una honda[4] transformación de la sociedad,
para hacer posible una distribución más equitativa de la riqueza.   Las
reformas sociales son urgentes no sólo por razones políticas y humanitarias,
sino también por razones económicas.

Las inversiones domésticas y el crédito exterior han constituido las principales fuentes de financiación del déficit comercial.   El ritmo de las inversiones no ha bastado para asegurar el progreso rápido de la industrialización;
será necesario, por consiguiente, aumentar el crédito exterior extendido a
Hispanoamérica.   Sin el capital necesario no pueden importarse los bienes
de equipo y los otros productos indispensables para estimular la producción
industrial.

---

[1] **ingresos**, *income, revenue.*   [2] Read **nueve y medio**.   [3] **contrarrestar**, *to counteract, offset.*
[4] **honda**, *profound, far-reaching*.

Fabricando artículos de
cerámica, Oaxaca, México

Restaurante del Lago,
ciudad de México

Escuela de un distrito pobre del Perú

Patio del famoso palacio Torre Tagle, Lima, Perú

Interior de una casa, Arequipa, Perú

Con las reformas de los últimos años ha habido un aumento notable en las responsabilidades y obligaciones del gobierno. En algunos países el gobierno ha asumido directamente la operación de ciertas industrias. Estimulados por la Alianza para el Progreso (iniciada por el presidente Kennedy en 1961), algunos países han acelerado sus programas para satisfacer las aspiraciones del pueblo respecto de la educación, la sanidad,[1] la urbanización, etcétera. En pocos años se han construido miles de escuelas y de viviendas y se han distribuido miles de libros; muchos lugares ya tienen servicios de alcantarillado,[2] hospitales y centros de salud. Para realizar estas mejoras ha sido necesario introducir cambios en el sistema burocrático y, sobre todo, en el sistema tributario.[3] Los esfuerzos de las clases poderosas por retardar reformas como las citadas revelan uno de los puntos más débiles en la nueva estructuración de Hispanoamérica: se está emprendiendo un vasto programa social* sin haber efectuado un cambio radical en la estructura de la sociedad.

No debemos olvidar que se presentan diversas etapas[4] de evolución económica y social en Hispanoamérica. En algunos países—México, Bolivia y Cuba—los procesos[5] revolucionarios han producido cambios radicales en la estructura social. En otros países van surgiendo diversos tipos de sociedades,* caracterizados, en general, por una fuerte clase media, con ingresos relativamente elevados. Hay que reconocer, sin embargo, que la mayoría de los hispanoamericanos todavía viven bajo regímenes en que el poder y la riqueza se encuentran concentrados en pocas manos. Para asegurar el bienestar de los países hispanoamericanos y fortalecer el desarrollo de los sistemas democráticos, habrá que emprender una serie de reformas económicas y sociales que eliminen los privilegios y la discriminación, den énfasis a la movilidad social y proporcionen a las generaciones jóvenes la motivación suficiente para adquirir la preparación científica y técnica que necesiten para competir en la sociedad moderna.

Como ya hemos indicado, será difícil que los países hispanoamericanos puedan llevar a cabo programas como los descritos si continúan dentro de sus estrechas fronteras actuales. La integración económica de Hispanoamérica es necesaria no sólo para estimular las relaciones comerciales, sino también para hacer posibles las vastas operaciones científicas y técnicas que habrá que emprender en el futuro—operaciones que sólo pueden ser realizadas por naciones de grandes recursos económicos. Sin la integración discutida,

---

[1] **sanidad,** *health, sanitation.*   [2] **alcantarillado,** *sewage system.*   [3] **tributario,** *of (pertaining to) taxation.*   [4] **etapas,** *stages.*   [5] **procesos,** *processes, progressive movements.*

los países hispanoamericanos no podrán asumir el puesto que les corresponde en la comunidad de naciones.

Es grato observar que se han dado ya los primeros pasos hacia la integración económica. La creación del Banco Centroamericano de Integración Económica, por ejemplo, ha estimulado las relaciones comerciales en Centroamérica. Un paso aún* más importante ha sido el establecimiento, en 1960, por el Tratado de Montevideo, de la Asociación Latinoamericana de Libre Comercio, cuyo objeto es el libre comercio en la América latina. Se espera que el libre comercio acelere la industrialización y contribuya al desarrollo económico general, ampliando los mercados y estimulando* las inversiones. Nueve naciones han aprobado el Tratado: la Argentina, el Brasil, Chile, Colombia, el Ecuador, México, el Perú, el Paraguay y el Uruguay. En conjunto, forman uno de los mercados más importantes del mundo, con una población de más de 222 millones. En la práctica parece que México ha sido el país que se ha beneficiado más del[1] Tratado.

Entre las entidades internacionales que han contribuido a elevar el nivel de vida de Hispanoamérica y a fomentar el desarrollo económico general, la más importante es la Organización de los Estados Americanos (OEA). El resultado de un proceso evolutivo que se inició hace más de un siglo, la OEA fue creada, en su forma actual, en 1948 como un organismo regional dentro de las Naciones Unidas. Desde entonces la OEA ha cumplido sus objetivos de manera ejemplar, manteniendo la paz entre sus miembros, esforzándose por resolver los problemas políticos, jurídicos, sociales y económicos de los respectivos países e impulsando su desarrollo económico, social y cultural.

Entre las otras instituciones que han contribuido al mejoramiento de la economía y de la vida en general hay que citar el Banco Interamericano de Desarrollo y la Organización Panamericana de la Salud.

Al concluir esta larga, pero incompleta, discusión hay que insistir en el hecho de que los problemas que hemos descrito son nuestros también; las soluciones y remedios que encuentren los países hispanoamericanos afectarán sus relaciones con todas las naciones del mundo libre. Los Estados Unidos ha demostrado que quiere cooperar en la busca de dichas[2] soluciones—pero sin imponer condiciones y sin el papel dominante que ha dañado nuestras relaciones en el pasado. Es preciso que las dos Américas alcancen el máximo grado posible de cooperación y ayuda mutua.

---

[1] **se ha beneficiado más de,** *has benefitted most from, has taken most advantage of.*   [2] **dichas,** *the aforementioned.*

Madre e hijo en un mercado
de Pátzcuaro, Michoacán,
México

PRÁCTICAS ORALES

A. Diálogos originales

Dos estudiantes prepararán un diálogo original, de unas doce líneas, para recitar
en clase, empleando las frases y preguntas siguientes como elemento inicial:

1. «Una discusión en la clase de español»

PROFESOR. Hoy vamos a discutir algunos de los problemas sociales y económicos
de los países hispanoamericanos. ¿Cuál es el problema más
evidente que estos países tendrán que resolver?

ESTUDIANTE. El problema más evidente es el de la debilidad económica y política
de los países hispanoamericanos frente a los Estados Unidos.

2. «En la Casa de Correos»

(*Dos estudiantes se encuentran en la Casa de Correos y charlan un rato antes de separarse.*)

ESTUDIANTE 1°   Veo que has recibido una carta de Bolivia. ¿Es de nuestro amigo boliviano que estudió con nosotros el año pasado?

ESTUDIANTE 2°   No. Es de un amigo que está trabajando en un proyecto de la Alianza para el Progreso.

3. «En la Residencia de Estudiantes»

(*Dos estudiantes acaban de volver a su cuarto. Charlan un poco acerca de la clase de español.*)

ESTUDIANTE 1°   Le hemos pedido al profesor que dediquemos un día más a la discusión de los problemas de Hispanoamérica.

ESTUDIANTE 2°   ¡Hombre! ¡Cuánto me alegro! No hemos prestado bastante atención a las necesidades de las generaciones jóvenes.

B. Para formular preguntas en español

Formúlense preguntas sobre la segunda parte de la Lectura VI (a partir del párrafo en la página 262 que comienza, «Con las reformas de los últimos años . . .», para que las contesten los demás estudiantes de la clase.

EJERCICIOS ESCRITOS

A. Uso de modismos y frases hechas

Usen los modismos y frases siguientes en oraciones completas:

a pesar de	llevar a cabo
al ritmo actual	oponerse a
deberse a	pasar de
en perjuicio de	respecto de

B. Para expresar en español

1. In the last third of the twentieth century the Spanish American countries will have to solve many economic and social problems which are extremely serious. 2. The economic and political weakness of most of those countries is due in part to the

geographic division of the territory and to strong nationalistic feelings which have opposed unification.   3. Other urgent problems are that of the unjust distribution of wealth and power, that of the rapid increase of population, and the lack of economic resources.   4. Besides stimulating industrialization and the export of manufactured products, it will be necessary to diversify and to increase agricultural production. 5. It is true that a certain attention has been given to the education of the masses and that thousands of schools have been built, but, unfortunately, the rate of illiteracy still exceeds fifty per cent in many Spanish American countries.   6. And it is evident that domestic investments and foreign credit are necessary in order that the governments of those countries can carry out reforms in the future.   7. Also, in spite of the progress which has been made in the last few years, they will have to introduce radical changes in the bureaucratic system, in the system of taxation, and in the social structure of Spanish America.   8. Even though a strong middle class is gradually arising, especially in the large cities, one must remember, nevertheless, that wealth and power are still concentrated in relatively few hands and that democracy is not practiced in many countries.   9. Among various solutions and remedies, Spanish America must undertake the necessary reforms which may provide the young generations sufficient motivation to acquire the technical preparation which they will need in order to compete in modern society.   10. Two of the first steps which have been taken in order to enlarge markets and to stimulate investments is the creation of the Central American Bank of Economic Integration and the establishment of the Latin American Association of Free Trade.   11. The Organization of American States, created in 1948, has contributed a great deal to raise the standard of living in the Spanish American countries, to maintain peace among its members, and to encourage their economic, social, political, and cultural development.   12. By means of cooperation and mutual aid the two Americas can contribute much to the solution of present problems, provided that the United States does not continue imposing conditions which have harmed our relations in the past.

C. Temas para un informe o composición

Escriban un informe o composición, de unas 120 palabras, sobre uno de los temas siguientes:

1. La industrialización en la América española.
2. La integración económica de Hispanoamérica.
3. Composición libre sobre un tema relacionado con la Lectura VI.

REPASO GENERAL

A. Repitan cada frase, pronunciándola en dos grupos fónicos (*breath-groups*) y fijándose en la entonación; luego, repítanla otra vez, omitiendo (*omitting*) el segundo substantivo de la frase:

1. Estas flores y las flores que tienes.
2. Esa tarjeta y la tarjeta que ella me envió.
3. Este cuento y el cuento que me contaste.
4. Estos dibujos y los dibujos que vimos ayer.
5. Aquella señorita y la señorita del pelo rojo.
6. Aquel jardín y el jardín de mi mamá.
7. Aquella mujer y la mujer del vestido amarillo.
8. Esos discos y los discos de música americana.
9. Esta orquesta y la orquesta que tocó anoche.
10. Estas melodías y las melodías que acabamos de oír.

B. Dictado.   (The teacher will select lines from page 258 for dictation.)

C. Para repetir, cambiando la forma del verbo a los tiempos indicados:

Pretérito
1. Marco el número de teléfono.
2. Juan nunca hace nada.
3. Yo le entrego a Ana el pan.
4. Vamos a la reunión el sábado.
5. ¿Les dicen Uds. lo importante?
6. ¿Duermen la siesta por la tarde?

Imperfecto
7. Él va al café a menudo.
8. Yo los veo todos los días.
9. Es preciso practicar mucho.
10. ¿Puedes hablar con ella a veces?
11. Hay muchos niños en la piscina.
12. Nos vemos todas las noches.

Futuro
13. Hacen eso con mucho gusto.
14. ¿Les dices tú la verdad?
15. Tengo mucho cuidado con el coche.
16. ¿Vale más esperar en la esquina?

D. Para repetir, y luego cambiar la forma de los verbos al pretérito o al imperfecto:

1. Son las cinco cuando mi padre vuelve de su oficina.
2. Le pregunto a Bárbara si quiere dar un paseo conmigo.

3. Yo sé que los niños juegan en el parque todas las tardes.
4. En esta carta mi tía dice que espera visitarnos pronto.
5. Yo estoy seguro de que Luisa se siente mejor.
6. La profesora quiere saber si la composición está bien escrita.
7. Elena me escribe que va a hacer una excursión a la sierra.
8. Dorotea entra en su cuarto y se sienta a estudiar.

E. Para repetir, y luego cambiar a la forma negativa:

1. Hay alguien en el patio.
2. Inés tiene algo en las manos.
3. Alguien acaba de llamar.
4. Siempre nos envían algo bonito.
5. Alguna de ellas seguirá cantando.
6. Algún muchacho traerá las flores.
7. Alguno de los cuadros es de Juan.
8. ¿Has estado alguna vez en México?
9. ¿Has visto a alguien esta tarde?
10. Él se da prisa también.
11. Ella escogerá alguna de las casas.
12. Alguien siempre nos da algo.

F. Para repetir, y luego cambiar a la construcción reflexiva (para expresar el sujeto indefinido o la voz pasiva):

1. En este país viajan mucho en avión.
2. ¿Cómo dicen eso en español?
3. ¿A qué hora cierran la oficina?
4. ¿Abren los edificios a las diez?
5. No estacionan coches en esta calle.
6. Han escrito muchos buenos artículos.
7. ¿Han presentado películas mexicanas?
8. Siempre servían buen café allí.

G. Para contestar afirmativamente, substituyendo el substantivo en cursiva con el pronombre correspondiente:

1. ¿Le ha dado Ud. a Marta *el regalo*?
2. ¿Les darás a los niños *la revista*?
3. ¿Dejó Ud. *la cinta* sobre la mesa?
4. ¿Tendrás que lavarte *las manos*?
5. ¿Ya han traído Uds. *los discos*?
6. ¿Están leyendo ellos *el cuento*?
7. ¿Saldrán Uds. de *casa* temprano?
8. ¿Pudo Ud. comprar *la bolsa* para Ana?

H. Para contestar, empleando formas de mandato con **Ud**(**s**)., primero la forma afirmativa y luego la negativa:

1. ¿Me pongo el abrigo?
2. ¿Me siento en esta fila?
3. ¿Se lo devuelvo a ellos ahora?
4. ¿Se los llevo a él mañana?
5. ¿Nos quedamos allí un rato?
6. ¿Nos acercamos a la pared?
7. ¿Se lo entregamos a ella hoy?
8. ¿Le traemos a Ud. las fotos?

Contesten las preguntas 1–4, empleando formas de mandato con **tú**, primero afirmativa, y luego negativamente.

I. Para contestar afirmativamente, usando en la contestación **estar** con el participio pasado:

1. ¿Has escrito los artículos?
2. ¿Has cerrado la cámara?
3. ¿Ha puesto Ud. la mesa?
4. ¿Ha abierto Ud. las ventanas?
5. ¿Han roto la bicicleta?
6. ¿Han envuelto los paquetes?

J. Repitan la oración; luego, al oír una frase con la conjunción **que**, usen la frase en una nueva oración:

1. Prefiero ir al museo de arte.   (que Ud.)
2. ¿Quieres tocar unos discos de música clásica?   (que Ana)
3. Ellos insisten en apagar las luces.   (en que yo)
4. José teme no llegar a tiempo.   (que nosotros)
5. Es lástima no conocerle mejor.   (que tú)
6. Nos alegramos de tener un televisor nuevo.   (que Pablo)

7. Era extraño no verlos en el centro.   (que Uds.)
8. Yo esperaba encontrar otra marca de radio.   (que tú)
9. No estábamos seguros de poder visitarlos a menudo.   (de que Marta)
10. Sentíamos no saber esa canción mexicana.   (que los estudiantes)

K. Después de oír una oración, oirán una oración incompleta; formen una nueva oración introducida por la oración incompleta.

MODELO: José irá allá.   (Déjele Ud.)   Déjele Ud. a José que vaya allá.

1. Felipe traerá los billetes lo más pronto posible.   (Dígale Ud.)
2. Pablo vendrá mañana por la noche.   (Aconséjele Ud.)
3. Isabel escogerá un vestido esta tarde.   (Le pediré)
4. Ricardo seguirá buscando un puesto.   (Le he aconsejado)
5. Roberto conducirá el coche esta noche.   (No le permita Ud.)

6. Ella pudo ir de compras con su prima.   (Me alegré de que)
7. Jaime tenía dolor de cabeza.   (Fue lástima que)
8. Antonio estaba muy ocupado.   (Yo no creía que)
9. Nuestra mamá se puso enferma durante el invierno.   (Temíamos que)
10. Ellos le permitieron quedarse allí un mes.   (Yo dudaba que)

L. Repitan cada oración; luego, al oír el comienzo de otra oración, completen la nueva, haciendo los cambios necesarios.

MODELO: Tienen una casa que es grande.   Tienen una casa que es grande.
    (Buscan)   Buscan una casa que sea grande.

1. Juan tiene un puesto que le gusta.   (Juan quiere)
2. Conozco a alguien que toca música española.   (¿Conoces . . . ?)
3. Vemos a un hombre que sabe arreglar la máquina.   (Buscamos un hombre)
4. He hablado con alguien que ha viajado por Chile.   (No he hablado con nadie)
5. Yo tengo una secretaria que habla español.   (Yo necesito)

6. Él quiere encontrar a alguien que haya vivido en México.   (Él quería)
7. No vemos a nadie que pueda llevarle al médico.   (No vimos)
8. ¿Hay alguien que haga la excursión con Miguel?   (¿Había . . . ?)
9. No hay nada en la tienda que nos guste.   (No había)
10. ¿Han leído ustedes algo que sea típico del país?   (¿Habían leído ustedes . . . ?)

M. Repitan la oración; luego, al oír el comienzo de otra oración, completen la nueva, haciendo los cambios necesarios.

MODELOS: Él salió aunque llovía.   Él salió aunque llovía.
    (Él saldrá)   Él saldrá aunque llueva.
    Yo le saludo cuando le veo.   Yo le saludo cuando le veo.
    (Yo le saludaré)   Yo le saludaré cuando le vea.

1. Les enseñé las fotografías cuando los vi.   (Les enseñaré)
2. Fuimos a ver a mis abuelos en cuanto fue posible.   (Iremos a ver)
3. Me quedé hasta que volvieron Ana e Isabel.   (Me quedaré)
4. Tuvimos que marcharnos aunque hacía mal tiempo.   (Tendremos que marcharnos)
5. El profesor habla claramente de modo que le entendemos.   (El profesor hablará)
6. Me gusta charlar con el señor Díaz cuando está aquí.   (Me gustará charlar)

N. Escuchen la oración; luego, formen una frase condicional usando las dos formas del imperfecto de subjuntivo en la cláusula introducida por **si**.

MODELO: Él lo haría, pero no está aquí.   Si él estuviera (estuviese) aquí,
                                             lo haría.

1. Yo le daría el billete, pero no le veo.
2. Me pondría el sombrero, pero no está lloviendo.

3. Ellos llegarían para las cinco, pero no se dan prisa.
4. Iríamos al concierto con ustedes, pero no tenemos tiempo.
5. Le daría a Marta las gracias, pero ella no ha vuelto.
6. Pablo haría el viaje, pero no ha ganado bastante dinero.

O. Repitan la frase o la pregunta; luego, repítanla otra vez, substituyendo las palabras en cursiva con el pronombre posesivo:

1. *Nuestro jardín* es muy bonito.
2. Les gustan *nuestras maletas.*
3. Quisieran mirar *mi cámara.*
4. Dame *tu bolsa.*
5. Llévale tú a él *su billete.*
6. No dejes allí *tus esquíes.*

7. Fueron por *su coche.*
8. Quítate *tus guantes.*
9. Yo traje *el equipaje de él.*
10. Estacione Ud. *el coche de ella.*
11. No te olvides de dejar *mis llaves.*
12. Me gusta muchísimo *el traje de Ud.*

13. Esta cámara es *de ellos.*
14. Esta blusa blanca es *de ella.*

15. ¿Son *de Ud.* estas rosas?
16. ¿Es *de Uds.* este coche rojo?

P. Para contestar en español:

1. ¿Qué tiempo hace hoy? 2. ¿Qué tiempo hace aquí en la primavera? 3. ¿Cuál de las estaciones le gusta a usted más? 4. ¿Qué planes tiene usted para las vacaciones? 5. ¿Qué deporte prefiere usted? 6. ¿Sabe usted jugar al golf? 7. ¿Tiene usted radio de onda corta? 8. ¿Escucha usted programas mexicanos a veces? 9. ¿Dónde puede uno comprar el libro de español? 10. ¿Cuántos estudiantes hay en esta clase? 11. ¿Cuántos estudiantes hay en esta universidad? 12. ¿Cuál es la fecha de hoy? 13. ¿Qué día de la semana es hoy? 14. ¿Cuántos años hace que estudia usted aquí? 15. ¿Soy yo menor o mayor que usted? 16. ¿Tiene usted hermanos mayores? 17. ¿Dónde se divierte usted el sábado por la noche? 18. ¿Con quién habla usted por teléfono? 19. ¿Tiene usted mucho sueño en clase a veces? 20. ¿Qué hago yo cuando veo que alguien tiene sueño? 21. ¿Qué parte del periódico universitario prefiere usted leer? 22. ¿Le gusta a usted mucho la música popular? 23. ¿Qué se necesita para sacar fotografías? 24. ¿Qué le gustaría a usted hacer si fuera millonario? 25. Si usted pudiera ir a México, ¿qué parte del país le gustaría visitar?

Q. Para expresar en español:

1. By the way, where did Mary go? 2. She went to Jane's by bus a while ago.
3. I arrived home at about ten o'clock. 4. We were supposed to wait here fifteen minutes. 5. You must be very tired (*two ways*) tonight. 6. Henry and Caroline

must have gone to the concert. 7. It was about five o'clock when Tom called me. 8. What do you think of this green dress? Do you like it? 9. We have been studying Spanish about six months. 10. How long have you been living in this city? 11. My grandfather had been working in Argentina five years when he returned to the United States. 12. We ran across Barbara and a friend (*f.*) of hers downtown. 13. What's the matter with George? Does he have a headache (*two ways*)? 14. Most of the students sleep late on Sundays, don't they? 15. Jane's parents are about to leave for South America.

R. Para expresar en español:

1. Don't call (*fam.*) Dorothy, but Martha. 2. We were cold and hungry after skiing all afternoon. 3. Although the sun is shining this morning, it is very windy. 4. We like to take walks through the park when the moon is shining. 5. It took him more than four hours to reach San Francisco. 6. Charles has only five dollars; therefore, he cannot buy the shirt. 7. It costs more than he thought. 8. What a beautiful suit! But how expensive it is! 9. How sorry I am not to be able to buy it! 10. It is the prettiest one in the store. 11. People say that Mr. Molina's country house is smaller than this one. 12. Is yours (*f.*) as large as the one we looked at last week? 13. That novel was written by a friend of ours. 14. I should like (*two ways*) to accompany you (*pl.*), but I have to work. 15. What do you (*pl.*) intend to do during the summer?

S. Para expresar en español:

1. Let's sit down; we can wait here until Charles comes to pick us up. 2. How glad we are that you (*pl.*) are going to Argentina! May you have a good time on the excursion! 3. Tell the girls to get dressed right away if they want to arrive on time. 4. Is there anyone who will take a friend of mine to the doctor's office? 5. It will be necessary for us to leave for the airport before Mr. López returns home. 6. We shall have to go to the lecture even though it may rain tonight. 7. We do not believe that Betty will be ready before a quarter of eight. 8. All the students will meet near the Student Center provided that it is good weather. 9. Martha is very sorry that her mother has not been able to visit her this month. 10. Paul called Richard in order that the latter might help him to select a new camera. 11. Did you (*fam.*) ask him to put a roll of film in the camera in order to try it? 12. Jane said that she was looking for a dress that might cost less than the one that she bought last week. 13. Would that Margaret were here with us! Perhaps she will come later, but I doubt it. 14. If my sister had not been ill, she would have gone shopping with us. 15. If we had the money, we would take a long trip through Mexico during vacation.

LECTURAS

Lectura I

Indiquen, por medio de las palabras *verdad* o *mentira*, si las oraciones siguientes son verdaderas o falsas:

1. Enciso guió la expedición de Núñez de Balboa a Panamá en el año 1510.
2. Hablando con los indios, los españoles oyeron hablar de un mar enorme en el cual navegaban los barcos de una nación poderosa.
3. Balboa tardó solamente tres días en atravesar el istmo de Panamá.
4. Pedrarias Dávila tomó posesión del Mar Pacífico en nombre del rey de España el 29 de septiembre de 1513.
5. Hernán Cortés, que llegó a la costa de México en 1519, fundó una nueva colonia.
6. Al acercarse Cortés y sus soldados a la capital azteca, el emperador Moctezuma salió a recibirlos y les permitió entrar en la ciudad.
7. Al poco tiempo los españoles le arrojaron al emperador una piedra que le causó la muerte.
8. Pizarro, acompañado de cuatro hermanos suyos, salió de Panamá para el Perú en enero de 1531.
9. El emperador inca, Atahualpa, aceptó la religión cristiana y reconoció el poderío del rey de España.
10. Después de tomar el Cuzco, la capital del imperio inca, Pizarro fundó la Ciudad de los Reyes el seis de enero de 1535.
11. Hernando de Soto había estado en Panamá y en el Perú antes de partir de Cuba para la Florida en 1539.
12. Después de explorar las regiones al norte y al oeste y de descubrir el río Misisipí, de Soto continuó hasta México.

Lectura II

Para completar:

1. Cuando Napoleón invadió a España en 1808, las colonias decidieron que _____.
2. Los dos grandes libertadores de la América del Sur fueron _____.
3. En el año _____ Bolívar volvió de España a Venezuela para tomar parte en la rebelión contra los españoles.
4. Por fin, Bolívar logró fundar la Gran Colombia, formada por las repúblicas actuales de _____.
5. El sueño de la vida de Bolívar fue la creación de _____.
6. La marcha de San Martín a través de _____ es una de las hazañas más notables de la historia militar.

7. Después de la conquista de Chile, San Martín ocupó a _____ y se proclamó _____.
8. Cuando San Martín se retiró de la lucha por la independencia del Perú, le tocó a _____ dar el golpe de muerte a las _____.
9. En México la revolución contra los españoles fue iniciada por _____.
10. Los revolucionarios mexicanos llevaban como bandera oficial la _____.
11. Aunque Hidalgo fracasó en sus planes, se le considera como _____.
12. Se celebra la fiesta nacional de México el _____.

Lectura III

Para identificar (*identify*) brevemente en español:

1. El siglo en que la novela y el cuento han llegado a tener una vida propia.
2. El representante más ilustre de la cultura sudamericana del siglo XIX.
3. La obra argentina que presenta un análisis magnífico del gaucho.
4. El mejor poema gauchesco, escrito por José Hernández.
5. El autor de *Tradiciones peruanas*.
6. El maestro reconocido de la poesía modernista.
7. El pensador uruguayo, autor de *Ariel*.
8. El género literario en que a veces la naturaleza viene a ser el protagonista.
9. La obra de Gallegos que trata de la vida de las llanuras de Venezuela.
10. El personaje de la obra anterior que simboliza el espíritu civilizador de la ciudad.
11. La novela colombiana en que la selva es el verdadero protagonista.
12. El cuentista que pasó muchos años en las selvas del norte de la Argentina.

Lectura IV

Indiquen, por medio de las palabras *verdad* o *mentira*, si las oraciones siguientes son verdaderas o falsas:

1. La obra y la personalidad de Rubén Darío determinaron la evolución de la poesía hispanoamericana en la primera parte del siglo XX.
2. Todos los poetas jóvenes que colaboraron con Darío quedaron fieles a las tendencias del modernismo.
3. A veces las preocupaciones políticas y sociales les llamaron la atención a los poetas.
4. Las obras de Gabriela Mistral son un reflejo de su vida de dolores y de sus esfuerzos contra las injusticias del mundo.
5. *El inglés de los güesos* fue la novela representativa del modernismo.
6. Güiraldes volvió las espaldas a lo americano en su obra, *Don Segundo Sombra*.

7. *Los de abajo* es la novela más célebre del período de la Revolución de 1910 en México.
8. En *El indio* y en *El mundo es ancho y ajeno* los autores protestan contra el abuso y la explotación de los indios.
9. La obra maestra de la novela indianista es *El hermano asno*.
10. Tanto Gabriela Mistral como Miguel Ángel Asturias recibieron el Premio Nobel de Literatura.
11. En *Al filo del agua* el mexicano Agustín Yáñez describe la vida moderna de la capital de su patria.
12. Entre los ensayistas de nuestro tiempo el erudito Alfonso Reyes es tal vez el autor más distinguido.

Lectura V

Para completar:

1. Al introducir en América la civilización europea, los españoles dieron una importancia especial a _____.
2. En el siglo XVII y en la primera parte del siglo siguiente, los edificios son de estilo _____, que muestra una fuerte influencia de _____.
3. Uno de los ejemplos más bellos del arte barroco es _____ en Taxco, México.
4. _____ es el centro más importante de actividad escultórica en la época colonial.
5. En el siglo XIX el valenciano Manuel Tolsá, escultor y arquitecto, terminó _____.
6. Cuatro grandes muralistas mexicanos del siglo actual son _____.
7. Las ideas sociales y políticas de Rivera le llevaron a hacer de la pintura _____.
8. José Sabogal, jefe del movimiento indígena en _____, ha buscado su inspiración en _____.
9. En 1928 el pintor uruguayo Joaquín Torres García creó un estilo nuevo, de formas _____.
10. En cuanto a la música, desde la época colonial ha habido dos corrientes distintas: _____ y _____.
11. Algunos de los compositores contemporáneos que han desarrollado una música de auténticos temas americanos son _____.
12. El fundador de la Orquesta Sinfónica de México es _____, que en su música se ha dedicado a integrar las diversas fuentes de _____.

Lectura VI

Para identificar brevemente en español:

1. El problema más evidente al compararse la América latina con los Estados Unidos.

2. El problema relacionado con la riqueza y el poder.

3. El ritmo actual del aumento de la población.

4. El medio que se ha considerado como el más eficaz para elevar el nivel de vida.

5. Uno de los obstáculos más importantes que encuentra la industrialización.

6. Las principales fuentes de financiación del déficit comercial.

7. La organización iniciada por el presidente Kennedy en 1961.

8. Tres países en que los procesos revolucionarios han producido cambios radicales en la estructura social.

9. La integración que se necesita para estimular las relaciones comerciales.

10. Dos pasos que se han dado ya para acelerar la integración económica.

11. El país que se ha beneficiado más de los cambios en los últimos años.

12. La entidad internacional que se ha esforzado mucho por resolver los problemas de las dos Américas.

CARTAS ESPAÑOLAS

In the following pages some of the essential principles for personal and business letters in Spanish will be given. Even though many formulas used in Spanish letters are less formal and flowery than formerly, in general, they are still less brief and direct than in English letters, and at times they may seem rather stilted. No attempt is made to give a complete treatment of Spanish correspondence, but study of the material included should suffice for ordinary purposes.

The new words and expressions whose English equivalents are given in this section (including the **Vocabulario útil**, pages 283–284) are not listed in the Spanish–English vocabulary, unless used elsewhere in the text.

A. Address on the envelope

The title of the addressee begins with **señor** (**Sr.**), **señora** (**Sra.**), or **señorita** (**Srta.**). **Sr. don** (**Sr. D.**) may be used for a man, **Sra. doña** (**Sra. Dª.**) for a married woman, and **Srta.** for an unmarried woman:

> **Señor don Carlos Morelos**   **Sr. D. Pedro Ortega y Moreno**
> **Srta. Isabel Alcalá**   **Sra. Dª. María López de Martín**

In the third example note that Spanish surnames often include the name of the father (**Ortega**), followed by that of the mother (**Moreno**). Often the mother's name is dropped (first two examples). A woman's married name is her maiden name followed by **de** and the surname of her husband (fourth example).

The definite article is not used with the titles **don** and **doña**, which have no English equivalents.

Two complete addresses follow:

> **Sr. D. Luis Montoya**   **Srta. Elena Pérez**
> **Calle de San Martín, 25**   **Avenida Bolívar, 245**
> **Santiago, Chile**   **Caracas, Venezuela**

Business letters are addressed to a firm:

> **Suárez Hermanos (Hnos.)**   **Señores (Sres.) López Díaz y Cía., S.A.**
> **Apartado (Postal) 867**   **Paseo de la Reforma, 12**
> **Buenos Aires, Argentina**   **México, D.F., México**

In an address in Spanish one writes first **Calle** (**Avenida**, *avenue*; **Paseo**, *boulevard*; **Camino**, *road*; **Plaza**, *square*), then the house number. **Apartado** (**Postal**), *post office box*, may be abbreviated to **Apdo.** (**Postal**). The abbreviation **Cía.** = **Compañía**; **S.A.** = **Sociedad Anónima**, equivalent to English *Inc.* (*Incorporated*); and **D.F.** = **Distrito Federal**, *Federal District.*

Air mail letters are marked **Vía aérea**, **Correo aéreo**, or **Por avión**. Special delivery letters are marked **Urgente**, and registered letters, **Certificada**.

B. Heading of the letter

The usual form of the date line is:

México, D.F., 27 de enero de 1971

The month is usually not capitalized unless it is given first in the date. For the first day of the month 1° (**primero**) is commonly used; the other days are written 2, 3, 4, etc. Other less common forms for the date line are:

Lima, Junio 15 de 1970
Bogotá, 1° agosto 1971

The address which precedes the salutation of the business and formal social letter is the same as that on the envelope. In familiar letters only the salutation need be used.

C. Salutations and conclusions for familiar letters

Forms used in addressing relatives or close friends are:

Querido hermano (Luis):	**(Mi) querida hija:**
Querida amiga mía:	**Queridísima[1] mamá:**

In conclusions of familiar letters a great variety of formulas may be used. Some commonly used endings for letters in the family are:

(Un abrazo[2] de) tu hijo,   *(one boy signs)*
Tu hijo (hija), que te quiere,   *(one boy or girl signs)*
Con todo el cariño[3] de tu hermano (hermana),   *(one boy or girl signs)*

---

[1] **Queridísima**, *Dearest.*   [2] **abrazo**, *embrace.*   [3] **cariño**, *affection.*

For friends (also for the family) the following, with many possible variations, are suitable:

> **Un abrazo de tu (su) amiga, que te (le) quiere,**
> **Tuyo (Suyo) afectísimo (afmo.),**[1] *or* **Tuya (Suya) afectísima (afma.),**
> **Cariñosos saludos**[2] **de tu amigo (amiga),**
> **(Con el cariño de) tu buen amigo (buena amiga),**
> **Sinceramente,** *or* **Afectuosamente,**[3]

In the first few letters to a Spanish friend one normally uses the polite forms of address; as the correspondence continues, more familiar forms may be used.

D. Salutations for business letters or those addressed to strangers

Appropriate salutations, equivalent to "My dear Sir," "Dear Sir," "Dear Madam," "Gentlemen," etc., are:

> **Muy señor (Sr.) mío:** (*from one person to one gentleman*)
> **Muy señor nuestro:** (*from a firm to one gentleman*)
> **Muy señores (Sres.) míos:** (*from one person to a firm*)
> **Muy señores nuestros:** (*from one firm to another firm*)
> **Muy señora (Sra.) mía:** (*from one person to a woman*)
> **Muy señorita nuestra:** (*from a firm to a young woman*)

Formulas which may be used in less formal letters are:

> **Muy estimado Sr. Salas:** Dear Mr. Salas:
> **Estimada amiga (Isabel):** Dear friend (Betty):
> **Mi distinguido amigo (colega):** Dear Friend (Colleague):

E. Conclusions for informal social and business letters

Common forms equivalent to "Sincerely yours," "Cordially yours," "Affectionately yours," are:

> **Suyo afectísimo (afmo.),** *or* **Suyos afectísimos (afmos.),**
> **Queda**[4] **(Quedo) suyo afmo. (suya afma.),**
> **Le saluda cariñosamente (muy atentamente),**
> **Se despide afectuosamente tu amigo,**

---

[1] **Tuyo (Suyo) afectísimo,** *Affectionately yours.*   [2] **Cariñosos saludos,** *Affectionate greetings.*   [3] **Afectuosamente,** *Affectionately, Sincerely.*   [4] **Queda** is in the third person if the signee is the subject. Also note the next examples.

Other phrases which may accompany these formulas are:

Dé (Da) mis mejores recuerdos a toda su (tu) familia,
   Give my best regards to all your family,
Salude afectuosamente de mi parte a sus padres,
   Give my affectionate (cordial) greetings to your parents,
Con mis mejores deseos para usted y los suyos, me despido,
   With best wishes for you and your family, I am (remain),

F. The body of business letters

The Spanish business letter usually begins with a brief sentence which indicates the purpose of the letter.   A few examples, with English translations, follow.   Note that the sentences cannot always be translated word for word:

Acabo (Acabamos) de recibir su carta del 10 de septiembre.
   I (We) have just received your letter of September 10.
Le doy a usted las gracias por el pedido que se sirvió hacerme . . .
   Thank you for the order which you kindly placed with me . . .
He recibido con mucho agrado su amable carta . . .
   I was very glad to receive your (good) letter . . .
Le acusamos recibo de su atenta[1] del 2 del corriente . . .
   We acknowledge receipt of your letter of the 2nd (of this month) . . .
Mucho agradeceré a usted[2] el mandarme . . .
   I shall thank you if you will send me . . .
Le envío giro postal por \$3.00 . . .
   I am sending you a postal money order for \$3.00 . . .
Con fecha 8 del actual me permití escribir a usted, informándole . . .
   On the 8th (of this month) I took the liberty of writing to you, informing you . . .
Tengo el agrado de dirigirme a usted para agradecerle el envío de . . .
   I have the pleasure of writing to thank you for sending me . . .

Some proper conclusions which might accompany such salutations are:

**Muy agradecidos por la buena atención que se dignará usted prestar a la
   presente, saludamos a usted con nuestro mayor aprecio y consideración,**
   Thanking you for your kind attention to this letter, we remain,
                                                                         Very truly yours,

---

[1] **Carta** is often replaced with **favor, grata, atenta.**   [2] Since **usted** is technically a noun (coming from **vuestra merced,** *your grace*), the object pronoun **le** may be omitted before the verb.   This practice is noted particularly in letter writing.

En espera de su envío y con gracias anticipadas, quedo de usted atto. S. S.,[1]
Awaiting the shipment and thanking you in advance, I remain,

Sincerely yours,

Aprovechamos esta ocasión para ofrecernos sus attos. y ss. ss.,
We take advantage of this opportunity to remain,

Yours truly,

Quedamos de ustedes afmos. attos. y Ss. Ss.,
We remain,

Very truly yours,

Me repito[2] **su afmo. s. s.,** *or* **Nos repetimos sus afmos. ss. ss.,**
I (We) remain,

Sincerely,

Le saluda muy cordialmente su servidor y amigo,

Cordially yours,

As noted above, the Spanish conclusion usually requires more than a mere "Very truly yours," or "Sincerely yours." However, there is a tendency nowadays to shorten conclusions of business letters, particularly as correspondence continues with an individual or firm.

Great care must be taken to be consistent in the agreement of salutations and conclusions of letters, keeping in mind whether the letters are addressed to a man or a woman, or to a firm, and whether the letters are signed by one person or by an individual for a firm.

---

[1] **Seguro servidor** (*sing.*) may be abbreviated to **S. S.** or **s. s.; seguros servidores** (*pl.*) to **SS. SS., Ss. Ss.,** or **ss. ss.** **Atto. = atento; attos. = atentos.** [2] After the first letter (where the verb **aprovechar** may have been used) **Me repito** is a good follow-up.

G. Sample letters

The following letters translated freely from Spanish to English will show how natural, idiomatic phrases in one language convey the same idea in another. Read the following letters aloud for practice, and be able to write either of them from dictation. The teacher may want to test comprehension by asking questions in Spanish on the content of the letters. At the end of this section are listed some words and phrases, not all of which are used in the sample letters, which should be useful in composing original letters.

1

12 de marzo de 1971

Librería de Porrúa Hnos. y Cía.
Apartado 7990
México, D.F., México

Muy señores míos:

Tengo el gusto de avisarles a ustedes que acabo de recibir su atenta del 8 del actual y el ejemplar de su catálogo con la lista de precios que se sirvieron remitirme por separado.

Sírvanse ustedes enviarme a la mayor brevedad posible la lista de libros que envío anexa. También hallarán adjunto un cheque por pesos 96,40[1] en pago de la factura del 20 del pasado.

Quedo de ustedes su atto. y S. S.,

March 12, 1971

Porrúa Brothers and Co., Bookstore
Post Office Box 7990
Mexico City, Mexico

Gentlemen:

I am glad to inform you that I have just received your letter of March 8 and the copy of your catalogue with the list of prices which you kindly sent me under separate cover.

Please send me as soon as possible the list of books which I am including (in this letter). Also you will find enclosed a check for $96.40 (96.40 pesos) in payment of your bill of February 20 (of the 20th of last month).

Sincerely yours,

---

[1] Read **noventa y seis pesos, cuarenta centavos**. While the comma between the **pesos** and **centavos** has largely been replaced in Spanish by a period, it is still used. The English comma is often written as a period in Spanish: **pesos** 1.250,35.

2

16 de marzo de 1971

Muy señor nuestro:

Acusamos recibo. de su favor del 12 del presente, en que hallamos adjunto su cheque por pesos 96,40, que abonamos en su cuenta, y por el cual le damos a usted las gracias.

Hoy le enviamos a vuelta de correo el pedido de libros que se sirvió hacernos, cuyo importe cargamos en su cuenta.

En espera de sus nuevos gratos pedidos, nos repetimos sus afmos. attos. y ss. ss.,

March 16, 1971

Dear Sir:

We acknowledge receipt of your letter of March 12, in which we found enclosed your check for 96.40 pesos, which we are crediting to your account, and for which we thank you.

Today we are sending by return mail the order for books which you kindly sent us (made of us), the amount of which we are charging to your account.

Awaiting other kind orders from you, we remain,

Sincerely yours,

VOCABULARIO ÚTIL

abonar   to credit
adjunto, -a   enclosed, attached
agradecer   to be grateful for, thank for
anexo, -a   enclosed, attached
aprovechar   to take advantage of
la cantidad   quantity, amount
cargar   to charge
la casa de correos   post office
el catálogo   catalogue
certificar   to register
comunicar   to inform, tell
dirigir   to address, direct
el ejemplar   copy
el envío   shipment, remittance
la factura   bill, invoice
la firma   signature
el folleto   folder, pamphlet
el franqueo   postage
el gerente   manager

el giro   draft
grato, -a   kind, pleased
el importe   cost, amount
la muestra   sample
las noticias   news, information
ofrecer(se)   to offer, be, offer one's services
el pago   payment
el pasado   last month
el pedido   order
permitirse   to take the liberty (to)
el recibo   receipt
remitir   to remit, send
rogar (ue)   to ask, beg
servirse (i, i)   to be so kind as to
el saldo   balance
el sello   stamp
el sobre   envelope
la solicitud   request
suplicar   to beg, ask

acusar recibo de   to acknowledge receipt of
a la mayor brevedad posible   as soon as possible
a vuelta de correo   by return mail
al cuidado de (a/c)   in care of (c/o)
anticipar las gracias   to thank in advance
de acuerdo con   in compliance with
del corriente (actual)   of the present month
echar al correo   to mail
en contestación a   in reply to
en espera de   awaiting
en pago de   in payment of
en su cuenta   to one's account
estar encargado, -a de   to be in charge of
giro postal   money order
hacer un pedido   to place (give) an order
haga(n) Ud(s). el favor de + *inf.*   please + *inf.*
lista de precios   price list
(nos) es grato   (we) are pleased
me repito (nos repetimos)   I (we) remain
paquete postal   parcel post
por separado   under separate cover
sírva(n)se + *inf.*   to please, be pleased + *inf.*
tener el agrado (gusto) de + *inf.*   to be pleased + *inf.*
tener la bondad de + *inf.*   to have the kindness to, please + *inf.*

Ejercicio

Suggestions for original letters in Spanish:

1. Write to a foreign student, describing some of your daily activities.   Try to use words which you have had in this text or some previous text.
2. Write to a member of your family, describing some shopping you have done.
3. Assume that you are the Spanish secretary for an American exporting firm. Write a reply to a Spanish American firm which has asked for a recent catalogue and prices.
4. Write to an individual, thanking him for his check, which has been received in payment of an invoice of a certain date.   Give the balance which remains in his account.

MAPS
APPENDICES

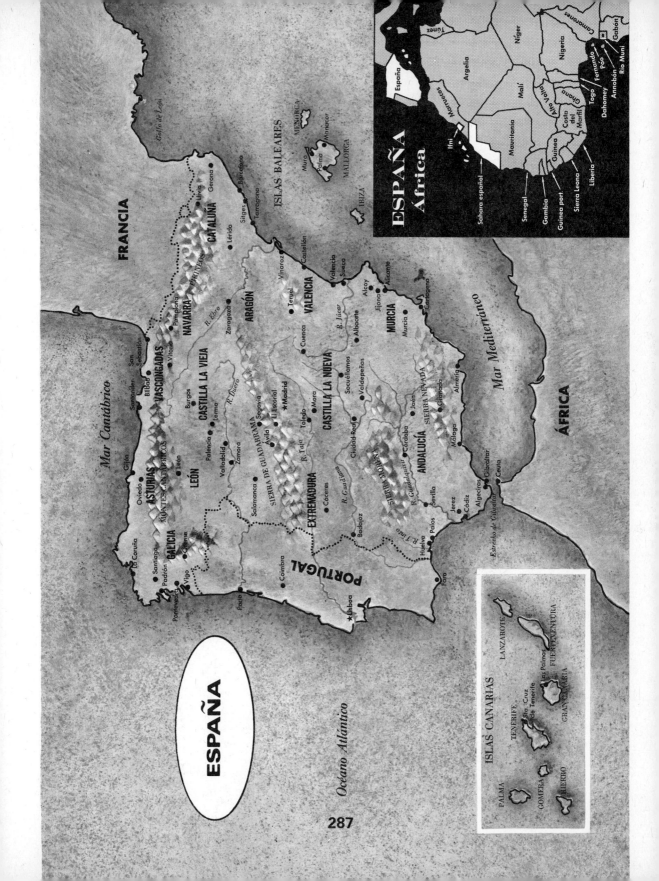

ESPAÑA

287

LA AMÉRICA CENTRAL Y EL CARIBE

Océano Atlántico

Golfo de México

Miami

La Habana

CUBA

Santiago

HAITÍ REP. DOMINICANA

Port au Prince Santo Domingo

San Juan

MÉXICO

Belize

BRITISH HONDURAS

GUATEMALA

Guatemala

HONDURAS

San Salvador Tegucigalpa

EL SALVADOR

NICARAGUA

Managua

JAMAICA Kingston

PUERTO RICO

Mar Caribe

COSTA RICA San José

Canal de Panamá Panamá

PANAMÁ

Océano Pacífico

La América del Sur

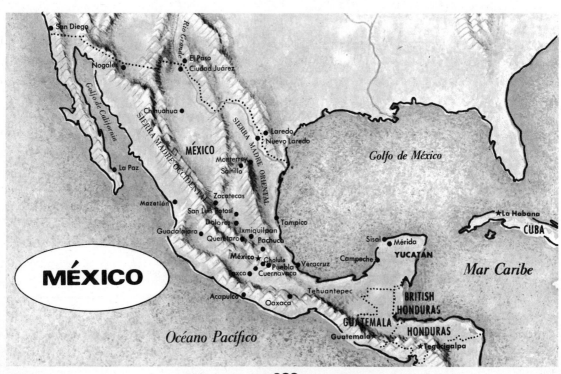

MÉXICO

San Diego

Río Grande

Nogales

El Paso Ciudad Juárez

Chihuahua

SIERRA MADRE OCCIDENTAL

Golfo de California

MÉXICO

La Paz

SIERRA MADRE ORIENTAL

Laredo Nuevo Laredo

Golfo de México

Monterrey Saltillo

Zacatecas

Mazatlán

San Luis Potosí

Dolores

Guadalajara Ixmiquilpan Pachuca

Querétaro

México Cholula Puebla

Taxco Cuernavaca

Acapulco Oaxaca

Tampico

Sisal Mérida

Campeche

YUCATÁN

Veracruz

Tehuantepec

GUATEMALA

Guatemala

Mar Caribe

CUBA

La Habana

BRITISH HONDURAS

HONDURAS

Tegucigalpa

Océano Pacífico

288

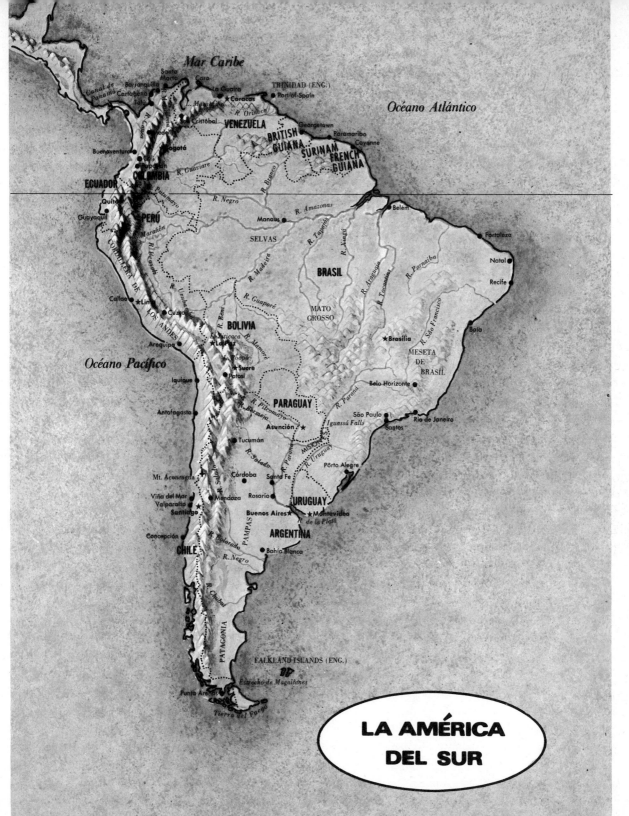

Mar Caribe

Océano Atlántico

Santa Marta
Barranquilla
Canal de Panamá
Cartagena
Tolú
Coro
La Guaira
★Caracas
TRINIDAD (ENG.)
Port-of-Spain

R. Cauca
Cristóbal
R. Orinoco
VENEZUELA
BRITISH
GUIANA
Georgetown
Paramaribo
SURINAM
FRENCH
GUIANA
Cayenne
Medellín
Buenaventura
Cali
Popayán
Bogotá
COLOMBIA
R. Guaviare
R. Branco

ECUADOR
Quito
Guayaquil
Putumayo
R. Negro
Manaus
R. Amazonas
Belém
Fortaleza

PERÚ
Marañón
SELVAS
R. Tapajós
R. Xingú
Natal
Recife

R. Ucayali
R. Madera
BRASIL
R. Araguaia
R. Tocantins
R. Parnaíba

Callao
★Lima
Cuzco
R. Urubamba
R. Guaporé
R. Beni
MATO
GROSSO
★Brasília
R. São Francisco
Baía

Arequipa
CORDILLERA DE
L. Titicaca
BOLIVIA
★La Paz
R. Mamoré
Cochabamba
Oruro
★Sucre
Potosí
MESETA
DE
BRASIL

Océano Pacífico

Iquique
LOS ANDES
PARAGUAY
R. Paraná
Belo Horizonte
São Paulo
Santos
Río de Janeiro

Antofagasta
R. Pilcomayo
R. Bermejo
Asunción ★
Iguassú Falls

Tucumán
R. Salado
MISIONES
R. Uruguay
Pôrto Alegre

Mt. Aconcagua
Córdoba
Santa Fe
Rosario
URUGUAY

Viña del Mar
Valparaíso
Mendoza
Buenos Aires★
★Montevideo
R. de la Plata

Santiago
PAMPAS
ARGENTINA

Concepción
R. Colorado
R. Negro
Bahía Blanca

CHILE
R. Chubut

PATAGONIA

FALKLAND ISLANDS (ENG.)

Estrecho de Magallanes
Punta Arenas
Tierra del Fuego

LA AMÉRICA DEL SUR

289

APPENDIX A

PRONUNCIATION

THE SPANISH ALPHABET

LETTER	NAME	LETTER	NAME	LETTER	NAME
a	a	j	jota	r	ere
b	be	k	ka	rr	erre
c	ce	l	ele	s	ese
ch	che	ll	elle	t	te
d	de	m	eme	u	u
e	e	n	ene	v	ve, uve
f	efe	ñ	eñe	w	doble ve
g	ge	o	o	x	equis
h	hache	p	pe	y	ye, i griega
i	i	q	cu	z	zeta

In addition to the letters used in the English alphabet, **ch, ll, ñ,** and **rr** represent single sounds in Spanish and are considered single letters. In dictionaries and vocabularies words or syllables which begin with **ch, ll,** and **ñ** follow words or syllables that begin with **c, l,** and **n,** while **rr,** which never begins a word, is alphabetized as in English. **K** and **w** are used only in words of foreign origin. The names of the letters are feminine: **la be,** *(the) b;* **la jota,** *(the) j.*

The Spanish alphabet is divided into vowels (**a, e, i, o, u**) and consonants. The letter **y** is a vowel when final in a word, and when used as the conjunction **y,** *and.*

The Spanish vowels are divided into two groups: strong vowels (**a, e, o**) and weak vowels (**i, u**).

GENERAL REMARKS.   DEFINITION OF PHONETIC TERMS

Even though Spanish uses practically the same alphabet as English, few sounds are identical in the two languages. In describing the Spanish sounds, it will sometimes be necessary to make comparisons between the familiar English sounds and the unfamiliar Spanish ones in order to show how Spanish is pronounced. The student should avoid, of course, the use of English sounds in Spanish words; he should strive to follow the explanations of the text and imitate the pronunciation of the teacher and of the tapes.

In general, Spanish pronunciation is much clearer and more uniform than the English. The vowel sounds are clipped short and are not followed by the diphthongal glide which is commonly heard in English, as in *no (no*ᵘ*), came (ca*ⁱ*me), why (why*ᵉ*).* Even

291

unstressed vowels are pronounced clearly and distinctly; the slurred sound of English *a* in *fireman*, for example, never occurs in Spanish.

Spanish consonants, likewise, are usually pronounced more precisely and distinctly than English consonants, although a few (especially **b, d,** and **g** between vowels) are pronounced very weakly. Several of them (**t, d, l,** and **n**) are pronounced farther forward in the mouth, with the tongue close to the upper teeth and gums. The consonants **p, t,** and **c** (before letters other than **e** and **i**) are never followed by the *h* sound that is often heard in English: *pen* (*pʰen*), *task* (*tʰask*), *can* (*cʰan*).

To allow for greater accuracy in the description of Spanish speech sounds, it will be helpful to be familiar with the phonetic terms explained in the following paragraphs.

Voiced and voiceless sounds. A sound is said to be voiceless when, during its articulation, the breath passes through the larynx without the vibration of the vocal cords. When the sound is accompanied by the vibration of the vocal cords, it is called voiced. All vowels are normally voiced sounds; consonants, however, may be voiced or voiceless.[1]

Stop and continuant consonants. A stop consonant is one in the making of which the passage of the air through the mouth is for a brief moment entirely stopped, after which the stoppage is released and the air is allowed to pass; such are the consonants in English *pat, cub, dog*. Continuants are consonants in the production of which there is a continuous passage of air and, consequently, a continuous sound, capable of being prolonged, such as the consonants in English *thief, save*.

Place of articulation. Sounds are also classified according to the position or place where the chief obstruction to the passage of the breath is made. If this obstruction is formed between the two lips, the sound is called bilabial: *p* in English *pen*. If the obstruction is made between the teeth, the sound is called interdental: English *th* in *thin*. If the tip of the tongue forms the obstruction back of the teeth, the sound is called dental: *t* in Spanish **tú**. If the obstruction is formed at the alveolar ridge (that is, the ridge that covers the base of the upper teeth), the sound is called alveolar: *t* in English *ten*. If the obstruction is between the tongue and the hard palate, the sound is called palatal: *ch* in English *church*. If it is between the tongue and the soft palate or velum, the sound is called velar: *c* in English *cut*.

DIVISION OF WORDS INTO SYLLABLES

Spanish words are hyphenated at the end of a line and are divided into syllables according to the following principles.

a. A single consonant (including **ch, ll, rr**) is placed with the vowel which follows: **pa-pel, mu-cho, ca-lle, pi-za-rra**.

b. Two consonants are usually divided: **tar-de, es-pa-ñol, tam-bién**. Consonants

---

[1] The following Spanish consonants are normally voiced: **b, d, g, l, ll, m, n, ñ, r, rr, v,** and **y**. One can easily learn to perceive the distinction between voiced and voiceless consonants by covering the ears with one's hands during the articulation of the sounds. After covering the ears, pronounce first, for example, the *z* of English *daze* and then the *ss* of English *hiss*; the distinction between voiced *z* and voiceless *ss* can be readily felt.

followed by **l** or **r**, however, are generally pronounced together and go with the following vowel: **li-bro, pa-dre, a-pren-do**. Exceptions are the groups **nl, rl, sl, tl, nr**, and **sr**: **Car-los, En-ri-que**.

c. In combinations of three or more consonants only the last consonant or the two consonants of the inseparable groups just mentioned (consonant plus **l** or **r**, with the exceptions listed) begin a syllable: **ins-pi-ra-ción, in-glés, en-tra**.

d. Two adjacent strong vowels (**a, e, o**) are in separate syllables: **le-o, tra-e, cre-e**.

e. Combinations of a strong and weak vowel (**i, u**) or of two weak vowels normally form single syllables. Such combinations of two vowels are called *diphthongs*. (See page 296 for further discussion of diphthongs.) Examples: **bue-nos, bien, es-tu-dio, gra-cias, ciu-dad, Luis**.

f. In combinations of a strong and weak vowel, a written accent mark on the weak vowel divides the two vowels into separate syllables: **dí-a, pa-ís, tí-o**. An accent on the strong vowel of such combinations does not result in two syllables: **lec-ción, tam-bién**.

WORD STRESS[1]

a. Most words which end in a vowel, and in **n** or **s** (plural endings of verbs and nouns, respectively), are stressed on the next to the last syllable: *cla*-se, *to*-mo, *ca*-sas, *en*-tran, *or*-den.

b. Most words which end in a consonant, except **n** or **s**, are stressed on the last syllable: **pro-fe-*sor*, ha-*blar*, pa-*pel*, ciu-*dad*, es-pa-*ñol***.

c. Words not pronounced according to these two rules have a written accent on the stressed syllable: **ca-*fé*, in-*glés*, lec-*ción*, tam-*bién*, *lá*-piz**.

The written accent is also used to distinguish between two words spelled alike but different in meaning (**si**, *if*, **sí**, *yes*; **el**, *the*, **él**, *he*, etc.), and on the stressed syllable of all interrogative words (**¿qué?** *what?*).

VOWELS

a is pronounced between the *a* of English *ask* and the *a* of *father*: *ca*-sa, *ha*-bla, *A*-na.

e is pronounced like *e* in *café*, but without the glide sound that follows the *e* in English: *me*-sa, *cla*-se, us-*ted*.

i (**y**) is pronounced like *i* in *machine*: Fe-*li*-pe, **sí**, *dí*-as, **y**.

o is pronounced like *o* in *obey*, but without the glide sound that follows the *o* in English: *no*, *so*-lo, cho-co-*la*-te.

u is pronounced like *oo* in *cool*: us-*ted*, *u*-no, a-*lum*-no.

---

[1] In this and the following four subsections the stressed syllable of Spanish examples is italicized.

The vowels **e** and **o** also have sounds like *e* in *let* and *o* in *for*. These sounds, as in English, generally occur when the **e** and **o** are followed by a consonant in the same syllable: *él, ser, son,* **es-pa-***ñol*. In pronouncing the **e** in **él** and **ser**, and the **o** in **son** and **español**, the mouth is opened wider, and the distance between the tongue and the palate is greater, than when pronouncing the **e** in **mesa** and **clase**, and the **o** in **no** and **solo**. These more open sounds of **e** and **o** occur also in contact with the strongly trilled **r** (**rr**), before the **j** sound (written **g** before **e** or **i**, and **j**), and in the diphthongs **ei** (**ey**) and **oi** (**oy**). Pay close attention to the teacher's pronunciation of these sounds.

CONSONANTS

b and **v** are pronounced exactly alike. Each has two different sounds, a voiced stop sound, and a voiced continuant sound. At the beginning of a breath-group (see page 297), or after **m** or **n** (also pronounced **m** in this case), whether within a word or between words, Spanish **b** (or **v**) is a voiced bilabial stop, similar to English *b* in *boy*, but somewhat weaker: *bien, bue-***nas**, *va-***mos**, *un va-***so**. In all other positions, it is a voiced bilabial continuant; the lips do not close completely, as in stop **b**, but allow the breath to pass between them through a very narrow passage: *li-***bro**, *Cu-***ba**, *no va-***mos**. When between vowels, the articulation is especially weak. Avoid the English *v* sound. Note the two different sounds in **vi-***vir*, **be-***ber*.

c before **e** and **i**, and **z** in all positions, are pronounced like the English hissed *s* in *sent* in Spanish America and in southern Spain. In northern and central Spain this sound is like *th* in *thin*. Examples: **cen-***ta***-vo, *ci-***ne**, **gra-***cias*.

c before all other letters, **k**, and **qu** are like English *c* in *cat*, but without the *h* sound that often follows the *c* in English: *ca-***sa**, *cla-***se**, **ki-***ló***-me-tro, *que-***so**, *par-***que**. Note both sounds of **c** in **cin-co**, **lec-***ción*.

ch is pronounced like English *ch* in *church*: *mu-***cho**, *le-***che**, **cho-co-***la***-te**.

d has two sounds, a voiced stop sound and a voiced continuant sound. At the beginning of a breath-group, or when after **l** or **n**, Spanish **d** is a voiced dental stop, like a weak English *d*, but with the tip of the tongue touching the inner surface of the upper front teeth rather than the ridge above the teeth, as in English: *dos, mun-***do**, **sal-***dré*. In all other cases the tongue drops even lower, and the **d** is pronounced as a voiced interdental continuant, like a weak English *th* in *this*: *ca-***da**, *pa-***dre**, *to-***do**. The sound is especially weak in the ending **-ado**, and when final in a word before a pause: **es-***ta***-do, us-***ted**, **Ma-***drid*.

f is pronounced like English *f*: *ca-***fé**, **Fe-***li***-pe**.

g before **e** and **i**, and **j** in all positions, have no English equivalent. They are pronounced approximately like a strongly exaggerated *h* in *halt* (rather like the rasping German *ch* in *Buch*): *gen-***te**, *hi-***jo**, *Jor-***ge**, *re-***gión**. (The letter **x** in the words **México** and **mexicano**, spelled **Méjico** and **mejicano** in Spain, is pronounced like Spanish **j**.)

g in other positions, and **gu** before **e** or **i**, are pronounced alike.   Each has two sounds, a voiced stop sound, and a voiced continuant sound.   At the beginning of a breath-group, or when after **n**, Spanish **g** (written **gu** before **e** or **i**) is a voiced velar stop, like a weak English *g* in *go*: **gra-cias**, **gui-*ta*-rra**, **ten-go**.   In all other cases, except before **e** or **i** in the groups **ge**, **gi**, Spanish **g** is a voiced velar continuant; that is, the sound is much weaker, and the breath continues to pass between the back of the tongue and the palate: **a-*pa*-ga**, **ha-go**, **la gui-*ta*-rra**.   (In the combinations **gua** and **guo** the **u** is pronounced like English *w* in *wet*: **a-gua**, ***len*-gua**, **an-*ti*-guo**; when the diaeresis is used over **u** in the combinations **güe**, **güi**, the **u** has the same sound: **ver-*güen*-za**, **ni-ca-ra-*güen*-se**.)

h is always silent: **ha-*blar***, ***ham*-bre**, ***hoy***.

l is pronounced like *l* in *leap*, with the tip and front part of the tongue well forward in the mouth: ***Li*-ma**, **pa-*pel***.

ll is pronounced like *y* in *yes* in most of Spanish America and in some sections of Spain; in other parts of Spain it is somewhat like *lli* in *million*: **e-lla**, ***ca*-lle**, **lla-*mar***.

m is pronounced like English *m*: ***to*-ma**, ***me*-sa**.

n is pronounced like English *n*: ***no***, **a-*pren*-den**.   Before **b**, **v**, **m**, and **p**, however, it is pronounced like *m*: **un-po-co**, **con-*Bár*-ba-ra**.   Before **c**, **qu**, **g**, and **j** it is pronounced like English *n* in *sing*: ***blan*-co**, ***ten*-go**, **con-Jua-*ni*-ta**.

ñ is somewhat like the English *ny* in *canyon*: **se-*ñor***, **ma-*ña*-na**, **es-pa-*ñol***, **ca-*ñón***.

p is pronounced like English *p*, but without the *h* sound that often follows the *p* in English: ***pe*-lo**, **pa-*pel***.

q (always written with **u**): see page 294, under **c**, **k**, and **qu**.

r and **rr** represent two different sounds.   Single **r**, except when initial in a word and when after **l**, **n**, or **s**, is a voiced, alveolar, single trill; that is, it is pronounced with a single tap produced by the tip of the tongue against the gums of the upper teeth.   The sound is much like *dd* in *eddy* pronounced rapidly: ***ca*-ra**, **o-ro**, **ha-*blar***.   When initial in a word, when after **l**, **n**, or **s**, and when doubled, the sound is a multiple trill, the tip of the tongue striking the gums in a series of very rapid vibrations: ***ri*-co**, ***ro*-jo**, **pi-*za*-rra**, **En-*ri*-que**.

s is a voiceless, alveolar continuant, somewhat like the English hissed *s* in *sent*: ***ca*-sa**, ***es*-tos**.   Before the voiced **b**, **d**, **g**, **l**, **ll**, **m**, **n**, **ñ**, **r**, **v**, and **y**, however, Spanish **s** becomes voiced and is pronounced like English *s* in *rose*: **es-bo-*zar***, **des-*gra*-cia**, ***mis*-mo**, **los *li*-bros**, **es ver-*dad***.

t is pronounced with the tip of the tongue touching the back of the upper front teeth (rather than the ridge above the teeth, as in English); it is never followed by the *h* sound that is often heard in English: ***to*-do**, ***tar*-des**, ***tiem*-po**.

v: see page 294, under **b**.

x is pronounced as follows: (1) Before a consonant it is pronounced like Spanish **s**; that is, it is a voiceless alveolar continuant sound, similar to English hissed *s* in *sent*: **ex-plo-*rar***, **ex-tran-*je*-ro**; (2) between vowels it is usually a double sound, consisting of a Spanish velar continuant **g** (as in **a-gua**) followed by a voiceless, hissed *s*: **e-*xa*-men** (**eg-*sa*-men**), **é-xi-to** (**ég-si-to**); (3) in a few words **x** may be pronounced **s** (a voiceless alveolar continuant sound) even between vowels, as in **e-*xac*-to**, **au-xi-*liar*** (and in words built on these words).

y is pronounced like a strong English *y* in *you*: **ya**, **yo**, **ma-yo**.   The conjunction **y**, *and*, when combined with the initial vowel of a following word, is similarly pronounced: *Car*-los-*y* A-na.

DIPHTHONGS

As stated on page 293 the weak vowels **i** (**y**) and **u** may combine with the strong vowels **a**, **e**, **o**, or with each other, to form single syllables.   Such combinations of two vowels are called diphthongs.   In diphthongs the strong vowels retain their full syllabic value, while the weak vowels, or the first vowel in the case of two weak vowels, lose part of their syllabic value.

As the first element of a diphthong, unstressed **i** is pronounced like a weak English *y* in *yes*, and unstressed **u** is pronounced like *w* in *wet*.   The Spanish diphthongs which begin with unstressed **i** and **u** are: **ia, ie, io, iu**; **ua, ue, ui, uo**, as in *gra*-cias, *bien*, a-*diós*, ciu-*dad*; *cua*-tro, *bue*-no, *Luis*, an-*ti*-guo.

The diphthongs in which unstressed **i** and **u** occur as the second element of the diphthong are nine orthographically, but phonetically only six, since **i** and **y** have the same sound here.   They are: **ai, ay**; **au**; **ei, ey**; **eu**; **oi, oy**; **ou**.   They are pronounced as follows:

  ai, ay like a prolonged English *i* in *mine*: ***bai*-le**, ***hay***
  au like a prolonged English *ou* in *out*: **au-*tor***, ***cau*-sa**
  ei, ey like a prolonged English *a* in *fate*: ***seis***, ***ley***
  eu has no close equivalent in English.   It consists of a clipped *e*, as in English *eh*, followed closely by a glide sound which ends in *oo*, to sound like *ehoo*: **Eu-*ro*-pa**
  oi, oy like a prolonged English *oy* in *boy*: ***sois***, ***soy***
  ou like a prolonged English *o* in *note*: **lo u-*sa*-mos**

Remember that two adjacent strong vowels within a word do not combine in a single syllable, but form two separate syllables: *le*-e, **Do-ro-*te*-a**.   Likewise, when a weak vowel adjacent to a strong vowel has a written accent, it retains its syllabic value and forms a separate syllable: *dí*-a, pa-*ís*.   An accent mark on a strong vowel merely indicates stress: **lec-*ción***, **tam-*bién***.

TRIPHTHONGS

A triphthong is a combination in a single syllable of a stressed strong vowel between two weak vowels.   Four combinations are of frequent use: **iai, iei, uai** (**uay**), **uei** (**uey**), as in **es-tu-*diáis***, **Pa-ra-*guay***.   To indicate the mew of a cat and the bark of a dog the triphthongs **iau** and **uau** occur: *miau*, *guau*.   In linking vowels between words, four and five vowels may be pronounced in one syllable.

LINKING OF WORDS

In reading or speaking Spanish, words are linked together, as in English, so that two or more may sound as one long word. These groups of words are called breath-groups. The pronunciation of certain Spanish consonants depends upon their position at the beginning of, or within, a breath-group. Similarly, the pronunciation of many individual sounds will be modified depending on the sounds with which they are linked within the breath-group. Since the words that make up the breath-group are pronounced as if they formed one long word, the principles which govern the structure of the syllable must be observed throughout the entire breath-group.

In speech, words normally are uttered in breath-groups. Thus it is necessary to practice pronouncing phrases and even entire sentences without a pause between words. Frequently a short sentence will be pronounced as one breath-group, while a longer one may be divided into two or more groups. The meaning of what is being pronounced will help you to determine where the pauses ending the breath-groups should be made.

The following examples illustrate some of the general principles of linking. The syllabic division in parentheses shows the correct linking; the syllable or syllables italicized bear the main stress.

a. Within a breath-group the final consonant of a word is joined with the initial vowel of the following word and forms a syllable with it: **el alumno** (e-la-*lum*-no).

b. Within a breath-group when two identical vowels of different words come together, they are pronounced as one: **el profesor de español** (el-pro-fe-*sor*-de es-pa-*ñol*).

c. When unlike vowels between words come together within a breath-group, they are usually pronounced together in a single syllable. Two cases occur: (1) when a strong vowel is followed or preceded by a weak vowel, both are pronounced together in a single syllable and the result is phonetically a diphthong (see page 296): **su amigo** (su a-*mi*-go), **Juan y Elena** (*Jua*-n y E-*le*-na), **mi padre y mi madre** (mi-*pa*-dre y-mi-*ma*-dre); (2) if both vowels are strong, each loses a little of its syllabic value and both are pronounced together in one syllable: **vamos a la escuela** (*va*-mo-sa-la es-*cue*-la); **¿Cómo está usted?** (*¿Có*-mo es-*tá* us-ted?).

INTONATION

The term intonation refers to the variations in pitch which occur in speech. Every language has its characteristic patterns of intonation. The intonation of Spanish is quite different from that of English.

The alternate rise and fall of the pitch depends upon the particular meaning of the sentence, the position of stressed syllables, and whether the sentence expresses command, affirmation, interrogation, exclamation, request, or other factors. In general, three meaningful levels of pitch can be distinguished in Spanish: one below the speaker's normal pitch (level 1); the speaker's normal tone (level 2), and a tone higher than the normal one (level 3). With respect to the use of these levels, the following basic principles should be observed:

a. At the beginning of a breath-group the voice begins and continues in a relatively low pitch (level 1) as long as the first accented syllable is not reached.

b. When the first accented syllable of a breath-group is reached, the voice rises to the speaker's normal tone (level 2) and continues in the same pitch as long as the last accented syllable is not reached.

c. When the last accented syllable of the breath-group is reached, the voice falls or rises, depending on the following circumstances:

(1) At the end of a declarative statement, the voice falls to a pitch even lower than that of the initial unaccented syllable or syllables.

(2) At the end of an interrogative sentence, or of an incomplete sentence interrupted by a pause, the voice rises to a pitch above the normal tone (level 3).

d. In exclamations, and in questions which begin with an interrogative word, the voice begins in a pitch above the normal tone (level 3) and gradually falls in the following syllables as long as the final accented syllable is not reached; when the last accented syllable is reached, the voice falls to a pitch even lower than that of the initial unaccented syllable or syllables, as in the case of the end of a simple declarative sentence, unless special interest or courtesy is intended, in which case the voice rises to the normal tone or even higher.

For additional remarks on Spanish intonation, and for a few intonation patterns, see pages 17–18, 23–24, and 45.

PUNCTUATION

Spanish punctuation is much the same as English.   The most important differences are:

1. Inverted question marks and exclamation points precede questions and exclamations.   They are placed at the actual beginning of the question or exclamation, not necessarily at the beginning of the sentence:

¿Hablan Carlos y Juan?	Are Charles and John talking?
¡Qué muchacha más bonita!	What a pretty girl!
Usted es español, ¿verdad?	You are a Spaniard, aren't you?

2. In Spanish a comma is not used between the last two words of a series, while in English it usually is:

Tenemos plumas, libros y lápices.   We have pens, books, and pencils.

3. A dash is generally used instead of quotation marks to denote a change of speaker in dialogue.   It appears at the beginning of each speech, but is omitted at the end.

— ¿**Es usted peruano?**	"Are you a Peruvian?"
— **Sí, señor. Soy de Lima.**	"Yes, sir. I am from Lima."

If Spanish quotation marks are used, they are placed on the line, as in the example which follows.   In current practice English quotation marks are widely used in Spanish.

Juan dijo: «Buenos días.»	John said, "Good morning."

CAPITALIZATION

Only proper names and the first word of a sentence begin with a capital letter in Spanish. The subject pronoun **yo** (*I* in English), names of months and days of the week, adjectives of nationality and nouns formed from them, and titles (unless abbreviated) are not capitalized.   In titles of books or works of art, only the first word is ordinarily capitalized.

Juan y yo hablamos.	John and I are talking.
Hoy es lunes.	Today is Monday.
Buenos días, señor (Sr.) Pidal.	Good morning, Mr. Pidal.
Son españoles.	They are Spanish.
Los de abajo.	The Underdogs.

APPENDIX B

FRASES PARA LA CLASE *(Classroom Expressions)*

A number of expressions and grammatical terms which may be used in the classroom and laboratory are listed below.   They are not included in the end vocabularies unless used in the preceding lessons.   Other common expressions are used in the text.

Voy a pasar lista.	I am going to call the roll.
Presente.	Present.
¿Qué lección tenemos hoy?	What lesson do we have today?
Tenemos la Lección primera (dos).	We have Lesson One (Two).
¿En qué página empieza?	On what page does it begin?
¿Qué línea (renglón)?	What line?
(La lectura) empieza en la página . . .	(The reading) begins on page . . .
Al principio de la página . . .	At the beginning of (the) page . . .
En el medio (Al pie) de la página . . .	In the middle (At the bottom) of (the) page . . .
Abra(n) usted(es) el (los) libro(s).	Open your book(s).
Cierre(n) usted(es) el (los) libro(s).	Close your book(s).
Lea usted en español.	Read in Spanish.
Empiece usted a leer.	Begin to read.
Siga usted leyendo.	Continue (Go on) reading.
Traduzca usted al español (inglés) . . .	Translate into Spanish (English) . . .
Repita usted la frase modelo.	Repeat the model sentence.
Pronuncie usted . . .	Pronounce . . .
Basta.	That is enough, That will do.
Conteste(n) (la pregunta) en español.	Answer (the question) in Spanish.
Vaya(n) usted(es) *or* **Pase(n) usted(es) a la pizarra.**	Go to the (black)board.
Escuche(n) las instrucciones.	Listen to the directions.
Escriba(n) usted(es) (al dictado).	Write (at dictation).
Usted ha hecho una falta (un error).	You have made a mistake.
Corrija(n) usted(es) la falta.	Correct the mistake.
Borre(n) usted(es) la frase.	Erase the sentence.
Vuelva(n) usted(es) a su(s) asiento(s).	Return to your seat(s).
Siénte(n)se usted(es).	Sit down, Be seated.
Haga(n) usted(es) el favor de (+ *inf.*) . . .	Please (+ *verb*) . . .
Está bien.	All right, That's fine.

¿Qué significa (quiere decir) la palabra . . .?	What does the word . . . mean?
¿Quién quiere hacer una pregunta?	Who wants to ask a question?
¿Cómo se dice . . .?	How does one (do you) say . . .?
Escuche(n) usted(es) bien.	Listen carefully.
Preste(n) usted(es) atención.	Pay attention.
Prepare(n) usted(es) para mañana . . .	Prepare for tomorrow . . .
Ha sonado el timbre.	The bell has rung.
La clase ha terminado.	The class has ended.
Ustedes pueden marcharse.	You may leave (You are excused).

PALABRAS Y EXPRESIONES PARA EL LABORATORIO (*Words and Expressions for the Laboratory*)

el	**alto parlante**	loud speaker
la	**audición**	playback
los	**auriculares (audífonos)**	ear(head)phones
la	**cabina**	booth
el	**carrete**	reel
la	**cinta (magnetofónica)**	(magnetic) tape
la	**cinta maestra (matriz)**	master tape
la	**corriente (eléctrica)**	power; (electric) current
el	**disco (fonográfico)**	disc, (phonograph) record
	empalmar	to splice
el	**enchufe**	plug
la	**entrada**	input
la	**grabadora (de cinta)**	(tape) recorder
	grabar	to record
el	**interruptor**	switch
el	**micrófono**	microphone
la	**perilla**	knob
	reparar	to repair
la	**salida**	output
el	**sonido**	sound
el	**volumen**	volume

Acérquese (Ud.) más al micrófono.	Get closer to the microphone.
Aleje más el micrófono.	Move the microphone away from you.
Apriete el botón.	Push the button.
Aumente el volumen.	Turn it louder (Increase the volume).
Cuelgue los auriculares.	Hang up the headphones.

Empuje el interruptor hacia la derecha (la izquierda).	Push the switch to the right (left).
Escuche la grabación.	Listen to the recording.
Hable en voz más alta (más baja, natural).	Speak in a louder (lower, natural) voice.
Hable más rápido (despacio).	Speak faster (slower).
Imite usted lo que oiga.	Imitate what you hear.
Mi máquina no funciona.	My machine does not work.
Pare (Apague) su máquina.	Stop (Turn off) your machine.
Ponga en marcha (Encienda) . . .	Start (Turn on) . . .
Póngase (Quítese) los audífonos.	Put on (Take off) your headphones.
Repita usted la respuesta.	Repeat the answer.
Se oirá (Usted oirá) cada frase una vez (dos veces), seguida de una pausa.	You will hear each sentence once (twice), followed by a pause.
Se oirá (Usted oirá) luego la respuesta (correcta).	You will hear the (correct) answer later.
¿Se oye la señal claramente?	Is the signal clear?
Vuelva a enrollar la cinta.	Rewind the tape.

TÉRMINOS GRAMATICALES (*Grammatical Terms*)

el adjetivo	adjective
demostrativo	demonstrative
posesivo	possessive
el adverbio	adverb
el artículo	article
definido	definite
indefinido	indefinite
el cambio ortográfico	change in spelling
la cláusula	clause
la comparación	comparison
el comparativo	comparative
el complemento	object
directo	direct
indirecto	indirect
la composición	composition
la concordancia	agreement
la conjugación	conjugation
la conjunción	conjunction
la consonante	consonant
el diptongo	diphthong

el género	gender
masculino	masculine
femenino	feminine
el gerundio	gerund, present participle
el infinitivo	infinitive
la interjección	interjection
la interrogación	interrogation, question
la letra	letter (*of the alphabet*)
mayúscula	capital
minúscula	small
el modo indicativo (subjuntivo)	indicative (subjunctive) mood
el nombre (substantivo)	noun (substantive)
el nombre propio	proper noun
el número	numeral, number
cardinal (ordinal)	cardinal (ordinal)
el objeto	object
directo	direct
indirecto	indirect
la palabra (negativa)	(negative) word
las partes de la oración	parts of speech
el participio pasado (presente)	past (present) participle
la persona	person
primera	first
segunda	second
tercera	third
el plural	plural
la posición	position
el predicado	predicate
la preposición	preposition
el pronombre	pronoun
interrogativo	interrogative
personal	personal
relativo	relative
la puntuación	punctuation
la radical (raíz)	stem
el significado	meaning
la sílaba	syllable
penúltima	next to last
última	last
el singular	singular
el subjuntivo	subjunctive
el sujeto	subject
el superlativo (absoluto)	(absolute) superlative

la terminación	ending
el tiempo	tense
el tiempo simple (**compuesto**)	simple (compound) tense
presente	present
imperfecto	imperfect
pretérito	preterit
futuro	future
condicional	conditional
perfecto	perfect (present perfect)
pluscuamperfecto	pluperfect
futuro perfecto	future perfect
condicional perfecto	conditional perfect
el triptongo	triphthong
el verbo	verb
auxiliar	auxiliary
impersonal	impersonal
irregular	irregular
reflexivo	reflexive
regular	regular
(in)transitivo	(in)transitive
la vocal	vowel
la voz	voice
activa	active
pasiva	passive

SIGNOS DE PUNTUACIÓN (*Punctuation Marks*)

, coma
; punto y coma
: dos puntos
. punto final
. . . puntos suspensivos
¿ ? signo(s) de interrogación
¡ ! signo(s) de admiración

( ) (el) paréntesis
« » comillas
´ acento escrito
¨ (la) diéresis
~ (la) tilde
– (el) guión
— raya

ABREVIATURAS Y SIGNOS (*Abbreviations and Signs*)

| *adj.* | adjective | *cond.* | conditional |
| *adv.* | adverb | *conj.* | conjunction |

dir.	direct		*obj.*	object
e.g.	for example		*p.p.*	past participle
etc.	and so forth		*part.*	participle
f.	feminine		*pl.*	plural
fam.	familiar		*prep.*	preposition
fn.	footnote		*pres.*	present
i.e.	that is		*pret.*	preterit
imp.	imperfect		*pron.*	pronoun
ind.	indicative		*reflex.*	reflexive
indef.	indefinite		*sing.*	singular
indir.	indirect		*subj.*	subjunctive
inf.	infinitive		*trans.*	transitive
lit.	literally		*U.S.*	United States
m.	masculine			

( ) Words in parentheses are explanatory or they are to be translated in the exercises.

— In the general vocabularies a dash indicates a word repeated, while in the exercises it usually is to be supplied by some grammatical form.

+ = followed by.

APPENDIX C

CARDINAL NUMERALS

0	cero	28	veinte y ocho (veintiocho)
1	un(o), una	29	veinte y nueve (veintinueve)
2	dos	30	treinta
3	tres	31	treinta y un(o), -a
4	cuatro	40	cuarenta
5	cinco	50	cincuenta
6	seis	60	sesenta
7	siete	70	setenta
8	ocho	80	ochenta
9	nueve	90	noventa
10	diez	100	ciento (cien)
11	once	101	ciento un(o), ciento una
12	doce	110	ciento diez
13	trece	200	doscientos, -as
14	catorce	300	trescientos, -as
15	quince	400	cuatrocientos, -as
16	diez y seis (dieciséis)	500	quinientos, -as
17	diez y siete (diecisiete)	600	seiscientos, -as
18	diez y ocho (dieciocho)	700	setecientos, -as
19	diez y nueve (diecinueve)	800	ochocientos, -as
20	veinte	900	novecientos, -as
21	veinte y un(o), -a (veintiún, veintiuno, veintiuna)	1.000	mil
		1.020	mil veinte
22	veinte y dos (veintidós)	2.000	dos mil
23	veinte y tres (veintitrés)	100.000	cien mil
24	veinte y cuatro (veinticuatro)	200.000	doscientos, -as, mil
25	veinte y cinco (veinticinco)	1.000.000	un millón (de)
26	veinte y seis (veintiséis)	2.000.000	dos millones (de)
27	veinte y siete (veintisiete)	2.500.000	dos millones quinientos, -as, mil

Uno and numerals ending in **uno** drop **-o** before a masculine noun; **una** is used before a feminine noun: **un soldado**, *one soldier*; **treinta y un muchachos**, *thirty-one boys*; **veinte y una repúblicas**, *twenty-one republics*.

Ciento becomes **cien** before nouns and before **mil** and **millones**: **cien dólares**, *one hundred dollars*; **cien mil habitantes**, *one hundred thousand inhabitants*.

Un is regularly not used with **cien(to)** and **mil**: **mil estudiantes**, *1,000 students*; however, one must say **ciento un mil habitantes**, *101,000 inhabitants*.   **Un** is used with the noun **millón**, which requires **de** when a noun follows: **un millón de dólares**, *$1,000,000*.   For *$2,000,000* one says **dos millones de dólares**.

The hundreds agree with a feminine noun: **doscientas muchachas**, *200 girls*; **quinientas cincuenta palabras**, *550 words*.   Beyond nine hundred **mil** must be used in counting: **mil novecientos setenta**, *1970*.

Regardless of the English use of *and* in numbers, **y** is regularly used in Spanish only between multiples of ten and numbers less than ten: **diez y seis**, *16*; **noventa y nueve**, *99*; but **seiscientos seis**, *606*.

From 16 through 19, and 21 through 29, the numerals are often written as one word: **dieciséis**, *16*.   Note that an accent mark must also be written on the forms **veintiún**, **veintidós**, **veintitrés**, **veintiséis**.   Above 29 the one-word forms are not used.

In writing numerals in Spanish a period is often used where a comma is used in English, and a comma is used for the decimal point: *$1.500,75*.   In current commercial practice, however, the English method is being used more and more.

ORDINAL NUMERALS

1st **primero (primer), -a**	4th **cuarto, -a**	8th **octavo, -a**
2nd **segundo, -a**	5th **quinto, -a**	9th **noveno, -a**
3rd **tercero (tercer), -a**	6th **sexto, -a**	10th **décimo, -a**
	7th **séptimo, -a**	

Ordinal numerals agree in gender and number with the nouns they modify.   **Primero** and **tercero** drop final **-o** before a masculine singular noun: **el primer (tercer) edificio**, *the first (third) building*, but **los primeros días**, *the first days*, **la tercera parte**, *the third part (one-third)*.

The ordinal numerals may precede or follow the noun.   Contrast the following:

Lección primera	Lesson One (I)	**la primera lección**	the first lesson
el capítulo tercero	Chapter Three	**el tercer capítulo**	the third chapter
la Calle Cuarta	Fourth Street	**la cuarta calle**	the fourth street

A cardinal number precedes an ordinal when both are used together: **las tres primeras páginas**, *the first three pages*.   (Note that Spanish says *the three first,* not *the first three*, as in English.)

With titles, chapters of books, volumes, etc., ordinal numerals are normally used through *tenth*.   For higher numerals, they are regularly replaced by the cardinal numerals; in these cases all numerals follow the noun.   With names of rulers and popes the definite article is omitted in Spanish.

Felipe Segundo Philip II (the Second)   **el tomo segundo** Volume Two
la página sesenta page 60   **el siglo veinte** the twentieth century

DAYS OF THE WEEK

domingo	Sunday	**jueves**	Thursday
lunes	Monday	**viernes**	Friday
martes	Tuesday	**sábado**	Saturday
miércoles	Wednesday		

MONTHS

enero	January	**julio**	July
febrero	February	**agosto**	August
marzo	March	**septiembre**	September
abril	April	**octubre**	October
mayo	May	**noviembre**	November
junio	June	**diciembre**	December

SEASONS

la primavera	spring	**el otoño**	fall, autumn
el verano	summer	**el invierno**	winter

DATES

In expressing dates the ordinal numeral **primero** is used for the *first* (day of the month), and the cardinals are used in all other cases. The definite article translates *the*, *on the*, with the day of the month. (Remember that the definite article translates *on* with a day of the week: **Yo saldré el lunes,** *I shall leave (on) Monday.*)

Hoy es el primero de enero. Today is the first of January (January 1).
Nació el dos de mayo. He was born (on) the second of May (May 2).

A complete date is expressed:

el diez de abril de mil novecientos setenta y uno April 10, 1971.

TIME OF DAY

¿Qué hora es (era)?   What time is (was) it?

Es (Era) la una.   It is (was) one o'clock.

Son (Eran) las dos.   It is (was) two o'clock.

Es la una y cuarto (media).   It is a quarter after one (half-past one).

Son las nueve menos diez de la mañana.   It is ten minutes before nine A.M. (in the morning).

Son las tres de la tarde en punto.   It is three P.M. (in the afternoon) sharp.

Eran las ocho de la noche.   It was eight at night (in the evening).

Ella saldrá a la una (a las cuatro).   She will leave at one (at four) o'clock.

Acaba de dar la una.   It has just struck one.

Ya han dado las dos.   It has already struck two.

Faltan diez minutos para las once.   It is ten minutes to eleven.

Estarán aquí hasta las cinco.   They will be here until five.

Yo trabajo desde las ocho hasta las doce.   I work from eight until twelve.

APPENDIX D

REGULAR VERBS

INFINITIVE

tomar, *to take*   **comer**, *to eat*   **vivir**, *to live*

PRESENT PARTICIPLE

tomando, *taking*   **comiendo**, *eating*   **viviendo**, *living*

PAST PARTICIPLE

tomado, *taken*   **comido**, *eaten*   **vivido**, *lived*

THE SIMPLE TENSES

INDICATIVE MOOD

PRESENT

I take, do take, am taking, etc.	*I eat, do eat, am eating, etc.*	*I live, do live, am living, etc.*
tomo	como	vivo
tomas	comes	vives
toma	come	vive
tomamos	comemos	vivimos
tomáis	coméis	vivís
toman	comen	viven

IMPERFECT

I was taking, used to take, took, etc.	*I was eating, used to eat, ate, etc.*	*I was living, used to live, lived, etc.*
tomaba	comía	vivía
tomabas	comías	vivías
tomaba	comía	vivía
tomábamos	comíamos	vivíamos
tomabais	comíais	vivíais
tomaban	comían	vivían

PRETERIT

I took, did take, etc.	*I ate, did eat, etc.*	*I lived, did live, etc.*
tomé	comí	viví
tomaste	comiste	viviste
tomó	comió	vivió
tomamos	comimos	vivimos
tomasteis	comisteis	vivisteis
tomaron	comieron	vivieron

FUTURE

I shall (will) take, etc.	*I shall (will) eat, etc.*	*I shall (will) live, etc.*
tomaré	comeré	viviré
tomarás	comerás	vivirás
tomará	comerá	vivirá
tomaremos	comeremos	viviremos
tomaréis	comeréis	viviréis
tomarán	comerán	vivirán

CONDITIONAL

I should (would) take, etc.	*I should (would) eat, etc.*	*I should (would) live, etc.*
tomaría	comería	viviría
tomarías	comerías	vivirías
tomaría	comería	viviría
tomaríamos	comeríamos	viviríamos
tomaríais	comeríais	viviríais
tomarían	comerían	vivirían

SUBJUNCTIVE MOOD

PRESENT

(that) I may take, etc.	*(that) I may eat, etc.*	*(that) I may live, etc.*
tome	coma	viva
tomes	comas	vivas
tome	coma	viva
tomemos	comamos	vivamos
toméis	comáis	viváis
tomen	coman	vivan

-ra IMPERFECT

(that) I might take, etc.	*(that) I might eat, etc.*	*(that) I might live, etc.*
tomara	comiera	viviera
tomaras	comieras	vivieras
tomara	comiera	viviera
tomáramos	comiéramos	viviéramos
tomarais	comierais	vivierais
tomaran	comieran	vivieran

-se IMPERFECT[1]

(that) I might take, etc.	*(that) I might eat, etc.*	*(that) I might live, etc.*
tomase	comiese	viviese
tomases	comieses	vivieses
tomase	comiese	viviese
tomásemos	comiésemos	viviésemos
tomaseis	comieseis	vivieseis
tomasen	comiesen	viviesen

IMPERATIVE

take	*eat*	*live*
toma (tú)	come (tú)	vive (tú)
tomad (vosotros)	comed (vosotros)	vivid (vosotros)

THE COMPOUND TENSES

PERFECT INFINITIVE

haber tomado (comido, vivido), *to have taken (eaten, lived)*

PERFECT PARTICIPLE

habiendo tomado (comido, vivido), *having taken (eaten, lived)*

[1] There is also a future subjunctive, used rarely today except in proverbs, legal documents, etc., but which was common in Old Spanish. Forms are:
tomar: tomare tomares tomare tomáremos tomareis tomaren
comer: comiere comieres comiere comiéremos comiereis comieren
vivir: viviere vivieres viviere viviéremos viviereis vivieren
The future perfect subjunctive is: hubiere tomado (comido, vivido), etc.

INDICATIVE MOOD

PRESENT PERFECT	PLUPERFECT	PRETERIT PERFECT
I have taken, eaten, lived, etc.	*I had taken, eaten, lived, etc.*	*I had taken, eaten, lived, etc.*

he
has
ha } tomado
  comido
hemos } vivido
habéis
han

había
habías
había } tomado
  comido
habíamos } vivido
habíais
habían

hube
hubiste
hubo } tomado
  comido
hubimos } vivido
hubisteis
hubieron

FUTURE PERFECT	CONDITIONAL PERFECT
I shall (will) have taken, etc.	*I should (would) have taken, etc.*

habré
habrás
habrá } tomado
  comido
habremos } vivido
habréis
habrán

habría
habrías
habría } tomado
  comido
habríamos } vivido
habríais
habrían

SUBJUNCTIVE MOOD

PRESENT PERFECT	-ra AND -se PLUPERFECT
(that) I may have taken, etc.	*(that) I might have taken, etc.*

haya
hayas
haya } tomado
  comido
hayamos } vivido
hayáis
hayan

hubiera *or* hubiese
hubieras *or* hubieses
hubiera *or* hubiese } tomado
  comido
hubiéramos *or* hubiésemos } vivido
hubierais *or* hubieseis
hubieran *or* hubiesen

IRREGULAR PAST PARTICIPLES OF REGULAR VERBS

abrir: **abierto**	describir: **descrito**	escribir: **escrito**
cubrir: **cubierto**	descubrir: **descubierto**	romper: **roto**

COMMENTS CONCERNING FORMS OF VERBS

INFINITIVE decir	PRES. PART. **diciendo**	PAST. PART. **dicho**	PRES. IND. **digo**	PRETERIT **dijeron**
IMP. IND. decía FUTURE **diré** CONDITIONAL **diría**	PROGRESSIVE TENSES **estoy**, etc. **diciendo**	COMPOUND TENSES **he**, etc. **dicho**	PRES. SUBJ. **diga** IMPERATIVE **di** decid	IMP. SUBJ. **dijera** **dijese**

a. From five forms (infinitive, present participle, past participle, first person singular present indicative, and third person plural preterit) all other forms may be derived.

b. The first and second persons plural of the present indicative of all verbs are regular, except in the cases of **haber, ir, ser.**

c. The third person plural is formed by adding **-n** to the third person singular in all tenses, except in the preterit and in the present indicative of **ser.**

d. All familiar forms (second person singular and plural) end in **-s**, except the second person singular preterit and the imperative.

e. The imperfect indicative is regular in all verbs, except **ir** (**iba**), **ser** (**era**), **ver** (**veía**).

f. If the first person singular preterit ends in unaccented **-e**, the third person singular ends in unaccented **-o**; the other endings are regular, except that after **j** the ending for the third person plural is **-eron.** Eight verbs of this group, in addition to those which end in **-ducir**, have a **u**-stem preterit (**andar, caber, estar, haber, poder, poner, saber, tener**); four have an **i**-stem (**decir, hacer, querer, venir**); **traer** retains the vowel **a** in the preterit. (The third person plural preterit forms of **decir** and **traer** are **dijeron** and **trajeron**, respectively. The third person singular preterit form of **hacer** is **hizo.**) **Ir** and **ser** have the same preterit forms, while **dar** has second-conjugation endings in this tense.

g. The conditional always has the same stem as the future. Only twelve verbs have irregular stems in these tenses. Five drop **e** of the infinitive ending (**caber, haber, poder, querer, saber**): five drop **e** or **i** and insert **d** (**poner, salir, tener, valer, venir**); and two (**decir, hacer**) retain the Old Spanish stems **dir-, har- (far-).**

h. The stem of the present subjunctive of all verbs is the same as that of the first person singular present indicative, except for **dar, estar, haber, ir, saber, ser.**

i. The imperfect subjunctive of all verbs is formed by dropping **-ron** of the third person plural preterit and adding the **-ra** or **-se** endings.

j. The singular imperative is the same in form as the third person singular present indicative, except in the case of ten verbs (**decir, di**; **haber, he**; **hacer, haz**; **ir, ve**; **poner, pon**; **salir, sal**; **ser, sé**; **tener, ten**; **valer, val** *or* vale; **venir, ven**). The plural imperative is always formed by dropping final **-r** of the infinitive and adding **-d**. (Remember that the imperative is used only for familiar affirmative commands.)

k. The compound tenses of all verbs are formed by using the various tenses of the auxiliary verb **haber** with the past participle.

IRREGULAR VERBS

(Participles are given with the infinitive; tenses not listed are regular.)

1. **andar**, andando, andado, *to go, walk*

PRETERIT	**anduve**	**anduviste**	**anduvo**	**anduvimos**	**anduvisteis** **anduvieron**
IMP. SUBJ.	**anduviera**, etc.		**anduviese**, etc.		

2. **caber**, cabiendo, cabido, *to fit, be contained in*

PRES. IND.	**quepo**	cabes	cabe	cabemos	cabéis	caben
PRES. SUBJ.	**quepa**	**quepas**	**quepa**	**quepamos**	**quepáis**	**quepan**
FUTURE	**cabré**	**cabrás**, etc.		COND.	**cabría**	**cabrías**, etc.
PRETERIT	**cupe**	**cupiste**	**cupo**	**cupimos**	**cupisteis**	**cupieron**
IMP. SUBJ.	**cupiera**, etc.		**cupiese**, etc.		

3. **caer, cayendo, caído**, *to fall*

PRES. IND.	**caigo**	caes	cae	caemos	caéis	caen
PRES. SUBJ.	**caiga**	**caigas**	**caiga**	**caigamos**	**caigáis**	**caigan**
PRETERIT	caí	**caíste**	**cayó**	**caímos**	**caísteis**	**cayeron**
IMP. SUBJ.	**cayera**, etc.		**cayese**, etc.		

4. **dar**, dando, dado, *to give*

PRES. IND.	**doy**	das	da	damos	dais	dan
PRES. SUBJ.	**dé**	des	**dé**	demos	deis	den
PRETERIT	**di**	diste	dio	dimos	disteis	dieron
IMP. SUBJ.	**diera**, etc.		**diese**, etc.		

5. **decir, diciendo, dicho**, *to say, tell*

PRES. IND.	**digo**	**dices**	**dice**	decimos	decís	**dicen**
PRES. SUBJ.	**diga**	**digas**	**diga**	**digamos**	**digáis**	**digan**
IMPERATIVE	**di**				decid	
FUTURE	**diré**	**dirás**, etc.		COND.	**diría**	**dirías**, etc.
PRETERIT	**dije**	**dijiste**	**dijo**	**dijimos**	**dijisteis**	**dijeron**
IMP. SUBJ.	**dijera**, etc.		**dijese**, etc.		

6. **estar**, estando, estado, *to be*

PRES. IND.	estoy	estás	está	estamos	estáis	están
PRES. SUBJ.	esté	estés	esté	estemos	estéis	estén
PRETERIT	estuve	estuviste	estuvo	estuvimos	estuvisteis	estuvieron
IMP. SUBJ.	estuviera, etc.		estuviese, etc.			

7. **haber**, habiendo, habido, *to have* (auxiliary)

PRES. IND.	he	has	ha	hemos	habéis	han
PRES. SUBJ.	haya	hayas	haya	hayamos	hayáis	hayan
IMPERATIVE	he				habed	
FUTURE	habré	habrás, etc.		COND.	habría	habrías, etc.
PRETERIT	hube	hubiste	hubo	hubimos	hubisteis	hubieron
IMP. SUBJ.	hubiera, etc.		hubiese, etc.			

8. **hacer**, haciendo, **hecho**, *to do, make*

PRES. IND.	hago	haces	hace	hacemos	hacéis	hacen
PRES. SUBJ.	haga	hagas	haga	hagamos	hagáis	hagan
IMPERATIVE	haz				haced	
FUTURE	haré	harás, etc.		COND.	haría	harías, etc.
PRETERIT	hice	hiciste	hizo	hicimos	hicisteis	hicieron
IMP. SUBJ.	hiciera, etc.		hiciese, etc.			

Like **hacer**: satisfacer, **to satisfy**

9. **ir, yendo, ido**, *to go*

PRES. IND.	voy	vas	va	vamos	vais	van
PRES. SUBJ.	vaya	vayas	vaya	vayamos	vayáis	vayan
IMPERATIVE	ve				id	
IMP. IND.	iba	ibas	iba	íbamos	ibais	iban
PRETERIT	fui	fuiste	fue	fuimos	fuisteis	fueron
IMP. SUBJ.	fuera, etc.		fuese, etc.			

10. **oír, oyendo**, oído, *to hear*

PRES. IND.	oigo	oyes	oye	oímos	oís	oyen
PRES. SUBJ.	oiga	oigas	oiga	oigamos	oigáis	oigan
IMPERATIVE	oye				oíd	
PRETERIT	oí	oíste	oyó	oímos	oísteis	oyeron
IMP. SUBJ.	oyera, etc.		oyese, etc.			

11. **poder, pudiendo**, podido, *to be able*

PRES. IND.	puedo	puedes	puede	podemos	podéis	pueden
PRES. SUBJ.	pueda	puedas	pueda	podamos	podáis	puedan
FUTURE	podré	podrás, etc.		COND.	podría	podrías, etc.
PRETERIT	pude	pudiste	pudo	pudimos	pudisteis	pudieron
IMP. SUBJ.	pudiera, etc.		pudiese, etc.			

12. **poner**, poniendo, **puesto**, *to put, place*

PRES. IND.	**pongo**	pones	pone	ponemos	ponéis	ponen
PRES. SUBJ.	**ponga**	**pongas**	**ponga**	**pongamos**	**pongáis**	**pongan**
IMPERATIVE	**pon**				poned	
FUTURE	**pondré**	**pondrás**, etc.		COND.	**pondría**	**pondrías**, etc.
PRETERIT	**puse**	**pusiste**	**puso**	**pusimos**	**pusisteis**	**pusieron**
IMP. SUBJ.	**pusiera**, etc.		**pusiese**, etc.			

Like **poner**: componer, *to compose*; exponer, *to expose*; imponer, *to impose*; oponer, *to oppose*; proponer, *to propose*; suponer, *to suppose*.

13. **querer**, queriendo, querido, *to wish, want*

PRES. IND.	**quiero**	**quieres**	**quiere**	queremos	queréis	**quieren**
PRES. SUBJ.	**quiera**	**quieras**	**quiera**	queramos	queráis	**quieran**
FUTURE	**querré**	**querrás**, etc.		COND.	**querría**	**querrías**, etc.
PRETERIT	**quise**	**quisiste**	**quiso**	**quisimos**	**quisisteis**	**quisieron**
IMP. SUBJ.	**quisiera**, etc.		**quisiese**, etc.			

14. **saber**, sabiendo, sabido, *to know*

PRES. IND.	**sé**	sabes	sabe	sabemos	sabéis	saben
PRES. SUBJ.	**sepa**	**sepas**	**sepa**	**sepamos**	**sepáis**	**sepan**
FUTURE	**sabré**	**sabrás**, etc.		COND.	**sabría**	**sabrías**, etc.
PRETERIT	**supe**	**supiste**	**supo**	**supimos**	**supisteis**	**supieron**
IMP. SUBJ.	**supiera**, etc.		**supiese**, etc.			

15. **salir**, saliendo, salido, *to go out, leave*

PRES. IND.	**salgo**	sales	sale	salimos	salís	salen
PRES. SUBJ.	**salga**	**salgas**	**salga**	**salgamos**	**salgáis**	**salgan**
IMPERATIVE	**sal**				salid	
FUTURE	**saldré**	**saldrás**, etc.		COND.	**saldría**	**saldrías**, etc.

16. **ser**, siendo, sido, *to be*

PRES. IND.	**soy**	**eres**	**es**	**somos**	**sois**	**son**
PRES. SUBJ.	**sea**	**seas**	**sea**	**seamos**	**seáis**	**sean**
IMPERATIVE	**sé**				sed	
IMP. IND.	**era**	**eras**	**era**	**éramos**	**erais**	**eran**
PRETERIT	**fui**	**fuiste**	**fue**	**fuimos**	**fuisteis**	**fueron**
IMP. SUBJ.	**fuera**, etc.		**fuese**, etc.			

17. **tener**, teniendo, tenido, *to have*

PRES. IND.	**tengo**	**tienes**	**tiene**	tenemos	tenéis	**tienen**
PRES. SUBJ.	**tenga**	**tengas**	**tenga**	**tengamos**	**tengáis**	**tengan**
IMPERATIVE	**ten**				tened	
FUTURE	**tendré**	**tendrás**, etc.		COND.	**tendría**	**tendrías**, etc.
PRETERIT	**tuve**	**tuviste**	**tuvo**	**tuvimos**	**tuvisteis**	**tuvieron**
IMP. SUBJ.	**tuviera**, etc.		**tuviese**, etc.			

Like **tener**: contener, *to contain*; detener, *to detain, stop*; mantener, *to maintain*; obtener, *to obtain*.

18. **traer, trayendo, traído**, *to bring*

PRES. IND.	**traigo**	traes	trae	traemos	traéis	traen
PRES. SUBJ.	**traiga**	**traigas**	**traiga**	**traigamos**	**traigáis**	**traigan**
PRETERIT	**traje**	**trajiste**	**trajo**	**trajimos**	**trajisteis**	**trajeron**
IMP. SUBJ.	**trajera**, etc.		**trajese**, etc.			

Like **traer**: atraer, *to attract*.

19. **valer**, valiendo, valido, *to be worth*

PRES. IND.	**valgo**	vales	vale	valemos	valéis	valen
PRES. SUBJ.	**valga**	**valgas**	**valga**	**valgamos**	**valgáis**	**valgan**
IMPERATIVE	**val** (vale)			valed		
FUTURE	**valdré**	**valdrás**, etc.			COND. **valdría**	**valdrías**, etc.

20. **venir, viniendo**, venido, *to come*

PRES. IND.	**vengo**	**vienes**	**viene**	venimos	venís	**vienen**
PRES. SUBJ.	**venga**	**vengas**	**venga**	**vengamos**	**vengáis**	**vengan**
IMPERATIVE	**ven**			venid		
FUTURE	**vendré**	**vendrás**, etc.		COND. **vendría**		**vendrías**, etc.
PRETERIT	**vine**	**viniste**	**vino**	**vinimos**	**vinisteis**	**vinieron**
IMP. SUBJ.	**viniera**, etc.		**viniese**, etc.			

Like **venir**: convenir, *to be fitting*.

21. **ver**, viendo, **visto**, *to see*

PRES. IND.	**veo**	ves	ve	vemos	véis	ven
PRES. SUBJ.	**vea**	**veas**	**vea**	**veamos**	**veáis**	**vean**
PRETERIT	**vi**	viste	**vio**	vimos	visteis	vieron
IMP. IND.	**veía**	**veías**	**veía**	**veíamos**	**veíais**	**veían**

VERBS WITH CHANGES IN SPELLING

Changes in spelling are required in certain verbs in order to preserve the sound of the final consonant of the stem. The changes occur in only seven forms: in the first four types below the change is in the first person singular preterit, and in the remaining types in the first person singular present indicative, while all types change throughout the present subjunctive.

	a	o	u	e	i
Sound of *k*	ca	co	cu	que	qui
Sound of *g*	ga	go	gu	gue	gui
Sound of *s* (*th*)	za	zo	zu	ce	ci
Sound of Spanish **j**	ja	jo	ju	ge, je	gi, ji
Sound of *gw*	gua	guo		güe	güi

1. Verbs ending in **-car** change **c** to **qu** before **e**: **buscar**, *to look for*

| PRETERIT | **busqué** | buscaste | buscó, etc. | | |
| PRES. SUBJ. | **busque** | **busques** | **busque** | **busquemos** | **busquéis** | **busquen** |

Like **buscar**: acercarse, *to approach*; atacar, *to attack*; certificar, *to register*; colocar, *to place*; comunicar, *to inform*; convocar, *to convoke, call up*; criticar, *to criticize*; dedicar, *to dedicate*; destacar, *to make stand out*; diversificar, *to diversify*; educar, *to educate*; embarcarse, *to embark*; evocar, *to evoke*; explicar, *to explain*; identificar, *to identify*; indicar, *to indicate*; marcar, *to dial* (telephone); practicar, *to practice*; publicar, *to publish*; sacar, *to take out*; suplicar, *to beg*; tocar, *to play* (music).

2. Verbs ending in **-gar** change **g** to **gu** before **e**: **llegar**, *to arrive*

| PRETERIT | **llegué** | llegaste | llegó, etc. | | |
| PRES. SUBJ. | **llegue** | **llegues** | **llegue** | **lleguemos** | **lleguéis** | **lleguen** |

Like **llegar**: agregar, *to add*; apagar, *to turn off* (lights); cargar, *to charge*; colgar (ue),[1] *to hang* (up); entregar, *to hand* (over); jugar (ue), *to play* (a game); navegar, *to sail*; negar (ie), *to deny*; obligar, *to oblige, force*; pagar, *to pay* (*for*); rogar (ue), *to ask, beg*.

3. Verbs ending in **-zar** change **z** to **c** before **e**: **cruzar**, *to cross*

| PRETERIT | **crucé** | cruzaste | cruzó, etc. | | |
| PRES. SUBJ. | **cruce** | **cruces** | **cruce** | **crucemos** | **crucéis** | **crucen** |

Like **cruzar**: alcanzar, *to reach*; almorzar (ue), *to take* (*eat*) *lunch*; analizar, *to analyze*; caracterizar, *to characterize*; comenzar (ie), *to commence, begin*; empezar (ie), *to begin*; esbozar, *to sketch*; garantizar, *to guarantee*; industrializar, *to industrialize*; lanzar, *to hurl*; organizar, *to organize*; poetizar, *to poeticize*; realizar, *to realize, carry out*; rechazar, *to repulse, reject*; reforzar (ue), *to reinforce*; simbolizar, *to symbolize*; sintonizar, *to tune in*.

4. Verbs ending in **-guar** change **gu** to **gü** before **e**: **averiguar**, *to find out*

| PRETERIT | **averigüé** | averiguaste | averiguó, etc. | | |
| PRES. SUBJ. | **averigüe** | **averigües** | **averigüe** | **averigüemos** | **averigüéis** | **averigüen** |

5. Verbs ending in **-ger** or **-gir** change **g** to **j** before **a** and **o**: **coger**, *to pick* (*up*)

| PRES. IND. | **cojo** | coges | coge, etc. | | |
| PRES. SUBJ. | **coja** | **cojas** | **coja** | **cojamos** | **cojáis** | **cojan** |

Like **coger**: dirigirse, *to direct oneself, go*; escoger, *to choose, select*; regir (i, i), *to rule*; surgir, *to surge, arise*.

6. Verbs ending in **-guir** change **gu** to **g** before **a** and **o**: **distinguir**, *to distinguish*

| PRES. IND. | **distingo** | distingues | distingue, etc. | | |
| PRES. SUBJ. | **distinga** | **distingas** | **distinga** | **distingamos** | **distingáis** | **distingan** |

Like **distinguir**: conseguir (i, i), *to obtain, attain*; seguir (i, i), *to follow*.

[1] See pages 322–324 for verbs with stem changes.

7. Verbs ending in **-cer** or **-cir** preceded by a consonant change **c** to **z** before **a** and **o**: **vencer**, *to overcome, conquer*

PRES. IND.	**venzo**	vences	vence, etc.		
PRES. SUBJ.	**venza**	**venzas**	**venza**	**venzamos**	**venzáis**	**venzan**

Like **vencer**: ejercer, *to exert*.

8. Verbs ending in **-quir** change **qu** to **c** before **a** and **o**: **delinquir**, *to be guilty*

PRES. IND.	**delinco**	delinques	delinque, etc.		
PRES. SUBJ.	**delinca**	**delincas**	**delinca**	**delincamos**	**delincáis**	**delincan**

VERBS WITH SPECIAL ENDINGS

1. Verbs ending in **-cer** or **-cir** following a vowel insert **z** before **c** in the first person singular present indicative and throughout the present subjunctive: **conocer**, *to know, be acquainted with.*

PRES. IND.	**conozco**	conoces	conoce, etc.		
PRES. SUBJ.	**conozca**	**conozcas**	**conozca**	**conozcamos**	**conozcáis**	**conozcan**

Like **conocer**: agradecer, *to be grateful for*; aparecer, *to appear*; crecer, *to grow*; establecer, *to establish*; florecer, *to flourish*; fortalecer, *to strengthen*; merecer, *to merit*; nacer, *to be born*; ofrecer, *to offer*; parecer, *to seem*; prevalecer, *to prevail*; reconocer, *to recognize*.

2. Verbs ending in **-ducir** have the same changes as **conocer**, with additional changes in the preterit and imperfect subjunctive: **conducir**, *to conduct, drive.*

PRES. IND.	**conduzco**	conduces	conduce, etc.		
PRES. SUBJ.	**conduzca**	**conduzcas**	**conduzca**	**conduzcamos**	**conduzcáis**	**conduzcan**
PRETERIT	**conduje**	**condujiste**	**condujo**	**condujimos**	**condujisteis**	**condujeron**
IMP. SUBJ.	**condujera**, etc.		**condujese**, etc.			

Like **conducir**: introducir, *to introduce*; producir, *to produce*; reproducir, *to reproduce*; traducir, *to translate*.

3. Verbs ending in **-uir** (except **-guir** and **-quir**) insert **y** except before **i**, and change unaccented **i** between vowels to **y**: **huir**, *to flee.*

PARTICIPLES	**huyendo**		huido		
PRES. IND.	**huyo**	**huyes**	**huye**	huimos	huís	**huyen**
PRES. SUBJ.	**huya**	**huyas**	**huya**	**huyamos**	**huyáis**	**huyan**
IMPERATIVE	**huye**				huid	
PRETERIT	huí	huíste	**huyó**	huimos	huisteis	**huyeron**
IMP. SUBJ.	**huyera**, etc.		**huyese**, etc.			

Like **huir**: concluir, *to conclude, end*; constituir, *to constitute*; construir, *to construct*; contribuir, *to contribute*; destruir, *to destroy*; distribuir, *to distribute*; substituir, *to substitute*.

4. Certain verbs ending in **-er** preceded by a vowel replace unaccented **i** of the ending by **y**: **creer**, *to believe*.

PARTICIPLES	**creyendo**		**creído**		
PRETERIT	creí	**creíste**	**creyó**	**creímos**	**creísteis**	creyeron
IMP. SUBJ.	**creyera**, etc.		**creyese**, etc.		

Like **creer**: leer, *to read*.

5. Some verbs ending in **-iar** require a written accent on the **i** in the singular and third person plural in the present indicative and present subjunctive and in the singular imperative: **enviar**, *to send*.

PRES. IND.	**envío**	**envías**	**envía**	enviamos	enviáis	**envían**
PRES. SUBJ.	**envíe**	**envíes**	**envíe**	enviemos	enviéis	**envíen**
IMPERATIVE	**envía**				enviad	

Like **enviar**: esquiar, *to ski*; guiar, *to guide*; variar, *to vary*.   However, such common verbs as the following do not have the accented **i**: anunciar, *to announce*; apreciar, *to appreciate, esteem*; asfixiar, *to asphyxiate*; asociarse, *to associate*; beneficiarse, *to benefit*; cambiar, *to change*; comerciar, *to trade*; estudiar, *to study*; iniciar, *to initiate*; pronunciar, *to pronounce*.

6. Verbs ending in **-uar** have a written accent on the **u** in the same forms as verbs in section 5:[1] **continuar**, *to continue*.

PRES. IND.	**continúo**	**continúas**	**continúa**	continuamos	continuáis	**continúan**
PRES. SUBJ.	**continúe**	**continúes**	**continúe**	continuemos	continuéis	**continúen**
IMPERATIVE	**continúa**				continuad	

Like **continuar**: acentuar, *to emphasize*; efectuarse, *to carry out*; graduarse, *to graduate*.

7. Verbs whose stems end in **ll** or **ñ** drop the **i** of the diphthongs **ie**(**ié**) and **ió**.   Examples, not used in this text, are:

bullir, *to boil*

PRES. PART.	**bullendo**					
PRETERIT	bullí	bulliste	**bulló**	bullimos	bullisteis	**bulleron**
IMP. SUBJ.	**bullera**, etc.		**bullese**, etc.			

reñir (**i**, **i**), *to scold*

PRES. PART.	**riñendo**					
PRETERIT	reñí	reñiste	**riñó**	reñimos	reñisteis	**riñeron**
IMP. SUBJ.	**riñera**, etc.		**riñese**, etc.			

[1] **Reunir(se)**, *to gather, meet*, has a written accent on the **u** in the same forms as **continuar**:

PRES. IND.	**reúno**	**reúnes**	**reúne** . . . **reúnen**
PRES. SUBJ.	**reúna**	**reúnas**	**reúna** . . . **reúnan**
IMPERATIVE	**reúne**		

STEM-CHANGING VERBS

CLASS I (**-ar, -er**)

Many verbs of the first and second conjugations change the stem vowel **e** to **ie** and **o** to **ue** when the vowels **e** and **o** are stressed, *i.e.*, in the singular and third person plural of the present indicative and present subjunctive and in the singular imperative.   Class I verbs are designated: **cerrar (ie)**,[1] **volver (ue)**.[2]

cerrar, *to close*

PRES. IND.	**cierro**	**cierras**	**cierra**	cerramos	cerráis	**cierran**
PRES. SUBJ.	**cierre**	**cierres**	**cierre**	cerremos	cerréis	**cierren**
IMPERATIVE	**cierra**					

Like **cerrar**: atravesar, *to cross*; comenzar, *to commence, begin*; despertar, *to awaken*; empezar, *to begin*; gobernar, *to govern*; manifestarse, *to be manifest*; negar, *to deny*; pensar, *to think*; sentarse, *to sit down*.

perder, *to lose, miss*

PRES. IND.	**píerdo**	**pierdes**	**pierde**	perdemos	perdéis	**pierden**
PRES. SUBJ.	**pierda**	**pierdas**	**pierda**	perdamos	perdáis	**pierdan**
IMPERATIVE	**pierde**					

Like **perder**: defender, *to defend*; entender, *to understand*; extender, *to extend*.

contar, *to count*; *relate*

PRES. IND.	**cuento**	**cuentas**	**cuenta**	contamos	contáis	**cuentan**
PRES. SUBJ.	**cuente**	**cuentes**	**cuente**	contemos	contéis	**cuenten**
IMPERATIVE	**cuenta**					

Like **contar**: acordarse, *to remember*; acostarse, *to go to bed*; almorzar, *to take (eat) lunch*; aprobar, *to approve*; colgar, *to hang (up)*; costar, *to cost*; demostrar, *to demonstrate*; encontrar, *to find*; esforzarse por, *to strive to*; mostrar, *to show*; probar, *to try out, test*; recordar, *to recall*; reforzar, *to reinforce*; rogar, *to ask, beg*; sonar, *to sound, ring*; soñar, *to dream*.

---

[1] **Errar**, *to err, miss* (a shot), is designated: **errar (ye)**.   At the beginning of a verb the initial **i** of the diphthong **ie** is changed to **y**, since no Spanish word may begin with **ie**:

PRES. IND.	**yerro**	**yerras**	**yerra**	erramos	erráis	**yerran**
PRES. SUBJ.	**yerre**	**yerres**	**yerre**	erremos	erréis	**yerren**
IMPERATIVE	**yerra**					

[2] Forms of **oler (ue)**, *to smell* (an odor), not used in this text, follow.   Spanish words do not begin with **u** followed by **a**, **e**, or **o**; thus **h** is written before **ue**:

PRES. IND.	**huelo**	**hueles**	**huele**	olemos	oléis	**huelen**
PRES. SUBJ.	**huela**	**huelas**	**huela**	olamos	oláis	**huelan**
IMPERATIVE	**huele**					

volver,[1] *to return*

PRES. IND.	**vuelvo**	**vuelves**	**vuelve**	volvemos	volvéis	**vuelven**
PRES. SUBJ.	**vuelva**	**vuelvas**	**vuelva**	volvamos	volváis	**vuelvan**
IMPERATIVE	**vuelve**					

Like **volver**: devolver, *to return, give back*; doler, *to ache, pain*; envolver, *to wrap up*; llover, *to rain*; resolver, *to resolve*.

jugar, *to play* (a game)

PRES. IND.	**juego**	**juegas**	**juega**	jugamos	jugáis	**juegan**
PRES. SUBJ.	**juegue**	**juegues**	**juegue**	juguemos	juguéis	**jueguen**
IMPERATIVE	**juega**					

CLASS II (**-ir**)

Certain verbs of the third conjugation have the changes in the stem indicated below. Class II verbs are designated: **sentir (ie, i)**, **dormir (ue, u)**.

PRES. IND.	1, 2, 3, 6		PRES. PART.	
PRES. SUBJ.	1, 2, 3, 6 $\Big\}$ e > ie		PRETERIT	3, 6
IMPERATIVE	Sing. $\Big\}$ o > ue		PRES. SUBJ.	4, 5 $\Big\}$ e > i
			IMP. SUBJ.	1, 2, 3, 4, 5, 6 $\Big\}$ o > u

sentir, *to feel*

PRES. PART.	**sintiendo**					
PRES. IND.	**siento**	**sientes**	**siente**	sentimos	sentís	**sienten**
PRES. SUBJ.	**sienta**	**sientas**	**sienta**	**sintamos**	**sintáis**	sientan
IMPERATIVE	**siente**					
PRETERIT	sentí	sentiste	**sintió**	sentimos	sentisteis	**sintieron**
IMP. SUBJ.	**sintiera**, etc.		**sintiese**, etc.			

Like **sentir**: adquirir,[2] *to acquire*; advertir, *to notice*; consentir, *to consent*; convertir, *to convert*; diferir, *to differ*; divertirse, *to amuse oneself*; preferir, *to prefer*; referir, *to refer*.

---

[1] The past participles of **volver, devolver, envolver, resolver** are: **vuelto, devuelto, envuelto, resuelto**, respectively.

[2] Forms of **adquirir (ie)** are:

PRES. IND.	**adquiero**	**adquieres**	**adquiere**	adquirimos	adquirís	**adquieren**
PRES. SUBJ.	**adquiera**	**adquieras**	**adquiera**	adquiramos	adquiráis	**adquieran**
IMPERATIVE	**adquiere**					

dormir, *to sleep*

PRES. PART.	**durmiendo**					
PRES. IND.	**duermo**	**duermes**	**duerme**	dormimos	dormís	**duermen**
PRES. SUBJ.	**duerma**	**duermas**	**duerma**	**durmamos**	**durmáis**	**duerman**
IMPERATIVE	**duerme**					
PRETERIT	dormí	dormiste	**durmió**	dormimos	dormisteis	**durmieron**
IMP. SUBJ.	**durmiera**, etc.		**durmiese**, etc.			

Like **dormir**: morir,[1] *to die.*

CLASS III (**-ir**)

Certain verbs in the third conjugation change **e** to **i** in all forms in which changes occur in Class II verbs.　These verbs are designated: **pedir** (**i, i**).

pedir, *to ask*

PRES. PART.	**pidiendo**					
PRES. IND.	**pido**	**pides**	**pide**	pedimos	pedís	**piden**
PRES. SUBJ.	**pida**	**pidas**	**pida**	**pidamos**	**pidáis**	**pidan**
IMPERATIVE	**pide**					
PRETERIT	pedí	pediste	**pidió**	pedimos	pedisteis	**pidieron**
IMP. SUBJ.	**pidiera**, etc.		**pidiese**, etc.			

Like **pedir**: competir, *to compete*; concebir, *to conceive*; conseguir, *to obtain, attain*; despedirse, *to take leave*; regir, *to rule*; repetir, *to repeat*; seguir, *to follow*; servir, *to serve*; vestir, *to dress.*

reír, *to laugh*

PARTICIPLES	**riendo**		reído			
PRES. IND.	**río**	**ríes**	**ríe**	reímos	reís	**ríen**
PRES. SUBJ.	**ría**	**rías**	**ría**	**riamos**	**riáis**	**rían**
IMPERATIVE	**ríe**				reíd	
PRETERIT	reí	reíste	**rió**	reímos	reísteis	**rieron**
IMP. SUBJ.	**riera**, etc.		**riese**, etc.			

[1] Past participle: **muerto**.

APPENDIX E

VERBS FOLLOWED BY AN INFINITIVE AND THOSE WHOSE MEANINGS CHANGE WHEN USED REFLEXIVELY

I. VERBS FOLLOWED BY AN INFINITIVE, WITH OR WITHOUT A PREPOSITION

Many verbs in Spanish are followed directly by an infinitive, as in English. Also, many verbs, as well as certain adjectives and nouns, require a preposition, especially **a**, **con**, **de**, **en**, or **por**, before an infinitive. An occasional verb may be followed by more than one preposition. [Remember that an infinitive is used after many idiomatic expressions; for example, **hay** (**había**) **que**, *it is* (*was*) *necessary to*; **tener que**, *to have to, must*.] Since the list is long, only the verbs (including a few which appear in idiomatic expressions) used in this text are listed below.

A. Verbs which may be followed directly by an infinitive

aconsejar	to advise	**merecer**	to merit, deserve
bastar	to be enough, sufficient	**necesitar**	to need
conseguir (**i, i**)	to succeed in	**oír**	to hear
convenir	to be fitting, advisable	**olvidar**	to forget
deber	should, ought to, must	**parecer**	to appear, seem
decidir	to decide	**pensar** (**ie**)	to intend, plan
dejar	to let, allow, permit	**permitir**	to permit, allow to, let
desear	to desire, wish, want	**poder**	to be able, can
determinar	to determine	**preferir** (**ie, i**)	to prefer
esperar	to hope, expect	**prometer**	to promise
faltar	to be lacking	**querer**	to wish, want
gustar	to like, be pleasing to	**resolver** (**ue**)	to resolve
hacer	to make, have	**resultar**	to result, turn out (to be)
importar	to matter, be important	**saber**	to know how (to), can
intentar	to try, attempt	**sentir** (**ie, i**)	to regret, be sorry
interesar	to interest	**temer**	to fear
lograr	to succeed in	**tocar** (**a uno**)	to fall to one's lot
mandar	to command, have, order	**ver**	to see

B. Verbs followed by certain prepositions before an infinitive, or other objects

a. Verbs which require **a** before an infinitive are:

acudir a	to resort (come) to	**aprender a**	to learn to
animar a	to encourage to	**aprestarse a**	to prepare oneself to

325

aproximarse a   to come near to
aspirar a   to aspire to
atreverse a   to dare to
ayudar a   to help (aid) to
bajar a   to come (go) down to
comenzar (ie) a   to commence to
contribuir a   to contribute to
correr a   to run to
decidirse a   to make up one's mind to
dedicarse a   to dedicate (devote) oneself to
dirigirse a   to turn to, direct oneself to
empezar (ie) a   to begin to
enseñar a   to teach (how) to, show to

enviar a   to send to
incorporarse a   to incorporate into
invitar a   to invite to
ir a   to go to
limitarse a   to limit oneself to
llegar a   to come to, become
llevar (a uno) a   to lead (one) to
negarse (ie) a   to refuse to
obligar a   to oblige (force) to
oponerse a   to oppose
pasar a   to go to
referirse (ie, i) a   to refer to
salir a   to go (come) out to
venir a   to come to
volver a   to return to; to . . . again

Verbs which require **a** before an object are:

acercarse a   to approach
asistir a   to attend
corresponder a   to correspond to
dar a   to face

echar a   to throw (toss) into
llegar a   to reach, arrive (at)
unirse a   to join

b. Verbs which require **con** before an infinitive (but more commonly before an object) are:

conformarse con   to be satisfied with
preocuparse con   to be concerned with (about), be preoccupied with

relacionarse con   to be related to
soñar (ue) con   to dream of

In addition to the four verbs mentioned, other verbs which require **con** before an object are:

acabar con   to put an end to
encontrarse (ue) con   to run across

reunirse con   to join

c. Verbs which require **de** before an infinitive are:

acabar de   to have just
acordarse (ue) de   to remember to
alegrarse de   to be glad to
beneficiarse de   to benefit from
cansarse de   to become tired of
deber de   must (*probability*)

dejar de   to stop (cease), fail to
disfrutar de   to enjoy
haber de   to be (be supposed) to
olvidarse de   to forget to
tratar de   to try to
tratarse de   to be a question of

Verbs which require **de** before an object are:

apoderarse de	to take possession of	**partir de**	to leave
burlarse de	to make fun of	**pasar de**	to exceed
constar de	to consist of	**salir de**	to leave
despedirse (i, i) de	to take leave of	**servir de**	to serve as (a)
llenar de	to fill with	**tratar de**	to treat of, deal with

d. Verbs which require **en** before an infinitive are:

consentir (ie, i) en	to consent to, agree to	**pensar (ie) en**	to think of (about)
insistir en	to insist on	**tardar en**	to delay in, take long to

Verbs which require **en** before an object are:

convertirse (ie, i) en	to be converted into	**entrar en**	to enter
echar en	to throw (toss) into	**fijarse en**	to notice

e. Verbs followed by **por** before an infinitive are:

esforzarse (ue) por	to make an effort to, strive for	**interesarse por**	to become interested in
estar por	to be inclined to	**preocuparse por**	to worry about, be concerned with

II. VERBS (NOT LISTED IN LECCIÓN DOS) WHOSE MEANINGS CHANGE WHEN USED REFLEXIVELY

decidir	to decide	**decidirse a**	to make up one's mind to
dedicar	to dedicate	**dedicarse a**	to dedicate oneself to
desarrollar	to develop	**desarrollarse**	to be developed
destacar	to make stand out, emphasize	**destacarse**	to stand out
dirigir	to direct, address	**dirigirse a**	to direct oneself (turn) to
distinguir	to distinguish	**distinguirse**	to become distinguished
encontrar (ue)	to find	**encontrarse (ue)**	to find oneself, be
entregar	to hand (over)	**entregarse (a)**	to abandon oneself (to)
establecer	to establish	**establecerse**	to establish oneself, settle
interesar	to interest	**interesarse (por)**	to become interested (in)
ir	to go	**irse**	to go away, leave
limitar	to limit	**limitarse a**	to limit oneself to
llevar	to take, carry	**llevarse**	to take away, take (with oneself)

marchar   to march
negar (**ie**)   to deny
preparar   to prepare

presentar   to present, introduce

quitar   to remove, take away
referir (**ie, i**)   to refer
reunir   to collect
sentir (**ie, i**)   to feel, regret
tratar de   to try to
ver   to see
volver   to return

marcharse   to leave, go away
negarse (**ie**) **a**   to refuse to
prepararse   to be prepared, get under way
presentarse   to present oneself, appear
quitarse   to take off (oneself)
referirse (**ie, i**) **a**   to refer to
reunirse   to meet, gather
sentirse (**ie, i**) (**bien**)   to feel (well)
tratarse de   to be a question of
verse   to be (seen)
volverse   to become

VOCABULARIES

VOCABULARY

A

a   to, at, in, on, from, by, *etc.*; *not translated when used before a personal dir. obj.*

abajo   below, underneath

   Los de abajo   The Underdogs

abandonar   to abandon, leave

abierto, -a *p.p. of* **abrir** *and adj.*   open, opened

el abogado   lawyer

abominable   abominable, detestable

la abreviatura   abbreviation

el abrigo   topcoat, overcoat

abril   April

abrir   to open

absorber   to absorb; engross completely; take in (up)

abstracto, -a   abstract

el abuelo   grandfather; *pl.* grandparents

la abundancia   abundance

abundante   abundant

el abuso   abuse

acabar   to end, finish

   acabar con + *obj.*   to put an end to, wipe out

   acabar de + *inf.*   to have just + *p.p.*

acaso   perhaps

acelerar   to accelerate

acentuar   to accentuate, emphasize

aceptar   to accept

acerca de   about, concerning

acercar   to bring near

   acercarse (**a** + *obj.*)   to approach, draw near, move toward

acompañado, -a (**de**)   accompanied (by)

acompañar   to accompany, go with

aconsejar   to advise

acordarse (**ue**) (**de** + *obj.*)   to remember, recall

acostar (**ue**)   to put to bed; *reflex.* go to bed

la activación   activation, promotion

la actividad   activity

el acto   act

actual *adj.*   present, present-day

   el actual   the present one (*m.*)

   las actuales   the present ones (*f.*)

acudir a   to resort (come) to

la acumulación   accumulation

acumular   to accumulate

la acusación (*pl.* **acusaciones**)   accusation

adelante   ahead

   más adelante   later (farther) on

además *adv.*   furthermore, in addition

   además de *prep.*   besides, in addition to

adiós   goodbye

adjetivo, -a   adjective, adjectival

el adjetivo   adjective

admirable   admirable

admirar   to admire

admitir   to admit

adonde   (to) where

¿adónde?   where? (*with verbs of motion*)

adornado, -a   adorned, decorated

adquirir (**ie**)   to acquire

adverbial *adj.*   adverb(ial)

el adverbio   adverb

advertir (**ie, i**)   to notice

el aeropuerto   airport

afectar   to affect

afirmativamente   affirmatively

afirmativo, -a   affirmative(ly)

la agonía   agony

agosto   August

   por agosto   sometime in August

331

agradable   agreeable, pleasant
agrandar   to enlarge, exalt
agregar   to add
agrícola (*m. and f.*)   agricultural
el **agua** (*f.*)   water
  vaso para agua   water glass
la **aguadora**   water bearer
el **águila** (*f.*)   eagle
    Caballero Águila   Eagle Knight
  Agustín   Austin, Augustine
  ¡ah!   ah! oh!
  ahora   now
    ahora mismo   right now, right away
    por ahora   for now (the present)
  ahorrar   to save
el **ahorro**   economy; *pl.* savings
  aislado, -a   isolated
  ajeno, -a   alien, foreign, another's
  al = a + el   to the
    al + *inf.*   on (upon) + *pres. part.*
el **alarde**   display, show
  Alberto   Albert
el **alcantarillado**   sewage
    servicios de alcantarillado   sewage
      systems
  alcanzar   to reach, attain
  alegrar   to make glad
    alegrarse (**de** + *obj.*)   to be glad (to)
    ¡cuánto me alegro (**de**)!   how glad
      I am (to)!
    ¡cuánto me alegro de que!   how
      glad I am that!
    me alegro mucho de   I am very
      glad to (of)
  alegremente   happily, joyfully
  Alemania   Germany
  Alfonso   Alphonse
  algo *pron.*   something, anything; *adv.*
    somewhat, rather
  alguien   someone, somebody, anyone,
    anybody
  algún *used for* **alguno** *before m. sing. nouns*
  alguno, -a *adj. and pron.*   some, any,
    someone; *pl.* some, several, a few
    alguna cosa   something, anything
    sin razón alguna   without any reason
      at all
el **aliado**   ally

la **alianza**   alliance
  Alianza para el Progreso   Alliance
    for Progress
  alimenticio, -a   (of) food
el **alma** (*f.*)   soul, heart
  almorzar (**ue**)   to eat (take) lunch
el **almuerzo**   lunch
    para el almuerzo   for lunch
    tomar el almuerzo   to take (eat)
      lunch
  aló   hello (*telephone*)
  alrededor *adv.*   around
  alto, -a   tall, high, upper
    el Alto Perú   Upper Peru
    en voz alta   aloud
la **altura**   height
la **alumna**   pupil, student (*girl*)
el **alumno**   pupil, student (*boy*)
  allá   there (*often after verbs of motion*)
  Allende: San Miguel de —,   *a city north*
    of Mexico City
  allí   there (*distant*)
    allí mismo   that very place
la **amargura**   bitterness
    con amargura   bitterly, with bitter-
      ness
  amarillo, -a   yellow
el **Amazonas**   Amazon (River)
el **ambiente**   atmosphere, environment
  América   America
    la América del Sur   South America
    la América española (**hispana**)
      Spanish America
    la América latina   Latin America
  americano, -a   American
    lo americano   what is (was) Amer-
      ican, the American scene
la **amiga**   friend (*f.*)
el **amigo**   friend
la **amistad**   friendship
el **amor**   love
  ampararse   to seek protection (help)
  ampliar   to amplify, enlarge, broaden
  Ana   Ann, Anne, Anna
el **analfabetismo**   illiteracy
el **(los) análisis**   analysis (*pl.*) analyses
  analizar   to analyze
  anatómico, -a   anatomical

ancho, -a   wide, broad

andaluz, -uza   Andalusian (*of southern Spain*)

andar   to go, walk

   andar + *pres. part.*   to be (*progressive form*) + *pres. part.*

los Andes   Andes (*mountains in South America*)

la anécdota   anecdote

el anhelo (*also pl.*)   yearning, longing

el animal   animal

animar   to animate, give life to

   animar a + *inf.*   to encourage to

anoche   last night

el antagonismo   antagonism

ante *prep.*   before (*position*)

anterior   anterior, earlier, preceding

antes *adv.*   before, formerly

   antes de *prep.*   before (*time*)

   antes (de) que *conj.*   before

antiguo, -a   ancient, old

Antonio   Anthony, Tony

anunciar   to announce

el año   year

   al año   yearly, each year

   al año siguiente   (in) the following year

   ¿cuántos años hace que (estudia Ud.)?   how long have you been (studying)?

   ¿cuántos años tiene (él)?   how old is (he)?

   de los últimos años   of the last (past) few years

   en los últimos años   ′in the last few years, recently

   tener . . . años   to be . . . years old

apagar   to turn off, lower (*lights*)

el aparato   set

   aparato (de radio)   (radio) set

aparecer   to appear, show up

apartado, -a de   separated (away) from

el apartamento   apartment

la apatía   apathy

apenas   scarcely, hardly

la aplicación   application

el Apocalipsis   Apocalypse (*revelation made to the Apostle John*)

apoderarse de   to seize, take possession of

la apreciación   appreciation

apreciar   to appreciate, esteem

aprender (a + *inf.*)   to learn (to)

   aprender de memoria   to memorize, learn from memory (by heart)

aprestarse a   to prepare oneself to

aprobar (ue)   to approve

apropiado, -a a   appropriate to (at), suitable (for)

aproximadamente   approximately

aproximarse a   to approximate, come near to

la aptitud   aptitude

apurarse   to hurry (up)

aquel, aquella (-os, -as) *adj.*   that, those (*distant*)

aquél, aquélla (-os, -as) *pron.*   that (one), those; the former

aquello *neuter pron.*   that

aquí   here

   por aquí   (around, by) here

Araure   *section of Venezuela where Bolívar defeated the Spaniards*

el árbol   tree

arcaico, -a   archaic, very old

la Argentina   Argentina

argentino, -a (*also noun*)   Argentine

el argumento   plot (*of music or drama*)

el arma (*f.*)   arm, weapon

   armas de fuego   firearms

armado, -a de   armed with

el arquitecto   architect

arquitectónico, -a   architectural

la arquitectura   architecture

arrebatado, -a   carried away

arreglar   to arrange, settle; fix, repair

arrojar   to throw, hurl

el arte   art; (*f. pl.*) arts, crafts

   (clase) de arte   art (class)

   las bellas artes   (the) fine arts

el artículo   article

el (la) artista   artist

artístico, -a   artistic

Arturo   Arthur

asegurar   to assure

asfixiar   to asphyxiate, suffocate

así   so, thus
    así como   just as, as well as
    así que *conj.*   as soon as
el **asiento**   seat
    asimilar   to assimilate
    asistir a   to attend
la **asociación**   association
    asociarse con   to join, form a partnership with
el **aspecto**   aspect, point
la **aspiración** (*pl.* **aspiraciones**)   aspiration
    aspirar a   to aspire to
    asumir   to assume
    atacar   to attack
    Atahualpa   *Inca leader at time of Spanish conquest*
la **atención**   attention
    llamar la atención (**a uno**)   to attract (one's) attention
    prestar atención (**a**)   to pay attention (to)
    atractivo, -a   attractive
    atraer   to attract
    atrasado, -a   backward, poor
    atravesar (**ie**)   to cross, traverse
    atreverse (**a**)   to dare (to)
    aumentar   to increase, augment
el **aumento**   increase
    aun, aún   even, still
    aunque   although, even though, even if
el **auricular**   receiver (*telephone*)
la **ausencia**   absence
    ausentarse   to absent oneself, get away
    ausente   absent
    auténtico, -a   authentic, real
el **autobús**   bus
    en autobús   by (in a) bus
el **autor**   author
el **autorretrato**   self-portrait
la **autoridad**   authority
    auxiliar *adj.*   auxiliary
el **avión** (*pl.* **aviones**)   (air)plane
    avión (**de las dos**)   (two-o'clock) plane
    en avión   by plane
    avisar   to advise, inform; warn
    Ayacucho   *Andean city in Peru*

ayer   yesterday
    ayer por la mañana (**tarde**)   yesterday morning (afternoon)
la **ayuda**   aid, help
    ayudar (**a** + *inf.*)   to help (to), aid (to)
el **azteca**   Aztec
el **azúcar**   sugar

B

¡bah!   bah!
la **bahía**   bay
    bailar   to dance
el **baile**   dance
    bajar   to come (go) down (downstairs), decline
    bajo *prep.*   below, under
    bajo, -a   low, lower
    piso bajo   first floor
el **balboa**   *monetary unit of Panama*
    Baltasar   Balthasar
el **banco**   bank
la **bandera**   banner, flag
el **banquete**   banquet
    bañarse   to take a bath, go swimming
    barato, -a   inexpensive, cheap
    Bárbara   Barbara
la **barbarie**   barbarism, lack of culture
el **barco**   boat
el **barril**   barrel
    barroco, -a   baroque
    basar   to base; *reflex.* be based
la **base**   base, basis
    servir (**i, i**) **de base**   to serve as a basis
    básico, -a   basic
    bastante *adj. and adv.*   quite, rather, enough, sufficient
    bastar   to be enough, be sufficient
    basta por ahora   that's enough for now
la **batalla**   battle
el **batido de leche**   milk shake
    beber   to drink
la **belleza**   beauty
    bello, -a   beautiful, pretty; fine
    las bellas artes   (the) fine arts

beneficiarse de   to benefit from, take advantage of

Bernardo   Bernard

la **Biblia**   Bible

la **biblioteca**   library

la **bicicleta**   bicycle

bien *adv.*   well

los **bienes**   wealth, goods

  bienes de equipo   capital goods

el **bienestar**   well-being, welfare

la **bienvenida**   welcome

  dar la bienvenida a   to welcome

el **billete**   ticket

blanco, -a   white

la **blusa**   blouse

Bolívar, Simón (1783–1830)   *Venezuelan liberator of northwest South America*

boliviano, -a   Bolivian

la **bolsa**   purse

el **bolsillo**   pocket

bonito, -a   pretty, beautiful

el **bosque**   forest, woods

el **Brasil**   Brazil

brasileño, -a   Brazilian

el **brazo**   arm

breve   brief, short

brevemente   briefly

brillante   brilliant

la **broma**   joke

buen   *used for* **bueno** *before m. sing. nouns*

bueno *adv.*   well, well now, fine, all right, good

  ¡bueno!   hello! (*telephone*)

bueno, -a   good, well

  lo bueno   what is good, the good thing (part)

burlarse (de)   to make fun (of)

burocrático, -a   bureaucratic

la **busca**   search

  en busca de   in search of

buscar   to look (for), search (for), seek

  buscar a uno   to come (go) for one, pick one up

C

el **caballero**   gentleman, Sir

el **caballo**   horse

  a caballo   on horseback

la **cabeza**   head

  (le) duele la cabeza   (his) head aches

  tener dolor de cabeza   to have a headache

el **cabo**   end

  llevar a cabo   to carry out

cada   each

caer   to fall

el **café**   café; coffee

  taza para café   coffee cup

Cajamarca   *city in northern Peru*

calcular mal   to misjudge, miscalculate

caliente *adj.*   warm, hot

el **calor**   heat, warmth

  hacer (mucho) calor   to be (very) warm (*weather*)

  tener (mucho) calor   to be (very) warm (*living beings*)

el **Callao**   Callao (*port near Lima, Peru*)

la **calle**   street

la **cama**   bed

  guardar cama   to stay in bed

la **cámara**   camera

  cámara de cine (de treinta y cinco milímetros)   movie (35 millimeter) camera

cambiar   to change

el **cambio**   change

el **camino**   road, way, path, course

la **camisa**   shirt

el **campeón** (*pl.* **campeones**)   champion

el **campeonato**   championship

el **campesino**   countryman, farmer, peasant; *pl.* countryfolk

el **campo**   country, field

  casa de campo   country house

el **Canadá**   Canada

la **canción** (*pl.* **canciones**)   song

el **candidato**   candidate

cansado, -a   tired

cansar   to tire (*someone*); *reflex.* become (get) tired

cantar   to sing

el **cañón** (*pl.* **cañones**)   cannon

la **capacidad**   capacity

el **capital**   capital (*money*)

la **capital**   capital (*city*)
el **capitán** (*pl.* **capitanes**)   captain
el **capítulo**   chapter
la **capota**   top (*of automobile*)
la **cara**   face
el **carácter** (*pl.* **caracteres**)   character
la **característica**   characteristic
característico, -a   characteristic
caracterizar   to characterize
¡caramba!   gosh! confound it!
Caribe *adj.*   Caribbean
la **caricatura**   caricature
Carlos   Charles
   Carlos I (**de España**) **y V** (**de Alemania**)   *king of Spain, 1515–1556*
   Carlos IV   *king of Spain, 1788–1808*
Carlota   Charlotte
caro, -a   expensive
Carolina   Caroline, Carolina (*state*)
la **carrera**   career
la **carretera**   highway, road
el **carro**   car (*railroad*)
la **carta**   letter
la **casa**   house, home; firm
   a casa de (**Ana**)   to (Ann's)
   casa comercial   business firm
   casa de campo   country house (home)
   Casa de Correos   Post Office
   en casa de (**Juan**)   at (John's)
   (**estar**) **en casa**   (to be) at home
   (**ir**) **a casa**   (to go) home
   (**salir**) **de casa**   (to leave) home
casado, -a (**con**)   married (to)
el **casado**   married man
casarse (**con** + *obj.*)   to marry, get married (to)
casi   almost
el **caso**   case
la **catedral**   cathedral
la **causa**   cause
   a causa de   because of
causar   to cause
celebrado, -a   celebrated; praised, extolled
celebrar   to celebrate, hold
célebre   celebrated, famous

cenar   to take (eat) supper
censurar   to censure, condemn
el **centavo**   cent (*U.S.*); *also Spanish American monetary unit*
el **centenar**   hundred
central   central
el **centro**   center
   Centro de Estudiantes   Student Center
   centro de salud   health center
   (**hallar**) **en el centro**   (to find) downtown
   (**ir**) **al centro**   (to go) downtown
Centroamérica   Central America
centroamericano, -a   Central American
la **cerámica**   ceramics, pottery
cerca de *prep.*   near, close to
cero   zero
cerrado, -a   closed
cerrar (**ie**)   to close
científico, -a   scientific
ciento (**cien**)   one (a) hundred
cierto, -a   (a) certain
   por cierto   certainly, of course
la **cifra**   cipher, figure
el **cigarro**   cigar
cinco   five
cincuenta   fifty
el **cine**   movie(s)
   cámara de cine   movie camera
   cinético, -a   kinetic (*consisting in or depending upon motion*)
la **cinta**   tape
   grabadora de cinta   tape recorder
el **círculo**   circle
citado, -a   cited, above-mentioned
   las citadas   the ones mentioned (listed)
citar   to cite, mention
la **ciudad**   city
   ciudad de México   Mexico City
civil   civil
la **civilización** (*pl.* **civilizaciones**)   civilization
civilizador, -ora   civilizing
Clara   Clara, Clare
claramente   clearly

claro, -a   clear, evident
  ¡claro!   clearly! certainly! of course!
la clase   class, kind
  clase (de español)   (Spanish) class
  compañero (compañera) de clase   classmate
  en clase   in class
  ¿qué clase de ...?   what kind of ...?
  sala de clase   classroom
clásico, -a   classic
el claustro   cloister
la cláusula   clause
el clérigo   cleric, priest
el club   club
la cocina   kitchen
el coche   car
  en coche   by (in a) car
codicioso, -a   covetous, greedy
coger   to take, pick (up)
colaborar   to collaborate
la colección (*pl.* **colecciones**)   collection
colgar (ue)   to hang (up)
la colocación   position, place
colocar   to place
Colombia: Gran —,   Greater Colombia
colombiano, -a (*also noun*)   Colombian
la colonia   colony
colonial   colonial
el colonizador   colonizer
el colono   colonist
la columna   column
la coma   comma
  punto y coma   semicolon
combinar   to combine
la comedia   play, comedy
el comedor   dining room
comenzar (ie) (a + inf.)   to commence (to), begin (to)
comer   to eat, dine
comercial   business, commercial
  casa comercial   business firm
comerciar   to trade, have commercial relations
el comercio   trade, commerce
  comercio exterior (interior)   foreign (domestic) trade
la comida   food, meal, dinner

el comienzo   beginning
como   as, like; since
  así como   just as, as well as
  como si   as if
  tanto ... como   both ... and; as much ... as
  tanto, tanta (-os, -as) ... como   as (so) much (many) ... as
¿cómo?   how? what?
¡cómo no!   of course! certainly!
cómodo, -a   comfortable
la compañera   companion (*f.*)
  compañera de clase   classmate (*f.*)
  compañera de cuarto   roommate (*f.*)
el compañero   companion
  compañero de clase (cuarto)   classmate (roommate)
la Compañía = (la) Compañía de Jesús   Society of Jesus
comparable   comparable
la comparación   comparison
comparativo, -a   comparative
competir (i, i)   to compete
completamente   completely
completar   to complete
completo, -a   complete
componer   to compose
la composición   composition
el compositor   composer
la compra   purchase
  ir de compras   to go shopping
comprar   to buy, purchase
comprender   to understand, comprehend
compuesto, -a *p.p. of* **componer** *and adj.* compound
compuso *pret. of* **componer**
común (*pl.* **comunes**)   common
la comunidad   community
con   with; to
  con tal (de) que   provided that
concebir (i, i)   to conceive
concentrar   to concentrate
la concesión (*pl.* **concesiones**)   concession
el concierto   concert
concluir   to conclude, end
la concordancia   agreement

la **concordia**   concord, harmony; agreement

condenar   to condemn

    condenar a muerte   to condemn to death

la **condición** (*pl.* **condiciones**)   condition

condicional (*also m. noun*)   conditional

conducir   to drive, conduct

la **confederación**   confederation

la **conferencia**   lecture; conference

el **conferenciante**   lecturer, speaker

la **confianza**   confidence

la **conflagración**   conflagration

el **conflicto**   conflict, strife

conformarse (**con**)   to be satisfied (with)

la **confusión**   confusion

la **conga**   conga (*a dance*)

el **congreso**   congress

la **conjunción** (*pl.* **conjunciones**)   conjunction

el **conjunto**   whole, entirety

    de conjunto   general

    en conjunto   as a whole

conmigo   with me

conocer   to know, be acquainted with, meet; recognize

    más conocido, -a   best known

    mucho gusto en conocerle(-la) a Ud.   (I'm very) pleased to meet (know) you

la **conquista**   conquest

el **conquistador**   conqueror

conquistar   to conquer

conseguir (**i, i**)   to get, obtain, attain, succeed in

consentir (**ie, i**) **en**   to consent to, agree to

el **conservatorio**   conservatory

considerar   to consider

    se le considera   (he) is considered

consigo   with himself, herself, etc.

consiguiente: por —,   consequently, therefore

el **conspirador**   conspirator

constar de   to consist of, be composed of

constituir   to constitute, establish, make up

la **construcción**   construction

constructivo, -a   constructive

construido, -a   constructed, built

construir   to construct, build

el **cónsul**   consul

consultar   to consult, discuss

contar (**ue**)   to count; tell, relate

contemporáneo, -a   contemporary

contener   to contain

contento, -a   contented, happy, pleased; *adv.* contentedly

la **contestación** (*pl.* **contestaciones**)   answer, reply

contestar   to answer, reply

el **contexto**   context

contigo   with you (*fam. sing.*)

el **continente**   continent

la **continuación**   continuation

continuar   to continue, go (keep) on

contra   against

el **contrario**   opposing player; *pl.* the opposing players, the other side

contrarrestar   to counteract, offset

el **contraste**   contrast

la **contribución** (*pl.* **contribuciones**)   contribution

contribuir   to contribute

convencido, -a de que   convinced that

la **convención** (*pl.* **convenciones**)   convention

convenir   to be fitting, be advisable

el **convento**   convent; monastery

convertir (**ie, i**)   to convert

    convertirse en   to become (be) converted (in)to

convocar   to convoke, call (together)

la **cooperación**   cooperation

cooperar   to cooperate

la **corbata**   necktie, tie

Coronado   *Spanish explorer of the southwestern U.S.*

correctamente   correctly, accurately

correcto, -a   correct, accurate

Correos: Casa de —,   Post Office

correr   to run, race, traverse

corresponder (**a**)   to correspond (to), belong (to), concern

correspondiente   corresponding

la **corriente**   current

cortar   to cut
cortés (*pl.* **corteses**)   courteous, polite
cortésmente   courteously, politely
corto, -a   short
la **cosa**   thing
  alguna cosa   anything, something
  cualquier cosa   anything (at all)
cósmico, -a   cosmic
la **costa**   coast
costar (**ue**)   to cost
costarricense *adj.*   Costa Rican
la **costumbre**   custom
el **costumbrismo**   *literature of customs and manners*
la **creación**   creation
crear   to create
crecer   to grow, increase
el **crédito**   credit
  crédito exterior   foreign credit
creer   to believe, think
  creer que sí   to believe (think) so
  ¡ya lo creo!   I should say so! of course!
cristiano, -a   Christian
la **crítica**   criticism, review
criticar   to criticize
cruel   cruel
la **crueldad**   cruelty
la **cruz** (*pl.* **cruces**)   cross
cruzar   to cross
el **cuaderno**   notebook
la **cuadra**   block (*city*)
el **cuadro**   picture, painting, scene
cual: el —, la — (**los, las cuales**)   that, which, who, whom
  lo cual   which (fact)
¿cuál(es)?   which one (ones)? what?
cualquier(a) (*pl.* **cualesquier**)   any *or* anyone (at all)
  cualquier cosa   anything (at all)
cuando   when
¿cuándo?   when?
cuanto: en —, *conj.*   as soon as
  en cuanto a *prep.*   as for, in regard to
cuantos, -as: unos, -as —,   a few, some (*few*)
¿cuánto, -a (**-os, -as**)?   how much (many)?
  ¿cuánto tiempo?   how long?

¿cuántos años?   how long (many years)?
¡cuánto + *verb*!   how!
cuarto, -a   fourth
el **cuarto**   quarter; room
  compañero (**compañera**) **de cuarto**   roommate (*m. and f.*)
  cuarto de estar   living (sitting) room, lounge
  (**las ocho**) **y cuarto**   a quarter after (eight)
cuatro   four
cubano, -a   Cuban
cubierto, -a (**de**)   *p.p. of* **cubrir** *and adj.* covered (with)
la **cuenta**   account, bill
  darse cuenta de   to realize
  por cuenta propia   by himself, on his own (account)
  tener en cuenta   to bear in mind
el **cuentista**   short story writer
el **cuento**   short story, tale
el **cuerpo**   body
el **cuidado**   care
  con cuidado   carefully
  tener (**mucho**) **cuidado**   to be (very) careful
la **culpa**   fault, blame
  tener la culpa   to be at fault, be to blame
cultivado, -a   cultivated, fostered
el **cultivador**   cultivator
cultivar   to cultivate
el **cultivo**   cultivation
culto, -a   cultured, learned
  la culta   the cultured one (*f.*)
la **cultura**   culture
cultural   cultural
la **cumbre**   summit
el **cumpleaños**   birthday
cumplir   to fulfil, perform, carry out, discharge
el **cura**   priest
cursiva: en —,   in italics
el **curso**   course
la **curva**   curve
cuyo, -a   whose, of whom, of which
el **Cuzco**   Cuzco (*Andean city in Peru, former capital of the Inca empire*)

Ch

Chacabuco   *town on Andean slopes near Santiago, Chile*
charlar   to chat, talk
Chávez, Carlos (1899–)   *Mexican composer and conductor*
el **cheque**   check
chileno, -a (*also noun*)   Chilean
churrigueresco, -a   Churrigueresque

D

la **danza**   dance
dañar   to harm, hurt
dar   to give
   dar a   to face
   dar gritos   to cry out, shout
   dar la bienvenida a   to welcome
   dar las gracias a   to thank
   dar un paseo (**una vuelta**)   to take a walk *or* stroll
   dar un paso   to take a step
   darse cuenta de   to realize
   darse prisa   to hurry
Darío, Rubén (1867–1916)   *Nicaraguan modernist poet*
de   of, from, about, by, to, concerning, with, as; in (*after a superlative*); than (*before numerals*)
deber   to owe; must, ought to, should
   deber de + *inf.*   must, probably + *verb*
   deberse a   to be due to
debiera   (I) should, ought to
débil   weak
la **debilidad**   weakness
la **década**   decade
decadente   decadent
decidir   to decide; *reflex.* make up one's mind
decir   to say, tell
   diga, dígame   hello (*telephone*)
   es decir   that is, that is to say
   oír decir (**que**)   to hear (that)
declarar   to declare
decorar   to decorate

dedicar   to dedicate, devote
   dedicarse a   to dedicate (devote) oneself to
defender (**ie**)   to defend
el **defensa**   back (*in soccer*)
el (**los**) **déficit**   deficit(s)
definido, -a   definite
dejar *trans.*   to leave (behind), abandon; let, allow, permit
   dejar de + *inf.*   to stop (cease) + *pres. part.*; fail to + *inf.*
   no dejar de + *inf.*   not to stop + *pres. part.*; not to fail to + *inf.*
del = de + el   of (from) the
el **delantero**   forward (*in soccer*)
la **demanda**   demand
   demanda interior   domestic demand
demás: los (**las**) **—,**   the other, the rest of the
demasiado *adv.*   too, too much
demasiado, -a *adj. and pron.*   too much (many)
la **democracia**   democracy
democrático, -a   democratic
demostrar (**ue**)   to demonstrate, show
demostrativo, -a   demonstrative
dentro de *prep.*   in, inside, within
el **departamento**   department
el **dependiente**   clerk
el **deporte**   sport
   sección de deportes   sports section
el **derecho**   right
la **derivación** (*pl.* **derivaciones**)   derivation
derrotar   to rout, defeat
desalentado, -a   discouraged
desanimarse   to become (get) discouraged
desarrollar   to develop; *reflex.* develop, be developed
el **desarrollo**   development
el **desastre**   disaster, catastrophe
desayunarse   to eat (take) breakfast
el **desayuno**   breakfast
descansar   to rest
desconocido, -a   unknown
el **descontento**   discontent
describir   to describe

descrito *p.p. of* **describir** *and adj.*
    los descritos   the ones described
descubierto *p.p. of* **descubrir**
el descubridor   discoverer
descubrir   to discover, find out about
desde   from, since; for (*time*)
    desde hace una hora   for an hour
    desde . . . hasta   from . . . (up) to
desear   to desire, wish, want
el desenlace   ending, denouement
desesperadamente   desperately, madly
la desgracia   misfortune
    por desgracia   unfortunately
desgraciadamente   unfortunately
deshacer   disband, destroy
el desierto   desert
designar   to designate, denote
desilusionado, -a   disillusioned
despacio   slowly
    lo más despacio posible   the slowest possible
despedirse (i, i) (de)   to take leave (of), say goodbye (to)
despertar (ie)   to awaken, wake up; *reflex.* wake up (oneself)
el despotismo   despotism
desprovisto, -a   devoid, deprived
después *adv.*   afterward(s), later, then
    después de *prep.*   after
    después (de) que *conj.*   after
    poco después   shortly afterward(s)
    poco después de   shortly after
destacar   to emphasize, make stand out; *reflex.* stand out
el destino   destiny
la destrucción   destruction
destruir   to destroy
el detalle   detail
detener   to detain, arrest, stop
determinar   to determine
detrás de *prep.*   behind
devolver (ue)   to return, give back
devuelto *p.p. of* **devolver**
D.F. = Distrito Federal   Federal District
el día   day
    al día siguiente   (on) the following day

    buenos días   good morning (day)
    de nuestros días   in (of) our time, of today
    en nuestros días   today, in our time
    hasta nuestros días   up to today, up to the present time
    hoy día   nowadays, today
    otro día   another day
    todo el día   all (the) day
    todos los días   every day
el diálogo   dialogue
    la aplicación del diálogo   dialogue adaptation
la diapositiva   slide, transparency
el dibujo   drawing
el diccionario   dictionary
diciembre   December
el dictado   dictation
el dictador   dictator
dicho *p.p. of* **decir** *and adj.*   said, aforementioned
    lo dicho   what is (was) said
dieciocho   eighteen
dieciséis   sixteen
Diego   James
diez   ten
diferente   different
diferir (ie, i)   to differ
difícil   difficult, hard
    lo difícil   what is difficult, the difficult thing (part)
    lo difíciles que (son)   how difficult (they are)
la dificultad   difficulty
el diminutivo   diminutive
dinámico, -a   dynamic
el dinero   money
Dios   God
    ¡Dios mío!   for heaven's sake!
    ¡por Dios!   for heaven's sake!
la dirección   direction
directamente   directly
directo, -a   direct
el director   director
dirigir   to direct, address (*a letter*)
    dirigirse (a + *obj.*)   to turn (to), direct oneself (to), go (to), address (*a person*)

el disco   record (*phonograph*)
la discordia   discord, disagreement
la discriminación   discrimination
la discusión   discussion
discutir   to discuss, talk about
disfrutar (de + *obj.***)**   to enjoy
la disminución   diminution, decrease
la disparidad   disparity, inequality
disperso, -a   scattered, separated
disputar   to contend (for), dispute
la distancia   distance
   a poca distancia (de)   at a short
      distance (from)
distinguido, -a   distinguished, famous
distinguir   to distinguish; *reflex.* distinguish oneself, become distinguished
distinto, -a   distinct, different
la distribución   distribution
distribuir   to distribute
diversificar   to diversify
la diversión (*pl.* **diversiones**)   diversion,
   amusement
diverso, -a   diverse, different
divertir (ie, i)   to amuse; *reflex.* amuse
   oneself, have a good time
   divertirse mucho   to have a very
      good time
doce   twelve
la docena   dozen
   docena de estudiantes   dozen stu-
      dents
el doctor   doctor (*title*)
documentar   to document
el dólar   dollar (*U.S.*)
doler (ue)   to ache, pain, hurt
   le duele (la garganta)   (his throat)
      hurts
el dolor   ache, pain, sorrow, grief
   tener dolor de cabeza   to have a
      headache
doméstico, -a   domestic
la dominación   domination
dominante   dominant, dominating, pre-
   vailing
dominar   to dominate, subdue, control,
   prevail
Domingo   Dominic
   Santo Domingo   St. Dominic

el domingo   (on) Sunday
el dominicano   Dominican (*of the Dominican Republic*)
dominico, -a   Dominican, of the Dominican Order
don   Don (*title used before first names of
   men*)
donde   where, in which
¿dónde?   where?
   ¿por dónde se va . . .?   how does
      one go . . .? (*by what route?*)
doña   Doña (*title used before first names of
   women*)
dormir (ue, u)   to sleep; *reflex.* fall
   asleep, go to sleep
   dormir la siesta   to take a nap
Dorotea   Dorothy
dos   two
   los (las) dos   the two, both
el drama   drama
el dramaturgo   dramatist
la duda   doubt
   sin duda   doubtless, without a doubt
dudar   to doubt
dudoso, -a   doubtful
duramente   harshly
durante   during
duro, -a   hard

E

e   and (*used for* **y** *before* **i-**, **hi-**, *but not*
   hie-)
el eco   echo
la economía   economy
   economía política   political econo-
      my, economics
económicamente   economically
económico, -a   economic
el Ecuador   Ecuador
ecuatoriano, -a   Ecuadorian, of Ecuador
ecuestre   equestrian
echar (en, a)   to throw *or* toss (into)
la edad   age
el edificio   building
editorial *adj.*   editorial

Eduardo Edward
la **educación** education
el **educador** educator
educar to educate
efectuar to effect, carry out
eficaz efficacious, effective
ejemplar exemplary
el **ejemplo** example
por ejemplo for example
ejercer to exert, exercise
el **ejercicio** exercise
el **ejército** army
el (*pl.* **los**) the (*m.*)
del (de los) que than
el (los) de that (those) of, the one(s) of (with, in)
el (los) que that, who, which, he (those) who (whom), the one(s) who (that, which)
él he; him, it (*m.*) (*after prep.*)
la **elección** (*pl.* **elecciones**) election
elegante elegant
el **elemento** element, part
Elena Helen, Ellen
elevado, -a elevated, high
elevar to elevate, raise, lift
eliminar to eliminate
ella she; her, it (*f.*) (*after prep.*)
ellos, -as they, them (*after prep.*)
ellos, (-as) todos, (-as) all of them, they all
todos, (-as) ellos, (-as) all of them, they all
embarcarse to embark
embargo: sin —, nevertheless
emigrar to emigrate
la **emisora** broadcasting station
la **emoción** (*pl.* **emociones**) emotion
emocionante exciting, thrilling
el **emparedado** sandwich
emparedado de jamón (queso) ham (cheese) sandwich
empatar to tie (*in game or elections*)
el **emperador** emperor
empezar (ie) (a + *inf.*) to begin (to)
el **empleado** employee
emplear to employ, use
emplumado, -a feathered

emprender to undertake
se está emprendiendo (it) is being undertaken
en in, on, at, to, into, of
en casa at home
encantado, -a delighted
¡encantado, -a! (I'll be) delighted (to)!
encantar to charm, delight
encima: por — de *prep.* over, above
Enciso, Martín Fernández de *Spanish geographer and colonizer in America*
encontrar (ue) to encounter, find, meet; *reflex.* be, be found, find oneself, meet
encontrarse con to run across (into), meet
el **enemigo** enemy
enérgico, -a energetic
enero January
el **énfasis** emphasis
la **enfermedad** sickness
enfermo, -a ill, sick; sickly (*with* **ser**)
el **enfoque** focus(ing)
enfrente de *prep.* in front of
la **enhorabuena** congratulations
¡enhorabuena! congratulations (to you)!
enorme enormous, large
Enrique Henry
ensayar to attempt, try
el **ensayista** essayist
el **ensayo** essay
la **enseñanza** teaching, education
enseñar (a + *inf.*) to teach *or* show (how to)
entender (ie) to understand
la **entidad** entity, body, organization
la **entonación** intonation
entonces then
entrante coming, next
entrar (en + *obj.*) to enter, come (go) in
entre between, among
entregar to hand (over), turn in, deliver
entregarse a to abandon oneself to, surrender (to)

el entrenador   coach, trainer
la entrevista   interview
enviar   to send
envolver (ue)   to wrap (up)
envuelto *p.p. of* **envolver**
la Epifanía   Epiphany (*January 6*)
la época   epoch, period, time
el equipaje   baggage, luggage
el equipo   team
  los bienes de equipo   capital goods
equitativo, -a   equitable
equivalente *adj. and m. noun*   equivalent
Ernesto   Ernest
errar (ye)   to miss (*a shot*), err
la erre   *the letter* "r"
el erudito   scholar
esbozar   to sketch, outline
la escalera   stairway
la escena   scene
  música de escena   background music
escoger   to choose, select
esconder   to hide; *reflex.* hide (oneself)
escondido, -a   hidden
escribir   to write
  está por escribir   (it) is to be written
escrito, -a *p.p. of* **escribir** *and adj.* written
  lo escrito   what is (was, has been) written
el escritor   writer
la escritora   writer (*woman*)
escuchar   to listen (to)
la escuela   school
el escultor   sculptor
escultórico, -a   sculptural
la escultura   sculpture
ese, esa (-os, -as) *adj.*   that, those (*nearby*)
ése, ésa (-os, -as) *pron.*   that (one), those
la esencia   essence
esforzarse (ue) por   to strive to, make an effort to
el esfuerzo   effort
eso *neuter pron.*   that
  a eso de   at about (*time*)
  por eso   therefore, because of that, for that reason, that's why

el espacio   space, room
la espalda   back
  volver (ue) las espaldas a   to turn one's back on, reject
España   Spain
  la Nueva España   New Spain (= Mexico)
español, -ola (*also noun*)   Spanish; Spaniard
el español   Spanish (*language*)
  (departamento) de español   Spanish (department)
la Española   Hispaniola (*island on which Haiti and the Dominican Republic are situated*)
especial   special
especialmente   especially
la esperanza (*also pl.*)   hope
esperar   to wait, wait for; hope, expect
  esperar mucho   to wait long (a long time)
  no esperar más   not to wait (any) longer
el espíritu   spirit
  el Espíritu Santo   Holy Spirit
espiritual   spiritual
la espiritualidad   spirituality
espontáneo, -a   spontaneous
la esposa   wife
el esquí (*pl.* **esquíes**)   ski
esquiar   to ski
  ir a esquiar   to go skiing
la esquina   corner (*street*)
establecer   to establish, set up; *reflex.* establish oneself, settle
el establecimiento   establishment
la estación (*pl.* **estaciones**)   season; station
estacionar   to park (*a car*)
el estado   state
  los Estados Unidos   United States
estallar   to break out, explode
la estampa   image, print
la estancia   ranch
estar   to be; look, taste, feel
  cuarto de estar   living room, lounge
  está bien   all right, that's fine
  ¿está (Carlos)?   is (Charles) at home?

estar para   to be about to
estar por   to be inclined to, feel like
está por escribir   (it) is to be written
la **estática**   static
la **estatua**   statue
este, esta (-os, -as) *adj.*   this, these
éste, ésta (-os, -as) *pron.*   this (one), these; the latter
el **estilo**   style
estimar   to esteem
estimular   to stimulate
el **estímulo**   stimulus
esto *neuter pron.*   this
esto es   that is
estrecho, -a   narrow, close, rigid
estrenar   to perform (present) for the first time
el **estreno**   première, first performance
la **estructura**   structure, development, organization
la **estructuración**   building process
el **(la) estudiante**   student
Centro de Estudiantes   Student Center
Residencia de Estudiantes   Student Residence Hall (Dormitory)
estudiar   to study
el **estudio**   study; *pl.* studies, courses
estudio de palabras   word study
la **etapa**   stage
etcétera   etcetera, etc., and so forth
eterno, -a   eternal
ético, -a   ethical
Europa   Europe
europeo, -a *(also noun)*   European
evidente   evident, obvious
evocar   to evoke, call up
la **evolución**   evolution
evolutivo, -a   evolutionary
exactamente   exactly, correctly
exacto, -a   exact
la **exageración**   exaggeration
exagerar   to exaggerate
el **examen** (*pl.* **exámenes**)   examination
examinar   to examine
exceder   to exceed, surpass
excelente   excellent, fine
excesivo, -a   excessive

la **exclamación** (*pl.* **exclamaciones**)   exclamation
la **excursión** (*pl.* **excursiones**)   excursion, trip
hacer una excursión   to make (take) an excursion
exhibir   to exhibit, show
existente   existent, extant
existir   to exist, be in existence
el **éxito**   success
la **expedición**   expedition
experimentar   to experiment
explicar   to explain
la **exploración** (*pl.* **exploraciones**)   exploration
el **explorador**   explorer
explorar   to explore
la **explotación**   exploitation
explotar   to exploit
el **exponente**   exponent
exponer   to expose, expound, advance
la **exportación** (*pl.* **exportaciones**)   export, exportation
la **exposición** (*pl.* **exposiciones**)   exhibition
expresar   to express
la **expresión** (*pl.* **expresiones**)   expression
expulsar   to expel, drive out
exquisito, -a   exquisite
extender(se) (ie)   to extend, spread (out)
extendido, -a   extended
extenso, -a   extensive, large
exterior   exterior; foreign
comercio (crédito) exterior   foreign trade (credit)
extranjero, -a   foreign
extraño, -a   strange, unusual
lo extraño   the unusual (strange)
extraordinario, -a   extraordinary

F

fácil   easy
fácilmente   easily
facturar   to check (*baggage*)

falso, -a   false
la **falta**   lack, want
faltar (**a uno**)   to lack, be lacking (to one), be missing, need, be in need of
la **fama**   fame, reputation
la **familia**   family
famoso, -a   famous
la **farmacia**   pharmacy, drugstore
la **fase**   phase
el **favor**   favor
   por favor   please (*at end of request*)
la **fe**   faith
febrero   February
la **fecha**   date
felicitar   to congratulate
Felipe   Philip
feliz (*pl.* **felices**)   happy; *adv.* happily
el **ferrocarril**   railroad
la **fiebre**   fever
fiel   faithful
fielmente   faithfully
la **fiesta**   fiesta, festival, party, holiday
la **figura**   figure, person
figurar entre   to figure (be) among
fijarse en   to notice, turn one's attention to
la **fila**   row
el **filo**   edge
filosófico, -a   philosophical
el **fin**   end
   a fin de que *conj.*   in order that
   a fines de   toward(s) (at) the end of
   desde fines   since *or* toward(s) the end of
   para fines de   by the end of
   poner fin a   to put an end to
   por fin   finally, at last
final   final
la **financiación**   financing
la **flor**   flower
florecer   to flourish
la **Florida**   Florida
el **foco**   focus, center
fomentar   to foment, promote, encourage, foster
el **fondo**   background
fónico, -a   phonic
   grupo fónico   breath-group

la **forma**   form
la **formación**   formation; training
formar   to form, make (up)
   formar parte de   to form (a) part of
formular   to formulate, make up
   formúlense   formulate
fortalecer   to strengthen, support
la **fortuna**   fortune (*money*)
la **foto**   photo
   sacar (**fotos**)   to take (photos)
la **fotografía**   photograph
fracasar   to fail
el **fraccionamiento**   fractioning, division
el **fragmento**   fragment
el **fraile**   friar, monk
francés, -esa *adj.*   French
el **francés**   French (*language*)
franciscano, -a   Franciscan, of the Order of St. Francis
Francisco   Francis
San Francisco   St. Francis
la **frase**   phrase, sentence
   frases hechas   fixed phrases
la **frecuencia**   frequency
   con frecuencia   frequently
   frecuencia modulada   FM (*radio*)
frente a *prep.*   opposite, in the face of, in the presence of
fresco, -a   cool, fresh
el **fresco**   coolness, fresh air
   hacer (**mucho**) **fresco**   to be (very) cool (*weather*)
frío, -a   cold
el **frío**   cold
   hacer (**mucho**) **frío**   to be (very) cold (*weather*)
   tener (**mucho**) **frío**   to be (very) cold (*living beings*)
la **frontera**   frontier
la **frustración**   frustration
la **fruta**   fruit
el **fuego**   fire
   armas de fuego   firearms
la **fuente**   fountain; source
fuerte   strong; powerful
fuertemente   strongly
la **fuerza**   force, strength; *pl.* forces, (military) forces

la **fuga**   flight
el **fugitivo**   fugitive
la **fundación**   foundation, founding
el **fundador**   founder
  fundar   to found, establish
la **furia**   fury
el **fusil**   rifle, gun
  fusilar   to shoot
la **fusión**   fusion
el **fútbol**   football
la **futilidad**   futility
  futuro, -a   future
el **futuro**   future, future tense

G

la **gana**   desire
  tener ganas de   to feel like, be anxious to
  ganar   to gain, earn, win
la **ganga**   bargain
  garantizar   to guarantee
  García Lorca, Federico (1898–1936) *Spanish poet and dramatist*
la **garganta**   throat
la **gasolina**   gasoline
  estación de gasolina   gas (service) station
  gastar   to waste, use (up), spend (*money*)
el **gato**   cat
  gauchesco, -a   gaucho, of (pertaining to) the gaucho
el **gaucho**   gaucho, (South American) cowboy
la **generación** (*pl.* **generaciones**)   generation
  general *adj.*   general
  en (por lo) general   in general, generally
el **general**   general
  generalmente   generally
  generativo, -a   generating
el **género**   gender; genre, type (*literary*)
el **genio**   genius
la **gente**   people
  mucha gente   many people
  geográfico, -a   geographical

  germinar   to germinate, begin to grow, sprout
la **gloria**   glory
  glotón, -ona   gluttonous
el **gobernador**   governor
  gobernar (ie)   to govern
el **gobierno**   government
el **gol**   goal (*soccer*)
el **golf**   golf
el **golpe**   blow
  golpe de muerte   death blow
  gótico, -a   Gothic
la **grabadora**   recorder
  grabadora de cinta   tape recorder
  grabar   to tape, record
  gracias   thanks, thank you
  dar las gracias a   to thank
el **grado**   degree, level
  graduarse   to graduate
  gramatical   grammatical
  gran   great, large (*used for* **grande** *before a sing. noun*)
  Gran Colombia   Greater Colombia
  Granada: Nuevo Reino de —,   New Kingdom of Granada (*name given to the Spanish colony and later viceroyalty in northwestern South America*)
  grande   large, big, great
  grato, -a   pleasing, pleasant
  grave   grave, serious
  gravísimo, -a   very grave (serious)
  Gregorio   Gregory
  gritar   to shout, cry out
el **grito**   shout, cry
  dar gritos   to cry out, shout
el **grupo**   group, class
  Guadalupe: Virgen de —,   Virgin of Guadalupe (*patron saint of the Mexican Indians*)
el **guante**   glove
  guapo, -a   pretty, good-looking, handsome
  guardar   to guard, keep
  guardar cama   to stay in bed
  guatemalteco, -a   Guatemalan
  Guayaquil   *port and commercial city of Ecuador*
la **guerra**   war

el **güeso** = el **hueso** (*in rustic speech*)   bone
guiar   to guide, lead
Guillermo   William
la **guitarra**   guitar
gustar   to be pleasing (to), like
  gustar más   to like more (better), prefer
  (**me**) **gustaría**   (I) should like
el **gusto**   pleasure, delight
  con (**mucho**) **gusto**   with (much) pleasure, (very) gladly
  mucho gusto en conocerle (**-la**) **a Ud.** (I'm very) pleased to meet (know) you
  tener mucho gusto en   to be very glad (pleased) to

H

la **Habana**   Havana
haber   to have (*auxiliary*); be (*impersonal*)
  ha habido   there has (have) been
  haber de + *inf.*   to be (be supposed) to
  había   there was (were)
  habrá   there will be
  hay   there is (are)
  hay (**había, habrá**) **que** + *inf.*   it is (was, will be) necessary to, one must (should)
  que haya   that there may be
  ¿qué hay de nuevo?   what's new?
hábil   skilful, talented
el **habitante**   inhabitant
hablador, -ora   talkative
hablar   to talk, speak
  habla (**Carlos**)   this is (Charles), (Charles) is speaking
  oír hablar de   to hear of (about)
hacer   to do, make; be (*weather*)
  desde hace una hora   for an hour
  hace (**media hora**)   (a half hour) ago
  hace tiempo que no te veo   I haven't seen you for a long time
  hace una hora que llegué   it is an hour since I arrived

  hacer buen (**mal**) **tiempo**   to be good (bad) weather
  hacerlo poner   to have it put
  hacer un viaje (**una excursión**)   to make (take) a trip (an excursion)
  hacer una jugada prohibida contra   to foul (*in a game*)
  hacerse + *noun*   to become
  hacía casi un siglo   almost a century before
  hacía un mes que yo vivía aquí   I had been living here (for) a month
hacia   toward(s), about (*with date*)
hallar   to find; *reflex.* be, be found, find oneself
el **hambre** (*f.*)   hunger
  a buen hambre   when hunger is great
  muerto, -a de hambre   starving (to death)
  tener (**mucha**) **hambre**   to be (very) hungry
la **hamburguesa**   hamburger
hasta *prep.*   until, to, up to; *adv.* even
  desde . . . hasta   from . . . (up) to
  hasta la vista   I'll see you later, until I see you
  hasta luego   see you later, until later (I see you)
  hasta que *conj.*   until
hay   there is (are)
  hay que + *inf.*   one must + *verb*, it is necessary to
  ¿qué hay de nuevo?   what's new?
la **hazaña**   deed
hecho *p.p. of* **hacer** *and adj.*   done, made
  lo hecho   what is (was) done
  frases hechas   fixed phrases
el **hecho**   fact
  el hecho de que   the fact that
la **hermana**   sister
la **hermanita**   little sister
el **hermanito**   little brother
el **hermano**   brother; *pl.* brothers, brother(s) and sister(s)
hermosísimo, -a   very pretty (beautiful)
hermoso, -a   pretty, beautiful

Hernán, Hernando   Ferdinand
Hernández, José (1834–1886)   *Argentine poet of gaucho literature*
el **héroe**   hero
Hidalgo, Miguel (1753–1811)   *village priest and Mexican revolutionary leader*
el **hielo**   ice
la **hija**   daughter
el **hijo**   son; *pl.* children
hispano, -a   Hispanic, Spanish
  la **América hispana**   Spanish America
  Hispanoamérica   Spanish America
  hispanoamericano, -a (*also noun*) Spanish American
  hispanoparlante   Spanish-speaking
la **historia**   history
el **historiador**   historian
histórico, -a   historical
la **hoja**   leaf
¡hola!   hello!
el **hombre**   man
  ¡hombre!   man (alive)!
hondo, -a   deep, profound, far-reaching
hondureño, -a   Honduran
el **honor**   honor
  en honor de   in honor of
la **honra**   honor
honrado, -a   honorable, honest
honrar   to honor
la **hora**   hour, time (*of day*)
  ¿a qué hora?   at what time?
  ya es la hora   the hour is over
el **horror**   horror
el **hospital**   hospital
hostil   hostile
el **hotel**   hotel
hoy   today
  hoy día   nowadays, today
  hoy mismo   this very day
huir   to flee
la **humanidad**   humanity
el **humanista**   humanist
humanístico, -a   humanistic
humanitario, -a   humanitarian
humano, -a   human
  lo humano   the (what is) human
humilde   humble, lowly

el **humo**   smoke
el **huracán** (*pl.* **huracanes**)   hurricane

I

la **idea**   idea
ideal (*also m. noun*)   ideal
el **idealismo**   idealism
identificar   to identify
ideológico, -a   ideological
la **iglesia**   church
  a la iglesia   to church
la **igualdad**   equality
ilustre   illustrious, famous
la **imagen** (*pl.* **imágenes**)   image, picture
imaginario, -a   imaginary
imaginarse   to imagine
imaginativo, -a   imaginative
el **imitador**   imitator
la **imparcialidad**   impartiality
el **imperfecto**   imperfect (*tense*)
el **imperio**   empire
impersonal   impersonal
imponer   to impose
importado, -a   imported
la **importancia**   importance
importante   important
  lo importante   the important thing (part), what is important
importar   to be important, to matter; import
imposible   impossible
  lo imposible   the impossible (thing), what is impossible
impresionante   impressive, moving
impresionar   to impress
impresionista (*m. and f.*)   impressionist(ic)
impulsar   to impel, move, give impetus to
inca (*m. and f.; also noun*)   Inca
incompleto, -a   incomplete
la **incorporación**   incorporation
incorporarse a   to be incorporated in
indefinido, -a   indefinite
la **independencia**   independence
independiente   independent

indianista (*m. and f.*)   Indianist, of (pertaining to) the Indian

indicar   to indicate

el **indicativo**   indicative (*mood*)
imperfecto (**pretérito**) **de indicativo** imperfect (preterit) indicative

el **índice**   index, rate
indígena (*m. and f.*)   native, Indian, indigenous
indio, -a (*also noun*)   Indian
indirecto, -a   indirect
indispensable   indispensable

la **industria**   industry
industrial   industrial

la **industrialización**   industrialization
industrializar   to industrialize
Inés   Inez, Agnes

el **infinitivo**   infinitive
infinito, -a   infinite

la **influencia**   influence

el **informalismo**   informalism

el **informe**   report; *pl.* information
inglés, -esa *adj. and noun*   English; Englishman

el **inglés**   English (*language*)

los **ingresos**   income, revenue
inicial   initial
iniciar   to initiate, start

la **injusticia**   injustice
injusto, -a   unjust
inmaterial   immaterial
inmediatamente   immediately
inmenso, -a   immense, very large
insigne   famous, noted, renowned
insistir (**en** + *obj.*)   to insist (on)
insistir en que   to insist that

la **inspiración** (*pl.* **inspiraciones**)   inspiration

la **institución** (*pl.* **instituciones**)   institution

la **integración**   integration
integrar   to integrate
intelectual   intellectual
intensamente   intensely
intenso, -a   intense, intensive, active
intentar   to attempt, try; intend

el **intento**   intent, design, plan
interamericano, -a   inter-American

intercontinental   intercontinental

el **interés** (*pl.* **intereses**)   interest, attention, concern
interesante   interesting
interesar   to interest
interesarse por   to be (become) interested in
interior   interior; domestic
la demanda (**el comercio**) **interior** domestic demand (trade)

el **intermedio**   intermission
internacional   international

la **interpretación**   interpretation
interpretar   to interpret

el **intérprete**   interpreter
interrogativo, -a   interrogative
interrumpir   to interrupt
intrínseco, -a   intrinsic
introducir   to introduce
invadir   to invade

el **invasor**   invader

la **invención**   invention
inventivo, -a   inventive

la **inversión** (*pl.* **inversiones**)   inversion; *pl.* investments

el **invierno**   winter
deportes de invierno   winter sports

la **invitación** (*pl.* **invitaciones**)   invitation
invitar (**a** + *inf.*)   to invite (to)
ir (**a** + *inf.*) to go (to); *reflex.* go (away), leave
ir + *pres. part.*   to be (*progressive form*), go on, keep, be gradually (+ *pres. part.*)
ir al centro   to go downtown
ir de compras   to go shopping
vámonos   let's be going
vamos   we are going, let's go
vamos a + *inf.*   we are going to, let's + *verb*
voy a llegar tarde   I'll be (arrive) late

irregular   irregular
Isabel   Isabel, Betty, Elizabeth

la **isla**   island
Israel   Israel

el **istmo**   isthmus

J

jactarse (de)   to boast (of)
el **jaguar**   jaguar
Jaime   James
Jalisco   *state in west central Mexico*
jamás   ever, never, (not) . . . ever
el **jamón**   ham
    emparedado de jamón   ham sandwich
el **jarabe**   *a popular dance in Mexico*
el **jardín** (*pl.* **jardines**)   garden
el **jefe**   chief, leader, head
Jesús   Jesus
Joaquín   Joachim
Jorge   George
José   Joseph, Joe
joven (*pl.* **jóvenes**)   young
    el **joven**   young man
    los **jóvenes**   young men (people)
Juan   John
Juanita   Juanita, Jane
Juanito   Johnny
el **juego**   game
el **(los) jueves**   (on) Thursday(s)
jugada: hacer una — prohibida contra   to foul (*in a game*)
el **jugador**   player
jugar (**ue**) (**a** + *obj.*)   to play (*a game*)
    jugar al (**fútbol**)   to play (football)
julio   July
Julio   Julius
junio   June
junto con *prep.*   along with
juntos, -as   together
jurídico, -a   juridical, legal
la **juventud**   youth

K

el **kilogramo**   kilogram (*2.2 pounds*)
el **kilómetro**   kilometer ($\frac{5}{8}$ *mile*)

L

la (*pl.* **las**)   the (*f.*)
    de la(s) que   than

la(s) de   that (those) of, the one(s) of (with, in)
la(s) que   who, that, which, she who, the one(s) who (that, whom, which), those who (which, whom)
la *obj. pron.*   her, it (*f.*), you (*polite f.*)
la **labor**   labor, work
el **laboratorio**   laboratory
el **lado**   side
    al lado de   beside, at (on) the side of
    al otro lado   on the other side
lanzar   to hurl, launch, make (*accusation, etc.*)
el **lápiz** (*pl.* **lápices**)   pencil
largo, -a   long
    a lo largo de   throughout
    lo largas que (**son**)   how long (they are)
las *obj. pron.*   them (*f.*), you (*polite f.*) (*also see* **la**)
    a las (**seis**)   at (six) o'clock
la **lástima**   pity
    ¡qué lástima!   what a pity!
    ser lástima   to be a pity, be too bad
latino, -a   Latin
    la **América latina**   Latin America
latinoamericano, -a   Latin American
lavar   to wash; *reflex.* wash (oneself)
le *obj. pron.*   him, you (*polite m.*); to him, her, it, you
la **lección** (*pl.* **lecciones**)   lesson
    Lección primera   Lesson One
la **lectura**   reading, reading selection
la **leche**   milk
    batido de leche   milk shake
la **lechuga**   lettuce
leer   to read
leído *p.p. of* **leer** *and adj.*   read
    lo leído   what is (was) read
la **lengua**   language, tongue
Leopoldo   Leopold
les *obj. pron.*   (to) them, you (*polite*)
levantar   to raise, lift (up); *reflex.* get up, rise
la **ley**   law
la **leyenda**   legend
la **libertad**   liberty, freedom
el **libertador**   liberator

libre free
la **librería** bookstore
el **libro** book
  libro de texto text, textbook
la **liga** league
limeño, -a native (resident) of Lima
limitar to limit
  limitarse a to limit oneself (be limited) to
la **línea** line
lírico, -a lyric, lyrical
la **lista** list, roll (*class*)
listo, -a ready
la **litera** litter
literario, -a literary
la **literatura** literature
lo *neuter article* the; what is (was, *etc.*)
  de lo que than (what)
  lo (bueno) the *or* what is (good), the (good) part *or* thing
  lo (contentas) que están how (happy) they are
  lo más pronto posible the soonest possible, as soon as possible
  lo que what, that which
lo *obj. pron.* him, it (*m. and neuter*), you (*polite m.*); so
  lo es he (it) is
  no lo parece (he) doesn't seem so
  pregúntaselo a ella ask her
loco, -a crazy
el **lodo** mud
  haber (mucho) lodo to be (very) muddy
la **lógica** logic
lograr to get, obtain; + *inf.* succeed in + *pres. part.*
los the (*m.*)
  de los que than
  los de those of, the ones of (with, in)
  los que who, that, which, the ones *or* those who (that, whom, which)
los *obj. pron.* them (*m.*), you (*polite m.*)
la **lucha** struggle, struggling, fight(ing)
  en lucha in a (his) struggle
luchar to struggle, fight
luego then, next, later
  hasta luego see you later, until later (I see you)

luego que *conj.* as soon as
el **lugar** place, site
  tener lugar to take place
Luis Louis
Luisa Louise
la **luna** moon
  hay luna the moon is shining, it is moonlight
el **(los) lunes** (on) Monday(s)
la **luz** (*pl.* **luces**) light

Ll

la **llamada** call
llamar to call; *reflex.* be called, be named
  ¿cómo se llama . . .? what is the name of . . .? what is (his) name?
  llamar la atención (a uno) to attract (one's) attention
  llamar por teléfono to telephone, call by telephone
  se le llama (it) is called
el **llanero** plainsman
la **llanura** plain
la **llave** key
la **llegada** arrival
llegar (a) to arrive (at), reach, come (to)
  llegar a + *inf.* to come to (go so far as to) + *inf.*, succeed in + *pres. part.*
  llegar a ser to become, come to be
  llegar tarde to arrive (be) late
  voy a llegar tarde I'll be (arrive) late
llenar (de) to fill (with)
llevar to take, carry, lead; bear; wear; *reflex.* take (with oneself), take away
  llevar a cabo to carry out
llover (ue) to rain
la **lluvia** rain

M

el **machete** machete (*long knife*)
la **madera** wood
  de madera wooden, of wood

la **madre**   mother
  madre patria   mother country
  maestra: obra —,   masterpiece
la **maestría**   mastery, skill
el **maestro**   master, teacher
  magnífico, -a   magnificent, fine, wonderful
  majestuoso, -a   majestic
  mal *used for* **malo** *before m. sing. nouns*
  mal *adv.*   bad, badly
la **maleta**   suitcase, bag
  malísimo, -a   very bad (poor)
  malo, -a   bad; ill (*with* **estar**)
  lo malo   the bad thing (part), what is bad
la **mamá**   mama, mother
el **mandato**   command
  mandar   to send, order, command, have
  le mandó llamar   (he) had him called
la **manera**   manner, way
  de dos maneras   in two ways
  de manera ejemplar   in an exemplary way
  de manera que *conj.*   so that
  manifestarse (ie)   to be manifest, be observed
la **mano**   hand
  a manos de   at (by) the hand(s) of
la **manta**   blanket
  mantener   to maintain, keep
  Manuel   Manuel, Emanuel
  manufacturar   to manufacture
  mañana *adv.*   tomorrow
  mañana mismo   tomorrow
la **mañana**   morning
  (ayer) por la mañana   (yesterday) morning
  mañana por la noche   tomorrow night
  por la mañana   in the morning
el **mapa**   map
la **máquina**   machine
el **(la) mar**   sea
  alta mar   high seas
  baja mar   ebb (low) tide
  la mar de cosas   lots of things
  Mar del Sur   Southern Sea
  Mar Pacífico   Pacific Ocean (Sea)

  maravillosamente   marvelously
  maravilloso, -a   marvelous
la **marca**   brand, make, kind
  marcar   to dial (*telephone*), make (*a score*)
la **marcha**   march, journey
  ponerse en marcha   to set out, start out
  marchar   to march; *reflex.* leave, go away
  Margarita   Margaret, Marguerite
  María   Mary
  Marta   Martha
el **(los) martes**   (on) Tuesday(s)
  Martín   Martin
  más   more, most; longer
  más conocido, -a   best known
  no esperar más   not to wait (any) longer
  no . . . más de   not . . . more than (*before numeral*)
  no . . . más que   only
la **masa**   mass; *pl.* masses (*people*)
  matar   to kill
  matemático, -a   mathematical
la **materia**   matter, material
el **material** (*also pl.*)   material(s), matter; copy (*printing*)
  máximo, -a   maximum, highest
  mayo   May
  mayor   greater, greatest; older, oldest
  la mayor parte de   the greater part of, most (of)
  los mayores   older people, elders
la **mayoría**   majority
  la mayoría de   the majority of, most (of)
  me *obj. pron.*   me, to me, (to) myself
  mediados: a — de   about the middle of
la **medicina**   medicine
  médico, -a   medical
el **médico**   doctor, physician
  medio, -a   half, a half; middle
  hace media hora   a half hour ago
  la clase media   middle class
  (las siete) y media   half past (seven)
  un grado y medio   a degree and a half
el **medio**   medium, means; *pl.* means
  por medio de   by means of

el **mediodía**   noon
  al **mediodía**   at noon
el **medro**   advancement
  mejor   better, best
  lo **mejor**   what is better (best)
la **mejora**   improvement
el **mejoramiento**   betterment, improvement
  mejorarse   to improve, get better
la **melodía**   melody
la **memoria**   memory
  aprender **de memoria**   to mem-
    orize, learn from memory (by heart)
  mencionar   to mention
  menor   younger, youngest, smaller,
    smallest; lesser, least
  menos   less, least, fewer; except
  a **menos que** *conj.*   unless
la **mentira**   lie
  menudo: a —,   often, frequently
el **mercado**   market
la **merced**   mercy
  merecer   to merit, deserve
el **mes**   month
la **mesa**   table, desk (*classroom*)
  poner la mesa   to set the table
  meter   to put (in)
el **metro**   meter
Metropolitano, -a   Metropolitan
mexicano, -a   Mexican
México   Mexico
  la **ciudad de México**   Mexico City
  México, D.F.   Mexico City
mezclar   to mix, mingle
mi   my
mí *obj. pron.*   me, (to) myself
el **micrófono**   microphone
el **miedo**   fear
  tener miedo (de + *obj.*)   to be
    afraid (of, to)
  tener (mucho) miedo (de que)   to
    be (very) afraid *or* be (very) frightened
    (that)
el **miembro**   member
mientras (que) *conj.*   while, as long as
el **(los) miércoles**   (on) Wednesday(s)
Miguel   Michael, Mike
mil   one (a) thousand; *pl.* thousands

el **milímetro**   millimeter
militar *adj.*   military
el **militar**   military man, soldier
el **millón** (*pl.* **millones**)   million
  (**dos**) **millones de** (**habitantes**)
    (two) million (inhabitants)
el **millonario**   millionaire
el **mineral**   mineral
el **minuto**   minute
mío, -a *adj.*   my, (of) mine
  (**el**) **mío**, (**la**) **mía**, (**los**) **míos**, (**las**)
    mías *pron.*   mine
mirar   to look (at)
la **misa**   Mass
  llamar a misa   to call to Mass
miserable   miserable
Misisipí   Mississippi
mismo, -a   same, the same, very, very
  same, self-same; himself, *etc.*
  ahora mismo   right now, right away
  allí mismo   that very place
  él mismo   he himself
  el mismo (**papel**) **que**   the same
    (role) as
  ellos mismos   they themselves
  (**gobernarse**) **a sí mismas**   (to
    govern) themselves (*f.*)
  hoy mismo   this very day
  lo mismo   the same thing
  mañana mismo   tomorrow
misterioso, -a   mysterious
místico, -a   mystic
Misurí   Missouri
la **mitad**   half
Moctezuma   *leader of the Aztecs at time of
  Spanish conquest*
el **modelo**   model
moderado, -a   moderate, restrained
el **modernismo**   modernism
modernista (*m. and f.*)   modernist
moderno, -a   modern
el **modismo**   idiom
el **modo**   manner, way, means, mode;
  mood (*grammar*)
  de modo que *conj.*   so that
  de todos modos   at any rate, by all
    means
modulada: frecuencia —,   FM (*radio*)

el **momento**   moment; period, time
  apropiado al momento   appropriate at the moment, suitable for that period (time)
  en este (ese) momento   at this (that) moment
la **monarquía**   monarchy
la **moneda**   money, coin, currency
el **monólogo**   monologue
la **montaña**   mountain
  Montevideo   *capital of Uruguay*
  moral   moral
el **moribundo**   moribund, dying person
  morir (ue, u)   to die
el **moro**   Moor
  mostrar (ue)   to show
la **motivación**   motivation
la **movilidad**   mobility
el **movimiento**   movement
la **muchacha**   girl
el **muchacho**   boy
  muchísimo *adv.*   very much
  muchísimo, -a (-os, -as)   very much (many)
  mucho *adv.*   much, a great deal, hard
  (esperar) mucho   (to wait) long (a long time)
  mucho, -a (-os, -as)   much (many); very
  mucha gente   many people
  muchas veces   many times, often
  mucho tiempo   long, a long time
  mudar   to change
  mudarse (de)   to change (*one's clothing, etc.*)
  mudéjar *adj. and m. noun*   Mudejar (Spanish Moorish)
la **muerte**   death
  condenar a muerte   to condemn to death
  golpe de muerte   death blow
  muerto, -a *p.p. of* **morir** *and adj.*   died, dead
  muerto, -a de hambre   starving (to death)
la **mujer**   woman
  múltiple   multiple, manifold
la **multitud**   multitude, great number

  mundial *adj.*   world(-wide), universal
el **mundo**   world
  del mundo   world, of the world
  Nuevo Mundo   New World
  todo el mundo   everybody
  mural *adj. and m. noun*   mural
el **muralismo**   muralism (*painting of murals*)
  muralista (*m. and f.*)   muralist, of murals
  Murillo, Bartolomé Esteban (1618–1682)   *famous Spanish painter*
el **museo**   museum
la **música**   music
  concierto de — sinfónica   symphony concert
  musical   musical
el **músico**   musician
  mutuo, -a   mutual
  muy   very

N

  nacer   to be born
  nacido, -a   born
la **nación** (*pl.* **naciones**)   nation
  Naciones Unidas   United Nations
  nacional   national
  nacionalista (*m. and f.*)   nationalist(ic)
  nada *pron.*   nothing, (not) . . . anything; *adv.* (not) at all
  de nada   don't mention it, you're welcome
  nada de particular   nothing special
  nadar   to swim
  nadie   no one, nobody, (not) . . . anybody (anyone)
  Napoleón   Napoleon (Bonaparte) (1769–1821)   *French emperor*
el **narrador**   narrator
la **naturaleza**   nature
el **naturalismo**   naturalism
  naturalista (*m. and f.; also noun*)   naturalist, naturalistic
  naturalmente   naturally
la **navaja**   knife; razor
la **nave**   boat, ship
  navegar   to sail, navigate

la **Navidad**   Christmas
  las **Navidades**   Christmas time
la **neblina**   mist
  hay neblina   it is misty
necesario, -a   necessary
  lo necesario   what is necessary, the necessary thing (part)
la **necesidad**   necessity
necesitar   to need
negar (ie)   to deny
  negarse a   to refuse to
negativamente   negatively
negativo, -a   negative
  la **negativa**   the negative one (*f.*)
los **negocios**   business
  hombre de negocios   business man
negro, -a   black, Negro
nervioso, -a   nervous
neutro, -a   neuter
la **nevera**   refrigerator
ni   neither, nor
  ni . . . ni   neither . . . nor, (not) . . . either . . . or
nicaragüense   Nicaraguan
la **niebla**   fog
  hay niebla   it is foggy
la **nieve**   snow
ningún   *used for* **ninguno** *before m. sing. nouns*
ninguno, -a   no, no one, none, (not) . . . any (anybody, anyone)
la **niña**   little girl
el **niño**   little boy, child; *pl.* children
el **nivel**   level
  nivel de vida   standard of living
no   no, not
  (yo) no   not (I)
la **noche**   night, evening
  (el sábado) por la noche   (Saturday) evening *or* night
  esta noche   tonight
  todas las noches   every night (evening)
nombrar   to name, appoint
el **nombre**   name
  en nombre de   in the name of
la **norma**   norm, standard
el **norte**   north, northern part

Norteamérica   North America
norteamericano, -a (*also noun*)   (North) American
nos *obj. pron.*   us, to us, (to) ourselves, (*reciprocal pron.*) (to) one another, each other
nosotros, -as   we, us (*after prep.*); ourselves
  nosotros todos   we all, all of us
la **nota**   note
notable   notable, noteworthy
notar   to note, observe, see
la **noticia**   news, news item, notice
  sección de noticias   news section
la **novela**   novel
el **novelista**   novelist
novelístico, -a   novelistic, of (pertaining to) the novel
la **novia**   sweetheart, fiancée, girl friend
noviembre   November
el **novio**   sweetheart, fiancé, boy friend
nuestro, -a *adj.*   our, (of) ours
  (el) nuestro, (la) nuestra, (los) nuestros, (las) nuestras *pron.*   ours
  lo nuestro   our part, what is ours
nueve   nine
  diez y nueve   nineteen
nuevo, -a   new, brand-new; another, different
  de nuevo   again, anew
  la nueva   the new one (*f.*)
  Nueva España   New Spain (= Mexico)
  Nueva Granada   New Granada
  Nueva York   New York
  Nuevo México   New Mexico
  ¿qué hay de nuevo?   what's new?
el **número**   number, issue (*newspaper*)
numeroso, -a   numerous, large
nunca   never, (not) . . . ever

O

o   or
  o . . . o   either . . . or
Oaxaca *capital of state of Oaxaca, Mexico*
el **objetivo**   objective
el **objeto**   object, purpose

la **obligación** (*pl.* **obligaciones**) obligation, duty

obligar (**a** + *inf.*) to oblige *or* force (to + *inf.*)

la **obra** work (*art, literary, etc.*)

obra maestra masterpiece

la **observación** (*pl.* **observaciones**) observation

observar to observe, note, see

el **obstáculo** obstacle

obtener to obtain, get

la **ocasión** (*pl.* **ocasiones**) occasion, opportunity

el **océano** ocean

Océano Pacífico Pacific Ocean

ocultar to hide, conceal

ocultar a (**uno**) to hide from (one)

ocupado, -a occupied, busy

ocupar to occupy

ocurrir to occur

ochenta eighty

ocho eight

OEA = Organización de los Estados Americanos Organization of the American States

el **oeste** west

oficial *adj.* official

la **oficina** office

el **oficio** craft, trade

ofrecer to offer

O'Higgins, Bernardo (1778–1842) *Chilean general, later dictator* (1817–1823)

oír to hear

oír decir (**que**) to hear (that)

oír hablar de to hear of (about)

¡ojalá (**que**)! would that! I wish that!

el **ojo** eye

olvidar to forget

olvidarse (**de** + *obj.*) to forget

la **omisión** (*pl.* **omisiones**) omission

omitir to omit

once eleven

la **onda** wave

de onda corta short-wave

la **ópera** opera

la **operación** (*pl.* **operaciones**) operation

oponer to oppose, face

oponerse a to oppose

la **oportunidad** opportunity

el **optimismo** optimism

la **oración** (*pl.* **oraciones**) sentence; prayer; oration

oral oral

el **orden** (*pl.* **órdenes**) order, arrangement

de primer orden first-rate, excellent

la **orden** (*pl.* **órdenes**) order, command

por orden de at the order of

la **orfebrería** gold or silver work

el **organismo** organism, agency, organization

la **organización** organization

organizar to organize

el **origen** (*pl.* **orígenes**) origin

original original

la original the original one (*f.*)

el **oro** gold

de oro (of) gold

la **orquesta** orchestra

os *obj. pron.* you (*fam. pl.*), to you, (to) yourselves, (*reciprocal pron.*) (to) one another, each other

el **otoño** autumn, fall

otro, -a other, another; *pl.* other

el uno (**la una**) **al otro** (**a la otra**) (to) one another, each other

otra vez again

P

Pablo Paul

pacífico, -a pacific, peaceful

Mar Pacífico Pacific Ocean (Sea)

Océano Pacífico Pacific Ocean

el **Pacífico** Pacific (Ocean)

el **padre** father, priest; *pl.* parents

pagar to pay, pay for

la **página** page

el **país** country (*nation*)

el **paisaje** landscape

la **palabra** word

estudio de palabras word study

el **palacio** palace

Palacio Nacional National Palace (*where the Mexican president has his offices*)

el **palo**   stick, club
la **pampa**   pampa, plain (*of Argentina*)
el **pan**   bread
Panamá   Panama
panameño, -a   Panamanian
panamericano, -a   Pan American
el **panorama**   panorama
la **pantalla**   screen (*movie*)
el **papá**   father, papa, dad
el **papel**   paper; role
representar el mismo papel que   to play the same role as
el **paquete**   package
el **par**   pair
un par de   a pair (couple) of, two
para   for, to, in order to, by (*time*)
estar para   to be about to
¿para qué?   why? for what purpose?
el **(los) parabrisas**   windshield
la **parada**   stop
el **Paraguay**   Paraguay
paraguayo, -a   Paraguayan
parar *trans.*   to stop
parecer   to seem, appear (to be)
(me) parece que   (I) think (believe) that
(me) parece que no   (I) think (believe) not
¿qué (te) parece . . .?   what do (you) think of . . .? how do (you) like . . .?
la **pared**   wall
el **(los) paréntesis**   parenthesis (*pl.* parentheses)
entre paréntesis   in (within) parentheses
el **parque**   park
el **párrafo**   paragraph
la **parte**   part
en gran parte   largely, in large measure
formar parte de   to form (a) part of
la mayor parte de   the greater part of, most (of)
el **participio**   participle
particular: nada de —,   nothing special
el **partido**   game, match
partido (de fútbol)   (football) game

partir (de + obj.)   to depart, leave (from)
partir para   to leave (depart) for
pasado, -a   passed, past, last
el **pasado**   past
pasar   to pass; happen; spend (*time*)
pasa (tú), pase(n) Ud(s).   come in
pasar a   to go to
pasar de   to exceed
pasar por   to pass (go, come) by *or* along
¿qué (le) pasa?   what's the matter with (him)?
el **paseo**   walk, ride, stroll; boulevard
dar un paseo   to take a walk (stroll)
la **pasión**   passion
pasivo, -a   passive
el **paso**   step
dar un paso   to take a step
el **patín** (*pl.* patines)   skate
patinar   to skate
el **patio**   patio, courtyard
patológico, -a   pathological
lo patológico   the pathological
la **patria**   native land, country (*where one is a citizen*)
madre patria   mother country
el **patriota**   patriot
la **pausa**   pause
el **payador**   gaucho singer
la **paz**   peace
pedir (i, i)   to ask, ask for, request
pedir a uno   to ask (of) one
Pedro   Peter
la **película**   film
el **pelo**   hair
la **penalidad**   trouble, hardship
penoso, -a   distressing
el **pensador**   thinker
pensar (ie)   to think; + *inf.* intend
pensar en + *obj.*   to think of (about)
peor   worse, worst
lo peor   what is worse (worst), the worse (worst) thing
pequeño, -a   small, little (*size*)
percibir   to perceive, see
perder (ie)   to lose, miss
la **perfección**   perfection

el **perfecto**   present perfect (*tense*)
  futuro perfecto   future perfect (*tense*)
el **periódico**   newspaper
el **periodista**   journalist
el **período**   period
el **perjuicio**   detriment, damage
  en perjuicio de   to the detriment of
el **permiso**   permission
  permitir   to permit, allow, let
    si me permites (ayudarte)   if you
      will let me (help you)
  pero   but
el **perro**   dog
la **persona**   person; *pl.* persons, people
el **personaje**   personage, character (*in a
    literary work*)
la **personalidad**   personality
el **Perú**   Peru
  el Alto Perú   Upper Peru
  peruano, -a   Peruvian
  pesar: a — de   in spite of, despite
el **pianista**   pianist
  pianístico, -a   piano (*adj.*)
la **piedra**   stone
    de piedra   (of) stone
el **pilar**   pillar
la **píldora**   pill
  pintar   to paint
el **pintor**   painter (*artist*)
la **pintura**   painting
la **piscina**   swimming pool
el **piso**   floor, story
    piso bajo   first floor
la **pizarra**   (black)board
el **plan**   plan
la **plana**   page (*printing*)
  plantear   to pose, set up
la **plata**   silver
  plateresco, -a (*also noun*)   Plateresque
la **plaza**   plaza, square
la **pluma**   pen
el **plural**   plural
el **pluscuamperfecto**   pluperfect (*tense*)
la **población**   population
el **poblador**   populator, settler
  pobre   poor
  poco, -a *adj., pron., and adv.*   little (*quan-
    tity*); *pl.* (a) few

  a poca distancia (de)   at a short
    distance (from)
  al poco rato   after a short while
  al poco tiempo   after (in) a short
    time
  poco a poco   little by little
  poco después *adv.*   shortly afterward(s)
  poco después de *prep.*   shortly after
  un poco   a little, a little while
poder   to be able, can, may
  puede (ser)   it may be
  ¿se puede entrar?   may I (we, one)
    come in?
el **poder**   power
  en poder de   in the hands (power) of
el **poderío**   power, might
  poderoso, -a   powerful; wealthy
el **poema**   poem
la **poesía** (*also pl.*)   poetry
el **poeta**   poet
  poético, -a   poetic, poetical
la **poetisa**   poetess
  poetizar   to make poetic, poeticize
la **política**   policy
  político, -a   political
    economía política   political econo-
      my, economics
el **político**   politician
el **polvo**   dust
  hay (mucho) polvo   it is (very) dusty
poner   to put, put in, place, turn on;
    reflex. put on (oneself)
  poner (el radio)   to turn on (the
    radio)
  poner fin a   to put an end to
  poner la mesa   to set the table
  ponerse + *adj.*   to become
  ponerse en marcha   to set (start) out
Popol-Vuh   *Popol-Vuh, sacred book of the
  Mayas*
popular   popular
  lo popular   the (what is *or* was)
    popular, that which pertains (pertained)
    to the people
por   for, during, in, through, along, by,
    because of, on account of, for the sake of,
    on behalf of, about, around, per, in ex-
    change for, as, (+ *inf.*) to

está por escribir   it is to be written
por aquí   (around) here
por encima de   over, above
por eso   because of that, therefore, for that reason, that's why
¿por qué?   why? for what reason?
por lo tanto   therefore
por último   finally, ultimately
porque   because, for
portátil   portable
la **portería**   goal (*soccer*)
el **portero**   goalkeeper (*soccer*)
portorriqueño, -a   Puerto Rican
el **portugués**   Portuguese (*language*)
la **posesión**   possession
posesivo, -a   possessive
posible   possible
   lo más pronto posible   the soonest possible, as soon as possible
   lo posible   what is possible
la **posición**   position
positivo, -a   positive
posterior   later
postrer(o), -a   last
la **práctica**   practice, skill
practicar   to practice
precedido, -a de   preceded by
el **precio**   price
precisamente   precisely, exactly
la **precisión**   precision
preciso, -a   necessary
preferir (**ie, i**)   to prefer
la **pregunta**   question
preguntar   to ask (*a question*)
   preguntar por   to ask for (about), inquire about
prehispánico, -a   pre-Hispanic (*before the Spanish discoveries in America*)
el **prejuicio**   prejudice, bias
preliminar   preliminary
el **premio**   prize, award
prender   to seize
la **preocupación** (*pl.* **preocupaciones**) (**por**)   preoccupation, concern, worry (with, about)
   preocuparse con (**por**)   to worry about, be concerned with (about), be (become) preoccupied with

la **preparación**   preparation
preparar   to prepare, fix; *reflex.* be prepared, get under way
   prepararse para   to prepare oneself to
la **preposición**   preposition
preposicional   prepositional
la **presentación**   presentation, introduction
presentar   to present, introduce, give (*a performance*); *reflex.* present oneself, appear
presente *adj.*   present
el **presente**   present (*time*), present tense
la **presidencia**   presidency
el **presidente**   president
   El señor presidente   Mr. President
prestar   to lend
   prestar atención (**a**)   to pay attention (to)
el **pretérito**   preterit (*tense*)
prevalecer   to prevail
la **prima**   cousin (*f.*)
la **primavera**   spring
   día de primavera   spring day
primer *used for* **primero** *before m. sing. nouns*
primero *adv.*   first
primero, -a   first
   Lección primera   Lesson One
   por primera vez   for the first time
el **primo**   cousin (*m.*)
principalmente   principally, mainly
el **principio**   principle; beginning
   a principios de   at *or* toward(s) the beginning of
la **prisa**   haste
   darse prisa   to hurry
   tener prisa   to be in a hurry
el **prisionero**   prisoner
el **privilegio**   privilege
la **probabilidad**   probability
probable   probable
probar (**ue**)   to try out, test; *reflex.* try on
el **problema**   problem
la **procedencia**   origin, source
el **procedimiento**   procedure, process

el **proceso**   process, progressive movement
proclamarse   to proclaim oneself
la **producción** (*pl.* **producciones**)   production, work
producir   to produce
el **producto**   product
el **productor**   producer
la **productora**   producer
el **profesor**   professor, teacher, instructor (*man*)
la **profesora**   professor, teacher, instructor (*woman*)
profundo, -a   profound, deep
el **programa**   program
progresar   to progress
el **progreso**   progress
Alianza para el Progreso   Alliance for Progress
prohibida: hacer una jugada — contra   to foul (*in a game*)
prometer   to promise
el **pronombre**   pronoun
pronto   soon, quickly
lo más pronto posible   the soonest possible, as soon as possible
la **pronunciación**   pronunciation
pronunciar   to pronounce
la **propaganda**   propaganda
propio, -a   proper, suitable, own, (of) one's own
ellos propios   they themselves
por cuenta propia   by himself, on his own (account)
proponer   to propose
proporcionalmente   proportionally
proporcionar   to furnish, provide
propósito: a —,   by the way
propuesto, -a *p.p. of* **proponer** *and adj.*   proposed
propuso *pret. of* **proponer**
la **prosa**   prose
el **protagonista**   protagonist, central figure
el **protector**   protector
la **protesta**   protest
protestar   to protest
la **provincia**   province
la **provisión** (*pl.* **provisiones**)   provision

próximo, -a   next
el **proyecto**   project, plan
el **proyector**   projector
la **prudencia**   prudence, wisdom, sound judgment
psicológico, -a   psychological
publicar   to publish
la **publicidad**   publicity
público, -a   public
Puebla   *Mexican city east of the capital, famous for pottery*
el **pueblecito**   small town, village
el **pueblo**   town, village; people, populace
la **puerta**   door
puertorriqueño, -a   Puerto Rican
pues *adv.*   well, well now (then); why; *conj.* since, because
el **puesto**   place, position, job, post
el **púlpito**   pulpit
la **pulsera**   bracelet
reloj de pulsera   wrist watch
el **pulso**   pulse
el **punto**   point; period (*punctuation*)
dos puntos   colon
en punto   sharp (*time*)
punto y aparte   new paragraph
punto y coma   semicolon
la **puntuación**   punctuation
puro, -a   pure

Q

que   that, which, who, whom; than; since; *indir. command* have, let, may, etc.
del (de la, de los, de las) que   than
de lo que   than (what)
el mismo (papel) que   the same role as
el (la, los, las) que   that, which, who, whom, he (she, those) who (*etc.*), the one(s) who (*etc.*)
lo que   what, that which, whatever
lo (+ *adj. or adv.*) **que**   how
¿qué?   what? which?
¿para qué?   why? for what purpose?
¿por qué?   why? for what reason?
¡qué + *adj. or adv.*!   how! what!; + *noun* what a (an)!

quedar(se)   to remain, stay; be
  si queda (algo)   if (anything) is left
    or remains
quejarse (de)   to complain (of)
quemar   to burn
querer   to wish, want
  no quisieron esperar   (they) re-
    fused to *or* would not wait
  querer (a)   to love, like
  ¿quieres (quiere Ud.) + *inf.*?   will
    you + *verb*?
  quiso hacer eso   (he) tried to do that
  (yo) quisiera   (I) should like
querido, -a   dear
el **queso**   cheese
  emparedado de queso   cheese sand-
    wich
quien (*pl.* **quienes**)   who, whom, he
  (those) who, the one(s) who
¿quién(es)?   who? whom?
  ¿a quién?   whom?
  ¿de quién(es) es?   whose is (it)?
quinto, -a   fifth
quisiera   (I) should *or* would like
quitar   to remove, take off (away);
  reflex. take off (*oneself*)
Quito   *capital of Ecuador*
quizá(s)   perhaps

R

el **rabo**   tail
racionalista (*m. and f.*)   rationalist
radical   radical; stem
el **radio**   radio (*set*)
la **radio**   radio (*communication*)
Ramón   Raymond
rápidamente   rapidly, fast
  lo más rápidamente posible   the
    fastest possible, as fast (rapidly) as
    possible
la **rapidez**   rapidity, speed
rápido, -a   rapid, fast
el **rato**   while, short time (while)
  al poco rato   after a short while
la **raza**   race

la **razón** (*pl.* **razones**)   reason
  no tener razón   to be wrong
  sin razón alguna   without any rea-
    son at all
  tener razón   to be right
la **realidad**   reality
el **realismo**   realism
realista (*m. and f.*)   realistic
realizar   to realize, carry out
rebelarse contra   to rebel against
la **rebelión**   rebellion
el **recado**   message
recibir   to receive, welcome
recitar   to recite, give
reconocer   to recognize; acknowledge
recordar (**ue**)   to recall, remember,
  remind (one of)
rectangular   rectangular
rectángulo, -a   rectangular
el **rectángulo**   rectangle
la **rectoría**   rector's (president's) office
el **recuerdo**   memory, remembrance
el **recurso**   recourse, resource; *pl.* resources, means
rechazar   to repulse, drive back; reject
redundante   redundant
referir (**ie, i**)   to refer
  referirse a   to refer to
reflejar   to reflect
el **reflejo**   reflection
reflexivo, -a   reflexive
la **reforma**   reform
reforzar (**ue**)   to reinforce
el **refrán** (*pl.* **refranes**)   proverb
el **refresco**   refreshment, cold (soft) drink
regalar   to give (*as a gift*)
el **regalo**   gift
el **régimen** (*pl.* **regímenes**)   regime, rule
la **región** (*pl.* **regiones**)   region
regional   regional
  lo regional   the (what is *or* was)
    regional, that which pertained to the
    region
regir (**i, i**)   to rule, govern
regresar   to return, come back
regular   regular
reinar   to reign
el **reino**   kingdom

reír (i, i) to laugh

la relación (*pl.* **relaciones**) relation
  en relación con in relation to
relacionar (con) to relate (to)
  relacionarse (con) to be related (to)
relatar to relate, tell
relativamente relatively
relativo, -a relative
el relato story, tale; report
la religión religion
religioso, -a religious
el reloj watch
  reloj de pulsera wrist watch
el remedio remedy
reñido, -a hard-fought
repasar to review
  para repasar for review
el repaso review
repetidamente repeatedly
repetir (i, i) to repeat
el representante representative
representar to represent, play
  representar el mismo papel que to play the same role as
representativo, -a representative
reproducir to reproduce
la república republic
reservar to reserve
el resfriado cold (*disease*)
la residencia residence
  Residencia de Estudiantes Student Residence Hall (Dormitory)
resolver (ue) to resolve, solve, settle
respectivo, -a respective
respecto de in (with) regard to, concerning
la responsabilidad responsibility
el resto rest
el resultado result
resultar to result, be, turn out (to be)
el resumen (*pl.* **resúmenes**) summary
retardar to retard, slow down
retirarse to retire, withdraw (oneself)
la reunión (*pl.* **reuniones**) meeting, gathering
reunir to collect; *reflex.* meet, gather, get together
  reunirse con to join

revelar to reveal, make known; develop (*film*)
revisar to check
la revista magazine, journal
la revolución revolution
revolucionario, -a revolutionary
el rey king; *pl.* kings, king(s) and queen(s)
  los Reyes Wise Men (Kings)
ricamente richly
Ricardo Richard
rico, -a rich, wealthy; (*food*) tasty
el Rimac *a river in Peru on which Lima was founded*
el río river
la riqueza wealth, riches, richness; *pl.* wealth, riches
el ritmo rhythm; rate
  al ritmo (actual) at the (present) rate
Roberto Robert
rodear to surround
Rodó, José Enrique (1872–1917) *Uruguayan essayist and thinker*
rojo, -a red
el rollo roll (*of film*)
el romanticismo romanticism
romper to break
la ropa clothes, clothing
  mudarse de ropa to change one's clothing
la rosa rose
roto, -a *p.p. of* **romper** *and adj.* broken
rubio, -a blond(e)
la rumba rumba (*a dance*)
rural rural
la ruta route

S

el sábado (on) Saturday
saber to know (*a fact*), know how, can (*mental ability*); *in pret.* learn, find out
  al saber upon learning (finding out)
sacar to take, take out
  sacar (fotos) to take (photos)
sagrado, -a sacred
el Sagrario sacrarium, sanctuary; shrine

la **sala de clase**   classroom
salir (**de** + *obj.*)   to leave, go out, set out
  salir a   to go (come) out to
  salir de casa   to leave home
la **salsa**   sauce
la **salud**   health
  centro de salud   health center
saludar   to greet, speak to
El **Salvador**   El Salvador
san *used for* **santo** *before m. saint name not beginning with* **Do-** *or* **To-**
San Agustín   St. Augustine
San Martín, José de (1778–1850)   *Argentine general and liberator of Chile and Peru*
San Miguel de Allende   *a city north of Mexico City*
San Roque (1295?–1327)   *a French saint venerated for his work in a plague in Italy*
San Sebastián   St. Sebastian (*Christian martyr at hands of the Romans, 3rd century, A.D.*)
sangriento, -a   bloody
la **sanidad**   health, sanitation
la **santa**   saint (*f.*)
Santa Prisca   St. Prisca (*Christian martyr at hands of the Romans in 1st or 3rd century, A.D.*)
santo, -a   saint, holy
  el Espíritu Santo   Holy Spirit
Santo Domingo   Hispaniola (*island on which Haiti and the Dominican Republic are situated*)
el **santo**   saint (*m.*)
satisfacer   to satisfy
se *pron. used for* **le** *or* **les**   (to) him, her, it, them, you (*polite*); *reflex. pron.* (to) himself, herself, *etc.*; *reciprocal pron.* (to) each other, one another; *indef. subject* one, people, *etc.*
Sebastián   Sebastian (*see* **San Sebastián**)
la **sección** (*pl.* **secciones**)   section
seco, -a   dry
la **secretaria**   secretary (*woman*)
el **sector**   sector
la **sed**   thirst
  tener (**mucha**) **sed**   to be (very) thirsty

seguida: en —,   at once, immediately
  vuelvo en seguida   I'll be right back, I'll return at once
seguido, -a de   followed by
seguir (**i, i**)   to follow, continue, go (keep) on
según   according to
segundo, -a   second
seguro, -a   sure, certain
  estar seguro, -a de + *obj.*   to be sure of
  estar seguro, -a de que   to be sure that
seis   six
  diez y seis   sixteen
seiscientos, -as   six hundred
la **selva**   forest
la **semana**   week
semejante   similar
el **semestre**   semester
sencillamente   simply
sencillo, -a   simple
la **sensibilidad**   sensibility, sensitivity
sentado, -a   seated
sentar (**ie**)   to seat; *reflex.* sit down
el **sentido**   sense, meaning
el **sentimiento**   feeling, sentiment
sentir (**ie, i**)   to feel, regret, be sorry
  ¡cuánto lo sentimos!   how sorry we are!
  sentirlo mucho   to be very sorry
  sentirse bien   to feel well
señor   Mr., sir
  El **señor presidente**   *Mr. President*
  los señores (**Gómez**)   Mr. and Mrs. (Gómez)
señora   Mrs., madam
la **señora**   lady, woman
señorita   Miss
la **señorita**   Miss, young lady (woman)
separado, -a por   separated by
separarse   to separate (oneself)
septiembre   September
ser   to be
  puede (**ser**)   it may be
  ¿qué ha sido de . . .?   what has become of . . .?
el **ser**   being

la serie series
la serpiente serpent
el servicio service
   servicios de alcantarillado sewage systems
   servir (i, i) to serve
     ¿en qué puedo servirle(s)? what can I do for you?
     ¿para qué sirven los amigos? what are friends for?
   servir de to serve as (a)
   sesenta sixty
el seudónimo pseudonym
   si if, whether
   sí yes
   sí *reflex. pron.* himself, herself, *etc.*
     (gobernarse) a sí mismas (to govern) themselves (*f.*)
   siempre always
     siempre que *conj.* provided that
la sierra mountain range, mountains
la siesta nap
   dormir (ue, u) la siesta to take a nap
   siete seven
el siglo century
el significado meaning
el signo sign, mark
   siguiente following, next
     al año (día) siguiente (in) the following year (day)
     las siguientes the following ones (*f.*)
el silencio silence
la silla chair
el simbolismo symbolism
   simbolizar to symbolize
el símbolo symbol
la simetría symmetry
   Simón Simon
la simpatía sympathy
   simpático, -a likeable, charming, nice
   sin *prep.* without
     sin que *conj.* without
la sinceridad sincerity
   sinfónico, -a symphony, symphonic
el singular singular
   sino but
     no sólo ... sino que not only ... but

     no sólo ... sino (también) not only ... but (also)
     sino que *conj.* but
la sintaxis syntax
   sintonizar to tune in
el sistema system
el sitio site, place
la situación situation
   soberbio, -a proud
   sobre on, upon, on top of, about
     sobre todo especially, above all
   sobrenatural supernatural
     lo sobrenatural the supernatural
la sobrina niece
   social social
la sociedad society
el sol sun
   hace *or* **hay (mucho) sol** it is (very) sunny, the sun is shining (brightly)
   solamente only
el soldado soldier
   sólido, -a solid
   solo, -a sole, single, alone
   sólo only
     no sólo ... sino que not only ... but
     no sólo ... sino (también) not only ... but (also)
el soltero bachelor
la solución (*pl.* **soluciones**) solution
la sombra shade, shadow
el sombrero hat
   sonar (ue) to sound, ring
   soñar (ue) con to dream of
   sórdido, -a sordid
   sorprender to surprise; catch
   sorprendido, -a surprised
la sorpresa surprise
   Sr. = señor
   Sra. = señora
   Srta. = señorita
   su(s) his, her, your (*polite*), its, their
   subdesarrollado, -a underdeveloped
   subir to climb, rise, go up
     iba subiendo (it) was rising
   subjuntivo, -a subjunctive (*mood*)
el subjuntivo subjunctive
   el (presente) de subjuntivo (present) subjunctive

la **sublevación**   revolt, uprising
sublevarse   to revolt, rebel, rise up
subordinado, -a   subordinate
subrayar   to underline, emphasize
substantivo, -a (*also noun*)   noun
substituir   to substitute
    substitúyan(lo)   substitute (it)
el **sucursal**   branch office
sudamericano, -a   South American
el **sudoeste**   southwest
el **suelo**   ground, floor
el **sueño**   sleep; dream
    tener sueño   to be sleepy
la **suerte**   luck
    ¡qué suerte has tenido!   how lucky
      (fortunate) you have been!
    tener (mucha) suerte   to be (very)
      lucky *or* fortunate
suficiente   sufficient, adequate
suficientemente   sufficiently
el **sufrimiento**   suffering
sufrir   to suffer, endure
el **sujeto**   subject
sumamente   extremely, exceedingly
superar   to surpass, exceed
superior   superior
suplir   to supply
suponer   to suppose
supuesto: por —,   of course, certainly
el **sur**   south, southern part
    el Mar del Sur   Southern Sea
    la América del Sur   South America
surgir   to surge, arise, appear
el **suroeste**   southwest
el **surrealismo**   surrealism (*literary and
artistic type of the 20th century*)
surrealista (*m. and f.*)   surrealist
suyo, -a *adj.*   his, her, its, your (*polite*),
    their, of his (hers, its, yours, theirs)
    (el) suyo, (la) suya, (los) suyos, (las)
      suyas *pron.*   his, hers, its, yours
      (*polite*), theirs
    lo suyo   what is his (hers, *etc.*); his
      (her, *etc.*) part

T

la **táctica**   tactics (*military*)

tal   such, such a
    con tal (de) que *conj.*   provided that
    ¿qué tal?   how are you? how goes it?
    tal vez   perhaps
también   also, too
tampoco   neither, (not *or* nor) . . . either
    ni (a mí) tampoco   nor (I) either
tan   as, so, such
    tan + *adj. or adv.* + **como**   as (so) . . . as
    ¡un día tan hermoso!   such a
      beautiful day!
tanto, -a (-os, -as) *adj. and pron.*   as (so)
    much (many); *adv.* as (so) much
    por lo tanto   therefore
    tanto . . . como   both . . . and, as
      much . . . as
    tanto, -a (-os, -as) + *noun* + **como**
      as (so) much (many) . . . as
tardar   to delay
    tardar (mucho) en   to take (very
      long) to, be (long) in, delay (long) in
tarde   late
    lo más tarde posible   the latest
      possible, as late as possible
la **tarde**   afternoon
    (ayer) por la tarde   (yesterday)
      afternoon
    por la tarde   in the afternoon
    toda la tarde   all afternoon
    todas las tardes   every afternoon
la **tarjeta**   card (*postal*)
Taxco   *city south of Mexico City*
el **taxi**   taxi
    en taxi   by (in a) taxi
la **taza**   cup
    taza para café (té)   coffee (tea) cup
te *pron.*   you (*fam.*), to you, (to)
    yourself
el **té**   tea
    taza para té   teacup
el **teatro**   theater
la **técnica**   technique
técnico, -a   technical
tecnológico, -a   technological
el **tejido**   textile, weaving
el **teléfono**   telephone
    llamar por teléfono   to telephone,
      call by telephone

número de teléfono telephone number

por (el) teléfono by (on the) telephone

la **telepatía** telepathy

la **televisión** television, TV

programa de televisión television program

el **televisor** television set

el **tema** subject, theme, topic

temer to fear

la **temperatura** temperature

el **templo** temple

temprano early

la **tendencia** tendency

tener to have (*possess*), hold; *in pret.* get, receive

aquí lo tienes (tiene Ud.) here it is

¿cuántos años tiene (él)? how old is (he)?

no tener razón to be wrong

¿qué tiene (él)? what's the matter (what's wrong) with (him)?

tener . . . años to be . . . years old

tener en cuenta to bear in mind

tener la culpa to be at fault, be to blame

tener lugar to take place

tener mucho gusto en to be very glad (pleased) to

tener que + *inf.* to have to (must) + *inf.*

tener razón to be right

tener suerte to be lucky

tuve (una carta) I got *or* received (a letter)

Tenochtitlán *Aztec capital on site of present Mexico City*

la **tensión** tension

la **teoría** theory

Tepotzotlán *town about 30 miles north of Mexico City*

tercer *used for* **tercero** *before m. sing. nouns*

tercero, -a third

por tercera vez for the third time

el **tercio** third

terminar to end, finish, terminate

el **término** term

el **territorio** territory

el **texto** text

libro de texto text, textbook

ti *pron.* you (*fam.*), yourself (*after prep.*)

la **tía** aunt

el **tiempo** time (*in general sense*); tense; weather; half (*of a game*)

al poco tiempo after (in) a short time

con el tiempo in (in the course of) time

¿cuánto tiempo? how long (much time)?

en tiempo de at (in) the time of

hace tiempo for a long time, a long time ago

hacer buen (mal) tiempo to be good (bad) weather

(llegar) a tiempo (to arrive) on time

más tiempo more time, longer

mucho tiempo long, a long time

¿qué tiempo hace? what kind of weather is it?

la **tienda** store, shop

la **tierra** land, earth

el **tinte** dye, dyeing

tintóreo, -a dyeing, tinctorial

el **tío** uncle; *pl.* uncle(s) and aunt(s)

típicamente typically

típico, -a typical

el **tipo** type

el **tiro** shot

el **título** title

el **(los) tocadiscos** record player

tocar to play (*music*)

tocarle a uno to fall to one's lot, be one's turn

todavía still, yet

todavía no not yet

todo, -a all, every; *pl.* all, all of them, everybody, everyone; *pron.* all, everything

sobre todo above all, especially

toda la (lección) all the (the whole) lesson

todas las noches (tardes) every night (afternoon)

todos (-as) ellos (-as) *or* **ellos (-as)**
todos (-as)   all of them, they all
todos los (días)   every (day)
todos nosotros   all of us, we all
tomar   to take, eat, drink
Tomás   Thomas, Tom
el **tomate**   tomato
la **tonada**   air, song
el **tono**   tone
el **tormento**   torment, anguish, torture
total   total, entire
trabajar   to work
trabajar mucho   to work hard (much)
el **trabajo**   work
la **tradición** (*pl.* **tradiciones**)   tradition
tradicional   traditional
la **traducción**   translation
ejercicio de traducción   translation exercise
traducir   to translate
para traducir al español   to translate into Spanish
traer   to bring
trágico, -a   tragic
la **traición**   treachery
traicionar   to betray
el **traidor**   traitor
el **traje**   suit
la **transformación**   transformation, change
transformar   to transform, change
la **transparencia**   transparency, slide
el **tratado**   treaty
tratar (**de** + *obj.*)   to treat (of), deal (with)
tratar de + *inf.*   to try to
tratarse de   to be a question of
través: a — de   across, through
treinta   thirty
treinta (y seis)   thirty(-six)
tres   three
la **tribu**   tribe
tributario, -a   of (pertaining to) taxation
triste   sad
tristemente   sadly
triunfante   triumphant

triunfar   to triumph
el **triunfo**   triumph
el **trono**   throne
la **tropa**   troop
tropical   tropical
el **trópico**   tropic(s), tropical region
tu   your (*fam.*)
tú   you (*fam.*)
el **tubo**   tube
tuyo, -a *adj.*   your (*fam.*), of yours
(el) tuyo, (la) tuya, (los) tuyos, (las) tuyas *pron.*   yours

U

U   or (*used for* **o** *before* **o-, ho-**)
Ud(s). = **usted(es)**   you (*polite*)
último, -a   last (*in a series*), latest
en estos últimos días   during these last few days
de los últimos años   of the last (past) few years
en los últimos años   during (in) the last few years, recently
por último   finally, ultimately
el **ultraísmo**   ultraism (*literary type of the 20th century*)
un, una, uno   a, an, one
hasta la una   until one o'clock
uno (-a) a otro (-a)   (to) one another, each other
la **unidad**   unity
unido, -a   united
los Estados Unidos   the United States
Naciones Unidas   United Nations
la **unificación**   unification
la **unión**   union
unirse a   to join, unite with
universal   universal
la **universidad**   university
periódico de la universidad   university newspaper
universitario, -a   university
unos, -as   some, any, a few, several; a pair of; about (*quantity*)
unos (-as) a otros (-as)   (to) one another, each other

la **urbanización**   urbanization, city growth (planning)
urgente   urgent
el **Uruguay**   Uruguay
uruguayo, -a (*also noun*)   Uruguayan
usar   to use
el **uso**   use
usted   you (*polite*)
útil   useful
utópico, -a   Utopian

V

las **vacaciones**   vacation
la **vacuidad**   emptiness, vacuity
valenciano, -a   Valencian, native of Valencia (Spain)
valer   to be worth
más vale (**vale más**)   it is better
valer más   to be better
valiente   valiant, brave
valioso, -a   valuable
el **valor**   value; valor, courage
el **valle**   valley
vamos   we are going, let's go
vamos a + *inf.*   we are going to, let's + *verb*
vanguardista (*m. and f.*)   vanguardist (*term applied to many "new" movements in the 20th century*)
vano: en —,   in vain
variado, -a   varied, diverse
variar   to vary
la **variedad**   variety
varios, -as   several, various
vasco, -a   Basque (*of northern Spain*)
el **vaso**   glass
vaso para agua   water glass
vasto, -a   vast, huge, very large
Vd(s). = **usted(es)**   you (*polite*)
el **vecino**   neighbor
la **vegetación**   vegetation
veinte   twenty
vencer   to conquer, overcome
el **vendaval**   windstorm
la **vendedora**   vendor (*woman*)

vender   to sell
venerar   to venerate
venezolano, -a   Venezuelan
venir (**a** + *inf.*)   to come (to)
(**el verano**) **que viene**   next (summer)
venir + *pres. part.*   to be (*progressive form*) + *pres. part.*
venir a ser   to come to be, become
la **ventana**   window
la **ventanilla**   ticket window
ver   to see; *reflex.* be (seen)
a ver   let's see
nos vemos   we'll be seeing each other
Veracruz   *city on Gulf of Mexico*
el **verano**   summer
veras: de —,   really, truly
el **verbo**   verb
la **verdad**   truth
es verdad   it is true
¿(no es) verdad?   isn't it (true)? aren't (you)? doesn't (he)?
verdadero, -a   true, real
vergonzoso, -a   shameful
la **vergüenza**   shame
tener vergüenza   to be ashamed
la **versatilidad**   versatility
el **vestíbulo**   vestibule, lobby, hall
el **vestido**   dress
vestir (**i, i**)   to dress (*someone*); *reflex.* dress oneself, get dressed
la **vez** (*pl.* **veces**)   time (*in a series*)
a veces   at times
alguna vez   some time, ever, (at) any time
dos veces   twice, two times
en vez de   instead of, in place of
muchas veces   often, many times
otra vez   again, another time
por primera (**tercera**) **vez**   for the first (third) time
tal vez   perhaps
el **viaje**   trip, journey; *pl.* travels, journeys
hacer un viaje   to take (make) a trip
el **viajero**   traveler
Vicente   Vincent
el **vicio**   vice, bad habit

la **víctima**   victim
la **victoria**   victory
la **vida**   life
    el nivel de vida   standard of living
  viejo, -a   old
el **viento**   wind
    hacer (mucho) viento   to be (very) windy
el **(los) viernes**   (on) Friday(s)
el **vigor**   vigor, strength
la **violencia**   violence
  violeta (*m. and f.*)   violet
la **Virgen** (*pl.* **Vírgenes**)   Virgin
el **virreinato**   viceroyalty
el **virrey**   viceroy
la **visión**   vision, view
la **visita**   visit
  visitar   to visit, call on
la **vista**   sight, view
    hasta la vista   I'll see you later, until I see you
  visual   visual
la **vitalidad**   vitality
la **vivienda**   dwelling, house
  vivir   to live
el **vocabulario**   vocabulary
la **vocal**   vowel
el **voluntario**   volunteer
  volver (ue)   to return, come back; turn
    volver a (levantar)   (to lift) again
    volver las espaldas a   to turn one's back on, reject
    volverse   to become
    vuelvo en seguida   I'll be right back, I'll return at once

vosotros, -as *pron.*   you (*fam. pl.*), to you, yourselves
la **voz** (*pl.* **voces**)   voice
  en voz alta   aloud
la **vuelta**   return
    dar una vuelta   to take a walk (stroll)
  vuestro, -a *adj.*   your (*fam. pl.*), of yours
    (el) vuestro, (la) vuestra, (los) vuestros, (las) vuestras *pron.*   yours

Y

y   and
ya   already, now, soon, presently, then; *sometimes used for emphasis and not translated*
  no es ya   (he) is no longer
  ya es la hora   the hour is over
  ¡ya lo creo!   I should say so! of course!
  ya no   no longer
yo   I
Yucatán   Yucatan (*peninsula, eastern Mexico*)

Z

Zacatecas   *capital of the state of Zacatecas, Mexico*
el **zapateado**   clog (tap) dance
el **zapato**   shoe
la **zona**   zone

VOCABULARY

ENGLISH–SPANISH

A

a, an   un, una; *often not translated*
abandon   abandonar
able: be —,   poder
about *prep.*   de, acerca de, sobre, (*before pl. numerals*) unos, -as
    at about   (*time*) a eso de
    be about to   estar para
    it was about (five o'clock)   serían (las cinco)
absent   ausente
abuse   el abuso
accept   aceptar
accompanied by   acompañado, -a de
accompany   acompañar
ache   doler (ue)
    (my) head aches   (me) duele la cabeza, (tengo) dolor de cabeza
acquire   adquirir (ie)
across: run —,   encontrarse (ue) con
activity   la actividad
admire   admirar
advise   aconsejar
afraid: be — (that)   tener miedo (de que)
after *prep.*   después de; (*in giving time*) y
    after a short while (time)   al poco rato (tiempo)
    at a quarter after (eight)   a las (ocho) y cuarto
    it is a quarter after (nine)   son las (nueve) y cuarto
    shortly after   poco después de
afternoon   la tarde
    all afternoon   toda la tarde
    good afternoon   buenas tardes
    (yesterday) afternoon   (ayer) por la tarde
afterward(s) *adv.*   después
    shortly afterward(s)   poco después

against   contra
ago: (three months) —,   hace (tres meses)
agricultural   agrícola (*m. and f.*)
aid   la ayuda
air   (*music*) la tonada
airport   el aeropuerto
all   todo, -a
    all (day)   todo (el día)
    not at all bad   (no) . . . nada malo, -a
along with   junto con
already   ya
also   también
although   aunque
always   siempre
America   América
    Central America   Centroamérica
    Latin America   la América latina
    South America   la América del Sur
    Spanish America   la América española (hispana), Hispanoamérica
    the Americas   las Américas
American   americano, -a
    American States   los Estados Americanos
    Central American   centroamericano, -a
    South American   sudamericano, -a
    Spanish American   hispanoamericano, -a
among   entre
amuse   divertir (ie, i)
analyze   analizar
and   y, (*before* i-, hi-, *but not* hie-) e
    both . . . and   tanto . . . como
Andes   los Andes
Ann   Ana
another   otro, -a
    (visit) one another   (visitar)se
    (write) to one another   (escribir)se

any *adj. and pron.*   alguno, -a, *(before m. sing. nouns)* algún, *(after negative)* ninguno, -a (ningún); *often not translated*
  any man (**at all**)   cualquier hombre
  at any rate   de todos modos
anyone   alguien, *(after negative or comparative)* nadie
anything   algo, alguna cosa, *(after negative)* nada, ninguna cosa
appear   aparecer, surgir
April   abril
architectural   arquitectónico, -a
architecture   la arquitectura
Argentina   la Argentina
Argentine *adj. and noun*   argentino, -a
arise   surgir
  (**it**) **is gradually arising**   va surgiendo
army   el ejército
arrange   arreglar
arrival   la llegada
arrive   llegar (a + *obj.*)
  arrive home   llegar a casa
  arrive in (**at**)   llegar a
  arrive on time   llegar a tiempo
art   el arte; *pl.* las artes
  art (**exhibition**)   (la exhibición) de arte
  these popular arts   estas artes populares
Arthur   Arturo
article   el artículo
artist   el artista
artistic   artístico, -a
as   como, tan; que
  as + *adj. or adv.* + **as**   tan . . . como
  as if   como si
  just as   así como
  serve as (**a**)   servir (i, i) de
  so much (**many**) + *noun* + **as**   tanto, -a (-os, -as) . . . como
  the same . . . as   el mismo (la misma) . . . que
ask   *(question)* preguntar; *(request)* pedir (i, i)
  ask for   pedir (i, i)
  I did not ask him (**it**)   no se lo pregunté
association   la asociación
at   a, en
  at about   a eso de
  at home   en casa
attain   conseguir (i, i)

attend   asistir a
attention   la atención
August   agosto
aunt   la tía
authentic   auténtico, -a
author   el autor
awaken   *(someone)* despertar (ie)
away: right —,   ahora mismo
Aztec   el azteca

B

back   *(soccer)* el defensa, *(body)* la espalda
  turn one's back on (**one**)   volver (ue) las espaldas a (uno)
bad   malo, -a, *(before m. sing. nouns)* mal
  not at all bad   (no) . . . nada malo, -a
bank   el banco
Barbara   Bárbara
barbarism   la barbarie
bargain   la ganga
baroque   barroco, -a
  the Baroque   el barroco
basis   la base
  serve as a basis   servir (i, i) de base
battle   la batalla
be   estar, ser; encontrarse (ue), hallarse; *(visible phenomena)* haber; *(weather)* hacer
  be able   poder
  be about to   estar para
  be afraid (**that**)   tener miedo (de que)
  be at fault   tener la culpa
  be better   ser mejor, valer más
  be fortunate   tener suerte
  be good weather   hacer buen tiempo
  be hungry (**thirsty**)   tener hambre (sed)
  be in a hurry   tener prisa
  be necessary to   haber que (ser necesario *or* preciso) + *inf.*
  be to, be supposed to   haber de + *inf.*
  be (**very**) **lucky**   tener (mucha) suerte
  be (**very**) **sleepy**   tener (mucho) sueño
  be (**very**) **windy**   hacer (mucho) viento
  here (**it**) **is**   aquí (lo) tienes (tiene Ud.)
  isn't it (**he**)**?**   ¿(no es) verdad?
  it was about five o'clock   serían las cinco

that is (to say)   es decir
there has (have) been   ha habido
there is (are)   hay
there is probably   habrá
there was (were)   había
there would be   habría
what time can it be?   ¿qué hora será?
bear in mind   tener en cuenta
beautiful   bonito, -a, hermoso, -a, bello, -a
because   porque
become + *noun*   hacerse, llegar (venir) a
ser, volverse (ue)
bed   la cama
  go to bed   acostarse (ue)
  put to bed   acostar (ue)
  stay in bed   guardar cama
before *prep.*   antes de; *conj.* antes (de) que
begin (to)   comenzar (ie) (a + *inf.*),
empezar (ie) (a + *inf.*)
believe   creer
  believe so   creer que sí
besides *prep.*   además de
best   mejor
  the best thing   lo mejor
betray   traicionar
better   mejor
  be better   ser mejor, valer más
Betty   Isabel
block   (*city*) la cuadra
blouse   la blusa
blow   el golpe
  death blow   golpe de muerte
blue   azul
  the blue one (*m.*)   el azul
book   el libro
bookstore   la librería
  at the bookstore   en la librería
born: be —,   nacer
both   los (las) dos
  both . . . and   tanto . . . como
boy   el muchacho
brand   la marca
breakfast   el desayuno
  take (eat) breakfast   desayunarse, tomar
el desayuno
brilliant   brillante
bring   traer
brother   el hermano

build   construir
building   el edificio
burn   quemar
bureaucratic   burocrático, -a
bus   el autobús
  by bus   en autobús
  the ten-o'clock bus   el autobús de las
  diez
business *adj.*   comercial
  business firm   las casa comercial
but   pero, (*after negative*) sino, (*after negative
  before inflected verb form*) sino que
  not only . . . but also   no sólo . . . sino
  también
buy   comprar
by   por, de, para
  by (plane)   en (avión)
  by the end of   para fines de
  by the way   a propósito
  by working   trabajando

C

café   el café
call   llamar
camera   la cámara
  (movie) camera   cámara (de cine)
can   poder, (*mental ability*) saber
car   el coche
card   (*postal*) la tarjeta
career   la carrera
Caroline   Carolina
carry out   realizar, llevar a cabo
cease to   dejar de + *inf.*
cent: per —,   por ciento
center   el centro, el foco
  Student Center   el Centro de Estudiantes
central   central
  Central America   Centroamérica
  Central American   centroamericano, -a
century   el siglo
ceramics   la cerámica
certain: (a) —,   cierto, -a
champion   el campeón (*pl.* campeones)
championship   el campeonato
change   el cambio
  change clothes   mudarse de ropa

character   el carácter (*pl.* caracteres)
characteristic   la característica
Charles   Carlos
chat   charlar
check   revisar
children   los niños
chocolate   el chocolate
choose   escoger
church   la iglesia
  to church   a la iglesia
city   la ciudad
  Mexico City   la ciudad de México, México, D.F.
civilization   la civilización (*pl.* civilizaciones)
civilizing   civilizador, -ora
class   la clase
  middle class   la clase media
  Spanish class   la clase de español
  to class   a clase
classmate   el compañero (la compañera) de clase
classroom   la sala de clase
clean   limpiar
clerk   el dependiente
close   cerrar (ie)
closed   cerrado, -a
clothes   la ropa
  change clothes   mudarse de ropa
coach   el entrenador
coast   la costa
coffee   el café
cold *adj.*   frío, -a
cold   el frío, (*disease*) el resfriado
  be cold   (*living beings*) tener frío
  be (very) cold   (*weather*) hacer (mucho) frío
collaborate   colaborar
colonizer   el colonizador
colony   la colonia
column   la columna
come   venir
  come to (have)   venir *or* llegar a (tener)
compete   competir (i, i)
composer   el compositor
composition   la composición (*pl.* composiciones)

concentrated   concentrado, -a
concern   la preocupación
concert   el concierto
  musical concert   el concierto de música
condemn   condenar
  condemn to death   condenar a muerte
condition   la condición (*pl.* condiciones)
confusion   la confusión
conquer   conquistar, vencer
conqueror   el conquistador
conquest   la conquista
consider   considerar
  he has been considered   ha sido considerado
  he is considered as   se le considera como
contemporary   contemporáneo, -a
continent   el continente
continue   seguir (i, i), continuar
  (he) continues being (to be)   sigue (continúa) siendo
contribute (to)   contribuir (a)
contribution   la contribución (*pl.* contribuciones)
cool   fresco, -a; (*m. noun with* **hacer**)
  be cool   (*weather*) hacer fresco
cooperation   la cooperación
cost   costar (ue)
could   podía, podría, pudo
country   el campo, (*nation*) el país, (*homeland*) la patria
  country house   la casa de campo
  mother country   la madre patria
course   el curso
courteous   cortés (*pl.* corteses)
cousin   el primo, la prima
create   crear
creation   la creación
credit   el crédito
  foreign credit   el crédito exterior
cross   cruzar, atravesar (ie)
cultivate   cultivar
cultural   cultural
culture   la cultura
current   la corriente
custom   la costumbre
cut   cortar
Cuzco   el Cuzco

D

dance el baile
day el día
  all day todo el día
  every day todos los días
deal: a great —, mucho, muchísimo
dear querido, -a
death la muerte
  condemn to death condenar a muerte
  death blow el golpe de muerte
December diciembre
decorate decorar
dedicate oneself to dedicarse a
deep profundo, -a, hondo, -a
defeat derrotar
definite definido, -a
democracy la democracia
demonstrate demostrar (ue)
deny negar (ie)
describe describir
desert el desierto
determine determinar
develop desarrollar
development el desarrollo
dialogue el diálogo
dictator el dictador
die morir (ue, u)
different diferente, diverso, -a, distinto, -a
difficult difícil
discover descubrir
distinct distinto, -a
distinguished distinguido, -a
distribution la distribución
diversify diversificar
division el fraccionamiento
do hacer; *not translated as auxiliary*
  don't (they)? ¿(no es) verdad?
  what can I do for you? ¿en qué puedo servirle(s)?
doctor el médico
dollar (*U.S.*) el dólar
domestic doméstico, -a
door la puerta
Dorothy Dorotea
doubt dudar
down: sit —, sentarse (ie)

downtown el centro
  (be) downtown (estar) en el centro
  (go) downtown (ir) al centro
drawing el dibujo
dream el sueño; soñar (ue)
  dream of soñar con
dress el vestido; **dress (oneself)** vestirse (i, i)
dressed: get —, vestirse (i, i)
drive conducir
drugstore la farmacia
due: be — to deberse a
during durante

E

each cada
  (see) each other (ver)se
early temprano
easily fácilmente
easy fácil
eat comer
  eat (take) breakfast desayunarse
  eat (take) lunch almorzar (ue), tomar el almuerzo
  eat supper cenar
economic económico, -a
Ecuadorian ecuatoriano, -a
educate educar
education la educación
educator el educador
eight ocho
either o, (*after negative*) tampoco
elders: their —, los mayores
election la elección (*pl.* elecciones)
element el elemento
eleven once
emperor el emperador
empire el imperio
encounter encontrar (ue)
encourage fomentar
end el fin; terminar
  by the end of para fines de
  his military work ended terminada su obra militar
enemy el enemigo
enlarge aumentar

enormous   enorme
enter   entrar (en + *obj.*)
especially   especialmente, sobre todo
essay   el ensayo
essayist   el ensayista
establish   establecer
establishment   el establecimiento
Europe   Europa
European   europeo, -a
even *adv.*   aun, aún
   even though *conj.*   aunque
ever   jamás, alguna vez, (*after negative*)
   nunca, jamás, (*at any time*) alguna vez
every   todo, -a
   every (day)   todos (los días)
examination   el examen (*pl.* exámenes)
example   el ejemplo
exceed   pasar de, exceder
excellent   excelente
except   menos
exciting   emocionante
excursion   la excursión
   take (make) the excursion   hacer la
      excursión
exercise   el ejercicio
exhibition   la exhibición (*pl.* exhibiciones)
exist   existir
expedition   la expedición
expensive   caro, -a
exploitation   la explotación
explore   explorar
export   la exportación
expression   la expresión
extraordinary   extraordinario, -a
extremely   sumamente
eye   el ojo

F

fail   fracasar
   (not) to fail to   (no) dejar de + *inf.*
faithful   fiel
faithfully   fielmente
fall   el otoño
fall to one's lot   tocarle a uno
famous   famoso, -a, distinguido, -a, ilustre
fast   rápido, -a

father   el padre, el papá
fault   la culpa
   be at fault   tener la culpa
February   febrero
feel like (studying)   tener ganas de (es-
      tudiar)
   feel well   sentirse (ie, i) bien
feeling   el sentimiento
few: (a) —,   pocos, -as, unos, -as
   the last few years   los últimos años
fifteen   quince
fifty   cincuenta
figure   la figura
fill (with)   llenar (de)
film   la película
finally   por fin, por último
find   encontrar (ue), hallar
   find out (*in pret.*)   saber
finish   terminar, concluir
firm   la casa
   business firm   casa comercial
first   primero, -a, (*before m. sing. nouns*)
      primer
   first floor   el piso bajo
   the first one (*m.*)   el primero
first-rate   de primer orden
five   cinco
flee   huir
floor   el piso
   first floor   el piso bajo
Florida   la Florida
flower   la flor
following   siguiente
food   la comida
football   el fútbol
   football championship   el campeonato
      de fútbol
for   para, por
   for (an hour)   hace (una hora)
force   la fuerza
foreign   (*credit*) exterior
forest   el bosque, la selva
fortunate: be —,   tener suerte
   how fortunate (our team) is!   ¡qué
      suerte tiene (nuestro equipo)!
found   fundar
founder   el fundador
fountain   la fuente

four   cuatro
free   libre
freedom   la libertad
friend   el amigo, la amiga
friendship   la amistad
from   de, desde
fun: make — of   burlarse de
  make fun of each other   burlarse uno de otro
futility   la futilidad
future   el futuro

G

game   (*match*) el partido
  football game   partido de fútbol
garden   el jardín
gaucho *adj.*   gauchesco, -a; *noun* el gaucho
general   el general
generally   generalmente
generation   la generación (*pl.* generaciones)
gentleman   el señor
geographical   geográfico, -a
George   Jorge
get   conseguir (i, i), obtener
  get dressed   vestirse (i, i)
  get up   levantarse
gift   el regalo
girl   la muchacha
give   dar
glad: be — to   alegrarse de
  how glad we are!   ¡cuánto nos alegramos!
  how glad they are to . . .!   ¡cuánto se alegran de + *inf.*!
glove   el guante
go   ir (a + *inf.*)
  go home   ir a casa
  go out (of)   salir (de + *obj.*)
  go shopping   ir de compras
  go to bed   acostarse (ue)
  let's not go   no vayamos
goalkeeper   el portero
gold   el oro
  fill with gold   llenar de oro
  gold and silver work   la orfebrería
  gold (watch)   (reloj) de oro

good   bueno, -a, (*before m. sing. nouns*) buen
  good afternoon   buenas tardes
  have a (very) good time   divertirse (ie, i) (mucho)
Gothic   gótico, -a
  the Gothic   el gótico
government   el gobierno
gradually   *use* ir + *pres. part.*
  (it) is gradually arising   va surgiendo
graduate   graduarse
grandfather   el abuelo
great   gran (*used before sing. noun*); *pl.* grandes
  a great deal   mucho, muchísimo
  a great part of   gran parte de
greatest   mayor
green   verde
  the green one (*f.*)   la verde
greet   saludar
guitar   la guitarra

H

hair   el pelo
  the one (*m.*) **with red hair**   el del pelo rojo
half   medio, -a
  a half hour   media hora
hand   la mano
hand (over)   entregar
happy   contento, -a, feliz (*pl.* felices)
hard-fought   reñido, -a
harm   dañar
hat   el sombrero
have   tener; (*auxiliary*) haber
  have (*causative*) hacer *or* mandar + *inf.*
  have (*indir. command*)·   que + *pres. subj.*
  have a headache   tener dolor de cabeza, doler (ue) (a uno) la cabeza
  have a (very) good time   divertirse (ie, i) (mucho)
  have just   acabar de + *inf.*
  have time to   tener tiempo para + *inf.*
  have to   tener que + *inf.*
he   él
head   la cabeza
  my head aches   me duele la cabeza, tengo dolor de cabeza

headache: does he have a —?   ¿le duele la cabeza? ¿tiene dolor de cabeza?
hear   oír
  hear about   oír hablar de
  hear that   oír decir que
heavens!   ¡por Dios!
Helen   Elena
help   ayudar (a + *inf.*)
  help one another   ayudarse
Henry   Enrique
her *adj.*   su(s); su(s) *or* el (la, los, las) . . . de ella
her *dir. obj.*   la; *indir. obj.* le; *after prep.* ella
here   aquí
  here (it) is   aquí (lo) tiene Ud. (tienes)
hero   el héroe
hers *pron.*   (el) suyo, (la) suya, (los) suyos, (las) suyas *or* el (la, los, las) de ella
  of hers *adj.*   suyo(s), -a(s), de ella
highway   la carretera
him *dir. and indir. obj.*   le; *after prep.* él
his *adj.*   su(s); su(s) *or* el (la, los, las) . . . de él; *pron.* (el) suyo, (la) suya, (los) suyos, (las) suyas, *or* el (la, los, las) de él
  of his   suyo(s), -a(s), de él
hold   tener
home   la casa
  (be) at home   (estar) en casa
  (go) home   (ir) a casa
  leave home   salir de casa
hope   la esperanza; esperar
  his hopes to   sus esperanzas de + *inf.*
horror   el horror
horse   el caballo
hot *adj.*   caliente
hour   la hora
  (we have been here) for an hour   hace una hora (que estamos aquí)
house   la casa
  country house   casa de campo
how?   ¿cómo?
  how do you like (the idea)?   ¿qué le (te) parece (la idea)?
  how long?   ¿cuánto tiempo?
  how old is (he)?   ¿cuántos años tiene (él)?
  how + *adj. or adv.*!   ¡qué!
  how + *verb*!   ¡cuánto!

humanity   la humanidad
humble   humilde
hundred: one —,   ciento, (*before noun*) cien
hungry: be —,   tener hambre
hurry: be in a —,   tener prisa
hurry up   darse prisa, apurarse
hurt   doler (ue)
  does your (throat) hurt?   ¿le duele a Ud. (la garganta)?

I

I   yo
ice   el hielo
if   si
  as if   como si
ill   enfermo, -a, malo, -a
illiteracy   el analfabetismo
imagine   imaginarse
important   importante
  it is important   es importante, importa
impose   imponer
impossible   imposible
in   en, de, a, por; (*after a superlative*) de
  in order to   para
Inca *m. and f. adj.*   inca; *noun* el inca
incorporate (into)   incorporar (a)
  be incorporated into   incorporarse a
increase   el aumento; aumentar
independence   la independencia
Indian *adj.*   indio, -a; *noun* el indio
Indianist   indianista (*m. and f.*)
industrialization   la industrialización
Inez   Inés
influence   la influencia
inhabitant   el habitante
initiate   iniciar
insist that   insistir en que
inspiration   la inspiración
instead of   en vez de
institution   la institución (*pl.* instituciones)
integration   la integración
intend   pensar (ie) + *inf.*
intensely   intensamente
interest   el interés
interesting   interesante
international   internacional

interpret   interpretar
into   a, en
introduce   introducir
introduction   la introducción
invader   el invasor
investments   las inversiones
invite   invitar (a + *inf.*)
island   la isla
it *dir. obj.*   lo (*m. and neuter*), la (*f.*); *indir.*
  obj. le; (*usually omitted as subject*) él (*m.*) ella
  (*f.*); *after prep.* él (*m.*), ella (*f.*)
item: news —,   la noticia
its   su(s)

J

Jane   Juanita
  to Jane's   a casa de Juanita
January   enero
job   el puesto
John   Juan
Johnny   Juanito
join   reunirse con
journalist   el periodista
July   julio
June   junio
just as   así como
just: have —,   acabar de + *inf.*

K

king   el rey
  the City of Kings   la Ciudad de los Reyes
know   (*facts*) saber, (*be acquainted with*)
  conocer
  know how to   saber + *inf.*

L

laboratory   el laboratorio
lack   la falta; faltar
  be lacking   faltar
  is there anything lacking?   ¿falta algo?
lady: young —,   la señorita
land   la tierra
landscape   el paisaje

language   la lengua
large   grande
  larger ones (*m.*)   los más grandes
largely   en gran parte
last   pasado, -a, (*in a series*) último, -a
  last night   anoche
  last time   la última vez
  the (this) last one (*m.*)   el (este) último
  the last few years   los últimos años
late   tarde
later   más tarde, después
Latin   latino, -a
  Latin America   la América latina
latter: the —,   éste, ésta (-os, -as)
law   la ley
lawyer   el abogado
leader   el jefe
league   la liga
learn   aprender (a + *inf.*)
  (they) are (gradually) learning   van
  aprendiendo
learned   culto, -a
  the learned one (*f.*)   la culta
leave   salir (de + *obj.*), partir (de + *obj.*),
  irse, marcharse (de + *obj.*); (*trans.*) dejar
  leave for   salir (partir) para
  leave home   salir de casa
lecture   la conferencia
lecturer   el conferenciante
less   menos
lesson   la lección (*pl.* lecciones)
let   dejar, permitir
  let me + *verb*   déjeme (permítame) Ud.
  or déjame (permíteme) + *inf.*
  let's (let us) + *verb*   vamos a + *inf.*, *or*
  first pl. pres. subj.
  let's not go   no vayamos
  let's see   (vamos) a ver
library   la biblioteca
life   la vida
light   la luz (*pl.* luces)
like   como; gustar, (*person*) querer (a)
  how do you like (the idea)?   ¿qué le
  (te) parece (la idea)?
  (I) should like   (me) gustaría, (yo)
  quisiera
  like better (more)   gustar más, preferir
  (ie, i)

listen (**to**)   escuchar
literature   la literatura
literary   literario, -a
little *adj.*   (*size*) pequeño, -a, (*quantity*) poco, -a
  a little   un poco
live   vivir
living: standard of —,   el nivel de vida
long   largo, -a
  how long (**have you been here**)**?**   ¿cuánto tiempo hace (que Ud. está aquí)?
  wait longer   esperar más
  (**we had been waiting**) **for a long time**   hacía mucho tiempo (que esperábamos)
look at   mirar
look for   buscar
lose   perder (ie)
lot: fall to one's —,   tocarle a uno
Louis   Luis
Louise   Luisa
love   querer (a)
  love each other   quererse
  love (**for**)   el amor (por)
lucky: be (**very**) **—,**   tener (mucha) suerte
lunch   el almuerzo
  eat (**take**) **lunch**   almorzar (ue), tomar el almuerzo
  for lunch   para el almuerzo

M

machine   la máquina
made *adj.*   hecho, -a
magazine   la revista
maintain   mantener
make   (*brand*) la marca; hacer
  make (**have**) + *verb*   hacer (mandar) + *inf.*
  make fun of   burlarse de
  make the trip   hacer el viaje (la excursión)
man   el hombre
  the poor man   el pobre (hombre)
manufacture   manufacturar
many   muchos, -as
  as (**so**) **many** + *noun* + **as**   tantos, -as ... como

so many people   tanta gente, tantas personas
map   el mapa
march   la marcha; marchar
March   marzo
Margaret   Margarita
market   el mercado
Martha   Marta
marvelous   maravilloso, -a
Mary   María
masses   las masas
masterpiece   la obra maestra
matter: that — (**of John**)   lo (de Juan)
  what's the matter with...? ¿qué tiene ...? ¿qué le pasa a ...?
may (*indir. command*)   (*wish*) que + *pres. subj.*; *sign of pres. subj.*; poder
  it may be that   puede (ser) que
  you may sit down   Ud(s). puede(n) sentarse
May   mayo
me *dir. and indir. obj.*   me; *after prep.* mí
  with me   conmigo
means: by — of   por medio de
meet   (*gather*) reunirse, (*be introduced to*) conocer
meeting   la reunión (*pl.* reuniones)
member   el miembro
Mexican   mexicano, -a
  the Mexican ones   los mexicanos
Mexico   México
  Mexico City   la ciudad de México, México, D.F.
Michael   Miguel
middle   medio, -a
  middle class   la clase media
midnight   la medianoche
military *adj.*   militar
mind: bear in —,   tener en cuenta
mine *pron.*   (el) mío, (la) mía, (los) míos, (las) mías
  of mine *adj.*   mío(s), -a(s)
minute   el minuto
miserable   miserable
Miss   (la) señorita
Mississippi River   el río Misisipí
model   el modelo

modern   moderno, -a
modernism   el modernismo
modernist *adj.*   modernista (*m. and f.*)
moment   el momento
money   el dinero
month   el mes
  next month   el mes que viene, el mes próximo
  three months ago   hace tres meses
moon   la luna
  the moon is shining   hay luna
Moorish: the Spanish —,   (*architecture*) el mudéjar
more   más
morning   la mañana
  tomorrow morning   mañana por la mañana
most   más
  most (of)   la mayor parte de, la mayoría de
mother   la madre, la mamá
  mother country   la madre patria
motivation   la motivación
mountains   las montañas, la sierra
movement   el movimiento
movie   el cine
  at the movie   en el cine
  movie camera   cámara de cine
Mr.   (el) señor, Sr.
Mrs.   (la) señora, Sra.
much *adj.*   mucho, -a; *adv.* mucho
  so much as *adv.*   tanto como
  so much + *noun* (+ **as**)   tanto, -a . . . (como)
  very much *adv.*   mucho, muchísimo
mural *adj.*   mural
muralist *adj.*   muralista (*m. and f.*)
music   la música
musical *adj.*   musical, de música
musician   el músico
must   deber, haber de + *inf.*, tener que + *inf.*; *for probability use future* (*conditional, future perfect*) *or* deber de + *inf.*
  one must (remember)   hay que (recordar)
mutual   mutuo, -a
my   mi(s), mío, -a

N

name   el nombre
  in the name of   en nombre de
nap   la siesta
  take a nap   dormir (ue, u) la siesta
national   nacional
nationalistic   nacionalista (*m. and f.*)
native *adj.*   indígena (*m. and f.*)
nature   la naturaleza
near *prep.*   cerca de
necessary   necesario, -a, preciso, -a
  be necessary to   haber que (ser necesario *or* preciso) + *inf.*
need   necesitar
never   nunca, jamás
nevertheless   sin embargo
new   nuevo, -a
  New Spain   la Nueva España
  New York   Nueva York
news item   la noticia
newspaper   el periódico
next   próximo, -a
  next (month)   (el mes) que viene, (el mes) próximo
night   la noche
  last night   anoche
  tomorrow night   mañana por la noche
nine   nueve
nineteen   diez y nueve, diecinueve
no, not *adv.*   no; *adj.* ninguno, -a, (*before m. sing. nouns*) ningún; *often not translated*
none   ninguno, -a
noon   el mediodía
north   el norte
not   no
  not at all bad   (no) . . . nada malo, -a
notable   notable
note   la nota
nothing   nada, ninguna cosa
  it is nothing serious   no es nada grave
novel   la novela
novelist   el novelista
November   noviembre
now   ahora, ya
nowadays   hoy día
number   el número

O

observe   observar, notar
obtain   conseguir (i, i), obtener
occupy   ocupar
ocean   el océano, el mar
  Pacific Ocean   el Océano Pacífico
o'clock: at (ten) —,   a las (diez)
  before (seven) o'clock   antes de las
  (siete)
  be (nine) o'clock   ser (las nueve)
October   octubre
of   de
  before a quarter of (eight)   antes de
  las (ocho) menos cuarto
off: take —,   (*someone*) quitar, (*oneself*) quitarse
office   la oficina
often   a menudo, muchas veces
old: how — is (he)?   ¿cuántos años tiene
  (él)?
older   mayor
  older people   los mayores
on   en, sobre
  on (Sundays)   los (domingos)
  on the other side of   al otro lado de
  on time   a tiempo
  put on   (*oneself*) ponerse, (*someone*) poner
one   un, uno, una; *indef. subject* se
  one must (remember)   hay que (recordar)
  that one   (*near person addressed*) ése, ésa,
  (*distant*) aquél, aquélla
  the one in (of, with)   el (la) de
  the one(s) who (which, that)   el (la)
  que, *pl.* los (las) que, quien(es) (*persons
  only*)
  the last one   el último, la última
  this one   éste, ésta
  (visit) one another   (visitar)se
  which one(s)?   ¿cuál(es)?
only   solamente, sólo, no ... más que
  not only ... but also   no sólo ... sino
  también
open   abrir
oppose   oponerse a
or   o, (*before* o-, ho-) u
orchestra   la orquesta

order: in — that *conj.*   para que, de manera
  (modo) que
  in order to *prep.*   para
organization   la organización
original   original
other   otro, -a
  (see) each other   (ver)se
  the other one   el otro, la otra
ought to: (I) —,   (yo) debiera
our   nuestro, -a
ours *pron.*   (el) nuestro, (la) nuestra, (los)
  nuestros, (las) nuestras
  of ours *adj.*   nuestro(s), -a(s)
out: drive —,   expulsar
  go out (of)   salir (de + *obj.*)
over   sobre
own: of one's —,   propio, -a
  a life of their own   una vida propia

P

Pacific   Pacífico, -a
package   el paquete
page   la página, (*printing*) la plana
  first page   (*printing*) la primera plana
painter   el pintor
painting   la pintura
Panama   Panamá
parents   los padres, los papás
park   el parque; (*car*) estacionar
part   la parte
  a great part of   gran parte de
  take part   tomar parte
past   pasado, -a; *noun* el pasado
patio   el patio
Paul   Pablo
peace   la paz
peasant   el campesino
pencil   el lápiz (*pl.* lápices)
people   la gente (*requires sing. verb*), el pueblo
  (*requires sing. verb*), las personas; *indef. subject*
  se
  native people   el pueblo indígena
  older people   los mayores
  so many people   tanta gente, tantas
  personas
  young people   los jóvenes

per   por
  per cent   por ciento
perhaps   tal vez, quizá(s), acaso
period   el período, la época
Peru   el Perú
Peruvian   peruano, -a
philosophical   filosófico, -a
photo   la foto
photograph   la fotografía
  take photographs   sacar fotografías
pick up (**one**)   buscar a (uno)
picture   el cuadro, (*image*) la imagen (*pl.* imágenes)
place   el sitio, el lugar
plain   la llanura
plainsman   el llanero
plan   el plan
plane   el avión (*pl.* aviones)
  by plane   en avión
Plateresque   plateresco, -a
  the Plateresque   el plateresco
play   (*game*) jugar (ue), (*music*) tocar, (*a role*) representar
  play the same role . . . as   representar el mismo papel . . . que
player   el jugador
  record player   el (los) tocadiscos
please   (*after request*) por favor
poet   el poeta
poetess   la poetisa
poeticize   poetizar
poetry   la poesía
policy   la política
political   político, -a
pool   (*swimming*) la piscina
poor   pobre
  the poor man   el pobre (hombre)
popular   popular
  the popular one (*f.*)   la popular
population   la población
possession   la posesión
  take possession of   tomar posesión de, apoderarse de
possible   posible
  the soonest possible   lo más pronto posible
post   el puesto
power   el poder

practice   practicar
prefer   preferir (ie, i)
preparation   la preparación
prepare   preparar
present *adj.*   (*present-day*) actual
present   presentar
president   el presidente
pretty   hermoso, -a, bonito, -a, bello, -a
  the prettiest one (*m.*)   el más bonito (hermoso)
prevail   prevalecer
priest   el cura
principal   principal
prisoner   el prisionero
probably   *use future, conditional, or future perfect tense or* deber de + *verb*
  there is probably   habrá
problem   el problema
produce   producir
product   el producto
production   la producción
professor   el profesor, la profesora
program   el programa
progress   el progreso
projector   el proyector
promise   prometer
prose   la prosa
protagonist   el protagonista
protest   la protesta; protestar
provide   proporcionar
provided that *conj.*   con tal (de) que, siempre que
psychological   psicológico, -a
public   público, -a
put   poner
  let's not put on   no nos pongamos
  put in   meter, poner
  put on   (*oneself*) ponerse
  put on   (*someone else*) poner
  put to bed   acostar (ue)

Q

quarter   el cuarto
  at a quarter after (**eight**)   a las (ocho) y cuarto

before a quarter of (eight)   antes de las (ocho) menos cuarto
question   la pregunta

R

radical   radical
radio   (*set*) el radio
rain   llover (ue)
raise   elevar
rapid   rápido, -a
rapidly   rápidamente
rate   el índice
  at any rate   de todos modos
Raymond   Ramón
reach   llegar (a + *obj.*)
read   leer
ready   listo, -a
real   verdadero, -a
realism   el realismo
realize (that)   darse cuenta de (que)
rebel (against)   rebelarse (contra)
rebellion   la rebelión
recall   recordar (ue)
record   (*phonograph*) el disco
  record player   el (los) tocadiscos
recorder: tape —,   la grabadora (de cinta)
red   rojo, -a
  the red ones (*f.*)   las rojas
reform   la reforma
refuse to   negarse (ie) a + *inf.*, *negative pret. of* querer + *inf.*
region   la región
reign   reinar
related: be — to   relacionarse con
relation   la relación (*pl.* relaciones)
relatively   relativamente
religious   religioso, -a
remedy   el remedio
remember   recordar (ue), acordarse (ue) de
repeat   repetir (i, i)
report   el informe
represent   representar
representative   el representante
reproduce   reproducir

republic   la república
resolve   resolver (ue)
resources   los recursos
rest   descansar
return   (*come back*) volver (ue), regresar; (*give back*) devolver (ue)
review   la crítica
revolution   la revolución
revolutionary   revolucionario, -a
rhythm   el ritmo
rich   rico, -a
Richard   Ricardo
right   derecho, -a; *noun* el derecho
  be right   tener razón
  right away   ahora mismo
  to the right   a la derecha
  work for the rights   trabajar por los derechos
river   el río
Robert   Roberto
role   el papel
  play the same role . . . as   representar el mismo papel . . . que
roll   (*film*) el rollo
room   el cuarto
roommate   el compañero (la compañera) de cuarto
rose   la rosa
row   la fila
run across   encontrarse (ue) con
rural   rural

S

same   mismo, -a
  the same . . . as   el mismo (la misma, etc.) . . . que
say   decir
  I should say so!   ¡ya lo creo!
scene   la escena
scholar   el erudito
school   la escuela
sculpture   la escultura
sea   el mar
search   la busca
  in search of   en busca de
seat   sentar (ie)

second　segundo, -a
secretary　la secretaria
section　la sección
　sports section　la sección de deportes
see　ver, observar
　let's see　(vamos) a ver
　see each other　verse
seek　buscar
seem　parecer
select　escoger
sell　vender
semester　el semestre
send　enviar, mandar
　send for　enviar por
sentence　la frase, la oración (*pl.* oraciones)
September　septiembre
series　la serie
serious　grave
　it is nothing serious　no es nada grave
serve　servir (i, i)
　serve as (a)　servir de
set　el aparato
　television set　el televisor
settle　(*oneself*) establecerse
seven　siete
several　varios, -as
she　ella
shining: the moon is —,　hay luna
　the sun is shining　hace (hay) sol
ship　la nave
shirt　la camisa
shoe　el zapato
shopping: go —,　ir de compras
short: after a — while (time)　al poco rato (tiempo)
short story　el cuento
　short story writer　el cuentista
shortly after *prep.*　poco después de
　shortly afterward(s) *adv.*　poco después
should　*sign of cond. and imp. subj.*; (*softened statement*) debiera
show　enseñar (a + *inf.*), mostrar (ue)
side　el lado
　on the other side of　al otro lado de
silver　la plata
　gold and silver work　la orfebrería
sing　cantar
sir　señor

sister　la hermana
sit down　sentarse (ie)
　let's sit down　sentémonos, vamos a sentarnos
six　seis
skate　patinar
sketch　esbozar
ski　el esquí (*pl.* esquíes); esquiar
skill　la maestría
sleep　dormir (ue, u)
sleepy: be very —,　tener mucho sueño
slide　la transparencia, la diapositiva
slowly　despacio
small　pequeño, -a
　the smallest one (*f.*)　la más pequeña
snow　la nieve
so (*with adj. or adv.*)　tan
　believe so　creer que sí
　I should say so!　¡ya lo creo!
　so many people　tanta gente, tantas personas
　so much (as) *adv.*　tanto (como)
　so much (many) + *noun* + **as**　tanto, -a (-os, -as) . . . como
social　social
society　la sociedad
soldier　el soldado
solution　la solución (*pl.* soluciones)
solve　resolver (ue)
some *adj. and pron.*　alguno, -a, (*before m. sing. nouns*) algún; *pl.* algunos, -as, unos, -as; (*before numerals*) unos, -as; *often not translated*
someone　alguien
　someone (of them)　alguno, -a (de ellos, -as)
song　la canción (*pl.* canciones)
soon　pronto
　as soon as *conj.*　en cuanto, así que, luego que
　the soonest possible　lo más pronto posible
sorry: be (very) —,　sentir (ie, i) (mucho)
　how sorry I am . . . !　¡cuánto siento . . . !
source　la fuente
south　el sur
　South America　la América del Sur
　South American　sudamericano, -a
space　el espacio

Spain   España
  New Spain   la Nueva España
Spaniard   el español
Spanish *adj.*   español, -ola; (*language*) el
  español
  in Spanish   en español
  Spanish America   la América española
    (hispana), Hispanoamérica
  Spanish American   hispanoamericano,
    -a
  Spanish class   la clase de español
  Spanish Moorish   (*architecture*) el mudéjar
speak   hablar
spend   (*time*) pasar
spiritual   espiritual
spite: in — of   a pesar de
spontaneous   espontáneo, -a
sports section   la sección de deportes
spring   la primavera
stand out   destacarse
standard   el nivel
  standard of living   nivel de vida
state   el estado
  American States   los Estados Americanos
  United States   los Estados Unidos
stay   quedarse
  stay in bed   guardar cama
step   el paso
  take a step   dar un paso
still   todavía, aun, aún
stimulate   estimular
stop   la parada; parar
store   la tienda
story: short —,   el cuento
strange   extraño, -a
street   la calle
strong   fuerte
structure   la estructura
struggle   la lucha; luchar
  in his struggle with   en lucha con
student   el (la) estudiante, el alumno, la
  alumna
  Student Center   el Centro de Estudiantes
study   estudiar
style   el estilo
succeed in   lograr + *inf.*, conseguir (i, i) +
  inf., llegar (a + *inf.*)
such   tal; tan

such definite rhythms   ritmos tan
  definidos
sufficient   suficiente
suit   el traje
summer   el verano
summit   la cumbre
sun   el sol
  the sun is shining   hace (hay) sol
Sunday   el domingo
  on Sundays   los domingos
supper: eat —,   cenar
suppose   *use future or cond. for conjecture*
supposed: be — to   haber de + *inf.*
sure   seguro, -a
  be sure that   estar seguro, -a de que
surprise   la sorpresa; sorprender
symbol   el símbolo
sympathy (**for**)   la simpatía (por)
symphony   sinfónico, -a
system   el sistema

T

table   la mesa
take   tomar, (*carry*) llevar, (*photos*) sacar
  take a nap   dormir (ue, u) la siesta
  take a step   dar un paso
  take a trip   hacer un viaje *or* una
    excursión
  take a walk   dar un paseo
  take (**eat**) **breakfast**   tomar el desayuno
  take (**eat**) **lunch**   almorzar (ue), tomar el
    almuerzo
  take (**four hours**) **to**   tardar (cuatro
    horas) en + *inf.*
  take off   (*from someone*) quitar
  take off   (*from oneself*) quitarse
  take possession of   apoderarse de, tomar
    posesión de
talk   hablar, charlar
tape   la cinta; grabar
  tape recorder   la grabadora (de cinta)
tastes: (it) —,   está
taxation: of —,   tributario, -a
teacher   el profesor, la profesora
team   el equipo

technical   técnico, -a
telephone   el teléfono
  on the telephone   por teléfono
television set   el televisor
tell   decir
  I shall tell her (**it**)   se lo diré
temperature   la temperatura
ten   diez
tendency   la tendencia
territory   el territorio
textbook   el libro de texto
textile   el tejido
than   que, (*before numeral*) de, (*before clause*)
  del (de la, de los, de las) que, de lo que
thank (**one**) **for**   darle las gracias (a uno)
  por
that *adj.*   (*near person addressed*) ese, esa (-os,
  -as), (*distant*) aquel, aquella (-os, -as); *pron.*
  ése, ésa (-os, -as), aquél, aquélla (-os, -as),
  (*neuter*) eso, aquello; *relative pron.* que
  that is (**to say**)   es decir
  that of   el (la) de
  that which   lo que
  the one(**s**) **that**   el (la, los, las) que
  those that   los (las) que
the   el, la, los, las
theater   el teatro
their *adj.*   su(s), de ellos (-as)
theirs *pron.*   (el) suyo, (la) suya, (los) suyos,
  (las) suyas, *or* el (la, los, las) de ellos (-as)
  of theirs *adj.*   suyo(s), -a(s), de ellos (-as)
them *dir. obj.*   los, las; *indir. obj.* les, se; *after*
  prep. ellos, -as
theme   el tema
then   luego, después
there   (*near person addressed*) ahí, (*distant*)
  allí
  there is (**are**)   hay
  there was (**were**)   había
  there would be   habría
therefore   por eso, por lo tanto
these *adj.*   estos, estas; *pron.* éstos, éstas
they   ellos, ellas, *indef. subject* se
thing   la cosa
  the best thing   lo mejor
think   pensar (ie), creer
  I think it's (*f.*) **wonderful!**   ¡Me parece
  magnífica!

what do you think of . . .?   ¿qué le (te)
  parece . . .?
thinker   el pensador
third *adj.*   tercero, -a; *noun* el tercio
thirsty: be —,   tener sed
this *adj.*   este, esta; *pron.* **this** (**one**) éste,
  ésta, (*neuter*) esto
Thomas   Tomás
those *adj.*   (*near person addressed*) esos (-as),
  (*distant*) aquellos (-as); *pron.* ésos (-as),
  aquéllos (-as)
  those which   los (las) que
  those who   los (las) que, quienes
though: even —,   aunque
thousand: a (**one**) **—,**   mil; *pl.* miles
three   tres
throat   la garganta
  does your throat hurt?   ¿le duele a
  Ud. la garganta?
through   por
throw (**into**)   echar (en, a)
time   (*in general sense*) el tiempo; (*of day*) la
  hora; (*series*) la vez (*pl.* veces)
  after a short time   al poco tiempo
  at any time   (*in a question*) alguna vez
  at times   a veces
  at what time?   ¿a qué hora?
  for the first time   por primera vez
  have a (**very**) **good time**   divertirse
  (ie, i) (mucho)
  have time to   tener tiempo para +
  inf.
  in (**in the course of**) **time**   con el
  tiempo
  last time   la última vez
  on time   a tiempo
  we had been waiting for a long time
  hacía mucho tiempo que esperábamos
  what time can it be?   ¿qué hora
  será?
tired   cansado, -a
to   a, de, con, para, que
  have to   tener que + *inf.*
  to (**Jane's**)   a casa de (Juanita)
today   hoy, hoy día
  of today (**our time**)   de nuestro tiempo
  today's game   el partido de hoy
Tom   Tomás

tomorrow   mañana
  tomorrow morning (night)   mañana por la mañana (noche)
tone   el tono
tonight   esta noche
topcoat   el abrigo
toward(s)   hacia
town   el pueblo
trade   el comercio
traditional   tradicional
traveler   el viajero
trip   el viaje, la excursión
  take (make) the trip   hacer el viaje (la excursión)
triumph   triunfar
true: be —,   ser verdad
try (out)   probar (ue)
  try to   tratar de + *inf.*
tube   el tubo
turn in   entregar
turn off   apagar
turn on   (*radio*) poner
turn one's back on (one)   volver (ue) las espaldas a (uno)
twenty   veinte
two   dos
  the two   los (las) dos
  at two (o'clock)   a las dos
type   el tipo, (*literary*) el género

U

uncle   el tío
Underdogs: The —,   *Los de abajo*
undertake   emprender
unfortunately   por desgracia, desgraciadamente
unification   la unificación
union   la unión
united   unido, -a
  United States   los Estados Unidos
unity   la unidad
university *adj.*   universitario; *noun* la universidad
unjust   injusto, -a
unless *conj.*   a menos que
until *prep.*   hasta; *conj.* hasta que

up: get —,   levantarse
  pick (one) up   buscar (a uno)
  wake up   (*oneself*) despertarse (ie)
upon + *pres. part.*   al + *inf.*
urgent   urgente
us *dir. and indir. obj.*   nos; *after prep.* nosotros, -as
use   usar, emplear
Utopian   utópico, -a

V

vacation   las vacaciones
vain: in —,   en vano
value   el valor
variety   la variedad
various   varios, -as
Venezuelan   venezolano, -a
very *adv.*   muy, mucho; *adj.* mucho, -a
  very much   mucho, muchísimo
viceroyalty   el virreinato
visit   visitar
  visit one another   visitarse

W

wait (for)   esperar
  wait longer   esperar más
  we had been waiting for a long time   hacía mucho tiempo que esperábamos
wake up (oneself)   despertarse (ie)
walk   el paseo; andar
  take a walk   dar un paseo
wall   la pared
want   querer, desear
war   la guerra
warm *adj.*   caliente; *noun* el calor
  be warm   (*living beings*) tener calor
wash   lavar, (*oneself*) lavarse
watch   el reloj
  gold watch   reloj de oro
  wrist watch   reloj de pulsera
water   el agua (*f.*)
way   la manera
  by the way   a propósito
we   nosotros, -as

weakness   la debilidad
wealth   la riqueza
wear   llevar
weather   el tiempo
  be good weather   hacer buen tiempo
Wednesday   el miércoles
week   la semana
  all week   toda la semana
  next week   la semana próxima (que
    viene)
welcome: you are —,   de nada
well *adv.*   bien
west   el oeste
  to the west   al oeste
what *pron.*   lo que
what?   ¿qué? ¿cuál?
what a . . .!   ¡qué . . .!
  what a fast game!   ¡qué partido más
    (tan) rápido!
whatever   lo que
when   cuando
when?   ¿cuándo?
where   donde
where?   ¿dónde? (*with verbs of motion*);
  ¿adónde?
whether   si
which *relative pron.*   que, el (la) cual, los
  (las) cuales, el (la, los, las) que
  that which   lo que
  the one(s) which   el (la) cual, los (las)
    cuales, el (la, los, las) que
  those which   los (las) que
  which (fact)   lo cual (que)
which?   ¿qué? ¿cuál?
  which one(s)?   ¿cuál(es)?
while *conj.*   mientras (que); *noun* el rato
  a while ago   hace un rato
  after a short while (time)   al poco rato
    (tiempo)
white   blanco, -a
who *relative pron.*   que, quien(es), el (la) cual,
  los (las) cuales, el (la, los, las) que
  he (the one) who   quien, el (la) que
  those (the ones) who   quienes, los (las)
    que
who?   ¿quién(es)?
whom   que, a quien(es)
whom?   ¿quién(es)? ¿a quién(es)?

whose *relative adj.*   cuyo(s), -a(s)
whose?   ¿de quién(es)?
why?   ¿por qué? ¿para qué?
will   querer; *sign of future tense*
  will you + *verb?*   ¿quiere Ud. (quieres)
    + *inf?*
  won't you (write)?   ¿no quiere Ud.
    (quieres) (escribir)?
win   ganar
window   la ventana
windy: be (very) —,   hacer (mucho) viento
wish   querer, desear
with   con, de, en
withdraw   (*oneself*) retirarse
without *prep.*   sin
woman   la mujer
wonder   *use future or cond. for conjecture*
wonderful   magnífico, -a
word   la palabra
work   la obra, el trabajo; *pl.* trabajos, obras;
  trabajar
  by working   trabajando
  gold and silver work   la orfebrería
  (he) had been working (there) five years
    hacía cinco años que trabajaba (allí)
  his military work ended   terminada
    su obra militar
  work for (the rights)   trabajar por (los
    derechos)
world   el mundo
would   *sign of imperfect or cond. tense*
  would that!   ¡ojalá que + *subj.*!
wrist watch   el reloj de pulsera
write   escribir
writer   el escritor
  short story writer   el cuentista
written   escrito, -a

Y

year   el año
  the last few years   los últimos años
yellow   amarillo, -a
  the yellow one (*f.*)   la amarilla
yesterday   ayer
  yesterday afternoon   ayer por la tarde
yet   todavía

you (*fam. sing.*)   tú, (*pl.*) vosotros, -as; *dir. and indir. obj.* te, os; *after prep.* ti, vosotros, -as

you   (*polite*) *subject pron. and after prep.* usted (Ud.), ustedes (Uds.); *dir. obj.* le, la, los, las; *indir. obj.* le, les; *indef. subject* se

young   joven (*pl.* jóvenes)
    young lady   la señorita
    young people   los jóvenes
    younger   más joven, menor

your   (*fam.*) *adj.* tu(s), vuestro(s), -a(s); (*polite*) su(s), de Ud. (Uds.)

yours   (*fam.*) *pron.* (el) tuyo, (la) tuya, (los) tuyos, (las) tuyas, (el) vuestro, (la) vuestra, (los) vuestros, (las) vuestras; (*polite*) (el) suyo, (la) suya, (los) suyos, (las) suyas *or* el (la, los, las) de Ud. (Uds.)

  of yours *adj.* tuyo(s), -a(s), vuestro(s) -a(s); suyo(s), suya(s), de Ud. (Uds.)

INDEX

INDEX

LIST OF PHOTOGRAPHS AND CREDITS

José Sabogal "Water Bearers (Aguadoras)," 1951
Courtesy, San Francisco Museum of Art
Gift of Mr. and Mrs. Garfield Warner

"The Young King," 1936, by C. Mérida
Courtesy, Carlos Mérida
From the collection of Mr. and Mrs. Stanley Markus

Lithograph, from the *Popol-Vuh*, by C. Mérida
Fragment of Chapter XVI of the Sacred Book
Courtesy, Carlos Mérida

"The Eternal Present," 1944, by W. Lam
Courtesy, Museum of Art, Rhode Island School of Design,
Providence, R. I.

"Constructive Art," 1942, by J. Torres García
Courtesy, Museo Nacional de Bellas Artes, Buenos Aires,
Argentina

"1943 America," 1943, by J. Torres García
Courtesy, Museum of Art, Rhode Island School of Design,
Providence, R. I.

"The Sun in the Moon," 1964, by R. Vergara Grez
Courtesy, R. Vergara Grez, and Antonio R. Romera, Santiago,
Chile

"Dynamic Symmetry," by R. Vergara Grez
Courtesy, R. Vergara Grez, and Antonio R. Romera, Santiago,
Chile

"Green and Black Immaterial Curves," 1966, by J. Soto
(wood and metal construction)
Courtesy, Museum of Art, Rhode Island School of Design,
Providence, R. I.

"In Violet," 1966, by E. Mac Entyre
Courtesy, Museum of Art, Rhode Island School of Design,
Providence, R. I.

"Confessions of an Iconoclastic Sea Urchin," by P. Friedeberg
Courtesy, Mexican National Tourist Council, and
Galería Antonio Souza, Mexico City

"Self-portrait," by J. L. Cuevas
Courtesy, José Luis Cuevas, and Galería de Arte Mexicano

1 2 3 4 5 6 7 8 9 10